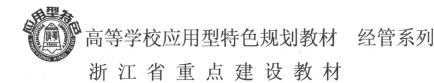

高等学校应用型特色规划教材　经管系列

浙江省重点建设教材

国 际 结 算

理论·实务·案例

(双语教材)(第二版)

International Settlement

主　编　蒋琴儿

副主编　管福泉　黄水灵　蒋瑞波
　　　　刘剑锋　董中辰

U0360553

清华大学出版社

北　京

内 容 简 介

本书是根据普通高等院校应用型特色规划教材编写计划，按照教育部应用型人才培养的教学要求编写的。全书分为中文部分与英文部分，系统地介绍了国际结算涉及的票据、结算方式、单据和进出口贸易融资方式，尽可能地反映了本学科发展的前沿动态，吸收了国际结算领域的最新成果。

相对于其他的国际结算教材，本书更加注重国际结算的实务操作，每一章都配有相关的案例与分析，并强化英语在国际结算领域的具体运用，从而突出应用型人才培养的特点，培养学生分析问题和解决问题的实际能力，具有覆盖面广、实用性强、案例丰富、内容新颖、难易适度等特点。

本书适合作为应用型本科或大专院校的经济或国际管理类国际经济与贸易、国际金融、电子商务等专业的教材，也可作为国际贸易、国际金融等相关领域从业人员的参考用书。

图书在版编目(CIP)数据

国际结算：理论·实务·案例(双语教材)/蒋琴儿主编；管福泉，黄水灵，蒋瑞波，刘剑锋，董中辰副主编. —2版. —北京：清华大学出版社，2012 (2024.8重印)
(高等学校应用型特色规划教材　经管系列)
ISBN 978-7-302-29160-2

Ⅰ. ①国… Ⅱ. ①蒋… ②管… ③黄… ④蒋… ⑤刘… ⑥董 Ⅲ. ①国际结算—双语教学—高等学校—教材 Ⅳ. ①F830.73

中国版本图书馆 CIP 数据核字(2012)第 135757 号

责任编辑：温　洁　汤涌涛
封面设计：杨玉兰
责任校对：周剑云
责任印制：宋　林
出版发行：清华大学出版社
　　　　　网　　址：https://www.tup.com.cn, https://www.wqxuetang.com
　　　　　地　　址：北京清华大学学研大厦 A 座　　　　邮　　编：100084
　　　　　社 总 机：010-83470000　　　　　　　　　　邮　　购：010-62786544
　　　　　投稿与读者服务：010-62776969, c-service@tup.tsinghua.edu.cn
　　　　　质量反馈：010-62772015, zhiliang@tup.tsinghua.edu.cn
　　　　　课件下载：https://www.tup.com.cn, 010-62791865
印 装 者：三河市君旺印务有限公司
经　　销：全国新华书店
开　　本：185mm×230mm　　　　印　张：24.25　　　字　数：543 千字
版　　次：2007 年 3 月第 1 版　2012 年 8 月第 2 版　印　次：2024 年 8 月第 18 次印刷
定　　价：68.00 元

产品编号：040193-03

出版说明

应用型人才是指能够将专业知识和技能应用于所从事的专业岗位的一种专门人才。应用型人才的本质特征是具有专业基本知识和基本技能，即具有明确的职业性、实用性、实践性和高层次性。应用型人才的培养，是"十二五"时期教育部关于进一步深化本科教学改革，全面提高教学质量的目标之一，也是协调高等教育规模速度与市场人才需求关系的重要途径。

教育部要求"十二五"期间有相当数量的高校致力于培养应用型人才，以满足市场对应用型人才的巨大需求。为了培养高素质应用型人才，必须建立完善的教学计划和高水平的课程体系。在教育部有关精神的指导下，我们组织全国高校的专家教授，努力探求更为合理有效的应用型人才培养方案，并结合我国当前的实际情况，编写了这套"高等学校应用型特色规划教材·经管系列"丛书。

为使教材的编写真正切合应用型人才的培养目标，我社编辑在全国范围内走访了大量高等学校，拜访了众多院校主管教学的领导以及教学一线的系主任和教师，掌握了各地区各学校所设专业的培养目标和办学特色，推进了优质教育资源进课堂，并广泛、深入地与用人单位进行交流，明确了用人单位的真正需求。这些工作为本套丛书的准确定位、合理选材、突出特色奠定了坚实的基础，同时逐步形成了反映时代特点、与时俱进的教材体系。

❖ 教材定位

- ➤ 以就业为导向。在应用型人才培养过程中，充分考虑市场需求，因此本套丛书充分体现"就业导向"的基本思路。

- ➤ 符合本学科的课程设置要求。以高等教育的培养目标为依据，注重教材的科学性、实用性和通用性，融入实践教学环节。

- ➤ 定位明确。准确定位教材在人才培养过程中的地位和作用，紧密结合学科专业发展和教育教学改革，正确处理教材的读者层次关系，面向就业，突出应用。

- ➤ 合理选材、编排得当。妥善处理传统内容与现代内容的关系，大力补充新知识、新技术、新工艺和新成果。根据本学科的教学基本要求和教学大纲的要求，制定编写大纲(编写原则、编写特色、编写内容、编写体例等)，突出重点、难点。

- ➤ 建设"立体化"的精品教材体系。提倡教材与电子教案、学习指导、习题解答、课程设计、毕业设计等辅助教学资料配套出版。

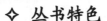

✧ 丛书特色

➢ 围绕应用讲理论，突出实践教学环节及特点，包含丰富的案例，并对案例作详细解析，强调实用性和可操作性。

➢ 涉及最新的理论成果和实务案例，充分反映岗位要求，真正体现以就业为导向的培养目标。

➢ 国际化与中国特色相结合，符合高等教育日趋国际化的发展趋势，部分教材采用双语形式。

➢ 在结构的布局、内容重点的选取、案例习题的设计等方面符合教改目标和教学大纲的要求，把教师的备课、授课、辅导答疑等教学环节有机地结合起来。

✧ 读者定位

本系列教材主要面向普通高等院校和高等职业技术院校，以满足培养应用型人才的高等院校的教学需要。

✧ 关于作者

丛书编委特聘请执教多年且有较高学术造诣和实践经验的教授参与各册教材的编写，其中有相当一部分的教材主要执笔者是各专业精品课程的负责人，本丛书凝聚了他们多年的教学经验和心血。

✧ 互动交流

本丛书的编写及出版过程，贯穿了清华大学出版社一贯严谨、务实、科学的作风。伴随我国教育教学改革的不断深入，要编写出满足新形势下教学需求的教材，还需要我们不断地努力、探索和实践。我们真诚希望使用本丛书的教师、学生和其他读者提出宝贵的意见和建议，使之更臻成熟。

清华大学出版社

前　　言

"国际结算"是从事国际贸易和国际金融工作必修的一门重要课程。本书紧扣应用型国际贸易与国际金融人才的培养目标，按照"宽口径、厚基础"的特点，结合国际贸易惯例、西方国家法律和我国的实际，系统阐述了国际结算的票据、结算方式、结算单据和进出口贸易融资方式，并融合了大量的相关案例。

随着国际贸易的发展变化，与国际结算相关的诸多法律与惯例已做了必要的修订与补充。例如，国际商会修订的《跟单信用证统一惯例》(国际商会第 600 号出版物，UCP600)于 2007 年 7 月 1 日正式实施，《国际贸易术语解释通则》(Incoterms 2010)于 2011 年 1 月 1 日正式实施，《见索即付保函统一规则》(URDG758)也于 2010 年 7 月 1 日正式实施。这些国际惯例的修订，对我国的国际贸易与结算带来了极大的影响。而本书的修订，及时反映了这些国际惯例的变化及其对国际贸易结算实践的具体影响。同时，本教材的修订力求保持与突出以下几个方面的特点。

(1) 系统性。力求反映国际结算最新法律和惯例的内涵，在保证理论完整性和系统性的前提下，深入浅出，化繁为简。同时，本书也尽可能地反映了本学科发展的前沿动态，吸收了国际结算领域的最新成果。

(2) 实用性。兼顾贸易和银行业务，从新从实，摒弃了一些陈旧的做法。在强调实务可操作性的同时，避免琐碎的文牍章程。

(3) 新颖性。采用中英双语体例编写，两部分在编排结构上紧密联系，强调了英语作为国际结算工作语言的重要性，有利于读者根据个人的具体需要选择学习。

(4) 真实性。本书每一章的内容都包含基本理论、实际操作和大量相关的真实案例，在每一个知识点上将理论与实践密切结合，在内容的广度、深度以及分量上注意符合应用型人才培养的教学要求。通过本书的学习，可以帮助学生理论联系实际，提高实际动手能力，使学生走上国际贸易和国际金融的工作岗位后能尽快适应相应的工作。

清华大学出版社的温洁编辑对本教材的编写给予了鼎力支持和热情帮助，在此表示由衷的敬意和感谢。

在本书的编写过程中，编者参阅了国内许多专家学者有关国际结算的著作，吸收和借鉴了其中的精华，在此向各位作者深表感谢。因水平有限，书中难免存在不足和遗漏，敬请读者批评指正，并期望得到大家的支持与帮助。

本书配有电子课件，以适应多媒体教学的需要。下载地址：www.tup.com.cn。

编　者

目　　录

Contents

第一章

国际结算概述

学习目标：掌握国际结算的概念；熟悉国际结算的种类、内容和涉及的法律与国际惯例；了解银行在国际结算中的作用、银行网络和资金转移网络。

关键概念：国际结算、国际贸易结算、非贸易结算、代理行、账户行、SWIFT、CHIPS、CHAPS

"国际结算"是一门理论与实践相结合的、新兴的国际经济应用课程。它以国际结算方式为研究对象，分析、评价各类结算方式的信用基础、实务操作与风险防范。国际结算有较长的历史演变过程，其业务的顺利开展有赖于银行与其海外分支机构或其代理行的共同协作。

第一节　国际结算的概念、基本种类与内容

一、国际结算的概念

假设中国 A 公司向美国 B 公司进口一批机器设备。两者之间的关系如图 1-1 所示。A 公司作为进口方，承担到期付款的义务；B 公司作为出口方，享有收取设备价款的权利。为平衡 A、B 两公司之间的"货、款"，必然会导致一笔货币资金从中国流向美国，从而得以清偿 A 与 B 公司之间的债权债务，这种金融活动称为国际结算。所谓国际结算，是指为清偿国际间的债权债务关系而发生在不同国家之间的货币收付活动。

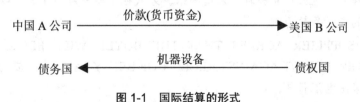

图 1-1　国际结算的形式

相对而言，如为清偿债权债务关系而发生在同一国内的货币收付活动，则属于国内结算的范畴。

二、国际结算的基本种类

根据发生国际间债权债务关系的原因，国际结算分为贸易结算和非贸易结算。

国际贸易结算是指有形贸易活动(即由商品的进出口)引起的货币收付活动，是国际结算的主要内容。其项目单一，但在国际收支中占有特殊地位，并具有结算方式多样化的特点。

国际非贸易结算是指由有形贸易以外的活动(包括国际资本流动、国际资金借贷、技术转让、劳务输出、侨民汇款、捐赠、利润与利息收支及国际旅游、运输、保险、银行业等活动)引起的货币收付活动。它的项目繁多，但结算方式简单，只涉及部分结算方式的内容。

三、国际结算的基本内容

国际结算包括四方面的内容：票据、国际结算方式、国际结算单据与国际结算融资。

票据是一种具有一定格式、由付款人到期对持票人或其指定人无条件支付确定金额的信用凭证。票据的用途是将贸易双方的信用关系转化为票据关系，因而票据是一种信用工具，就像国库券、政府债券等一样。信用工具是指用以证明债权人权利和债务人义务的书面契约凭证，它的主要特性是可流通转让。国际贸易结算所使用的信用工具主要是票据。

国际结算方式是指货币收付的手段和渠道，是国际贸易结算的中心内容，包括汇款、托收、信用证、银行保函和备用信用证。另外，有许多教材把福费廷(包买票据)和国际保理也称为国际结算方式，但这两者的功能应该说更多地体现在"融资"方面。

国际结算单据是指贸易结算中涉及的单据，例如发票、装箱单、货运单据、保险单、产地证、函抄与汇票等单据。

国际结算融资是指进出口商利用票据及(或)单据，结合结算方式进行特定方式的融资(或融物)，例如票据贴现、信托收据、进出口押汇、保理、出口信用保险项下融资等。

【案例 1-1】结算方式与单据

一家公司在开展进出口业务时，采用的结算方式也不是一成不变的。以瑞典某跨国公司购买合同中的支付条款为例。

(1) THE SUPPLIER AGREES THAT THE BUYER WILL EFFECT PAYMENTS UNDER THE TERM OF T/T AGAINST RECEIPT OF B/L BY FAX. (卖方应同意买方在收到提单传真件后采用电汇付款。)

(2) HONG KONG SUPPLIERS AGREE THAT THE BUYER WILL EFFECT PAYMENTS UNDER THE TERM OF CAD (CASH AGAINST DOCUMENTS). (香港卖方应同意买方采用凭单付款。)

(3)　ONLY IN CASE OF NEW SUPPLIERS AND FIRST ORDER TO THEM, THE BUYER MIGHT AGREE TO EFFECT PAYMENTS UNDER L/C TERMS. THE L/C CHARGES ON THE BUYER'S SIDE WILL BE BORN BY THE BUYER AND THE L/C CHARGES ON THE SUPPLIER'S SIDE WILL BE BORN BY THE SUPPLIER. THE BILL OF LADING WILL BE MADE OUT TO ORDER AND NOTIFY THE BUYER. (只有在初次交易时，买方会同意卖方采用信用证付款的要求。买方这边产生的信用证费用由买方承担，而卖方这边的信用证费用由卖方承担。提单须做成指示性抬头并通知买方。)

(4)　IN CASE THAT THE SUPPLIER STILL INSISTS ON L/C TERMS EVEN AFTER THE FIRST ORDER, THE SUPPLIER AGREES TO TAKE OVER ALL L/C CHARGES ON HIM AS WELL AS THE BUYER'S SIDE. IN THOSE CASES WE REQUEST A BILL OF LADING …(如在初次交易后，供应商仍然坚持采用信用证结算，则所有的信用证费用全部由他承担。在这种情况下，买方要求提单……)

T/T、CAD 与 L/C 均是结算方式。由上例可知，随着双方贸易的逐渐开展，采用的结算方式将发生变化。

【案例 1-2】结算方式与支付货币

有些进出口业务，支付货币不同，结算方式也会有差异。例如，以下进口合同规定：

Payment for Goods supplied from abroad(国外提供的货物价款支付):

(1)　Payment of foreign currency portion shall be made in *US Dollars* in the following manner(外币支付采用美元，并按以下方式分期支付)：

①　**Advance Payment:** Ten (10) percent of the Contract Price shall be paid within thirty (30) days of signing of the Contract, and upon submission of claim and a bank guarantee for equivalent amount valid until the Goods are delivered and in the form provided in the bidding documents or another form acceptable to the Purchaser.(预付款为合同价款的 10%，在签订合同后 30 天内支付，凭卖方提交的一份银行保函支付。银行保函的金额应与预付款金额相等，保函有效期为货物交付后，保函形式可为投标保函或购买者所能接受的其他保函形式。)

②　**On Shipment:** Eighty (80) percent of the Contract Price of the Goods shipped shall be paid through irrevocable confirmed letter of credit opened in favor of the Supplier in a bank in its country, upon submission of documents specified in GCC Clause 12.(装运支付：80%的合同价款采用不可撤销的保兑信用证支付。凭本合同条款第 12 条规定的单据，在供应方所在地的一家银行得到兑用。)

③　**On Acceptance:** Ten (10) percent of the Contract Price of Goods received shall be paid within thirty (30) days of receipt of the Goods upon submission of claim supported by the

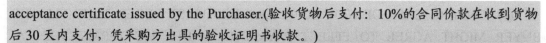

acceptance certificate issued by the Purchaser.(验收货物后支付：10%的合同价款在收到货物后 30 天内支付，凭采购方出具的验收证明书收款。)

(2) Payment of local currency portion shall be made in **AMD (Armenian Drams)** within thirty (30) days of presentation of claim supported by a certificate from the Purchaser declaring that the Goods have been delivered and that all other contracted Services have been performed.(本币支付采用亚美尼亚法定货币，卖方凭采购方出具的履约证明在收到证明的 30 日内收款。该履约证明应申明货物已经交付并且合同规定的其他义务已得到履行。)

因此，从本案例可以看出采购方支付贷款的方法相比案例 1-1 更为复杂。本案例的结算方式采用了预付、跟单信用证、银行保函、到付相结合的方式。同时，支付货币不同，结算方式也不相同。

第二节　国际结算的历史演变及其涉及的国际惯例

一、国际结算的历史演变

贸易结算的产生以商品贸易的产生和发展为前提。当商品流通跨越国界形成国际贸易时，国际贸易结算随之产生。

最初的国际贸易是易货贸易，金、银作为一般等价物行使货币的职能，国际结算确立了最初的方式，贸易双方一手交钱、一手交货，双方"钱货两讫"，我们称之为"现金结算"。由于长途运输金银风险大、费用高，占压资金时间长，而且金银很难辨别真伪，特别是交易量大、交易频繁时清点货币就更加困难，因此，现金结算不能适应国际贸易的进一步发展。公元 11 世纪，地中海沿岸的商人开始使用字据来代替黄金。需要运送现金的交易商，在本地将现金交付专门的从事货币兑换业务的兑换商，获得由兑换商开出的兑换证明。交易商可持兑换证明到异地的指定兑换商(往往是本地兑换商在异地的网点)出示兑换证明，要求兑换成现金，再向其贸易伙伴支付现金。在 16、17 世纪，这种字据逐渐发展成票据，得到广泛的运用。18 世纪，票据在国际贸易中使用十分普遍，并形成一套较为完善的制度。中国票据起源很早，唐代的飞钱和贴子便是汇票和支票的萌芽，南宋时代使用的交子是本票的雏形。

基于前文所述原因，国际结算逐渐从现金结算过渡到非现金结算。非现金结算的发展主要表现为凭单付款、贸易结算国际惯例的完善以及以银行为中介的国际结算体系的形成。航运业、保险业与商业相互分化，成为独立的行业，并出现提单、保险单等重要单据。这些单据不仅是一种货物收据或保险证明，而且可以转让，成为买卖的对象，"物权单据化"的概念被普遍接受。卖方交单，代表货物的交付和物权的转让；买方付款赎单，代表买方取得物权。同时，单据逐渐发展为商人凭以融资的抵押对象，凭单付款逐渐替代"凭货付款"。随着托收和跟单信用证等结算方式的产生与发展，特别是买方付款赎单的规则得以进一步的明确和运用，凭单付款成为非现金结算的主要付款方式。

二、国际结算涉及的法律与国际惯例

国际结算涉及的国际惯例是国际结算长期实践形成的习惯做法和普遍规则。国际惯例的形成与发展，保障了当事人各方的权益，保证了一定时期内国际贸易方式和规则的相对稳定性。国际惯例的运用，减少了国际贸易运作的环节，提高了国际结算的效率。

(一)与票据相关的法律和国际惯例

有关票据的主要法律如下所述。

(1)　《英国票据法》(Bills of Exchange Act，1882)，它是英美法系票据法的典型代表。

(2)　《日内瓦统一票据法》，它是大陆法系票据法的典型代表。

(3)　《中华人民共和国票据法》，它于1995年5月10日在第八届全国人民代表大会常务委员会第十三次会议通过。2004年8月28日在第十届全国人民代表大会常务委员会第十一次会议上通过了《关于修改〈中华人民共和国票据法〉的决定》，据此对《中华人民共和国票据法》进行了修正。

(二)与结算方式相关的国际惯例

有关结算方式的主要国际惯例如下所述。

(1)　《托收统一规则》(Uniform Rules for Collection，ICC Publication No. 522)于1996年1月1日正式实施，是关于约束托收各当事人权利与义务的国际惯例，简称URC522。URC522明确规定：除非另有规定，或与一个国家、一个地区或当地的法律、法规相抵触，否则本规则对托收的所有当事人均具有约束力。

(2)　《跟单信用证统一惯例》(Uniform Customs and Practice for Commercial Documentary Credits)，是关于约束信用证各当事人权利与义务的国际惯例。目前正在使用的是2007年7月1日正式实施的2007年修订本，即国际商会第600号出版物(2007 Revision，ICC Publication No. 600)，简称UCP600。世界各国的法院与国际仲裁机构都已经将该惯例作为处理和判决国际间信用证争端的法律规则。

(3)　《见索即付保函统一规则》。2010年7月1日，国际商会(ICC)发布的新版《见索即付保函统一规则》(URDG758)正式实施。URDG758是继UCP600之后的又一重要国际惯例，突出了见索即付保函的独立性和单据化特征，更加强调保函业务的"先赔付、再争论"的理念，从而在全球商界、企业界和金融界确立了共同遵从的国际惯例，已先后得到了国际咨询工程师联合会(FIDIC)、世界银行、联合国国际贸易法委员会等机构的支持和承认。

(三)与单据相关的国际公约与国际惯例

涉及单据的国际惯例有《海牙规则》(Hague Rules)、《汉堡规则》(Hamburg Rules)、《国际铁路货物运送公约》(International Convention Concerning the Transport of Goods by Rail)、《国际铁路货物联运协定》(Agreement on International Rail-Road through Transport of Goods)、《联合运输单证统一规则》(Uniform Rules for a Combined Transport Documents)、《伦敦保险协会货物保险条款》(Institute Cargo Clauses, ICC)、《国际贸易术语解释通则》(International Rules for Interpretation of Trade Terms, Incoterms 2010)、《联合国国际贸易法委员会仲裁规则》(UNCITRAL Arbitration Rules)等。

第三节　国际结算体系及银行网络

一、银行在国际结算中的作用

随着国际结算的不断发展，银行开始介入结算业务。银行的介入使国际结算进入新的发展时期。银行在国际结算中起中介作用，主要表现在以下三个方面。

(1) 银行资金雄厚、资信优良，可以为国际贸易结算提供信用保障，例如信用证和银行保函。国际贸易的开展建立在双方信用的基础上，商业信用起着决定性的作用。在贸易双方互不了解的情况下，买方担心付款后能否取得正确的货物，而卖方则担心供货后能否取得货款。纯粹以商业信用来开展业务，很难保证国际贸易的顺利开展。若银行介入贸易结算，为买方提供信用保障，担保付款，则有利于贸易在新领域的拓展，从而进一步推动国际结算业务的扩大。

(2) 银行可提供贸易融资，如开展出口押汇、单据贴现等融资业务。随着物权单据的普遍接受和凭单付款方式的完善，出口商以单据作为抵押对象向银行进行融资，可以帮助出口商解决资金周转的难题。银行的融资，使出口商增加了交易量，而银行本身拓展了新业务，两者相辅相成，形成一个以银行为中介的、贸易与融资为一体的结算体系。

【案例 1-3】银行在国际贸易中的作用

上海 TEX 出口公司在 2004 年广州春交会上结识了俄罗斯 Ladimir 公司，该公司求购节能灯，共计数量 3 个 40′FCL，总金额为 83 456.79 美元。俄方客户坚持采用"100%货款在装运后 30 天内汇付"。由于是初次交易，TEX 公司不敢贸然接受 100%商业信用的结算方式，要求修改结算方式为"100%货款采用即期信用证支付"，并要求在收到信用证后合同才开始生效。经反复磋商，双方达成了"100%货款凭信用证在装运后 30 天内付款"(100%

PAYMENT BY L/C WITHIN 30 DAYS FROM THE DATE OF BILL OF LADING)的结算方式。俄方客户按期通过德意志银行莫斯科分行开来了信用证，信用证指定中国银行上海分行为通知行(Advising Bank)和被指定银行(Nominated Bank)。TEX公司在收到信用证后开始组织生产。生产完毕后，按照合同和信用证的要求，及时向中国银行上海分行办理了交单。由于资金紧张，TEX公司同时向银行提出了融资的要求。中国银行上海分行审核单据后，认为"交单相符"，并在第二天接受了TEX的融资要求，给其办理了出口押汇。35天后，中国银行上海分行从开证行处收回了全部货款，该笔出口业务顺利完结。

　　采用不同的结算方式，对出口商的收汇保障是不一样的：汇付是进口商自行付款，体现商业信用；信用证直接体现的是银行信用。如进口商坚持采用汇付结算，这笔业务有可能不能成功，出口商的销售量不可能提高。采用信用证结算，出口商就敢于与新客户开展贸易往来。采用30天付款的远期信用证相比装运后30天付款的汇付，出口商收款的安全性大大加强，而且便于出口商向银行进行融资。对中国银行上海分行而言，可以从该笔业务中收取信用证通知费、银行议付费用和押汇利息等，拓展了业务范围。由于有出口商的单据(含物权单据)做抵押，提供融资的银行的风险大大降低。

　　(3) 银行拥有效率高、安全性强的银行网络与资金转移网络。银行在全球建立了分支机构以及代理行关系、账户关系，以拓展海外业务，加快资金的收付。

二、国际结算的银行网络

(一)商业银行的分支机构

　　商业银行在全世界往往有以下分支机构：①分行和支行(BRANCH & SUB-BRANCH)。分行和支行之间的关系称为"联行关系"(SISTER BANK)。②代表处(REPRESENTATIVE OFFICE)。它是商业银行在国外设立的非营业性机构，为总行或其国外分行提供当地信息，为开办分行建立基础。③经理处(AGENCY)。它是商业银行在海外设立的能办理汇款及贷款业务的机构，但被限制经营当地存款业务，是总行的一个组成部分，介于代表处和分行之间，不具有法人资格。资金来源只能是总行或者从东道国银行同业市场拆入。④子银行(SUBSIDIARY)。它是在东道国注册的独立金融机构，具有法人地位。⑤联营银行。⑥银团银行(CONSORTIUM BANK)。

(二)代理行

　　代理行(CORRESPONDENT BANK OR CORRESPONDENTS)是指相互间建立委托办理业务的，具有往来关系的银行。代理行的建立，一般经过三个步骤。第一，开展资信调查。主要考察对方银行的资信，通过多方渠道了解对方银行所在国的有关政策、法规、市场信息等。第二，在分析与评价的基础上，确定建立代理行关系的层次。代理行的层次分为一般代理关系、账户代理关系与议定透支额度关系。第三，签订代理行协议(AGENCY ARRANGEMENT)。代理行协议由双方银行负责人签署后才开始生效。代理行协议包括双方机构的总称(总行签订的代理协议是否包括分支行、包括几家分支行必须在协议中明确)、交换和确认控制文件(密押、签字样本和费率表)、代理业务的范围、业务往来头寸的调拨、融资便利的安排等内容。

密押(TEST KEY)是两家银行之间事先约定的专用押码，在发送电报时，由发送电报的银行在电文前加注，经接收电报的银行核对相符，用以确认电报的真实性。密押的机密性强，国际结算中的资金转移可通过电报或者电传进行，应由绝对可靠的人经管，使用1～2年后应当更换新的密押，以确保安全。

签字样本(BOOK OF AUTHORIZED SIGNATURE)是银行列示的每个有权签字人的授权签字额度、有权签字范围、有权签字组合方式以及亲笔签名字样，是代理行用以核对对方发来的电报、电传的真实性的凭证。银行之间的信函凭证和对外签发的票据、对外签订的协议，都必须经有权签字人签字才可生效。委托付款银行必须先核对信函、票据和凭证上的签字，然后才具体处理委办的业务。代理行签字样本由总行互换，包括总行及代理协议中所包括分行的有权签字人的签字式样。

费率表(SCHEDULE OF TERMS AND CONDITIONS)是银行办理各项业务的收费标准。一般由总行制定，分行和支行执行。我国银行办理委托业务时，按照对方银行的标准收费。收费应公平合理，避免过高而削弱代理行的竞争力。

(三)账户行

代理行建立代理关系后，就可以根据协议办理委办业务。但是，对于汇款、托收以及信用证业务，会涉及外汇资金的收付，需要双方建立账户处理资金的清算。因此，代理行之间单方或者双方互相在对方银行开设账户，称为账户代理行(DEPOSITORY CORRESPONDENTS)，简称账户行(DEPOSITORY BANK)。

经营国际业务的银行都在国际货币的清算中心开立账户，否则会影响货币收付的正常进行。例如美元，必须在美元的清算中心——纽约开立账户；日元，必须在日元的清算中心——东京开立账户。开立账户时，如果本国银行在境外其他银行开立账户的，称为往账(NOSTRO ACCOUNT 或 DUE FROM ACCOUNT)。往账通常开立的是境外货币的账户。例如：中国银行在纽约大通银行开立美元账户，在日本东京开立日元账户。若境外银行在国内开立账户的，称为来账(VOSTRO ACCOUNT 或 DUE TO ACCOUNT)。来账通常以本币开立，也可以用境外货币开立。例如，大通银行在北京开设人民币和美元账户。

账户行一定是代理行，代理行不一定是账户行。各银行开立账户的条件各不相同，在不同银行建立账户的成本费有大有小。账户条件大致有以下几种：①最低存款额；②存款利息；③透支额度及利息；④账户费用；⑤对账单。

> **【案例1-4】中国银行山东省分行与越南胡志明市分行联手解决信用证项下纠纷案**
>
> 中国银行山东省分行于 2006 年 3 月因一笔信用证项下付款一事，与越南某代理行反复交涉未果，后在中行越南胡志明市分行的鼎力协助下，成功收回大部分货款。这项纠纷的成功解决表明海内外分支机构的积极良好协作促进了各自业务的联动发展。
>
> 这笔信用证金额为 775 450.00 美元，受益人为我国某著名家电产业公司。越南开证行在收到单据后，未在合理时间内提出任何不符点，也不付款或承兑。在中行山东省分行的大力催收下，开证行先是借故拖延时间，进而干脆对中行山东省分行的电报置之不理。鉴于上述情况，山东省分行致电中行越南胡志明市分行，请求帮助催收。中行越南胡志明市分行积极配合，与开证行业务人员据理力争，并将和开证行交涉的注意事项及技巧、催收结果随时与中行山东分行进行沟通，内外联手共同向开证行施压。同时，山东出口商(受益人)在越南期间也得到了中行越南胡志明市分行的大力帮助。
>
> 通过海内外联动催收，该笔业务最终成功收回 705 055.00 美元，基本解决了该项纠纷，巩固了中国银行国际结算业务在客户心目中的地位，对中行维系优质客户、拓展业务进一步奠定了基础。

三、银行资金转移网络

目前，全世界有三大货币清算系统，保障了货币资金在全世界的安全、迅速转移。

(1) 纽约银行同业电子清算系统(Clearing House Interbank Payment System，CHIPS)。它是国际美元收付的计算机网络，总部设在纽约。

(2) 伦敦银行同业自动清算系统(Clearing House Automated Payment System，CHAPS)。它以高度计算机自动化代替票据交换，各商业银行在清算银行开设账户，总部设在伦敦。

(3) 环球银行金融电信协会(The Society for Worldwide Interbank Financial Telecommunication，SWIFT)。该系统可以自动储存信息、自动加押、自动核对密押。SWIFT因其费用低廉、安全、可靠、快捷、标准化、自动化等优点，已成为银行之间划拨资金、开立信用证和往来联系的主要通信工具。SWIFT 在银行界的广泛使用，对提高国际银行同业间的信息处理与交换具有深远的意义。目前，除世界少数落后国家外，银行之间的信息往来普遍采用 SWIFT 方式。

> **【案例1-5】电报、电传和 SWIFT 电文的费用比较**
>
> 发送电文的成本较低是 SWIFT 通信方式的一大特点。假设对发往美国的 300 字符(约

合 50 个单词)的电文进行价格上的比较：

电报(CABLE)：50 字 × CNY3.60/字=CNY180.00

电传(TELEX)：1 分钟 × CNY25.00/分钟=CNY25.00

SWIFT：以每 325 个字符为一个收费单位，每一收费单位的价格为 EUR0.315，约合 CNY2.27。

第四节 本书的结构体系

本书的结构体系如图 1-2 所示。

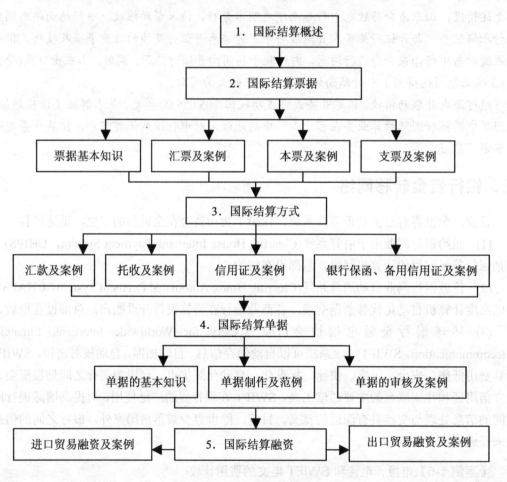

图 1-2 本书的结构体系

本 章 小 结

国际结算分为贸易结算和非贸易结算，贸易结算是本书学习的重点。国际贸易结算的主要内容包括票据、国际贸易结算方式、结算单据和进出口贸易融资。这四部分内容是相辅相成、紧密结合的。国际结算从现金结算发展到非现金结算，它有一个历史的演变过程。而这个过程与国际贸易的发展是紧密联系在一起的。国际惯例、银行、物权单据等极大地促进了国际结算的发展。学习国际结算，必须了解和熟悉国际结算涉及的主要法律和国际惯例。银行在国际结算中起着中介作用。银行自身的网络、高速安全的资金转移网络是国际结算坚强的后盾，银行的资金实力能为进出口贸易商提供必要的融资。

复习思考题

1. 国际结算的概念、基本种类以及基本内容是什么？
2. 国际结算涉及的法律和国际惯例有哪些？
3. 银行在国际结算中的作用是什么？它具备怎样的结算网络优势？

第二章

国际结算票据

学习目标: 重点掌握票据的性质与功能以及汇票、本票和支票的具体使用;结合两大票据法系统的分歧,熟悉汇票的必要事项及其具体记载,汇票当事人的责任和义务,汇票的行为及其具体表示;了解本票、支票与汇票的异同。

关键概念: 票据、汇票、本票、支票、出票、背书、承兑、保证、参加承兑、退票、保全手续、要式性、无因性、流通转让性、票据伪造、票据变造

第一节 票据基本知识

一、票据的种类与样本

当国际结算从现金结算过渡到非现金结算时,其使用的用以抵消国际间债权债务关系的信用工具就是票据。票据是适应商业需要而产生和发展起来的,经历了漫长的演变过程。为便于票据流通,各国都制定有票据法对其加以约束,使之发挥的作用越来越大。票据包括三种:汇票、本票和支票。

> **【案例 2-1】票据的具体运用**
>
> 假定纽约公司 A 向巴黎公司 B 采购一批物品,签约日期为 2010 年 5 月 13 日,订单(P/O)号码为 95E03LC001,金额为 10 000.00 美元,约定装运后 30 天付款,假定货物装运日期为 2010 年 7 月 10 日。巴黎公司 C 向纽约公司 D 采购一批商品,价值为 10 000.00 美元。而公司 B 与 C 之间刚好存在某种业务关系,如 C 向 B 借贷或提供商品与劳务给 C。它们之间的关系如图 2-1 所示。

票据产生以前,采用的是现金结算。对应的是一批现金从美国流向法国,然后再从法国流回美国。现金循环时间长,手续相对麻烦。如采用票据结算,则相对比较简单。

图 2-1 中 A、B、C 和 D 之间的债权债务关系的清算可以采用汇票、本票或支票中的任何一种来结算。

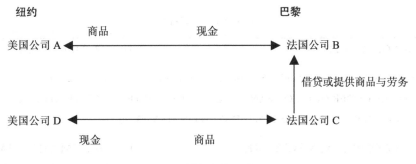

图 2-1 平行贸易示意图

(一)汇票

1. 汇票定义

《英国票据法》规定：汇票是一人向另一人开出的，由开出人签字，要求收件人对某一特定的人或其指定人或持票人即期或固定地，或在可以确定的未来某一日期支付一定货币金额的无条件支付命令(A BILL OF EXCHANGE IS AN UNCONDITIONAL ORDER OF WRITING, ADDRESSED BY ONE PERSON TO ANOTHER, SIGNED BY THE PERSON GIVING IT, REQUIRING THE PERSON TO WHOM IT IS ADDRESSED TO PAY ON DEMAND OR AT A FIXED OR DETERMINABLE FUTURE TIME A SUM CERTAIN IN MONEY TO OR TO THE ORDER OF A SPECIFIED PERSON, OR TO BEARER.)。

我国《票据法》第十九条：汇票是出票人签发的、委托付款人在见票时或者在指定日期无条件支付确定的金额给收款人或者持票人的票据。汇票分为银行汇票和商业汇票。

2. 汇票解决方案

图 2-1 中的法国公司 B 可以开立一张汇票(参见示样 2-1)，收款人是法国公司 C，受票人是美国公司 A。汇票开立后，B 将汇票交给 C，以此汇票解决 B 与 A、B 与 C 之间的债权债务关系。B 将其对 A 的债权转让给 C，委托 A 对 C 直接支付来解决其对 C 该履行的债务。

法国公司 C 收到汇票后，为了清偿其对美国公司 D 的债务，可以将以上汇票通过背书转让给 D，由 D 去向 A 提示汇票，要求 A 付款。这样一来，两笔国际间的债权债务关系通过一张汇票，最终在美国得以清偿，以票据的流通替代了现金的流通，非常简便。

示样 2-1　汇票样本

EXCHANGE FOR USD10,000.00　　　　　　　　　　JULY 13, 2010　PARIS AT THIRTY DAYS AFTER SHIPMENT DATE (SHIPMENT DATE: JULY 10, 2010) PAY TO THE ORDER OF C COMPANY THE SUM OF USD TEN THOUSAND ONLY DRAWN UNDER P/O NO. 95E03LC001 DATED ON MAY 13, 2010. TO:　A COMPANY, NEW YORK　　　　　　　FOR B COMPANY, PARIS 　　　　　　　　　　　　　　　　　　　　　　　　(MANUALLY SIGNED)

(二)本票

1. 本票定义

《英国票据法》关于本票的定义：本票是一人向另一人开出的，由出票人签字，保证对某一特定的人或其指定人或持票人即期或固定地，或在可以确定的未来某一日期支付一定货币金额的书面的无条件支付承诺(A PROMISSORY NOTE IS AN UNCONDITIONAL PROMISE IN WRITING MADE BY ONE PERSON TO ANOTHER, SIGNED BY THE MAKER, ENGAGING TO PAY ON DEMAND OR AT A FIXED OR DETERMINABLE FUTURE TIME A SUM CERTAIN IN MONEY TO OR TO THE ORDER OF A SPECIFIED PERSON, OR TO BEARER.)。

我国《票据法》第七十三条：本票是出票人签发的，承诺自己在见票时无条件支付确定的金额给收款人或者持票人的票据。我国《票据法》所称本票，是指银行本票。

2. 本票解决方案

图 2-1 的四方当事人的债权债务关系可以通过本票解决。美国公司 A 开立一张本票(参见示样 2-2)给 B，以此作为对 B 保证履行债务的债权凭证。

示样 2-2　　本票样本

PROMISSORY NOTE FOR USD10,000.00　　　　　　JULY 13, 2010 NEW YORK AT THIRTY DAYS AFTER SHIPMENT DATE (SHIPMENT DATE: JULY 10, 2010) WE PROMISE TO PAY B COMPANY OR ORDER THE SUM OF USD TEN THOUSAND ONLY FOR VALUE RECEIVED. 　　　　　　　　　　　　　　　　FOR A COMPANY, NEW YORK 　　　　　　　　　　　　　　　　　　(MANUALLY SIGNED)

B 将本票背书转让给 C 来履行其对 C 的债务。同样，C 可将该本票背书转让给 D 来履行其对 D 的债务。

(三)支票

1. 支票定义

《英国票据法》关于支票的定义：简单地说，支票是以银行为付款人的即期汇票。详细地说，支票是银行客户开出的，由银行客户签字，授权银行对某一特定的人或其指定人或者持票来人即期支付一定货币金额的书面的无条件支付命令(BRIEFLY SPEAKING, A CHEQUE IS A BILL OF EXCHANGE DRAWN ON A BANK PAYABLE ON DEMAND. DETAILEDLY SPEAKING, A CHEQUE IS AN UNCONDITIONAL ORDER IN WRITING, ADDRESSED BY THE CUSTOMER TO A BANK, SIGNED BY THAT CUSTOMER, AUTHORIZING THE BANK TO PAY ON DEMAND A SUM CERTAIN IN MONEY TO OR TO THE ORDER OF A SPECIFIED PERSON, OR TO BEARER.)。

我国《票据法》第八十一条：支票是出票人签发的，委托办理支票存款业务的银行或者其他金融机构在见票时无条件支付确定的金额给收款人或者持票人的票据。

2. 支票解决方案

假设美国 A 公司的资金账户银行为纽约 ABC 银行，A 公司可以通过开立支票(参见示样 2-3)来履行其对 B 的债务。对于装运日后 30 天付款的票据，由于支票都是即期的，其要反映远期付款的出票日期填写方法与本票或汇票不同。本例中，本票与汇票的出票日期可以同为 "JULY 13, 2010"，但支票需要填写 "AUG. 9, 2010"，即装运日 "JULY 10, 2010" 后 30 天满期的那天。

B 公司拿到支票后，可以将支票背书转让给 C 来履行其对 C 的债务。同样，C 可将该支票背书转让给 D 来履行其对 D 的债务。支票到期后，D 拿着票据到 ABC 银行提示付款，得到付款后，A、B、C 和 D 之间的债权债务关系全部得以清偿。

示样 2-3 支票样本

CHEQUE NO. __XXX__	NEW YORK AUG. 9, 2010
PAY TO THE ORDER OF B COMPANY THE SUM OF USD TEN THOUSAND ONLY	
	USD10,000.00
TO: ABC BANK, NEW YORK	FOR A COMPANY, NEW YORK
	(MANUALLY SIGNED)

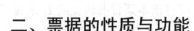

二、票据的性质与功能

(一)票据的性质

无论汇票、本票或支票，其作为票据，都具有设权性、要式性、文义性、无因性和流通转让性。

1. 设权性

所谓设权，是指持票人的票据权利随票据的设立而产生，离开了票据，就不能证明其拥有票据权利。要产生票据权利必须制作票据，转移权利时要交付票据，行使权利时要提示票据。这里的票据权利是指付款请求权、追索权及转让票据权。

示样 2-1 汇票样本中的 B COMPANY 作为汇票出票人，开立了这张汇票，并将这张汇票交给了 C COMPANY，从而使 C 作为持票人拥有了这张金额为 10 000.00 美元的汇票代表的票据权利。但如果这张汇票尚未被 B 开立或 B 开立汇票后自己保留汇票，并没有将汇票交给 C，那么 C 手中因无票据而不能证明其拥有票据权利。C 持有汇票，如果想自己实现票据权利，必须持票据先向 A 提示票据，这是获取票款的前提。如果 A 拒付，则 C 可以持票据向 B 进行追索。在汇票到期前，C 也可以将汇票转让给 D。票据离开了 C，C 也即失去了票据权利，而此时 D 拥有票据权利。因此，票据权利的实现离不开票据本身。

2. 要式性

票据的开立必须具备必要的法定条件才能产生票据的效力，即票据的形式必须符合规定。票据上需要记载的必要事项必须齐全，且符合票据法规定，才能使票据产生法律效力。对于票据上需要记载的必要事项，各国票据法都做了详细的规定。

一份要式齐备的汇票必须满足七个绝对必要事项，否则汇票无效。示样 2-1 汇票样本所具备的必要条件如下。

(1) 表明汇票字样，如 "DRAFT"，"BILL OF EXCHANGE" 或 "EXCHANGE"。

(2) 确定的金额。这份汇票到期付款的确定金额是 10 000.00 美元。

(3) 无条件的支付命令。一般记载为 "PAY TO…"。

(4) 受票人，即设定的 "付款人"。这份汇票记载的受票人是 "A COMPANY"。

(5) 收款人。这份汇票记载的收款人是 "THE ORDER OF C COMPANY"。

(6) 出票人签章。这份汇票的出票人是 "B COMPANY"，"MANUALLY SIGNED" 是其有权签字人的手签。

(7) 出票日期。本汇票的出票日期是 "JULY 13, 2010"。

其中，受票人、收款人和出票人合称为汇票的三个基本当事人。

3. 文义性

文义是指文字上的含义或其思想内容。票据的效力是由文字的含义来决定的，债权人和债务人只受文义的约束，债权人不得以票据上未记载的事项向债务人有所主张，债务人也不能用票据上未记载的事项对债权人有所抗辩。

示样 2-3 支票样本中的出票日期显示为"AUG. 9, 2010"，而实际出票日期为"JUL. 13, 2010"，则该支票只能以支票上显示的时间为准，B COMPANY 不得拿着这张支票在未到期时到 ABC 银行提示付款，要求 ABC 银行提前付款。

4. 无因性

"因"是指产生票据权利义务关系的原因。无因性是指债权人持票据行使权利时，可以不明示原因。只要要式齐全，受让人不需要了解票据产生或转让的原因，就能取得票据文义上载明的权利，而债务人也要自其票据行为完成之日起对正当持票人承担票据责任。

案例 2-1 中的美国 D COMPANY 无论取得汇票、本票，去向 A COMPANY 提示要求付款时，A 不需要过问其中的原因。A 付款后，保留本票或支票，以此作为其对 B 履行债务完毕的证明。如美国 D COMPANY 取得支票，去向 ABC 银行提示付款时，ABC 银行只要 A COMPANY 在其开设的账户上有足够的存款支付这张支票，且支票要式齐备，并在法定期限内提示即要付款，不需要过问持票人与支票出票人 A COMPANY 之间的原因关系。

5. 流通转让性

该特性与民法规定不同。

1) 票据权利转让不必要通知相关债务人

一般的债权在转让时，必须经过债务人的同意，但票据经过背书或交付就可以自由地转让、流通，其权利的转让无须通知债务人，债务人不能以没接到通知为由拒绝承担义务。

案例 2-1 中的法国公司 B COMPANY 将其对美国公司 A COMPANY 的 1 万美元债权转让给 C COMPANY，如果采用票据的形式，如汇票，则不需要事先通知 A。如不采用票据，而依民法来转让债权，则 B 必须向 A(债务人)发出债权转让通知，否则 A 不会直接向 C 履行其对 B 的债务。

2) 正当持票人权利不受前手权利缺陷的影响

票据受让人取得票据全部的权利，一旦拒付，受让人可以自己的名义对票据上的所有当事人起诉，且正当持票人的票据权利不受其前手权利缺陷的影响。所谓正当持票人是指取得或受让票据时是善意的，并给付对价。所谓对价，是指可以支持一项简单交易之物。

民法上，受让人与转让人的法律地位相同，受让人受让的债权受其前手权利缺陷的限制。

假定 B COMPANY 向 A COMPANY 销售价值 1 万美元的伪劣商品，B 将其 1 万美元债权转让给 C(参见图 2-2)。如依民法转让，当 C 要求 A 履行债务时，A 可以质量低劣为由，拒绝向 C 履行债务。民法上 C 的债权是从 B 转让而来，B 获得债权的权利有缺陷，C 作为受让人，其法律地位与 B 相同。

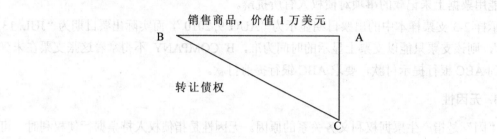

图 2-2　债权转让(B 将其对 A 的债权转让给 C)

假定 B 是通过汇票来转让债权，B 对 A 供货后开立一张汇票，以 A 为受票人，要求其付款给 C。如 C 得到这张汇票代表的债权是因为 C 向 B 供应商品生产的零部件，即 C 是正当持票人。当 C 持汇票向 A 提示要求付款时，A 不能以 B 提供的商品有质量问题为由拒绝给付。一般来说，A 有两种办法处理此类问题：一是拒付，C 遭拒付后按法定要求出具拒绝证书向 B 进行追索；二是 A 支付 C 款项后，对 B 提请诉讼，要求 B 赔偿其损失。实践中，A 往往选择拒付。

上述票据特性中，最重要的是流通转让性，它是票据的基本特性，其次才是无因性和要式性，它们是为流通转让性服务的。

(二)票据的功能

1. 结算功能

票据是非现金结算时使用的一种支付工具，利用它可以清偿债权债务。

2. 信用功能

票据本身不是商品，亦无所谓价值，它是建立在信用基础上的书面支付凭证。例如，图 2-1 中 A COMPANY 与 B COMPANY 之间进行商品交易时，如约定由 A COMPANY 开立支票或本票给 B COMPANY，这张支票或本票代表了买方 A COMPANY 到时付款的信用。

3. 支付和流通功能

票据作为一种支付工具，可以减少现金的使用，并且单据经过背书还可以连续转让，使票据在市场上广泛流通。

三、票据法(系)

(一)票据法范畴与渊源

票据法是调整票据关系的法律规范的总括性称谓。票据法有广义和狭义之分。

广义票据法，又称"实质票据法"，指一切有关票据的法律规范。广义的票据法不仅包括名为票据法的票据规范，还包括其他法律中对票据的规定，如民法中可以适用于票据的规范(人的行为能力制度、代理制度、动产物权制度等)、民事诉讼法中关于票据的规定(公示催告和除权判决、票据纠纷的诉讼等规范)、刑法中有关票据的规定(如伪造有价证券罪)、公证制度中关于拒绝证书的规定、破产法中关于票据当事人受破产宣告的规定、行政法规和规定中关于票据的规定。

狭义票据法，也叫"形式票据法"，是指由国家立法机关按照一定体系编制颁行的名为票据法的法律。

西方各国的票据法起源于欧洲。票据法在统一前，世界上有三大票据法系：法国法系、德国法系和英国法系。

法国法系的影响地区包括比利时、荷兰、葡萄牙、意大利等欧洲大陆国家和拉丁美洲各国。法国票据法仅将票据作为替代现金运输的工具，并作为证明原因关系的契约，强调票据当事人之间必须先有资金关系，对票据的形式要求并不严格，导致票据与原因关系不可分离，从而妨碍了票据的使用与流通。法国法系只注重票据的原始功能，即支付手段，限制了其发挥流通手段和信用工具的职能。

德国法系的影响地区有日本、土耳其、波兰、奥地利、丹麦、瑞士、瑞典等国家。德国票据法注重票据的流通功能和信用功能,将票据本身与票据产生的原因关系完全相分离，撇开当事人之间的资金关系，强调票据的无因性，规定严格的票据形式，强调票据的要式性和文义性。德国票据法相比法国票据法有了较大的进步，最终促使德国的票据法系成为大陆法系票据法的代表。

英国票据法是根据历来的习惯法、特别法以及各种判例编成的，比较强调保护票据流通和信用功能，制定了一套完整的票据流通制度，将票据本身与票据产生的基础关系严格区分。强调保护持票人尤其是正当持票人的权利，注重保护银行的权益。英国票据法的影响地区为加拿大、印度、澳大利亚、新西兰及其他原英属殖民地。

美国票据法属于英国法系，但各州并不统一。后该法被纳入美国的《统一商法典》(Uniform Commercial Code)中。

三大票据法系存在的分歧，阻碍了票据在国际间的使用和流通，从而影响国际结算的顺利完成。

(二)统一票据法

目前世界上存在两大票据法系：大陆法系与英美法系。大陆法系以《日内瓦统一票据法》为代表；英美法系以《英国票据法》为代表。两者在总体上有很多相似之处，但在具体条款上因各国商业习惯不同而有所不同，主要表现在四个方面：①对票据必要事项的要求；②伪造背书的处理；③对票据的对价观点上；④票据的分类。

(三)我国票据法

我国的票据起源虽然很早，但发展缓慢，一切票据行为及票据争议都以各地的习惯来处理。1928 年拟定票据法草案，1929 年正式颁布实施。1988 年实行《银行结算办法》。1995 年通过并颁布《中华人民共和国票据法》，该法于 2004 年 8 月修正，共 7 章 111 条，适用于境内的票据活动，对票据的出票、背书、承兑、保证、付款行为做出了规定，强调票据的无因性、要式性、文义性和独立性。

(四)票据的伪造、变造与抗辩

票据的伪造是指假冒他人名义所做的票据行为，如假冒出票人的名义而签发票据，假冒承兑人的名义而承兑票据，假冒背书人的名义而做背书等，均为票据的伪造。票据的伪造可分为票据的伪造和票据上签名的伪造。前者指假冒他人名义而做出票行为；后者指假冒他人名义而做出票行为以外的其他票据行为。由于被伪造的人并没有在票据上签名，所以不负任何票据责任；伪造人没有在票据上签上自己的真名，也不付票据责任，但在刑事上构成伪造有价证券罪，在民事上构成侵权行为，应受到法律的制裁。票据的变造是指无变更权限的人擅自变更票据上除签名以外的他人记载事项的一种行为，如变更金额、到期日、付款地等。

债务人提出抗辩以阻止债权人行使债权的权利，称为抗辩权。票据的抗辩是指票据债务人出于某种原因对票据债权人拒绝履行义务的行为，可分为对物的抗辩和对人的抗辩。前者基于票据本身的内容而产生，如票据缺乏必要事项、票据属于伪造、票据未到期或时效已过等；后者是特定的票据债务人对特定的票据债权人的抗辩行为，如甲以乙未依约交货而拒绝乙的提示付款等。债务人可以用抗辩这种手段保护自己，防止债权人滥签票据，但这种抗辩的理由必须是正当的。

第二节　汇　票

一、汇票的必要事项和任意记载事项

汇票内容包括必要事项和任意记载事项。其中，必要事项包括绝对必要事项和相对必要事项。绝对必要事项欠缺其一，汇票无效；相对必要事项尽管重要，如无记载，也不影响汇票的有效性。任意记载事项的内容相对不重要，有无记载都不影响汇票的有效性。

(一)汇票的绝对必要事项

(1) 表明"汇票"的字样(BILL OF EXCHANGE)，表示票的种类。《日内瓦统一票据法》要求汇票注明"BILL OF EXCHANGE"、"EXCHANGE"或"DRAFT"字样，《英国票据法》无此要求，但实务中一般都加注"汇票"字样。

(2) 无条件支付命令(UNCONDITIONAL ORDER)，即票据支付的文义不能附加某项条件及支付方式不能受限制，否则票据无效。票据必须采用书面形式，包括印刷、手写和打字等，但不能以铅笔或类似书写工具做成。支付命令用英语的祈使、命令的语气，如"PAY TO C CO. OR ORDER THE SUM OF U.S. DOLLARS TEN THOUSAND"，不能使用商量或请求语气书写(如"WE WOULD BE GLAD IF YOU WILL PAY..."或"WOULD YOU PLEASE PAY…")。

【案例 2-2】判断下列汇票中的文句是否构成票据的无条件支付委托

① PAY TO THE ORDER OF C COMPANY THE SUM OF USD TEN THOUSAND ONLY ON DELIVERY OF B/L NO. 123.

② PAY TO C COMPANY OR ORDER PROVIDED THE GOODS ARE COMPLIED WITH CONTRACT THE SUM OF USD TEN THOUSAND ONLY.

③ PAY TO C COMPANY OR ORDER THE SUM OF USD TEN THOUSAND ONLY AND CHARGE/DEBIT SAME TO APPLICANT'S ACCOUNT MAINTAINED WITH YOU.

④ PAY TO C COMPANY OR ORDER THE SUM OF USD TEN THOUSAND ONLY DRAWN UNDER P/O NO. 95E03LC001 DATED ON MAY 13, 2010.

⑤ PAY TO C COMPANY OR ORDER THE SUM OF USD TEN THOUSAND ONLY.

【分析】

以上①与②不构成无条件的支付委托，原因在于"ON DELIVERY OF B/L NO. 123"和"PROVIDED THE GOODS ARE COMPLIED WITH CONTRACT"构成了付款的条件，

不可接受。③支付命令虽然连接着借记某人账户，但可判定其是无条件的，可以接受。④支付命令连接着发生汇票交易的陈述也是无条件的，可以接受。汇票中是否写上"收到对价"(VALUE RECEIVED)也不影响汇票的有效性。⑤无条件支付委托。

(3) 确定的金额(AMOUNT)，包括确定的金额或可确定的金额，不能用大约或选择性的表达方式。金额中含利息或要求分期支付或要求以其他货币等值支付时，具体支付金额应能明确计算。

【案例 2-3】判定以下汇票文句是否构成确定的金额

① PAY TO THE ORDER OF C COMPANY THE SUM OF USD TEN THOUSAND ONLY PLUS INTEREST CALCULATED AT THE RATE OF 3% PER ANNUM FROM THE DATE HEREOF TO THE DATE OF PAYMENT(支付 C 公司的指定来人 1 万美元加上利息，利息按年息 3%计算，计息时间从出票日起至付款日止)。

② PAY TO THE ORDER OF C COMPANY THE SUM OF USD TEN THOUSAND ONLY BY TEN EQUAL CONSECUTIVE MONTHLY INSTALLMENTS(支付 C 公司的指定来人 1 万美元，连续 10 个月等额分期支付)。

③ PAY TO THE ORDER OF C COMPANY THE SUM OF USD TEN THOUSAND ONLY CONVERTED INTO HKD AT CURRENT RATE OF EXCHANGE(支付 C 公司的指定来人 1 万美元，可按当期汇率折算成港币支付)。

【分析】

① 构成确定的金额，因而汇票有效。如票据带有利息记载的，对不注明利率的汇票处理有两种情况：按照《日内瓦统一票据法》，该票据仍是有效票据；而按《英国票据法》，则视为无效票据。如果只注明利率，未注明起算日和止算日，根据《日内瓦统一票据法》第 5 条，从出票日起算，以付款日作为止算日，可以接受这样的汇票。

② 该汇票带有分期付款记载。《日内瓦统一票据法》不允许汇票分批付款，因而该汇票无效；而《英国票据法》承认汇票的分批付款，但是记载必须明确、具体，因而本汇票有效。如果汇票加注违约规定，如：任何一期付款违约时，其余未付各期则到期(PAY TO THE ORDER OF C CO. THE SUM OF US DOLLARS TEN THOUSAND BY TEN EQUAL CONSECUTIVE MONTHLY INSTALLMENTS WITHIN TWO YEARS AFTER THE DATE HEREOF PROVIDED THAT UPON DEFAULT IN PAYMENT OF ANY INSTALLMENT THE UNPAID BALANCE BECOMES DUE.)，可以接受。

③ 该汇票带有支付其他货币记载。无论是《日内瓦统一票据法》还是《英国票据法》，该项记载应明确货币的种类和凭以折算的汇率。因此，该汇票的文义满足条件，汇票有效。如未注明折算汇率，是不能接受的。

(4) 出票日期(DATE OF ISSUE)。出票日期即为汇票签发日期。列明出票日期有三个作用：①确定汇票到期日。如汇票付款期限为出票日后 30 天付款(AT 30 DAYS FROM THE DATE HEREOF)，而汇票出票日为"JUL. 13, 2010"，则汇票付款满期日为"AUG. 12, 2010"。②确定汇票提示期限，该期限是付款提示或承兑提示的依据。按照《日内瓦统一票据法》，见票即付的汇票，必须自出票日起 1 年内提示汇票，否则汇票失效，受票人可以拒付。③判定票据行为人能力。若出票时，出票人已宣告破产或被清算，则该汇票不能成立。若出票人是出票在先、宣告破产在后，则持票人在受票人拒付后可以持汇票作为一般债权人进入出票人的破产清算。

英美票据法认为出票日期不是必要事项。为避免混淆，出票日期建议使用月份的名称(如 JAN.、FEB.、MAR. 等或 JANUARY、FEBRUARY、MARCH 等)而不要使用数字。

(5) 受票人名称(NAME OF DRAWEE，ADDRESSEE)，也可称为付款人名称(NAME OF PAYER)。受票人是出票人出票指向的汇票付款人或承兑人。付款人名称和地址必须书写清楚，以便持票人向其提示要求付款或承兑。受票人是接受命令的人，他可以拒付，也可指定担当付款人付款，他不是确定付款之人。

《英国票据法》允许汇票开给两个付款人，但不允许两个付款人任择其一(A BILL DRAWN ON A OR B IS NOT PERMISSIBLE)，因为这样的付款人是不确定的。

(6) 收款人名称(NAME OF PAYEE)，又称为汇票抬头，有三种做法：限制性抬头、指示性抬头和来人抬头。

限制性抬头(RESTRICTIVE ORDER)。这种带有限制转让字样的汇票，不能以背书的方式转让，而只能以一般民法上债权让与的方式转让。常见的表示方法有：①PAY TO C COMPANY ONLY. ②PAY TO C COMPANY, NOT TRANSFERABLE. ③PAY TO C COMPANY, NOT NEGOTIABLE.

指示性抬头(DEMONSTRATIVE ORDER)。这种指示性抬头记载的汇票可以背书转让。常见的表示方法有：①PAY TO THE ORDER OF C COMPANY ONLY. ②PAY TO THE ORDER OF C COMPANY. ③PAY TO C COMPANY OR ORDER. 如汇票抬头记载为"PAY TO C COMPANY"，但没有加注限制转让字样，这种汇票应视为"指示性抬头"的汇票，可以背书转让。

来人抬头(BEARER ORDER)。这种汇票不记载收款人名称，而只写"付给持票人"，这种汇票可以流通转让，而且是仅凭交付就可转让。《日内瓦统一票据法》不允许以来人作为收款人，英国则允许，但都不允许留空。常见的记载方法有：①PAY TO BEARER. ②PAY TO C COMPANY OR BEARER. 我国《票据法》不允许做成"来人抬头"的汇票。

(7) 出票人签章(DRAWER'S SIGNATURE)，确定票据债务人必须承担票据债务的根本依据和票据是否有效成立的重要形式要件。出票人在开出汇票时，首先他要签字，承认自己的债务责任，汇票方可有效。如果签字是伪造的，或是未经授权的人签字，则汇票无效。出票人如为公司，应由公司法人代表签字(最好是手签)加盖公司公章，例如：

FOR ABC CO., LTD., NEW YORK
__JOHN SMITH, MANAGER__

受票人、收款人和出票人构成汇票的三个基本当事人。这三个当事人在同一汇票上的位置是相对固定的，如图 2-3 所示，三个当事人的关系体现了债权债务关系与结算关系。

图 2-3 汇票三个基本当事人的布局

一般来说，汇票的三个基本当事人应不重叠，但某些时候会发生变形，即汇票的某两个当事人的身份重叠，常见的有对己汇票与指己汇票。对己汇票是指受票人和出票人为同一个当事人；指己汇票是指出票人和收款人为同一个当事人。对于对己汇票，英美法认为持票人有权自由选择作为本票或汇票处理，而在其他国家，有些视为本票，有些视为汇票。各国法律都允许出票人与收款人为同一个人(指己汇票)，在转让时由出票人背书。变形汇票的产生与跨国公司内部贸易关系互不可分。

【案例 2-4】变形汇票的产生

西门子公司的全球结算中心设在新加坡，其上海分公司负责在中国的采购业务，而巴西分公司是制造企业。假设西门子上海分公司向杭州的 B 公司采购电子配件，货物由 B 公司直接装运给巴西的西门子公司。

【分析】

如采用汇票结算，理论上有如下方案。

① 方案 1：由西门子上海分公司出票，受票人是新加坡西门子，收款人为杭州 B 公司，这张汇票是对己汇票。

② 方案 2：由杭州 B 公司出票，受票人是新加坡西门子，收款人是 B 公司在海外的分公司或其本身，则这张汇票是指己汇票。

③ 方案 3：由杭州 B 公司出票，受票人是新加坡西门子，收款人是 B 公司的往来银行，这张汇票是一般汇票。

(二)汇票的相对必要事项

相对必要事项是否记载不影响汇票的有效性。

1. 付款日期(TENOR)

付款日期(TENOR)又称到期日，该日期是：①付款人履行付款义务的日期；②持票人行使或者保全票据权利的始期；③确定票据债务人何时履行其义务的依据；④决定票据权利时效的依据。汇票的付款期限有即期和远期之分。我国《票据法》规定：汇票上未记载付款日期的，为见票即付。

1) 即期付款的规定方法

常见的即期付款记载方法有三种：①"AT SIGHT PAY TO THE ORDER OF…"；②"ON DEMAND PAY TO THE ORDER OF…"；③"ON PRESENTATION PAY TO THE ORDER OF…"。

2) 远期付款的规定方法

常见的远期付款记载方式有四种：①定期付款(PAYABLE ON A FIXED FUTURE DATE)，例如"ON 09 AUG. 2010 PAY TO THE ORDER OF…"；②出票后定期付款(PAYABLE AT A FIXED TIME AFTER DATE)，例如"AT 30 DAYS AFTER DATE HEREOF PAY TO THE ORDER OF…"；③见票后定期付款(PAYABLE AT A FIXED TIME AFTER SIGHT)，例如"AT 30 DAYS AFTER SIGHT PAY TO THE ORDER OF…"；④某一特定事件发生后定期付款(PAYABLE AT A FIXED TIME AFTER THE HAPPENING OF A SPECIFIED EVENT)，例如"AT 30 DAYS AFTER BILL OF LADING DATE PAY TO THE ORDER OF…"。

3) 远期付款到期日计算

远期汇票到期日的算法有以下几种。

(1) AFTER。 AT XXX DAYS AFTER SIGHT/DATE/STATED DATE：算尾不算头，若干天的最后一天是到期日，如遇节假日顺延。不含所述日期，以次日为起算日。例如，见票后90天(AT 90 DAYS AFTER SIGHT)，见票日即承兑日，如为4月15日，则从4月16日起算，详细计算步骤如下：4月16日～4月30日，计15天；5月1日～5月31日，计31天；6月1日～6月30日，计30天；7月1日～7月14日，计14天，末尾一天是到期日，是90天的最后一天；若到期日适逢节假日，则顺延至下一个工作日。"AT XXX MONTH(S) AFTER SIGHT/DATE/STATED DATE"，应为付款之月的相应日期，如果没有相应日期，则以该月最后一日为到期日。如"AT 3 MONTHS AFTER 15 JAN."的到期日为4月15日；"AT 2 MONTHS AFTER 31 DEC."的到期日为2月28日。

(2) FROM。根据UCP600第三条的规定，"从……开始"(from)及"在……后"(after)

等词用于确定到期日时不包含提及的日期。

(3) 固定将来日期付款(PAYABLE ON A FIXED FUTURE DATE)：也称为板期付款汇票，需要提示承兑，以明确承兑人的付款责任，如固定在 6 月 30 日付款(ON JUNE 30 FIXED PAY TO...)。提单日后 XX 天付款可以转换成固定日期付款汇票，如"AT 30 DAYS AFTER B/L DATE/JUL. 15, 2004"可写成"ON AUG. 14, 2004 FIXED PAY TO..."。

(4) 不确定日期付款：凡注明"在某事件发生时付款"的汇票是无效汇票。例如：货物到达目的港时付款("ON ARRIVAL OF THE GOODS AT THE PORT OF DESTINATION PAY TO...")。

【案例 2-5】收款时间快慢比较

假定中国出口商 B 欲开立三张出票日为同一天的汇票，付款时间分别为提单日后 30 天付款、出票日后 30 天付款与见票后 30 天付款，受票人同为伦敦的 A 公司，收款人为中国银行浙江分行，并且 B 在同一天将这三张汇票交给中行。而中行在同一天将三张票据寄出，委托伦敦 EF 银行向 A 提示承兑和提示付款。同时，假定三张汇票在法定期限内被 A 在同一天承兑，试问：中行是否会在同一天收到三张汇票的款项？

【分析】

按照实务情况，在托收或信用证业务中，出口商一般是在装运货物取得货运单据后，汇集进口商或信用证所需要的全部单据，并开立汇票后向银行进行交单，因此提单日期在前，汇票出票日期在其后面。单据经过特快专递投递，到达 EF 银行。EF 银行在合理的工作期限内向 A 公司提示单据后，A 公司才可以见票。假定提单日为 7 月 13 日，出票日为 7 月 15 日，A 公司见票日为 7 月 21 日。因此，付款期限如下所示：

- 提单日后 30 天付款的汇票，A 公司付款满期日为 8 月 12 日(7 月有 31 天)。
- 出票日后 30 天付款的汇票，A 公司付款满期日为 8 月 14 日。
- 见票日后 30 天付款的汇票，A 公司付款满期日为 8 月 20 日。

由上可见，同为 30 天后付款的汇票，由于受票人计算付款法定期限的基数不同，收款人实际收款的时间有较大的差异。因此，选用提单日后定期付款的汇票方案对出口商最为有利。

2. 出票地(PLACE OF ISSUE)

出票地是出票人签发汇票的地点。出票地应与出票人地址相同，一般与出票日期相连，国际汇票应注明出票地，因各国均采用行为地法律原则，即按出票地的国家法律来确定必要事项是否齐全，汇票是否成立、有效。

我国《票据法》第二十三条规定：汇票上未记载出票地的，以出票人的营业场所、住所或者经常居住地为出票地。

3. 付款地(PLACE OF PAYMENT)

付款地是汇票金额的支付地点。付款地是确定出票人付款提示的地点、做成拒绝证书的地点。关于国际汇票的票据提示期限、拒绝证书的出具方式以及出具拒绝证书的期限，适用付款地法律。我国《票据法》规定，汇票上未记载付款地的，以付款人所在营业场所、住所或者经常居住地为付款地。

(三)票据的任意记载事项

票据的任意记载事项是否具备，并不影响汇票的有效性。

1. 担当付款行

担当付款行(A BANKER DESIGNATED AS PAYER)是指出票人根据与付款人的约定在出票时注明或者付款人在承兑时指定执行付款的银行，其目的是方便付款。担当付款行并不是票据的债务人，只是推定的受委托付款人。持票人应该先向付款人要求承兑，于到期日向担当付款行提示要求付款。例如，汇票付款人在承兑时可以加注担当付款行：

ACCEPTED

JUL. 21, 2010

PAYABLE AT BANK OF EUROPE

FOR A COMPANY, LONDON

_____(SIGNED)_____

汇票的承兑行为表示在汇票的正面。

2. 预备付款人

预备付款人(REFEREE IN CASE OF NEED)就是在汇票未获承兑或者未付款时，持票人可以请求承兑或者付款的对象，相当于第二付款人。

预备付款人被提示汇票后，可以参加承兑的称为票据债务人，于到期日参加付款，其一般表示在汇票正面受票人所在的位置。预备付款人要表明详细的地址，以方便持票人向其提示。例如：

TO: C COMPANY

IN CASE OF NEED REFER TO

ABC COMPANY, 129 BUFFEE STREET, LONDON

3. 免做退票通知或者放弃拒绝证书

出票人或者背书人可以在其签名旁记载放弃对持票人的某种要求，如免做退票通知或者放弃拒绝证书(NOTICE OF DISHONOR EXCUSED OR PROTEST WAIVED)。例如，B 公司在出票时，可以加列：

NOTICE OF DISHONOR EXCUSED

FOR B COMPANY

(SIGNED)

这表示持票人未获承兑或者未获付款时，不必做成退票通知，可以直接向 B 公司追索。不做退票通知，不影响持票人对该票据债务人的追索权。

4. 无追索权

《英国票据法》认为，出票人或者背书人可以通过免于追索的条款免除汇票被退票后受追索的责任。因此，出票人或者背书人可以在签章前加列无追索权(WITHOUT RECOURSE)条款。这实际上是免除了出票人或者背书人对汇票应承担的责任。其一般表示如下：

WITHOUT RECOURSE TO US

FOR B COMPANY

(SIGNED)

《日内瓦统一票据法》规定：出票人可以解除其保证承兑的责任，但是任何解除出票人的保证付款责任的规定，均视为无记载。

二、汇票的当事人

汇票的当事人有汇票进入流通领域前和汇票进入流通领域后之分。指示性抬头和来人抬头的汇票，可以进入流通领域；限制性抬头的汇票不能进入流通领域。汇票进入流通领域前，有三个基本当事人；汇票进入流通领域后，出现背书人、被背书人、保证人、参加承兑人或持票人等当事人，如图 2-4 所示。

1. 出票人

出票人是指签发并交付汇票的当事人。出票人在汇票上签章，即对汇票承担付款责任，向收款人或者持票人保证汇票在提示时，付款人一定付款或者承兑。若汇票未获付款或者未获承兑，则在持票人完成必要的法律程序后，出票人将偿付票款给持票人或者被迫付款的任何背书人。出票人在承兑前是主债务人，在承兑后是次债务人。

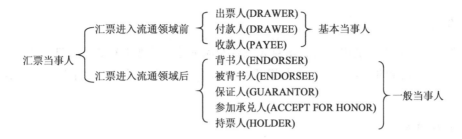

图2-4　汇票的基本当事人与一般当事人

2. 付款人

付款人是指接受无条件支付命令的当事人，即受票人(ADDRESSEE)。但是各国票据法均没有规定付款人一定承兑或者付款。付款人有选择不付款或者不承兑的权利。若付款请求权不能实现，持票人就可以对出票人等票据债务人行使追索权。远期汇票的付款人一旦承兑汇票，就成为票据的主债务人，即承兑人(ACCEPTOR)。承兑人在汇票上签章，表示接受出票人的无条件支付命令，应当保证按照其所承兑的文义于到期日付款。汇票的出票人、被迫付款的背书人或者出票人，均可凭票向承兑人主张权利。

3. 收款人

收款人是指收取票款的当事人。出票人签发并交付汇票给收款人，收款人就取得票据上的权利，即付款请求权和追索权，成为票据的债权人。收款人可以自己持票向付款人请求权利，实现票款，也可以将票据的权利通过背书转让给他人。

4. 背书人

背书人是指在票据背面作签章，将票据权利通过背书转让给他人的人。收款人将汇票背书转让给他人后成为第一背书人，受让人依此将票据背书再转让，相应成为第二背书人、第三背书人等。

背书人在票据背面作签章，即对受让人承担保证其所持汇票承兑和付款的责任。背书人在汇票得不到承兑或者付款时，应当向持票人或者被迫付款的后手背书人清偿票款。背书人是票据的次债务人。

5. 被背书人

被背书人是指接受票据背书转让的受让人。被背书人通过受让票据的权利，成为票据的债权人，有权持票对付款人或者其他票据债务人主张付款请求权和追索权。被背书人若不拟凭票取款，也可以转让汇票给其他人，而自己成为另一个背书人。

6. 保证人

保证人是指对汇票的出票人、承兑人或者参加承兑人的票据行为作保证的人。保证人必须在汇票上或者汇票的粘贴单上记载相应的保证事项。保证人的责任与被保证人相同。

7. 参加承兑人

参加承兑人是指当票据提示被拒绝承兑时，在票据上签章，表示参加承兑汇票的人。参加承兑人是票据的债务人，当票据到期，付款人拒绝付款时，由参加承兑人承担支付票款的责任。

8. 持票人

持票人是指现在正持有汇票的人。持票人可以是汇票的收款人，也可能是汇票流通过程中的被背书人或者来人。

《英国票据法》将持票人分为对价持票人(HOLDER FOR VALUE)和正当持票人(HOLDER IN DUE COURSE)，不同持票人享有票据权利不同。对价持票人获得的票据权利与其前手相同，不能超越其前手权利缺陷的限制。正当持票人取得票据的权利优于前手，不受前手权利缺陷影响，但是正当持票人必须保证其前手背书是真实的，汇票票面完整合格，取得汇票时尚未过期，对汇票是否曾经退票并不知悉，善意取得汇票并自己给付对价。

我国《票据法》第三十一条规定：以背书转让的汇票，背书应当连续。持票人以背书的连续，证明其汇票权利。

示样 2-1 中的汇票，B 是出票人，A 是受票人，C 是收款人，汇票抬头记载是"PAY TO THE ORDER OF C COMPANY…"。如 C 希望将汇票权利转让给 D，而 D 也可以将此汇票背书转让给 E，依此类推(参见图 2-5)。如果汇票在 J 手中，而 J 持有汇票是从 I 背书转让过来的，则 J 为持票人，又是被背书人。

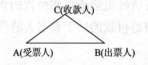

背书人	C		D		E		F		G		H		I
被背书人	D		E		F		G		H		I		J

图 2-5 汇票背书的连续性

三、汇票的票据行为

(一)出票

出票(DRAW, ISSUE)即票据的签发，包括两个环节：一是做成汇票，并由出票人本人或授权人签名；二是将汇票交付给收款人。交付是法律上的一个重要行为，若出票人仅有开票行为而无交付行为，汇票就是无效的。出票在票据诸行为中是主要的票据行为，其他的行为都是在出票的基础上进行的，称附属票据行为，如图 2-6 所示。

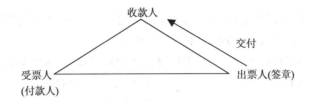

图 2-6　汇票的出票(包括汇票的做成与交付两个动作)

(二)背书

汇票的持有者在汇票背面加注签章并将汇票交给被背书人的行为称为背书(ENDORSEMENT)。背书的作用是表明票据权利由背书人转让给被背书人。背书包括两个动作：在汇票背面签字并交付被背书人。背书人对票据所负的责任与出票人是相同的，只不过他属"次债务人"，只有在汇票的主债务人即出票人或承兑人拒付时，才会被追索。背书包括完全背书、空白背书、限制性背书、附有条件的背书、委托收款背书、设质背书等。

1. 完全背书

完全背书，又称为特别背书(SPECIAL ENDORSEMENT)，背书人在汇票背面记有背书人的名称并作签章。此外，还应记有被背书人的名称。

PAY TO THE ORDER OF D COMPANY

FOR C COMPANY

(SIGNED)

D COMPANY 是被背书人，C COMPANY 是背书人。

2. 空白背书

空白背书(BLANK ENDORSEMENT)，又称不完全背书。背书人在汇票背面只记载背书人名称并作签章，未记载被背书人的名称。

FOR C COMPANY

(SIGNED)

我国《票据法》规定不允许空白背书，但是其在国际上非常盛行。对于空白背书后票据背书的连续性，需要借助法律上的推定认定，即后次背书的背书人视为前次空白背书的被背书人，依此类推，即使含有空白背书，也可认定背书的连续性。

做成空白背书的汇票，持票人仅凭交付完成转让。持票人在转让时不需要在票据上签章，可不承担票据责任，不受追索权人追索。持票人也可以在空白背书的签章前，添加被背书人的名称记载，将空白背书转化为完全背书后再做背书转让。

3. 限制性背书

背书人在汇票背面记载带有限制流通的文义，使汇票不可以再流通转让的背书，即为限制性背书(RESTRICTIVE ENDORSEMENT)。例如：

PAY TO D COMPANY ONLY	PAY TO D COMPANY NOT TO ORDER
FOR C COMPANY	FOR C COMPANY
(SIGNED)	(SIGNED)

4. 附有条件的背书

持票人在背书转让汇票时，其背书是带有条件的(CONDITIONAL ENDORSEMENT)，即为附有条件的背书。

PAY TO THE ORDER OF D COMPANY

ON DELIVERY OF BILL OF LADING NO. 123

FOR C COMPANY

(SIGNED)

根据汇票背书的无条件性，汇票背书所附的条件不发生汇票上的效力，而只对该次背书的背书人和被背书人有约束力。实际上，也只有条件完成后，背书人才将汇票交付给被背书人。

5. 委托收款背书

委托收款背书(ENDORSEMENT FOR COLLECTION)，是不以转让票据权利为目的的背书。背书人在票据背面除了附有被背书人的名称和自己的签章外，委托收款背书还带有以下类似的记载：

- FOR COLLECTION PAY TO THE ORDER OF BANK OF CHINA, SHANGHAI
- PAY TO THE ORDER OF BANK OF CHINA, SHANGHAI FOR DEPOSIT
- PAY TO THE ORDER OF BANK OF CHINA, SHANGHAI VALUE IN COLLECTION

委托收款背书是非权利转让背书，因此委托收款背书仅使被背书人获得代理权。我国《票据法》第三十五条规定："背书记载'委托收款'字样的，被背书人有权代背书人行使被委托的汇票权利。但是，被背书人不得再以背书转让汇票权利。"

6. 设质背书

设质背书(ENDORSEMENT IN PLEDGE)又称质权背书，是背书人以在票据权利上设定质权为目的而做成的背书。背书人为出质人，被背书人为质权人，设定的质权为权利质权。

我国《票据法》第三十五条规定："汇票可以设定质押，质押时应当以背书记载'质押'字样。被背书人依法实现其质权时，可以行使汇票权利。"设质背书的实用价值不大。受到期日限制，债权到期而票据未到期，或票据到期而债权未到期。

7. 回头背书

回头背书(REVERSE ENDORSEMENT)，又称为还原背书或逆背书。回头背书同样发生转让票据权利的效力，但票据权利会受到某种限制。如回头背书的被背书人为出票人，其仅享有对承兑人的付款请求权，而对其前手无追索权。背书人如为回头背书的持票人，对其后手均无追索权。如承兑人为回头背书的持票人，对任何人均无追索权。保证人以及参加承兑人为回头背书的持票人，其权利限制具体视保证人以及参加承兑人为何人而定。

回头背书的例子如图2-7所示。

顺序 当事人	第一次	第二次	第三次	第四次	第五次	第六次
背书人	C	D	E	F	G	B
被背书人	D	E	F	G	B	A

图2-7　回头背书

(注：第五次背书的被背书人B是汇票的出票人，而第六次背书的被背书人A是汇票的受票人。)

(三)提示

持票人将汇票交给受票人，要求付款或承兑的行为叫提示(PRESENTATION)。即期汇票在得到付款前要做付款提示。即期汇票的受票人如愿意付款，一经提示则要付款；远期汇票在得到付款前要做二次提示。第一次提示为"承兑提示"；在汇票到期时要做第二次提示，即"付款提示"。远期汇票的受票人如愿意付款，在第一次提示时要"承兑"汇票，在第二次提示时则要"付款"。提示一般在汇票记载的"付款地"或受票人所在营业场所进行，且须在合理时间内提示。

关于提示期限，我国规定即期汇票必须自出票日起一个月内提示付款，而《日内瓦统一票据法》则规定自出票日起一年内提示。远期汇票，我国规定承兑提示期限为出票日起一个月，《日内瓦统一票据法》则为出票日起一年。而对于远期汇票的付款提示期限，我国规定自到期日起十日内，《日内瓦统一票据法》为到期日或者前后两个营业日中之一日。

(四)承兑

1. 承兑的性质

承兑(ACCEPTANCE)是指远期汇票的受票人签章于汇票的正面，明确表示到期支付票据金额的一种行为。承兑行为一般做在汇票的正面或其粘贴单上。汇票正面记载的受票人因承兑行为的发生而成为汇票的承兑人，而该远期汇票则成为承兑汇票。远期汇票一经承兑，承兑人成为汇票的主债务人。

承兑包括两个动作：一是写成，二是交付。交付包括实际交付和推定交付。实际交付是指承兑人将承兑汇票交还给持票人；推定交付是指承兑人以发送一份承兑通知来替代交回承兑汇票。承兑人如通知持票人该汇票已于某日承兑就算交付。国际上习惯的做法是，对180天以内的远期汇票承兑后不退给持票人，而只是书面通知(发一个"承兑通知")。

付款人有权决定是否予以承兑，但应尽快决定同意承兑或者拒绝。付款人考虑的时间，即承兑时间，《日内瓦统一票据法》规定为第一次提示后的次日到第二次提示的这段时间，而我国《票据法》则规定收到提示承兑的汇票之日起3日内承兑或者拒绝。

2. 承兑的种类

1) 普通承兑

普通承兑即一般性承兑，是指承兑人对出票人的指示不加限制地予以确定且同意执行。具体做法如下，表明承兑人 A 完全接受出票人的无条件支付命令。该行为表明 A 公司在2010年7月21日承兑了汇票。

ACCEPTED

JULY 21, 2010

FOR A COMPANY

<u>(SIGNED)</u>

2) 保留性或限制性承兑

在承兑时，承兑人对汇票的到期付款加上一些保留条件，从而对票据文义进行了修改，包括有条件的承兑、部分承兑、限定地点的承兑、延长付款时间的承兑等。

(1) 有条件的承兑(CONDITIONAL ACCEPTANCE)。承兑人更改汇票付款的无条件性。

ACCEPTED

JULY 21, 2010

PAYABLE ON DELIVERY OF BILLS OF LADING

FOR A COMPANY

<u>(SIGNED)</u>

(2) 部分承兑(PARTIAL ACCEPTANCE)。承兑人表示同意对汇票的部分金额承担到期付款的责任(假定汇票金额为 10 000.00 美元)。

ACCEPTED

JULY 21, 2010

PAYABLE FOR AMOUNT OF USD 5000 ONLY

FOR A COMPANY

<u>(SIGNED)</u>

(3) 限制地点的承兑(LOCAL ACCEPTANCE)。承兑人限定支付票款的地点。

ACCEPTED

JULY 21, 2010

PAYABLE AT THE BANK OF EUROPE, LONDON AND THERE ONLY

FOR A COMPANY

<u>(SIGNED)</u>

(4) 延长付款时间的承兑(QUALIFIED ACCEPTANCE AS TO TIME)。下例假定票面记载的付款期限为见票后 90 天。

ACCEPTED

JULY 21, 2010

PAYABLE AT NINETY DAYS AFTER SIGHT

FOR A COMPANY

<u>(SIGNED)</u>

我国《票据法》规定：付款人承兑汇票，不得附有条件，承兑附有条件的，视为拒绝承兑。

【案例 2-6】远期汇票承兑与背书行为的表示

以下汇票是一份提单日后 90 天付款的汇票，出票日期为 2010 年 7 月 16 日。出票人 A 将汇票做成指示性抬头 "PAY TO BANK OF CHINA LTD., SHANGHAI OR ORDER"。

① "BANK OF CHINA LTD., SHANGHAI" 为方便收款，将汇票委托国外代理行向汇票的受票人提示承兑和付款，而在汇票背面做成空白背书，如图 2-8 所示。

BANK OF CHINA LTD., SHANGHAI
<u>SIGNATURE</u>

图 2-8 汇票的空白背书(做在汇票的背面)

② 受票人于2010年7月27日接受了持票人的第一次提示，并在汇票正面签章并做出承兑行为，如图2-9所示。

EXCHANGE FOR GBP5,000.00   JULY 16, 2010 SHANGHAI

AT NINETY DAYS AFTER B/L DATE/JULY 13, 2010 SIGHT OF THIS FIRST OF EXCHANGES (SECOND OF THE SAME TENOR AND DATE UNPAID)PAY TO BANK OF CHINA LTD., SHANGHAI OR ORDER THE SUM OF FIVE THOUSAND POUNDS ONLY.

DRAWN UNDER

TO: C COMPANY, LONDON

> ACCEPTED
> JULY 27, 2010
> FOR C COMPANY, LONDON
> SIGNED

FOR A COMPANY, SHANGHAI

(SIGNED)

图 2-9　汇票的承兑(由受票人 C 做在汇票的正面)

补充说明：

a. 实践中，汇票的收款人往往做成银行，原因有二：一是为满足汇票的一般形式(三个基本当事人)；二是出口企业要向银行进行融资，出口地银行采用押汇、议付等方式购进出口商手中票据，成为当然的收款人。

b. 出口地银行为便于代收行提示单据和代收款项，在寄出单据前在汇票背面作空白背书。

c. 托收项下汇票付款人做成进口商，而信用证项下是开证银行或其指定的付款行，不能是进口商本人。

d. 承兑做在汇票正面并穿过汇票，可以采用盖章的方式。

e. 出票地在中国上海，付款地在伦敦。

f. 汇票一般做成指示性抬头，不要做成记名抬头和来人抬头。

g. 付款命令必须是无条件的。

③ 这份汇票是提单日后90天付款的汇票，提单日为"JULY 13, 2010"，出票日期为"JULY 16, 2010"。以上汇票的付款日期填写方式为"AT NINETY DAYS AFTER B/L DATE/JULY 13, 2010"，实务中该汇票的付款日期还可以如下表示：

a. 出票日为"JULY 16, 2010"，付款日期为"AT NINETY DAYS AFTER JULY 13, 2010"(7月13日后90天付款)。

b. 出票日为"JULY 16, 2010"，付款日期为"AT NINETY DAYS AFTER B/L DATE (B/L DATE: JULY 13, 2010)"(提单日后90天付款，并在汇票表面的其他地方表明提单日为 JULY

13, 2010)。

c. 出票日为 "JULY 13, 2010"，付款日期为 "AT NINETY DAYS AFTER DATE HEREOF" (将汇票的出票日做成与提单日期为同一天，付款日期表示为出票日后 90 天)。

d. 出票日为 "JULY 16, 2010"，付款日期为 "ON OCT. 11, 2010"，即计算出提单日后 90 天的具体日期为 10 月 11 日。

另外，提单日应理解为装船日，即使装船日早于或晚于提单签发日期也是如此。

(五)付款

付款(PAYMENT)是指汇票的付款人于汇票到期日支付汇票金额以消灭票据关系的行为，是票据关系的最后一个环节，其具体过程是：汇票的持票人向付款人提示汇票，请求付款，然后付款人付款并收回汇票，从而使汇票上的法律关系结束。

(六)拒付

当持票人提示汇票要求承兑或付款时，遭到拒绝就叫拒付(DISHONOR)，也叫退票。事实上不可能的付款，如破产、死亡等也属于拒付。一旦发生拒付，持票人要及时通知前手，即发出退票通知(或称拒付通知)。这个通知可以是书面的，也可以由人传达，措辞不限，只要能说明是哪一张汇票遭退票即可。

为了使每一个前手都负责，持票人应在发生退票时，依此通知其前手，直至出票人。《英国票据法》规定退票通知应在退票后的一个营业日内发出，持票人未做通知或者未及时发出通知，则丧失追索权。《日内瓦统一票据法》规定：持票人未做通知或者未及时发出通知，不丧失追索权，但因未及时通知，造成前手损失的，应负赔偿责任，其赔偿金额以汇票金额为限。我国《票据法》规定持票人必须在退票后 3 日内，依法做成书面的退票通知。

退票通知在实践中有两种做法：第一种是依此通知其前手，第二种是持票人通知全体前手。此两种做法如图 2-10 所示。

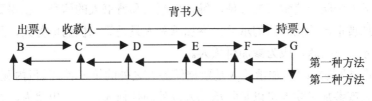

图 2-10　发出退票通知的办法

(七)追索

汇票遭拒付时，持票人要求前手偿还票款和费用的行为称为追索(RECOURSE)。持票人是主债权人，有权向背书人、承兑人、出票人及其他的债务人追索。持票人可以依背书人的次序，也可越过前手，向其中任何一个债权人请求偿还。为节省时间，甚至可以跨越所有的中间环节，向最主要的债务人追索。未承兑前向出票人追索；已承兑时，如承兑人拒付，也是向出票人追索。出票人清偿之后，还可向承兑人追索，承兑人若拟不付款，出票人可以向法院起诉。索偿的金额包括：①汇票金额，包括汇票上规定的利息；②损失的利息，即期汇票从付款提示日起计息，远期汇票从汇票到期日起计息；③做成拒绝证书和退票通知的费用。

索偿分期前索偿和期后索偿。

(1) 期前追索金额=票据金额-未到期利息+费用

(2) 期后追索金额=票据金额+利息+费用

若出票时注明"PROTEST WAIVED"或"NOTICE OF DISHONOR EXCUSED"字样，则出票人和全体背书人对拒绝证书和退票通知的费用免责。

(八)保证

指非汇票债务人对于出票、背书、承兑等行为予以保证(GUARANTEE 或 AVAL)，也是对汇票债务的担保。保证人一般是第三者，被保证人可以是出票人、承兑人、背书人等。保证人与被保证人所负的责任完全相同。经过保证后，票据的付款责任增强，促使票据更加易于流通转让。常见的汇票保证行为做法如下：

> PAYMENT GUANANTEED
>
> FOR ACCOUNT OF
>
> SIGNED BY＿＿＿＿＿＿＿
>
> DATED ON＿＿＿＿＿＿＿
>
> GOOD AS AVAL

(九)参加承兑和参加付款

非汇票债务人为防止追索权的行使，维护出票人和背书人的信誉，在得到持票人同意的前提下，参加被拒绝承兑汇票的承兑。参加承兑人只是第二性的债务人，只有在主债务人不付款时，才负责付款，成为参加付款人。

《英国票据法》规定："参加承兑人是票据债务人之外的第三者。"《日内瓦统一票据法》规定参加承兑人或参加付款人可以是除承兑人以外的任何人，包括出票人、背书人、保证人、预备付款人等。我国《票据法》没有这项规定。

参加承兑应在票据上记载，由参加人签章，并记载被参加人的姓名。参加承兑未记载的被参加承兑人视为出票人。参加承兑行为一般表示如下：

ACCEPTED FOR HONOR OF B COMPANY

JULY 26, 2010

FOR K COMPANY

(SIGNED)

持票人若接受其参加承兑，则持票人对被参加承兑人及其后手不得于到期日前行使追索权。参加承兑人对持票人以及被参加人后手，承担与承兑人相同的责任。如持票人到期向付款人做付款提示被拒付，参加承兑人应当承担付款责任。

四、汇票的主要种类

(一)商业汇票与银行汇票

根据汇票出票人身份的不同，可分为银行汇票(BANKER'S DRAFT)和商业汇票(COMMERCIAL DRAFT 或 TRADE BILL)。银行汇票以银行为出票人，委托国外分行或联行付款，出票人和付款人都是银行；商业汇票则以商号或商人为出票人。

(二)跟单汇票与光票

根据汇票是否附有货运单据，可分为跟单汇票(DOCUMENTARY BILL OR DRAFT)和光票(CLEAN BILL OR DRAFT)。跟单汇票指附有货运单据的汇票，光票指未附有任何货运单据的汇票。

根据交付单据的方式，跟单汇票可分为付款交单汇票(DOCUMENT AGAINST PAYMENT BILL)和承兑交单汇票(DOCUMENT AGAINST ACCEPTANCE BILL)。付款交单汇票指付款人付清票款后才对其交付货运单据的汇票，承兑交单汇票指付款人承兑汇票之后即对其交付货运单据的汇票。

(三)即期汇票与远期汇票

根据汇票付款期限的不同，可分为即期汇票(SIGHT BILL OR DRAFT, DEMAND BILL OR DRAFT)和远期汇票(TIME BILL OR DRAFT, USANCE BILL OR DRAFT)。即期汇票是付款人在见票或提示时立即就要付款的汇票，远期汇票是在将来若干时日付款的汇票。

远期汇票在付款前需要提示承兑。根据承兑人身份的不同，可分为商业承兑汇票(COMMERCIAL ACCEPTANCE BILL)和银行承兑汇票(BANKER'S ACCEPTANCE BILL)。若远期汇票的承兑人是进口商或其指定的个人，则此汇票是商业承兑汇票；若远期汇票的承兑人是银行，则此汇票为银行承兑汇票。

(四)国内汇票与外国汇票

根据汇票三个基本当事人居住地的不同，可以划分为国内汇票(INLAND BILL)和外国汇票(FOREIGN BILL)。出票人、付款人和收款人处在同一国的称为国内汇票，否则为外国汇票。

(五)一般汇票与变式汇票

根据汇票三个基本当事人身份的不同，可以分为一般汇票和变式汇票。一般汇票的三个基本当事人身份互不重叠，否则称为变式汇票。

另外，根据收款人抬头的记载可以分为记名汇票、指示汇票和无记名汇票。

第三节　本　　票

一、本票的必要事项

根据《日内瓦统一票据法》，本票必要事项如下：
(1) 表明"本票"的字样。
(2) 无条件支付的承诺。
(3) 付款日期，如未记载，视同见票即付。
(4) 付款地(未记载，以出票地或者出票人之住所为付款地)。
(5) 收款人或者其指定人的名称。
(6) 出票日以及出票地。
(7) 出票人的签章。

我国《票据法》第七十五条则规定本票必须记载下列事项：表明"本票"的字样，无条件支付的承诺，确定的金额，收款人名称，出票日期，出票人签章。"本票上未记载前款规定事项之一的，本票无效。"因此，与《日内瓦统一票据法》相比，我国《票据法》中将确定的金额列为绝对必要事项，而本票的付款地和出票地的记载视为相对必要记载事项。

二、本票与汇票的异同

(1) 本票行为有出票、背书、提示、付款、追索和保证，但是本票没有承兑行为。
(2) 本票出票是出票人根据票据法的规定做成本票并将其交付收款人的行为。其与汇票出票的相同点是出票包括做成与交付两个动作。与汇票出票的不同点如下所述。
① 法律效力不同：本票是自我支付承诺，是自付债券。

② 本票只有两个基本当事人，即出票人和收款人，没有受票人。

③ 本票没有承兑人，本票出票后，出票人就是主债务人，承担无条件的、绝对的、最终的票据责任。出票人的支付义务除因时效经过消灭外，不因持票人行使权利或保全权利的手续欠缺而免除。出票后收款人取得付款请求权和追索权。

④ 本票是单张签发的，汇票是成套签发，可以一式多份。

(3) 本票的提示是指本票的持票人必须在法定期限内提示票据，才能实现其票据权利。我国《票据法》规定：本票自出票日起，付款期限最长不得超过 2 个月。本票的持票人如果未在规定的期限内提示本票，则丧失对出票人以外的前手的追索权。本票持票人的前手仅指背书人或者保证人，不包括出票人；而汇票持票人的前手包括出票人。

(4) 本票的背书、保证、付款和追索与汇票相同。

三、本票的种类

(1) 根据出票人的不同，可分为商业本票(TRADER'S NOTE)和银行本票(BANKER'S NOTE)。

商业本票是指公司、企业或者个人签发的本票，分交易性的商业本票和融资性的商业本票。商业本票是商业信用。国际结算中使用的本票一般属于交易性的商业本票，目的是为了清偿债权债务。在出口贸易中，只有在出口方提供出口信贷的情况下，才接受进口商签发的分期付款的本票，并必须由进口国银行的背书保证。融资性的商业本票用于短期的资金融通，类似公司债券。

商业本票与商业信用密切相关，企业信用等级状况良好及资本运作管理制度完善是一国发展商业本票的基础。

银行本票是由银行签发的本票，通常被用于代替现金支付。即期银行本票是支付凭证，而不是信用工具。银行本票多为即期的，而各国为了加强对现金和货币市场的管理，一般对银行发行本票加以限制。我国《票据法》第七十三条规定："本法所称本票，是指银行本票。"

(2) 根据付款期限的不同，可分为即期本票和远期本票。我国《票据法》第七十八条规定："本票自出票日起，付款期限最长不得超过二个月。"

(3) 根据抬头的不同，可分为记名式本票、指示式本票和无记名式本票。

此外，公债、国库券、信用卡、旅行支票、银行券等也都属于本票。

第四节　支　票

一、支票的必要事项

根据《日内瓦统一票据法》，支票应记载以下事项：

(1) 表明"支票"的字样。

(2) 无条件支付一定金额的委托(我国《票据法》要求"确定的金额")。

(3) 付款人名称。

(4) 付款地(未记载的，以付款人地址为付款地)。

(5) 出票日期与出票地(未记载出票地，以付款人地址为出票地)。

(6) 出票人签章。

支票是最重要的支付工具，使用范围广泛。支票上的金额可以由出票人授权补记，未补记前的支票，不得使用。支票金额是相对必要记载事项，应当强调授权补记。

二、支票与汇票的异同

支票与汇票的异同如下所述。

(1) 支票的出票人是银行客户，付款人是开立账户的银行，支票是授权书；汇票的出票人、付款人是没有限定的任何人，汇票是委托书。

(2) 支票是支付工具，只有即期付款，没有远期付款，因而没有承兑，也没有到期日的记载；汇票是支付和信用工具，它有即期、远期之分，有承兑行为，也可能有到期日的记载。

(3) 支票的主债务人是出票人；汇票的主债务人在承兑前是出票人，在承兑后是承兑人。

(4) 支票可以保付；汇票没有保付的做法。

(5) 支票的出票人和付款人之间要有资金关系；而汇票的出票人和付款人之间不必先有资金关系。

(6) 支票可以划线；汇票一般不能划线。

(7) 支票可以止付；汇票承兑后，付款是不可撤销的。

(8) 支票只能开出一张；汇票可以开出一套。

三、支票的种类

支票有以下几种分类。

（1）按收款人的不同，支票可以分为记名支票和不记名支票。

（2）按照支票是否保付，分为保付支票(CERTIFIED CHEQUE)和普通支票。保付支票是由付款银行在支票上加"保付"字样并签字，以表明在支票提示时付款行一定付款。支票保付后，付款行就成为主债务人，出票人和背书人都可免除责任，免予追索。而且，对于保付支票，一般情况下不会退票，不会有止付的通知。

（3）按照支票是否划线，分为划线支票和非划线支票。支票不带划线者称为现金支票或非划线支票(OPEN CHEQUE)，持此类支票既可提取现金，也可通过往来银行代收转账。支票带有划线者称为划线支票(CROSSED CHEQUE)。这种支票在支票上划有两道平行线，可分为普通划线支票(GENERAL CROSSING)和特别划线支票(SPECIAL CROSSING)两种。一般划线支票是在平行线中不注明收款行名称的支票，收款人可通过任何一家银行代收转账；特别划线支票是在平行线中具体写有收款银行名称的支票，即付款银行只能将票款划付给划线中指定的银行，而不能像一般划线支票那样只要付给银行就行。非划线支票在由出票人、收款人、持票人加划横线后，或加注银行名称后，可成为一般划线支票或特别划线支票。但是不允许将划线支票转化成非划线支票，或将特别划线支票转化成一般划线支票。付款银行对划线支票和非划线支票所承担的责任是不同的。对划线支票，付款银行必须对真正的所有人付款或按划线的要求付款。

本 章 小 结

票据是用于清偿贸易双方债权债务关系的一种主要信用工具，分为汇票、本票和支票。票据具有七大特性，其中最主要的是要式性、无因性和流通转让性。由于票据本身代表一定的经济利益，世界各国基本上都有专门的票据法来调整票据项下债权人和债务人之间的权利与义务关系以及票据行为的法律关系，并最终形成了两大票据法系，即大陆法系和英美法系，而两大法系之间在某些方面有不可调和的分歧。

汇票票面记载的内容分为必要事项和任意记载事项，而必要事项又分为绝对必要事项和相对必要事项。汇票的必要事项必须记载，欠缺其一，汇票无效；汇票的相对必要事项尽管重要，但没有记载也不影响汇票的有效性；而汇票的任意记载事项记载与否不影响汇票的有效性。汇票、本票、支票的出票理念是不同的。汇票是出票人开立的，要求受票人在见票时或将来的某一可确定的日期付款给收款人或其指定来人或持票人的票据，有三个基本当事人。本票是一种自付债券，出票人开立本票后承诺自己付款，有两个基本当事人，本票没有承兑行为。支票是出票人委托银行付款给收款人或其指定来人或持票人的票据，有三个当事人，其中支票的付款人一定是银行。与汇票相比，支票都是即期的，而汇票有即期与远期之分。另外，还要注意汇票、本票、支票在票据的必要事项、票据行为方面的差异。

汇票行为有出票、背书、提示、承兑、保证、参加承兑、付款、拒付与追索，并且票据行为必须符合特定的法律规范。汇票的提示、承兑与付款必须在法定期限内进行。汇票在流通过程中，除注意汇票的出票是否有效外，还要注意汇票背书的连续性、正当持票人、对价持票人、票据变造与伪造等问题。

复习思考题

1. 汇票的绝对必要事项和相对必要事项有哪些？本票和支票的必要事项有哪些？

2. 本票、汇票和支票分别有哪些种类？

3. 票据有哪些特性？其中最主要的特性有哪几个？其具体含义是什么？

4. 汇票行为有哪些？分别应该注意哪些事项？汇票的背书、承兑、保证行为如何表示？

5. 两大票据法系关于付款人和持票人权利方面的规定有何差异？

第三章

汇款与托收

学习目标： 掌握汇款和托收的概念、分类、工作程序以及在具体操作时应注意的事项；熟知托收、汇款业务项下银行办理业务的要点；了解汇款的偿付和退汇、D/P 远期与 D/A 的关键不同点。

关键概念： 国际汇兑、顺汇、逆汇、电汇、票汇、托收、跟单托收、D/P、D/A、代收行、汇款行、预付

第一节　汇款基本知识

一、国际汇兑

商业银行的主要业务是存款、贷款和汇兑(拨头寸)。国际汇兑是指银行借助一定的结算工具在不同国家的两地之间进行资金的调拨，以结清两国客户间的债权债务关系。国际汇兑分动态的和静态的两种。动态(DYNAMIC)国际汇兑是指一国汇款人通过银行将资金汇付给另一国收款人，以实现国际债权债务清偿和国际资金的转移。汇是指国际货币资金转移，兑是两种不同货币资金的转换。静态(STATIC)国际汇兑主要是指外汇，即一国以外币表示的用以国际结算的支付手段。

国际汇兑按资金流向和结算工具流向的不同分为顺汇和逆汇两大类。

(一)顺汇

顺汇(REMITTANCE)，又称汇付，是指债务人主动将款项交给本国银行，委托该银行通过某种结算工具的使用将汇款汇付给国外债权人或者收款人。结算工具的流向和资金的流向相同，因此称为顺汇(如图 3-1 所示)。

(二)逆汇

逆汇(REVERSE REMITTANCE)是指债权人通过出具票据委托本国银行向国外债务人收取汇票金额的结算方式。因结算工具的流向和资金的流向相反，所以称为逆汇(如图 3-2 所示)。托收和信用证都为逆汇。逆汇通常由债权人签发汇票向债务人收款，这种方法称为

出票法。

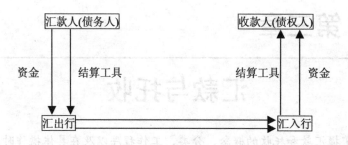

图 3-1 顺汇

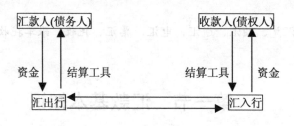

图 3-2 逆汇

二、汇款

(一)汇款定义

汇款采用顺汇的理念，即为"汇付"，是指银行根据汇款人或客户的委托，以一定的方式，通过其国外联行或代理行，将一定金额的货币支付给国外收款人或债权人的结算方式。

(二)汇款当事人

汇款具有四个基本当事人。

(1) 汇款人(REMITTER)，即付款人，是委托汇出行将款项汇交收款人的当事人。在进出口贸易中，一般是买方，汇款时需要填制汇款申请书。

(2) 汇入行或解付行(PAYING BANK)，是指接受汇出行委托，并解付一定金额给收款人的银行，一般是出口地银行。

(3) 汇出行(REMITTING BANK)，是指接受汇款人委托汇出款项的银行，通常是汇款人所在地银行，即进口地银行。

(4) 收款人或受益人(PAYEE OR BENEFICIARY)，是指收取汇款的当事人，一般是卖方。

(三)汇款的种类及其业务程序

以汇出行与汇入行之间委托付款指令的不同传递方式为依据进行划分，汇款业务可分有三种：电汇(TELEGRAPHIC TRANSFER, T/T)、信汇(MAIL TRANSFER, M/T)与票汇(REMITTANCE BY BANKER'S DEMAND DRAFT, D/D)。

1. 电汇(T/T)业务程序

电汇的业务程序如下所述，流程图参见图3-3。

(1) 买卖双方签订合同，约定以汇款方式结算。在合同中一定要规定汇款的具体种类。

(2) 汇款人，一般是进口方，填写汇款申请书(见示样3-1)，交付汇费。如采用电汇，汇款人则在汇款种类中选择电汇" X 电汇(T/T)"。国际贸易中选择有关单据内容的选项时一般标注"X"，标明该栏是选中项。

(3) 汇出行(进口方银行)如接受汇款人的汇款，在收妥汇款和银行费用后，在汇款申请书上签章，退回一份给汇款人，以此表明接受了汇款人的委托。汇出行将按照汇款人的要求，根据不同的传送方式通知汇入行，汇入行则根据汇出行的汇款指示向收款人解付汇款。

(4) 汇出行缮制汇款委托书，以加押电报、电传或 SWIFT 等电讯方式向汇入行发出汇款委托书，委托汇入行将款项支付给收款人。在汇款委托书上，汇出行告知汇入行该笔汇款的偿付方式，并以一定的方式将款项汇交汇入行。

(5) 汇入行收到汇款委托书(PAYMENT ORDER, P/O)，并收妥汇款后，向收款人发出电汇到账通知书，通知收款人前来解付汇款。

(6) 收款人到汇入行解付汇款。按照我国现行银行结算制度，银行在核对收款人身份后，按当日外汇牌价结汇入收款人账户。

(7) 汇入行向汇出行发出付讫通知。该笔汇款业务完结。

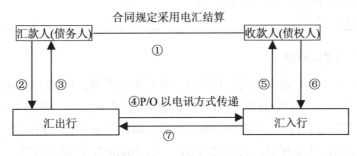

图 3-3　电汇业务程序

示样 3-1　汇款申请书

汇款申请书		
APPLICATION FOR OUTWARD REMITTANCE　□电汇(T/T)　□信汇(M/T)　□票汇(D/D)		
大写金额 AMOUNT IN WORDS	金额 AMOUNT	
收款人姓名 BENEFICIARY NAME		
收款人往来银行名称及账号 BENEFICIARY'S BANK & ACCOUNT NUMBERS		
收款人地址 BENEFICIARY ADDRESS		
汇款人姓名 REMITTER'S NAME 地址 ADDRESS	电话 TEL.	
汇款人附言 MESSAGE		

□上述汇款偿付办法 IN PAYMENT OF THE ABOVE REMITTANCE □请借记我行在贵行开立之账户、账号_____ PLEASE DEBIT MY/OUR ACCOUNT WITH YOU A/C NO._____ □付现金/支票 I/WE SEND YOU CASH/CHEQUE -------------------------------------- 申请人签名盖章(APPLICANT'S SIGNATURE) (请用留存本行之印鉴)	银行专用 FOR BANK USE ONLY	
	银行编号 BANK REF.	
	手续费 COMMISSION	
	邮电费 POSTAGE/CABLE	
	银行盖章	
	主管	复核
	核印	经办

2. 信汇(M/T)业务程序

信汇业务程序与电汇基本相同，只在以下几步中有差异：在第(1)步中，合同约定采用信汇结算，而非电汇；在第(2)步中，汇款人填写汇款申请书时，选择汇款种类为"信汇(M/T)"，而非"电汇(T/T)"；在第(4)步中，汇出行缮制汇款委托书后，以航空挂号信方式向汇入行邮寄发出汇款委托书。其余的第(3)、(5)、(6)和(7)步与电汇相同。

3. 票汇(D/D)业务程序

票汇的业务程序与电汇、信汇有很大的不同，流程参见图 3-4。

(1)　买卖双方签订合同，约定以票汇结算。

(2)　汇款人到其银行填写汇款申请书(见示样 3-1)，交付汇费。如采用票汇，汇款人则在汇款种类中选择"X 票汇(D/D)"。

(3)　汇出行(进口方银行)如接受汇款人的汇款，在收妥汇款和银行费用后，签发一张即期银行汇票交给汇款人。银行汇票以汇出行为出票行，汇入行为付款行，汇款收款人为汇票的受益人。

(4)　汇款人将银行即期汇票寄交收款人。

(5)　汇出行将汇款通知书(汇票一式五联中的第二联)，又称为"票根"寄汇入行，凭此将与收款人提交的汇票进行核对。近年来，银行已不寄出汇款通知书，汇票改为一式四联。

(6)　收款人向汇入行提示汇票，要求付款。

(7)　汇入行借记汇出行账户，取出头寸，凭票解付汇款给收款人。

(8)　汇入行将借记通知书寄汇出行，通知汇款解付完毕。

该笔汇款业务完结。

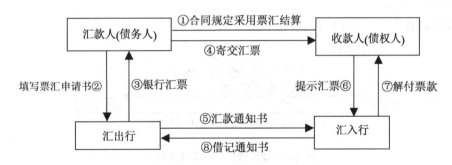

图 3-4　票汇业务程序

(四)汇款的偿付与退汇

1. 汇款的偿付

汇款的偿付是指汇出行办理汇出业务时应及时将汇款金额拨交给解付汇款的汇入行的行为。结合汇出行与汇入行开设账户的情况，汇款资金的拨付有以下四种不同的方式。

1)　主动贷记

汇出行在汇入行开有往来账户，汇出行在委托汇入行解付汇款时，汇出行会在支付委托书上注明偿付指示"IN COVER, WE HAVE CREDITED YOUR A/C WITH US"(作为偿付，我行已经贷记你行在我行开立的账户)，表明汇出行已主动将相应头寸贷记汇入行的账户。

汇入行收到支付委托书，知悉汇款头寸已拨入自己账户，即可使用拨妥的头寸解付汇款给收款人。

主动贷记的流程如图 3-5 所示。

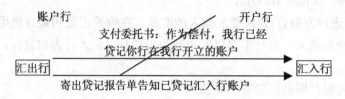

图 3-5　主动贷记汇款头寸拨付

2)　授权借记

汇出行在汇入行开有往来账户，汇出行在委托汇入行解付汇款时，汇出行会在支付委托书上注明偿付指示 "IN COVER, PLEASE DEBIT OUR A/C WITH YOU" (作为偿付，请借记我行在你行开立的账户)，表明授权汇入行借记在汇出行中的账户。

汇入行收到支付委托书后借记汇出行账户，拨出头寸解付汇款给收款人，并寄出借记报告单通知汇出行。

授权借记的流程如图 3-6 所示。

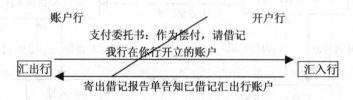

图 3-6　授权借记汇款头寸拨付

3)　共同账户行转账

汇出行和汇入行相互之间没有往来账户，但在同一代理银行均开设有账户时，为了偿付解款，汇出行可以在支付委托书上作偿付指示 "IN COVER, WE HAVE AUTHORISED X BANK TO DEBIT OUR A/C AND CREDIT YOUR A/C WITH THEM" (作为偿付，我行已授权 X 银行借记我行的账户同时贷记你行在他们银行所开立的账户)。

共同账户行转账的流程如图 3-7 所示。

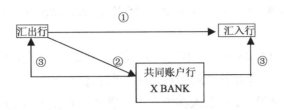

图 3-7　共同账户行转账汇款头寸拨付

注：①汇出行向汇入行发出支付委托书，并在支付委托书上作偿付指示"IN COVER，WE HAVE AUTHORIZED X BANK TO DEBIT OUR A/C AND CREDIT YOUR A/C WITH THEM"。②汇出行向共同账户行发出指示，授权共同账户行借记汇出行账户，并将头寸拨交汇入行账户。③共同账户行向汇入行邮寄贷记报告单同时向汇出行邮寄借记报告单。

4)　各自账户行转账

汇出行和汇入行相互之间没有往来账户，但他们各自的账户行之间有账户往来时，汇出行应在支付委托书上作偿付指示"IN COVER, WE HAVE INSTRUCTED X BANK TO PAY THE PROCEEDS TO YOUR ACCOUNT WITH Y BANK"(作为偿付，我行已指示 X 银行支付款项入你行在 Y 银行所开立的账户)。

各自账户行转账的流程如图 3-8 所示。

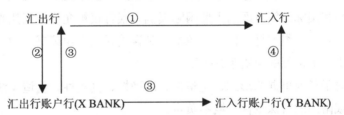

图 3-8　各自账户行转账汇款头寸拨付

注：①汇出行向汇入行发出汇款支付委托，并在支付委托书上作偿付指示"IN COVER, WE HAVE INSTRUCTED X BANK TO PAY THE PROCEEDS TO YOUR ACCOUNT WITH Y BANK"。②汇出行向其账户行发出指示，授权其账户行借记汇出行账户，并将款项汇给汇入行的账户行。③汇出行账户行向汇入行账户行邮寄贷记报告单，同时向汇出行邮寄借记报告单。④汇入行账户行贷记汇入行账户并邮寄贷记报告单给汇出行。

2. 汇款的退汇

退汇就是汇款在解付前的撤销。退汇可以是收款人提出，也可以是汇款人提出的。

1)　收款人退汇

信汇(M/T)和电汇(T/T)项下办理退汇，收款人只要通知汇入行，汇入行退回付款委托书给汇出行，汇出行通知付款人办理退汇。

票汇(D/D)项下办理退汇，收款人将票汇退回汇款人，由汇款人办理退汇手续。

2) 汇款人退汇

信汇(M/T)和电汇(T/T)项下办理退汇，汇出行接到退汇申请后立即通知汇入行停止解付，在撤销通知到达汇入行并且汇入行未解付汇款时才生效。

票汇(D/D)项下办理退汇，汇款人在未寄出汇票之前可以持汇票到汇出行退汇，汇出行发函通知汇入行将有关汇款通知书注销退回。但是，如果汇款人已将汇票寄出，则不能办理退汇。

若汇票遗失、被窃，汇款人应立即办理"挂失止付"手续。在办理手续时，汇款人应向汇出行出具担保书，担保若发生重付，由汇款人负责赔偿。汇出行收到担保书后即可通知汇入行挂失止付，待汇入行书面确认后，方可办理退汇手续或者办理补发汇票。

第二节　托收基本知识

一、托收国际惯例

由国际商会编写的《托收统一规则》(UNIFORM RULES FOR COLLECTION，URC522)是关于国际贸易和国际结算方面的重要国际惯例。银行仅被允许根据托收申请书的指示和URC522 办理委托，不得超越、修改、疏漏、延误委托人在申请书上的指示，否则引起的后果由银行负责。但银行的免责条款如下：

(1) 银行对于任何单据的形式、完整性、准确性、真实性、伪造及法律效力，或对于单据上规定的或附加的特殊条件，概不负责。

(2) 银行对于任何单据代表之货物的描述、数量、重量、质量、状况、包装、交货价值或存在，或对于货物的发货人、承运人、运输行、收货人或货物保险人或其他人的诚信、行为和/或疏忽、偿付能力、执行能力或信誉也概不负责。

(3) 银行对于任何发电、信件或单据在寄送途中的延误和/或丢失所引起的后果，或由于任何电讯工具在传递中产生的延误、残缺或其他错误，或对于专门术语在翻译或解释上的错误，不承担义务和责任。

(4) 银行对于自己所收到的指示因意思不明需澄清所引起的延误不负责任。

(5) 银行对于天灾人祸、暴动、内乱、叛乱、战争或他们所不能控制的任何其他原因，或罢工、停工致使营业中断所造成的后果，不承担义务或责任。

二、托收的定义及其当事人

(一)托收的定义

托收体现商业信用。出口商(或债权人)开立金融票据或商业单据或两者兼有，委托托收行通过其联行或代理行向进口商(或债务人)收取货款或劳务费用的结算方式。金融票据可以是汇票、本票、支票或付款收据；商业单据是指商业发票、运输单据、所有权单据或其他类似单据。

(二)托收业务当事人

托收业务有四个基本的当事人：委托人、托收行、代收行和付款人。根据业务需要，还可能出现另两个当事人：提示行和需要时的代理。

1. 委托人

委托人(PRINCIPAL)就是委托银行进行托收的当事人。委托人一般是出口商，根据票据法，即为出票人。当贸易合同确定结算方式为托收时，出口商托收货款受贸易合同和托收申请书的约束。

(1) 委托人的责任和义务如下：①根据合同规定交付货物，这是出口商最基本的义务，也是跟单托收的前提条件；②提交符合合同规定的单据。进口商提货前必须取得单据，单据代表货物所有权；③填写托收申请书，开立汇票，并将托收申请书(其具体内容见示样3-2)和汇票连同商业单据一并交给托收行。

(2) 托收申请书的内容：①委托人的名称、地址、有权印鉴；②付款人的名称、地址，或开户行的名称、地址、账号；③托收随附单据的名称和份数；④托收交单方式；⑤托收收妥后的收账要求；⑥托收拒付或者拒绝承兑时应采取的必要措施，如是否要做成拒绝证书、货物抵港后是否代办存仓保险等；⑦托收费用由谁承担；⑧有关托收的其他要求。

2. 托收行

托收行(REMITTING BANK)是接受委托人的委托并通过国外代理行办理托收的银行。托收行一般是出口商的往来银行。托收行根据委托人的指示办理，并对自己的过失负责。托收行的责任和义务如下：

(1) 缮制托收委托书(其具体内容见示样 3-3)。根据托收申请书的内容制作托收委托书，并将委托书和单据寄给国外的代理行，指示其向付款人收款。实践中，托收委托书与托收申请书内容基本一致，只是函头名称不一样。如出口托收申请书为"LETTER OF INSTRUCTION FOR OUTWARD COLLECTION"，而托收委托书是"COLLECTION

ORDER"。

(2) 核验单据。托收行应当审核实收单据的名称和份数是否与申请书填写的相同，但除此之外没有进一步审核单据的义务。托收行照常规处理业务，对自己的过失承担责任。选择代收行的费用和风险由委托人承担。

示样 3-2　托收申请书

出口托收申请书

LETTER OF INSTRUCTION FOR OUTWARD COLLECTION

| OUR REFERENCE NUMBER |
| FOR ALL COMMUNICATIONS |
| PLEASE ALWAYS QUOTE |

OFFICE:

ADDRESS:

DATE:

TELEX:

FAX:

DEAR SIRS,

WE ENCLOSE THE FOLLOWING DOCUMENTS FOR COLLECTION.

□DOCUMENTARY COLLECTION　　□CLEAN COLLECTION

| TO (COLLECTING BANK): | | | | | | DRAWER: | | | | |
| DRAWEE: | | | | | | AMOUNT: | | | | |

DOCUMENTS	DRAFT(S)	COMMERCIAL INVOICE	OCEAN B/L	N/N OCEAN B/L	AIRWAY BILL	INS. POLICY	P/W LIST	CERT. OF ORIGIN	G.S.P. FORM A	BENEFICIARY'S CERT.

DISPOSAL OF PROCEEDS UPON COLLECTION:

COLLECTION INSTRUCTIONS ARE MARKED WITH "X" AS BELOW:

□ DELIVER DOCUMENTS AGAINST □ PAYMENT □ ACCEPTANCE

□ ALL YOUR BANKING CHARGES ARE FOR ACCOUNT OF □ DRAWER □ DRAWEE

□ WAIVE BANKING CHARGES AND/OR INTEREST IF REFUSED BY DRAWEE.

□ DO NOT WAIVE BANKING CHARGES AND / OR INTEREST.

□ ADVISE US ACCEPTANCE OF DRAFT (S) AND GIVING DUE DATE BY TELETRANSMISSION.

□ HOLD DRAFT(S) AND DOCUMENTS PENDING FURTHER INSTRUCTIONS FROM US IN CASE
OF NON-PAYMENT /NON-ACCEPTANCE.

□ IN CASE OF DISHONOR, HAVE THE GOODS STORED IN BOND AND INSURED AGAINST
USUAL RISKS WHEN DEEMED NECESSARY, AND ADVICE US IMMEDIATELY TO THAT EFFECT.

□ IF PAYMENT IS DELAYED COLLECT INTEREST AT @ ____% P. A. FOR THE PERIOD OF SUCH
DELAY.

□ IN CASE OF NEED, REFER TO_____.

FOR _____

AUTHORIZED SIGNATURE(S)

示样 3-3　托收委托书

COLLECTION ORDER						ORIGINAL				

COLLECTION ORDER　　　　　　　　　　　**ORIGINAL**

OFFICE:

ADDRESS:　　　　　　　　DATE:_____

TELEX:

FAX:

DEAR SIRS,

WE ENCLOSE THE FOLLOWING DOCUMENTS FOR COLLECTION.

□DOCUMENTARY COLLECTION　　□CLEAN COLLECTION

OUR REFERENCE NUMBER
FOR ALL COMMUNICATIONS PLEASE ALWAYS QUOTE

TO (COLLECTING BANK):	DRAWER:
DRAWEE:	AMOUNT:

DOCUMENTS	DRAFT(S)	COMMERCIAL INVOICE	OCEAN B/L	N/N OCEAN B/L	AIRWAY BILL	INS. POLICY	P/W LIST	CERT. OF ORIGIN	G.S.P. FORM A	BENEFICIARY'S CERT

DISPOSAL OF PROCEEDS UPON COLLECTION:

COLLECTION INSTRUCTIONS ARE MARKED WITH "X" AS BELOW:

□ DELIVER DOCUMENTS AGAINST □ PAYMENT □ ACCEPTANCE

□ ALL YOUR BANKING CHARGES ARE FOR ACCOUNT OF □ DRAWER □ DRAWEE

□ WAIVE BANKING CHARGES AND/OR INTEREST IF REFUSED BY DRAWEE.

□ DO NOT WAIVE BANKING CHARGES AND / OR INTEREST.

□ ADVISE US ACCEPTANCE OF DRAFT (S) AND GIVING DUE DATE BY TELETRANSMISSION.

□ HOLD DRAFT(S) AND DOCUMENTS PENDING FURTHER INSTRUCTIONS FROM US IN CASE
　OF NON-PAYMENT /NON-ACCEPTANCE.

□ IN CASE OF DISHONOR, HAVE THE GOODS STORED IN BOND AND INSURED AGAINST USUAL
　RISKS WHEN DEEMED NECESSARY, AND ADVICE US IMMEDIATELY TO THAT EFFECT.

□ IF PAYMENT IS DELAYED COLLECT INTEREST AT @ _____% P. A. FOR THE PERIOD OF SUCH
　DELAY.

□ IN CASE OF NEED, REFER TO_____ .

　　　　　　　　　　　　　　　FOR _____

　　　　　　　　　　　　　　　AUTHORIZED SIGNATURE(S)

3. 代收行

代收行(COLLECTING BANK)是指接受委托行委托向付款人办理收款并交单的银行。
代收行在托收业务中所承担的责任与托收行基本相同，如核对单据的份数和名称，如有不符立即通知托收行，代收行在未经托收行同意前不得变更委托书上的任何条件，否则责任自负。除此以外，代收行还有以下责任。一是保管好单据。代收行在进口商按规定付款或承兑前不可以将单据发给进口商。付款人拒付，代收行应当通知托收行，若发出通知后90日仍未收到指示，将单据退回托收行。二是谨慎处理货物。代收行原则上无义务处理货物，只有在付款人拒付时，才会根据委托人指示办理存仓、保险手续。若代收行为了保护货物，在发生天灾人祸等紧急情况下即使未得到委托人的指示也可以对货物采取行动。

4. 付款人

付款人(DRAWEE)是根据托收委托书被提示单据要求付款的当事人，一般是进口商。依据票据法，即为受票人。付款人有权利审查单据以决定是否付款或承兑，但是拒付必须经得起委托人的抗辩，否则会遭受信誉和经济上的损失。

5. 非基本当事人

托收业务还可能出现其他当事人，主要有提示行和需要时的代理。

(1) 提示行(PRESENTING BANK)，是指向付款人提示单据要求付款人付款的银行。若代收行与付款人无账户关系或者两者不在同一城市，代收行必须转托另一家银行提示单据。

(2) 需要时的代理(REPRESENTATIVE IN CASE OF NEED)，是指委托人指定的代表。付款人在拒付或拒绝承兑后，需要时的代理可代理委托人办理货物存仓、保险、转售、运回或改变交单条件等事宜。委托人在托收指示中应明确完整地规定其权限，否则银行将不接受该代理的任何指示。

(三)托收的种类及其业务程序

1. 托收的种类

按托收项下是否随附商业单据，托收分为光票托收与跟单托收。

1) 光票托收

光票托收(CLEAN BILL FOR COLLECTION)是指出口商仅开立汇票而不附任何商业单据，委托银行收取货款的一种托收方式。一般用于收取货款尾数、代垫费用、佣金、样品费或者其他贸易从属费用。光票托收的汇票有即期和远期之分。采用即期汇票，代收行收到汇票后应立即向付款人提示，要求付款；采用远期汇票，代收行收到汇票后，应立即向付款人提示，先要求承兑，以确定到期付款的责任。承兑后，代收行收回汇票，于到期日再做提示要求付款。若付款人拒付或拒绝承兑，除托收委托书另有规定外，应由代收行在法定期限内及时将拒付情况通知托收行，转知委托人。

2) 跟单托收

跟单托收(DOCUMENTARY BILL FOR COLLECTION)按金融单据是否随附商业单据分为两种。一种是金融票据随商业单据的托收。这种托收是凭汇票付款，其他单据是汇票的附件，起"支持"汇票的作用。另一种是商业单据不附金融单据的托收。由于有些国家如日本、德国对汇票要征收印花税，为了减免税收负担而在信誉和信任度较高的公司之间采用后一种方式。跟单托收按其交单方式，分为付款交单(DOCUMENTS AGAINST PAYMENT，D/P)与承兑交单(ACCEPTANCE DOCUMENTS AGAINST PAYMENT，D/A)。

付款交单是指代收行必须在进口商付清票款后，才将商业单据包括提单交给进口商的一种交单方式。按出口商开立汇票付款期限的不同，付款交单分为即期付款交单与远期付款交单。即期付款交单(D/P AT SIGHT)是指代收行提示跟单汇票给进口商要求付款，进口商作为即期汇票的受票人见票即付后，代收行才交单给进口商。远期付款交单(D/P AT XX DAYS AFTER SIGHT/SHIPMENT DATE)是指代收行提示跟单汇票给进口商要求承兑，进口商作为远期汇票的受票人对汇票承兑后，代收行保管全套商业单据和承兑汇票，待汇票到期时提示付款，进口商付款后取得单据。

承兑交单(DOCUMENTS AGAINST ACCEPTANCE)是指代收行在进口商承兑远期汇票后，即把全套商业单据交给进口商，汇票到期时由进口商付款。

2. 托收业务程序

1) 即期付款交单业务程序

即期付款交单业务程序如图 3-9 所示。

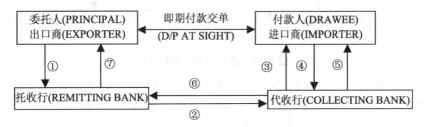

图 3-9 即期付款交单业务程序

注：在进出口贸易项下，贸易双方签订合同，规定货款结算方式为即期付款交单。其业务程序如下：①出口商按合同要求出运货物后，填写托收申请书(或交单委托书)，开立即期汇票后连同商业单据交托收行委托收款。②托收行接受委托后，核验出口商提交的单据后，填写托收委托书，并将汇票、商业单据等邮寄代收行。托收委托书的内容与托收申请书基本相同。③代收行按照托收委托书的指示向付款人提示汇票。④付款人审单无误后付款。⑤代收行向付款人交单。⑥代收行按托收委托书规定的方式将货款交付托收行。⑦托收行交付货款给出口商。

2) 远期付款交单业务程序

远期付款交单业务程序如图 3-10 所示。

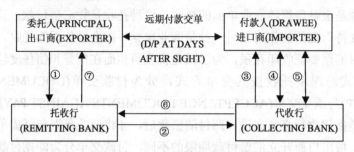

图 3-10 远期付款交单业务程序

注：在进出口贸易项下，贸易双方签订合同，规定货款结算方式为远期付款交单。其业务程序与即期付款交单相比，在①④⑤环节存在明显差异，但其他程序大致相似：①远期付款交单，出口商装运货物后开立的是远期汇票。④付款人审单无误后在汇票上加具承兑，代收行收回承兑汇票及所有提示的商业单据。⑤汇票到期后，代收行向付款人提示付款。付款人支付票款后，代收行向其交单。

3) 承兑交单业务程序

承兑交单业务程序如图 3-11 所示。

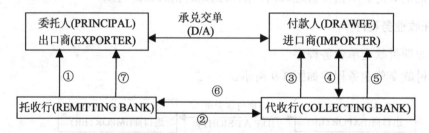

图 3-11 承兑交单业务程序

注：在进出口贸易项下，贸易双方签订合同，规定货款结算方式为承兑付款交单。其业务程序与远期付款交单相比，在④环节存在明显差异，但其他程序大致相似。其中④付款人审单无误后在汇票上加具承兑，代收行收回承兑汇票，并将单据交付给付款人。

第三节　汇款和托收结算方式具体运用及相关案例

一、汇款具体运用及应注意的问题

(一)汇款的具体运用

在汇款业务中，银行仅仅起服务中介的作用，买卖双方凭商业信用，资金负担不平衡。

但是，汇款具有速度快、费用低、使用灵活的特点。在国际贸易中，汇款一般用于预付和到付。预付项下，进口商资金负担重；而到付项下出口商资金负担重。

1. 预付

预付汇款是针对买方而言的，对卖方来说是在装运货物前或在交出货运单据前收取货款，具体细分为以下三种。

(1) 随订单付现(CASH WITH ORDER)，即订单签订后，买方就将全部货款预付给卖方。卖方收取预收款后，开始生产。买方需要承担买方是否能按期交货或质量等方面的全部风险，而卖方几乎不承担任何经营风险。

(2) 装运前 XX 天付款(PAYMENT TO BE EFFECTED AT LEAST XX DAYS BEFORE SHIPMENT)。买卖双方合同签订后，卖方开始安排生产。货物生产包装完毕后，将发货清单和预装运期通知买方，请其付款。货款收妥后，卖方才将货物装运出去。

(3) 装运后 XX 天付款，但进口商必须先付款后提货。此方法根据不同的情况，可细分为三种。

① PAYMENT WITHIN XX DAYS AFTER SHIPMENT, THE SHIPPING DOCUMENTS WILL BE RELEASED BY THE SELLER TO THE BUYER ON THE BASIS OF 100% PAYMENT RECEIVED BY THE SELLER. 在运输单据具有物权凭证性质的前提下(如海运提单，且提单抬头不能做成记名提单)可以操作。买卖双方签订合同后，卖方先安排生产，然后将货物装运出去。在进口商付清货款后，出口商再将全套商业单据(包括物权单据)寄交买方。

② CASH ON DELIVERY(COD)，即"代客收款"或"付款交货"。在运输单据不具有物权凭证性质前提下(如航空运输)，进口商坚持让出口商先装运后收款，而出口商坚持让进口商先付款后提货，则贸易双方可约定采用此种方式。出口商在装运货物前，必须先找到一家能提供代理收款业务的空运承运人或其代理，委托其将货物空运到目的地机场，待进口商来提货时，进口商必须将货款支付给该空运承运人后才能提取货物。

③ CASH AGAINST DOCUMENTS(CAD)，即"凭单付款"。该方法俗称"反托收"。在汇付方式下，进口商主动将货款预存在一家出口地银行，出口商将货物交付到进口商指定的仓库或将货物按照约定的方式装运出去后，凭包括提货单或运输单据在内的商业单据到存款银行换取货款。CAD 现在普遍用于边境贸易中。

以上(1)、(2)、(3)预付的共同点是在买方付清货款前，卖方掌握货物或货运单据。但是对于出口商而言，面临的风险是有差异的，(1)最小，(3)比较大，而(2)折中。

2. 到付

相对预付而言，到付是指买方先得到货物、后进行付款的汇款方式，具体有以下两种。

(1) 赊销(OPEN ACCOUNT，O/A)。卖方装运货物后，将全套货运单据寄交买方以便买方提取货物进行销售。在合同规定的付款期限内，不管买方是否已将货物售罄，应将全部货款支付给卖方的结算方式。

(2) 寄售(CONSIGNMENT)。在合同规定的付款期限内，买方可以仅付给卖方销售完毕的货物的价款。对未销售的部分货物，买方可以退货，也可以与卖方协商继续销售。相对售定来说，寄售项下出口商承担的风险进一步加重。

预付和到付项下贸易双方承担的风险不一样。随订单付现，进口商承担全部风险；寄售则由出口商承担全部风险。在贸易实践中，汇付除用于货款结算外，还广泛用于运保费、佣金、样品费和索赔、理赔款项及退补款结算。

(二)汇款具体运用应注意的事项

1. 政治风险与商业风险

对于汇款项下的进出口双方来说，政治风险与商业风险是他们面临的最主要风险。

(1) 政治风险。对于进出口双方来说，应密切关注进出口国家和中转运输国家的政治、经济局势的变化。如目的地国家政治局势动乱、发生战争等，则不宜与对方开展贸易往来。对出口方来说，如进口国存在政治风险，更不应该采用"先发货、后收款"的货款结算方式；对进口方来说，如出口国存在政治风险，则不应该采用预付货款的方式，以防出口商不能按期按质交货。

(2) 汇款是商业信用，出口商应加强对进口商的资信调查。对于新客户，我国的出口商一般都比较担心其商业信用，不会接受新客户"到付"的要求。但是，出口商却往往忽略对老客户的资信调查，从比较有利的结算方式改为"到付"，从而导致"货、款两空"的案例屡见不鲜。对于进口商来说，如对出口商的生产能力、货物品质等方面的情况不很了解，也不应采用装运前全额付款的结算方式，并最好争取能有合理机会在付款前对货物进行必要的检验，以保证出口商装运的货物符合合同和进口国的要求。

2. 我国出口商采用汇款方式应特别注意的事项

对于我国的出口商来说，采用汇款方式结算除注意以上问题以外，还应注意以下事项。

(1) 对出口商来说，由于"到付"风险太大，出口商一般不应接受"到付"。如出口商接受"到付"，应采取一定的保障措施，如采用"到付"与银行保函相结合、办理出口信用保险、保理或包买票据等办法，以转嫁一定的风险。

(2) 汇款项下不存在银行介入审核单据的问题。因此，在"预付"项下，出口商应掌握货款不到则不发货(装运前 XX 天付款)的原则，或者发货后取得提单，等电汇到账后再寄出单据，以平衡物权和货款(装运后 XX 天付款)。

（3）注意提单抬头的做法。除非出口商在装运前收妥货款，否则提单的以下抬头做法均不可取，以便在进口商拒付后，及时转卖货物或将货物运回。①TO ORDER OF SHIPPER, UNENDORSED；②TO ORDER OF SHIPPER, WITHOUT ENDORSEMENT；③TO ORDER OF ABC COMPANY(假定国外进口商的公司名称为 ABC COMPANY)；④ABC COMPANY。

（4）注意贸易术语的选择，并及时办理货物运输及投保运输险。

按照 Incoterms 2010，CFR 和 FOB 贸易术语项下，进、出口商均无投保责任。但是，货物自装运港装上指定的运输船只并越过船舷后，风险由进口商承担。如采用装运后收款的方式，万一货物在运输途中发生灭失，进口商因忘记保险而拒受货物，出口商将陷入困境。采用 FOB 贸易术语成交，是由进口商安排货物运输，实践中，进口商一般指定货运代理，而其代理资质与信用不被出口商所了解。货运代理往往是谁支付运费，就将货物交给谁。因此，FOB 项下往往存在"无单放货"问题，使得出口商尽管手中握有提单，但已失去货物所有权。因此，采用汇款方式时，出口商最好采用 CIF 或 CIP 贸易术语成交，并亲自安排货物运输并及时办理运输保险。货物一旦发生灭失，可以向保险公司索赔，也避免了"无单放货"问题。

二、托收具体运用及应注意的问题

(一)托收具体运用

光票托收一般用于贸易从属费用的结算以及佣金、样品费的结算等，金额较小。

对出口商来说，跟单托收中以即期付款交单风险最小，而以承兑交单风险最大。但是，进口商的选择则刚好相反。

相对于货到付款，跟单托收有比较强的安全性，出口商比较容易控制单据，进口商要在付款或承兑汇票后，才能取得单据。跟单托收业务中出口商的资金负担较重，但其可以利用单据向银行融通资金。

(二)托收具体运用应注意的事项

进出口双方面临的政治风险与商业风险在托收项下与在汇款项下基本相同。为防止进口商拒收货物，出口商同样应该注意提单的抬头与贸易术语的选择。相对于汇款，托收项下的出口商还应注意以下事项。

1. 谨慎选择代收行

托收项下，出口商是在装运货物后备齐单据，委托银行向进口商收取货款。银行的行为直接关系到出口商收汇的成功与否。按照 URC522，托收行必须完全按照出口商的指示，依据 URC522 的相关规定办理业务，不得越权或擅自变更出口商的要求。而代收行必须完全遵照托收行的指示，并妥善保管好单据。在必要的情况下，谨慎处理好货物。例如，在即期付款交单条件下，托收行必须指示代收行在货款收妥的情况下才能将单据交给进口商，否则单据将仍然控制在代收行手中。如代收行在收妥货款前，将单据先放给进口商，进口商到期拒付的风险要由代收行承担。代收行要为自己的过失承担责任。

2. 不宜接受 D/A 付款

由于 D/A 风险太大，出口商一般不应该接受 D/A。如采用 D/A，应采取一定的控制风险措施，如采用 D/A 与银行保函相结合的方法，或要求进口银行在汇票上保证，或采用办理出口信用保险、保理或包买票据等办法，以转嫁一定的风险。

3. 制单环节应谨慎

托收项下银行只是核验单据，而非审核单据。进口商为降低自己的风险，要仔细审核单据，以判定"单、货"、"单、同"、"单、单"是否一致。进口商从这三个"一致"来判定出口商装运的货物是否与合同要求相吻合。因此，出口商在制作单据时必须十分谨慎，以免出错，从而导致进口商拒收货物。

4. 特别注意远期付款交单

远期付款交单被国际商会视为不规范的做法。

远期付款交单的进口商在承兑汇票后，受票据法制约，成为汇票的主债务人，但进口商的承兑未能取得物权凭证(即对价)而有欠公平，进口商也没有获得相应的资金融通。货物在目的港(地)未及时办理进口清关会产生大量的滞港费用，最终导致进口商拒付货款。但是，远期付款交单的存在有一定的必然性，在具体运用时应注意以下事项。

(1) 注意某些国家远期付款交单的习惯做法。例如，澳大利亚商业银行将 D/P 远期视同 D/A；德国、挪威、阿拉伯联合酋长国的商业银行拒绝接受 D/P 远期；智利商业银行则采用拒绝或视同 D/A 的做法；加拿大商业银行明确表示只接受 D/P 即期，而泰国商业银行则表示可以接受 D/P 远期。

(2) 远期交单凭信托收据(TRUST RECEIPT, T/R)借单。远期付款交单的进口商在承兑汇票后，可凭信托收据向代收行先借得单据后，去目的港(地)先提取货物进行销售，等汇票到期后再将票款交回代收行，然后赎回信托收据。有时，出口商为了方便进口商提货，也会授权托收行同意进口商凭信托收据借单。如果进口商凭信托收据借单后，不将票款按期交回代收行，那么代收行的责任要以"同意进口商凭信托收据借单"的指示是否得到托收行的授权来判定。如代收行事先未得到托收行的授权，而是自行借单给进口商，则代收行应承担全部责任。

(3) 远期付款交单的付款期限。D/P 远期的付款期限规定，最好是货物抵达目的港(地)

之时，进口商的付款期限业已届满。这样，能避免大量滞港费用的产生。例如，某贸易合同采用 D/P 远期结算，货物是从中国上海运输到美国纽约。上海到纽约的海运方式有两种：一是全程海运，所花时间为 35 天左右；二是从上海到美国西岸(如长岛)走海运，运程一般为 15 天左右，从西岸到纽约采用公路运输，一般是 7 天左右，总运程 22 天左右。因此 D/P 付款期限的确定最好为 "D/P 30 DAYS FROM THE DATE OF B/L"。如货物是从上海通过海运运输到巴西的里奥格兰德，运程为 42 天左右，则采用 D/P 远期的规定方法最好为 "D/P 45 DAYS FROM THE DATE OF B/L" 或者 "D/P 30 DAYS AFTER SIGHT"。见票付款期限因要加上单据在途时间，故期限应比提单日后付款的期限稍短。当然，以上规定的时间最好能更短些，即期付款交单的风险要远远低于远期付款交单的风险。

(4) 由于远期付款交单项下，往往存在货到目的港而汇票付款期限未满期的情况。货物滞留在目的港会产生大量的滞港费用，而进口商有可能因市场行情下跌、目的港费用过高而拒付。因此，出口商往往授权托收行在托收委托书上加列以下条款。

① 列明计息条款，鼓励进口商提前付款。如 "DISCOUNT AT THE RATE OF____% PER ANNUM IS ALLOWED ON PAYMENT EFFECTED BEFORE THE DUE DATE OF THE DRAFT. IN CASE OF THE DRAFT BEING NOT DULY HONOURED BY THE DRAWEE AT MATURITY，KINDLY COLLECT FROM THE DRAWEE AN OVERDUE INTEREST AT THE RATE OF____% PER ANNUM FROM THE DUE DATE TO THE DATE OF ACTUAL PAYMENT" (汇票到期前付款，允许按年利率____%扣除贴现利息。如果汇票满期后付款人拒付，请按年利率____%加收从到期日开始至实际付款日的利息)。

② 列明分期付款、分批提货的条款，避免货款全部拒付和大量滞港费用的产生。如 "MERCHANDISE MAY BE PARTIALLY RELEASED AGAINST PARTIAL PAYMENT" (货物允许分批支付后，分批提货)。

三、与汇款结算方式相关的案例

(一)装运后 T/T 收汇失败案

1. 案例介绍

浙江宁波 A 出口公司与俄罗斯 B 进口公司签订了一份五金产品的 CIF 合同，两个 40′FCL。合同约定分两次等量装运，两次交货的间隔时间为 30 天，约定付款方式为在装运后 30 天内 T/T 付款。出口商收齐货款后将单据用快递邮寄给进口商供其提货。A 公司将第一个货柜的货物按时装运出口。30 天后，A 公司催 B 公司支付货款，B 公司先是推脱过几天付款，后又称其为代理商，正催促其委托人付款。A 公司继续催 B 公司付款，但 B 公司开始回避，最后索性不再接听 A 公司的去电或回复任何邮件。货到目的港两个月后，A

公司见催收无果，只得联系船公司将货物运回。由于货物在目的港滞港太久，造成大量的滞港费用，加上来回的运费和进出口国家的清关费用，使 A 公司遭受巨大的损失。而前一个货柜的拒收导致后一货柜只得转为库存。

2. 案例分析

(1) 信用风险。对出口方来说，无任何风险的汇款方式是随订单付现，其他付款方式或多或少都有一定的风险。即便是装运前电汇，如果进口商不及时付款，出口商将陷入尴尬境地。一是合同规定的装运期已过；二是出口方已将货物生产出来，如不装运，将转为库存，从而影响资金的周转和经济利益的实现。采用装运后付款，如果进口商以降价或拒付为要挟而不及时赎单，最终出口商将不得不接受进口商的要求，从而造成巨额损失。到付风险之大自不必说。

(2) 宁波到俄罗斯口岸的运输时间一般为 30 天左右。本案中的付款方式对进出口双方来说，"货、款平衡"应该是比较合理的。出口商在装运货物后，通过控制物权单据而掌握货物的所有权，得到货款后将单据转移给进口商而失去货物的所有权；进口商在货到目的港时付款，一方面避免滞港费用的产生，另一方面是减轻资金负担。但是，本案的出口商采用这种结算方式造成了巨额损失，其主要原因是因为汇款的本质(信用风险)所造成的。

(3) 出口商与资信情况不很了解的客户进行交易，最好不要采用装运后收款的方式，而应采用装运前付款的方式，或至少采用部分在装运前付款的方式。如出口商争取到在装运前预付 30%，在装运后付清余款赎单。在出口商装运货物后，如遇进口商拒付，出口商可以用预收的 30% 金额抵补货物因转卖、退运而造成的损失。而对进口商来说，该笔预付款将成为其损失，从而抑制进口商拒付的发生。如出口商迫不得已接收进口商的"先装运、后付款"要求，则可以投保出口信用险或续做保理来降低部分风险。

(4) 在商业信用的结算方式下，出口商应争取分批装运、分批收款，收妥前一单货款后，才能将第二单货物装运出去。

(5) 客人订做的货物或不通用的货物，最好采用全部或部分随订单付现的方式结算。部分随订单付现的比例不应太高或太低，太高不利于成交，太低则对进口商的约束作用不大。

(6) 如与俄罗斯、伊朗、非洲等高风险国家或地区开展贸易往来，最好采用信用证结算或预付，否则应采取一定的措施以降低风险，如投保出口信用险等。

(二)忽视对老客户资信调查造成拖欠案

1. 案例介绍

我国某服装进出口公司(A)和澳大利亚一家著名的女装进口批发商公司(B)7 年来一直保持良好的贸易合作关系。B 公司在澳洲纺织行业中有较高的声誉，几年来与中国的贸易额一直处于稳定的发展阶段。由于与 B 公司合作时间长，对方已是老客户，A 公司认为其信誉良好，就从小额订单开始放松了监督管理，采用装运前预付 20%，余 80% 为装货后 90 天付清的方式。截至 1999 年 3 月，B 公司累计有 60 万美元没有按时支付。有些款项拖欠达 3 年之久，B 公司还以种种理由继续拖欠。对于这笔欠款，A 公司既想催讨以解决资金周转不灵的问题，又怕损害和这个大客户的关系，最后请资信调查机构核实 B 公司的经营状况和拖欠理由是否属实，结果发现 B 公司正全力变卖固定资产，已处于破产边缘。经过强大的追讨攻势，总算及时挽回了 60 万美元的损失。A 公司后来了解到，若此案晚追讨 1 个月，追回欠款的可能性几乎为零。

2. 案例分析

(1) 本案中，客观上造成 B 公司拖欠的主要原因在于付款方式。因为货物余款的收取采用的是高风险的赊销(O/A)方式，本例中为装运后 90 天付款。出口商实际上是在收取 20% 货款后，就将货物的所有权转让给了进口商，并对进口商的付款欠缺必要的限制措施。

(2) 出口公司应加强应收账款的管理与监督。一旦发生进口商拖欠，出口商应立即停止供应货物，并要求修改付款方式。

(3) 一般来说，大公司、知名企业的资信当然相对可靠，但并不意味着可以不做资信调查。例如，一些大公司下面的子公司、孙子公司，虽然其有相同的商号，但资信状况差距却很大，而这些子公司因是独立法人，其债务与母公司无关。仅仅依赖商号的信誉很有可能产生信用风险。即便是大公司本身，也可能有不良的付款习惯。实际上，很多大公司尽管不会拒付货款，但往往拖欠货款，而出口公司又不愿意得罪这样的大主顾。因此，在同大公司开展业务往来之前，应该了解其付款习惯和记录，有助于在谈判时对付款条件进行掌控。

(4) 一旦发生拖欠，出口商应及时强有力地追讨货款，千万不要怕得罪客户。追讨措施要得当，必要时应委托国外专业追账公司进行，因为他们熟悉当地法律和司法程序。

(三)海关特殊规定导致无法安全收汇案

1. 案例介绍

我某出口商 C 公司与巴基斯坦 D 公司签订了一批总值 5 万多美元的出口服装合同，付款方式为先电汇 30%货款作为订金，剩余 70%货款装运后 10 天内支付。我方收到订金后按期装运了货物。装运货物后，我方及时将全套单据的复印件传真给了客户。十多天后，客户来电称由于市场行情急剧下跌，要求我方降价 40%才可以接受货物。我方不同意 D 公司的条件，决定将货物运回。我方联系船公司后，被告知无法办妥货物转运，原因在于巴基斯坦海关规定，退货必须征得原进口商的同意，否则无法退货。万般无奈之下，我方同意了 D 公司的要求才了结此案。

2. 案例分析

进口方当地的海关特殊规定是本案出口方遭受损失的重要原因。本案的焦点在于进口国的信用及进口商的信用。任何结算方式都会给出口商带来不同程度的潜在风险，必须采用相应的防范措施。首先，出口商在签订合同前后，应通过各种途径对进口商进行资信情况和经营作风方面的调查，尤其对初次成交的客户更应如此。其次，应事先了解进口国贸易管制、外汇管制和商业惯例等方面的有关法律法规(如海关特殊规定)，以免落入客户精心设计的圈套。再者，该出口商品应为大路货，不然，一旦商品积压或退运，就很难转售他人或做内销处理等。最后，业务人员在制单时应仔细认真，避免进口商因挑剔单据而拒收货物。

四、与托收结算方式相关的案例

(一)D/P AT SIGHT 收汇损失案

1. 案例介绍

某服装贸易公司与美国一家公司签订了一笔 10 万美元的服装出口合同，价格条件为 FOB 上海，支付条件为 D/P AT SIGHT，出口货代公司为买方指定的 ABC 公司。由于在此之前公司与该客户曾采用 L/C 支付方式通过该货代公司做过两笔订单，所以没有对该货代公司进行详细了解。该服装贸易公司将货物发出后，将包括三份正本货代提单在内的全套货运单据通过中国银行转交对方指定的代收行收款，但在规定的时间内没有收到货款。

在此后的一个多月内，对方一会儿说没见着单据，一会儿说正在和银行商量赎单，一会儿又传来一份真假难辨的银行付款底单。在忍无可忍的情况下，公司只好指示代收行将全套单据转让给公司在美国的分公司，让其先代收此货然后再与买方交涉，以避免大量滞港费的产生。当美国分公司拿着正本提单去提货时，发现货已被买方提走。公司与买方交涉，但对方既不回传真，也不接电话，随即公司派法律顾问带人赶往上海，准备对 ABC 公司采取行动。

赶到上海时，ABC 公司早已人去楼空，再到工商部门一调查，才发现该公司根本没有货代资质，仅为一家运输咨询公司。在万般无奈的情况下，该出口公司只好采取委托授权的方式，通过美国分公司请美国律师起诉进口方，但得知该客户已申请了破产保护。按美国的法律，该出口商只能参加破产清算，经计算，如参加清算，其所得可能还不够支付律师费用，公司只好撤诉。

2．案例分析

本案例中，由于出口商的失误给自己造成了巨大损失：不仅全部货款血本无归，而且还浪费了大量人力和其他额外的费用，损失巨大，其教训也十分深刻！如果出口商在出口贸易中采取适当的措施，则可在一定程度上减少风险。这也是出口方在今后的贸易中应注意的地方。

(1) 在 FOB 价格条款下以托收方式办理货款结算，使出口方承担了较大风险。所以如果可能，在出口贸易中应争取使用先结后出的 T/T 方式或 L/C 方式进行支付。安全主动的支付方式可以在一定程度上消除或减轻 FOB 价格条款所带来的风险。先收钱后给货的付款方式应该无风险可言，但要记住眼见为实，不要仅凭所谓的银行付款单的传真件就将货物付运，最起码要通过银行核实货款确实已付往你的账户。L/C 支付条件下要严把单据质量关，杜绝单据不符点，严格控制担保议付。虽说这还有风险，但毕竟主动权在自己手里，最起码可以通过努力在一定程度上去控制风险，毕竟 L/C 这种支付方式是银行信用代替了商业信用。

(2) 使用货代提单而且没有对货代资质进行深入调查，也是本案例中致使出口方受损的一个重要原因。应争取采用信誉度较高的船公司提单取代货代提单。船公司大多信誉良好，即便有时凭担保将货放给客户，一旦出现问题，也会凭借其信誉与实力，妥善地处理纠纷，其信誉度远非货代公司可比。如果不可避免地要通过对方指定的货代交易并使用货代提单，必须要对货代公司的资质进行审查。未在工商部门注册登记，并且也未得到外经贸部批准的非法货代公司坚决不用。如不行，就只好让对方在发货前预付全部货款。

(3) 拒绝接受"记名提单"和"凭进口商指定抬头"的提单(如 ABC COMPANY 和 TO ORDER OF ABC COMPANY)，在这两种提单项下，只有提单的收货人(ABC COMPANY)才有权对提单项下的货物进行处置。一旦双方发生争执，出口人就有可能不便行使甚至失去对滞于目的港码头的货物的处置权。因此，在 L/C 支付条件下，可接受在提单收货人一栏中注明"凭开证行或付款行指令"(TO ORDER OF XXX BANK)，在托收业务中使用"指示提单"(TO ORDER OF SHIPPER 或 TO ORDER)，出口商往往做成"空白背书"，避免因无单提货而导致的风险和纠纷，而发货人因故要将货物退运、转运或委托第三方提货等也比较方便。

(4) 针对不同的客户进行不同程度的风险控制。人们常说：只有完美的客户，没有完美的交易条件。应该说绝大多数外贸业内人士对此深有同感。在具体操作中，对于那些不知底细、信誉不良的客户，要严格遵守操作规定，高度警惕，严格把关，切不可操之过急，否则会事与愿违。但对于信誉较好的老客户，也不可过分地掉以轻心，要随时关注客户业务的变化，并设立风险控制底线，不可将口子开得太大，以免掉进恶性循环的泥潭。

(5) 投保"短期出口信用险"，以规避并转移风险。中国人民保险公司海外业务部已建立起一套信用调查体系和风险追偿体系，通过投保信用险，由保险公司帮你调查客户的信用，以规避可能出现的风险。在风险事故产生时，通过代位权的转移，由保险公司帮你通过不同的渠道对有关责任方进行追索，无论结果如何，你均可在规定的期限内得到一定程度的赔偿。这种方式不仅效果好，还省去了大量的人力和费用。

目前在我国外贸出口合同中，有相当大比例是按 FOB 或 CFR 价格条件成交的，其中有很大一部分客人来自于中东、南亚、非洲、美洲等地区，他们往往以中国的货运险费率过高为由，坚持按 FOB 或 CFR 成交，而实际操作中他们又往往不按规定去办理货运保险，而是待货物到港后直接赎单提货，以躲避保险费用的支出。一旦货物在运输途中发生任何损失，皆由出口人来承担。根据国际海洋货物运输的惯例与规则，承运人对其所承运的货物在运输过程中所产生的短少和灭失，仅承担有限的赔偿。在这种情况下，如果出口货物一旦发生海损，出口人将要承受的风险是可想而知的。所以投保"短期出口信用险"在一定程度上可以帮助出口企业解决出口中的一些实际困难。

(二)D/P AT SIGHT 的风险防范分析案例

1. 案例介绍

2004 年 5 月 D 公司开始与一美商开展贸易活动，并在 6 月成交一笔生意。美商进口一个 20 英尺货柜的台面板，条款为 L/C AT SIGHT。现在美商对该期货物质量反映良好，并发函预定另一 20 英尺货柜的台面板，条件为 D/P AT SIGHT，原因是做 D/P 比做 L/C 省钱。D 公司历来没做过 D/P AT SIGHT，所以担心有风险。那么，有哪些预防措施可以防患于未然？

2. 案例分析

(1) D/P AT SIGHT 与 L/C AT SIGHT 相比，缺少了银行信用的重要保证，银行虽参与其间，但只是提供服务，并无非收妥货款不可的保证，这对委托人(出口商)而言，是致命的弱点。因此，在 D/P AT SIGHT 结算方式中，付款人的信誉是最重要的。只有对付款人进行充分调查，认定付款人信誉可靠的基础上，才能以 D/P AT SIGHT 结算。在结算过程中，委托人还应注意以下几个问题。

① 与买方签订合同时，对于结算方式、单据名称、详细分类及份数、托收费用由谁

负责等条款必须清楚注明。

②　在委托银行办理托收时，未经银行事先同意，货物不能直接发至银行，也不能做成以银行为收货人的记名提单。根据 URC522(《托收统一规则》)，倘若货物直接发至银行，或者做成以银行为收货人的记名提单，然后由银行凭以付款或承兑或其他条件，将货物交给付款人，而没有事先征得该银行的同意，则银行没有提货的义务，货物的风险和责任由发货人承担。

③　委托人到银行办理托收时，在托收申请书上必须清楚地表明付款人的名称、地址及开户行的名称、地址，避免出现代收行找不到付款人的现象。

④　委托人可以在托收委托书上标明如遇拒付时应采取的必要措施，例如要求做成拒绝证书、货物抵港时要求代收行办理存仓保险等工作。如果国外银行声明不办理，那么当委托人遭拒付时，代收行就应设法代办，并将办妥结果告知托收行。

(2)　考虑与其他支付方式相结合。如果进口商的信誉有问题，货物到达目的地后，他不去银行赎单，乘机要求降价或称因为市场变化而拒收货物，那么，出口商就要在当地贱卖或将货物退运回来。在本案例中，进口商出现拒收货物的可能性很小，因为台面板是一个通用产品，市场变化应该不会很大，因此此案例的最大风险是进口商可能要求降价。当然，这种分析是基于遇到不良商人的情况。

如果要增加出口保险系数，就只能同其他支付方式相结合，如可以要求客户先以 T/T 方式预付部分货款，余额做 D/P，这样一来，既可以节省银行费用，又可以降低风险。因为只要市场不出现剧烈变动，客户一般不会宁可损失预付款而不去银行赎单的。

(3)　在细节上加强把握。

①　选择较有信誉的客户。

②　在出提单时一定要出以 "TO SHIPPER'S ORDER" 或 "TO ORDER" 为抬头的提单。

③　千万不要在市价走低时采用 D/P AT SIGHT。

④　考虑在以 CIF 或 CIP 成交时，投保 "卖方出口收汇险"，增加风险防范手段。

⑤　采用非 CIF 或 CIP 成交时，最好不要采用 D/P AT SIGHT 结算，而改为装运前 T/T 结算。

本 章 小 结

国际汇兑按资金流向和结算工具流向的不同分为顺汇和逆汇两大类。国际贸易结算方式中，汇款方式采用顺汇，而托收和信用证则采用逆汇。汇款是国外进口商主动将款项通过本国银行汇交出口商的付款方式，属于商业信用。汇款使用灵活，可以采用预付或到付的方式。买卖双方的风险分担与资金负担不平衡。如采用预付，进口商承担风险比较大，资金负担比较重；如采用到付，则出口商面临的风险比较大，资金负担也比较重。汇款方式有电汇、信汇和票汇，每一笔汇款业务都涉及四个基本当事人：汇款人、汇出行、汇入行和收款人。汇出行与汇入行之间汇款的偿付方法有四种：主动贷记、授权借记、共同账户行转账和各自账户行转账。汇款可以办理退汇。

托收属商业信用，分为光票托收和跟单托收，而跟单托收按照交单方式又分为付款交单和承兑交单。付款交单有即期与远期之分。交单方式不同，出口商面临的收汇风险也不一样。承兑交单的风险要远远高于付款交单。但是，在托收业务中，出口商要慎用远期付款交单，远期付款交单被国际商会认定为不规范的结算方式。在托收业务中，代收行是至关重要的一环，是业务成功的关键，所以还要谨慎选择代收行。

复习思考题

1. 简述电汇、信汇和票汇的工作流程。电汇和票汇业务应注意哪些事项？
2. 预付和到付的种类有哪些？出口商应如何选择？
3. 简述 D/P 即期、D/P 远期和 D/A 的工作流程。请特别注意代收行与进口商之间的"单、款衔接"环节。
4. D/P 远期应注意哪些事项？

第四章

跟单信用证

学习目标：结合 UCP600，掌握信用证的基本种类、各当事人的责任和义务、信用证业务的具体办理手续及其注意的事项；了解信用证的定义、性质、作用与内容。

关键概念：信用证、开证行、通知行、申请人、被指定银行、保兑行、UCP600、相符交单、交单人、不可撤销信用证、可转让信用证

第一节 信用证基本知识

一、信用证的定义、性质及其作用

信用证是国际结算的重要组成部分，尤其是跟单信用证在国际贸易结算中有着其他结算方式无法替代的功能。信用证业务集结算和融资为一体，为国际贸易提供综合服务。

(一)信用证适用的国际惯例

《跟单信用证统一惯例》2007 年修订本(国际商会第 600 号出版物)，简称 UCP600，于 2007 年 7 月 1 日正式生效。UCP600 是一套规则，适用于所有在其文本中明确表示受本惯例约束的跟单信用证(在可适用的范围内，包括备用信用证)。除非信用证明确修改或排除，UCP600 各条文对信用证所有当事人均具有约束力。UCP600 正式生效前，《跟单信用证统一惯例》使用的是 1993 年修订本(国际商会第 500 号出版物，简称 UCP500)。

(二)信用证的定义

UCP600 关于信用证的定义：信用证是指一项不可撤销的安排，无论其名称或描述如何，该项安排构成开证行对相符交单予以承付的确定承诺。

(三)信用证的性质

1. 开证行负第一性付款责任

开证行承担第一性的付款责任，但这是有条件的付款承诺。只要规定的单据提交给被

指定银行或开证行，并且构成相符交单，则开证行必须承付。如果信用证为以下情形之一，开证行负第一性付款责任。

(1) 信用证规定由开证行即期付款、延期付款或承兑。

(2) 信用证规定由被指定银行即期付款但其未付款。

(3) 信用证规定由被指定银行延期付款但其未承诺延期付款；或其虽承诺延期付款，但未在到期日付款。

(4) 信用证规定由被指定银行承兑，但其未承兑以其为付款人的汇票；或虽承兑了汇票，但未在到期日付款。

(5) 信用证规定由被指定银行议付但其未议付。

开证行自开立信用证之时即不可撤销地承付责任。只要受益人交单相符(A COMPLYING PRESENTATION)，开证行独立地履行其付款承诺，不受其他当事人的干扰。无论是被指定银行还是受益人向开证行交单，开证行必须履行其付款承诺，不管开证申请人是否有付款的意愿或者能力。信用证体现了银行信用。开证行以自己的信用做出付款保证，这种保证与一般担保业务不同。在一般的担保业务中，只有被担保人不履约时，担保人才承担付款义务，而信用证业务中的开证行承担第一性付款义务，只要交单相符，开证行必须付款，其付款不以进口人的付款为前提条件。

2. 信用证是自足文件

信用证是与买卖合同相分离的独立文件。信用证项下的开证申请人应具备的一种基本技能是能将贸易合同的条款全部转化为开证申请书上的条款。信用证的基础首先是买卖合同，其次是买方与开证行的开证申请书和担保协议，开证行在这两个文件的基础上才向受益人开立信用证。但是，这些文件是相互独立的，每个文件只能约束相关当事人。

UCP600第4条A、B款规定："就其性质而言，信用证与可能作为其开立基础的销售合同或其他合同是相互独立的交易，即使信用证中含有对此类合同的任何援引，银行也与合同无关，且不受其约束。因此，银行关于承付、议付或履行信用证项下其他义务的承诺，不受申请人基于其与开证行或与受益人之间的关系而产生的任何请求或抗辩的影响。受益人在任何情况下不得利用银行之间或申请人与开证行之间的合同关系。开证行应劝阻申请人试图将基础合同、形式发票等文件作为信用证组成部分的做法。"因此，信用证的特点就是独立于合同，并不受合同的限制。虽然信用证条款中出现了合同号，但银行并不对合同负责。合同条款是否与信用证条款一致，所交单据是否符合合同要求等，银行一律不过问。

3. 信用证是单据化业务

信用证业务是单据买卖。在信用证业务中所有各方，包括银行和商人所处理的都是单据，而非货物。受益人要保证收款就一定要提供与信用证相符的单据，开证行拒付只能以单据上的不符点为由。UCP600 第 6 条规定：银行处理的是单据，而不是单据可能涉及的货物、服务或履约行为。

信用证的独立性与抽象性一起，构成信用证大厦的两块基石。

【案例 4-1】合同与信用证有关货物的描述不一致导致的拒付案

1. 案例介绍

A 出口公司与 B 进口公司就 "金鸡牌" 某种货物订立合同，并规定采用信用证结算。但是，B 公司通过开证行开出的信用证上货物为 "金牌"。A 公司未仔细审核信用证就办理了交货，制作了全套单据向出口地银行办理交单议付，单据显示为 "金鸡牌"。出口地银行审核单据后予以拒付，其理由是单据的货物描述与信用证条款不符，而 A 公司坚持认为合同签订的货物为 "金鸡牌"，实际装运的货物也为 "金鸡牌"，因此银行拒付无理。

2. 案例分析

(1) 由于信用证规定 "金牌"，而提交的单据与合同相符，为 "金鸡牌"，交单不符成立，银行拒付是有理由的。至于说 "金鸡牌" 误为 "金牌"，应由买卖双方自行解决。因为信用证是独立于合同的保证文件，不受合同约束。

(2) 本案例拓展分析：

① 假设本案例中，A 出口公司实际装运的是 "金鸡牌"，但在单据上显示 "金牌"。这样一来，交单相符，开证行就会付款。

② 如果交单相符，而进口商付款赎单后发现实际收到的货物不符合合同要求(例如品质、包装有缺陷等)，进口方就不能要求开证行退回货款或要求开证行向出口方追索。货物有问题，买卖双方自行解决。对开证行来说，只要交单相符，就必须承付。银行的职能是提供信用和资金融通，不能要求银行具备商品交易的专门知识。如果银行卷入他们不熟悉的商业合同或货物问题中去，既超越了他们的职能，也超越他们的能力。事实上，银行面对大量的客户和业务，也不可能去过问客户的每笔交易合同及合同项下的货物。

③ 在信用证业务中，银行的付款责任不受申请人索赔或抗辩的影响。如交单相符，申请人不能由于受益人以前一笔出口货款的索赔尚未解决，而要求开证行拒付，用这笔货款来抵偿索赔款。

④ 如开证行误将申请书中的 "金鸡牌" 开成 "金牌"，申请人拒绝付款赎单，开证行不能因此不付款。

(四)信用证的用途

国际商会将信用证用途归纳如下：①购买外国货物时融通资金的极好工具；②有助于开证行向进口商提供资金融通，并控制资金的用途；③为商业交易提供信心和安全因素；

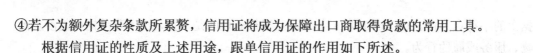

④若不为额外复杂条款所累赘，信用证将成为保障出口商取得货款的常用工具。

根据信用证的性质及上述用途，跟单信用证的作用如下所述。

1. 解决贸易双方互不信任的矛盾

信用证使用的前提是买卖双方缺乏相互满意的信任基础，需要借助银行信用实施国际贸易结算。采用信用证结算，由银行出面担保，只要卖方按合同规定交货就可拿到货款，而买方又无须在卖方履行合同规定的交货义务前支付货款。这种支付方式使不在交货现场的买卖双方在履行合同时处于同等地位，在一定程度上使他们重新找回了"一手交钱，一手交货"的现场交易所具有的安全感，解决了双方互不信任的矛盾。

2. 保证出口商安全收汇

对出口商来说，信用证可以保证出口商在履约交货后，按信用证条款的规定向银行交单取款，即使在进口国实施外汇管制的情况下，也可保证凭单收到外汇。

3. 保证进口商安全提货

对进口商来说，信用证可以保证进口商在支付货款时即可取得代表货物的单据，并可通过信用证条款来控制出口商按质、按量、按时交货。

4. 获得资金融通

对进口商来说，开证时只需缴纳部分押金，单据到达后才向银行赎单付清差额。如为远期信用证，进口商还可以凭信托收据向开证行借单先行提货出售，到期向开证行付款。对出口商来说，在信用证项下货物装运后即可凭信用证所需单据向出口地银行叙做押汇，取得全部货款。

二、信用证的格式与内容

1. 信用证的格式

国际商会推荐使用的跟单信用证格式，既考虑申请人与受益人的利益，便利了国际商界的沟通，又考虑到银行的利益，方便了国际银行之间的沟通。其内容包括：①不可撤销的跟单信用证申请书(IRREVOCABLE DOCUMENTARY CREDIT APPLICATION)(见示样 4-1)。申请书内容由正反两部分内容构成。②不可撤销的跟单信用证——给受益人的通知(IRREVOCABLE DOCUMENTARY CREDIT(ADVICE FOR THE BENEFICIARY))(见示样 4-2)。③不可撤销跟单信用证修改通知书(IRREVOCABLE DOCUMENTARY CREDIT AMENDMENT FORM)(见示样 4-3)。④不可撤销跟单信用证——给通知行的通知(IRREVOCABLE DOCUMENTARY CREDIT(ADVICE FOR THE ADVISING BANK))(见示样 4-4)。

示样 4-1　不可撤销的跟单信用证申请书

正面

IRREVOCABLE DOCUMENTARY CREDIT APPLICATION

TO:	DATE:
□ISSUE BY AIRMAIL　　□ISSUE BY EXPRESS DELIVERY □WITH BRIEF ADVICE BY TELETRANSMISSION □ ISSUE BY TELETRANSMISSION (WHICH SHALL BE THE OPERATIVE INSTRUMENT)	CREDIT NO. : DATE AND PLACE OF EXPIRY:
APPLICANT:	BENEFICIARY (FULL NAME AND ADDRESS):
ADVISING BANK:	AMOUNT:

PARTIAL SHIPMENTS	TRANSSHIPMENT	CREDIT AVAILABLE WITH
□ALLOWED	□ALLOWED	BY □ SIGHT PAYMENT　□ACCEPTANCE
□NOT ALLOWED	□NOT ALLOWED	□ NEGOTIATION　　□DEFERRED PAYMENT AT
LOADING ON BOARD/DISPATCH/TAKING IN CHARGE AT/FROM_____ NOT LATER THAN _____ FOR TRANSPORTATION TO: ____ □ FOB　□CFR　□CIF　OR　□ OTHER TERMS		AGAINST THE DOCUMENTS DETAILED HEREIN □ AND　BENEFICIARY'S DRAFT(S)　FOR _____ % OF INVOICE VALUE AT_____ SIGHT DRAWN ON _____

DOCUMENTS REQUIRED: (MARKED WITH X)

1. (　) SIGNED COMMERCIAL INVOICE IN __COPIES INDICATING L/C NO. __AND CONTRACT NO. _____.
2. (　) AIRWAY BILLS/CARGO RECEIPT/COPY OF RAILWAY BILLS ISSUED BY _____ SHOWING "FREIGHT [　] TO COLLECT/[　] PREPAID[　] " INDICATING FREIGHT AMOUNT AND CONSIGNED TO _____.
3. (　) INSURANCE POLICY/CERTIFICATE IN ____COPIES FOR ____% OF THE INVOICE VALUE SHOWING CLAIMS PAYABLE IN _____ CURRENCY OF THE DRAFT, BLANK ENDORSED, COVERING _____.
4. (　) PACKING LIST/WEIGHT MEMO IN _____ COPIES INDICATING QUANTITY, GROSS AND WEIGHTS OF EACH PACKAGE.
5. (　) CERTIFICATE OF QUANTITY/WEIGHT IN _____ COPIES ISSUED BY _____.
6. (　) CERTIFICATE OF QUALITY IN __COPIES ISSUED BY [ ] MANUFACTURER/[ ] PUBLIC RECOGNIZED SURVEYOR _____.
7. (　) CERTIFICATE OF ORIGIN IN _____ COPIES ISSUED BY _____.
8. (　) BENEFICIARY'S CERTIFIED COPY OF FAX / TELEX DISPATCHED TO THE APPLICANT WITHIN __ HOURS AFTER SHIPMENT ADVISING OF VESSEL, DATE OF SHIPMENT, NAME, QUANTITY, WEIGHT AND VALUE OF GOODS.

OTHER DOCUMENTS, IF ANY:

DESCRIPTION OF GOODS:

ADDITIONAL INSTRUCTIONS:

1. (　) ALL BANKING CHARGES OUTSIDE THE OPENING BANK ARE FOR BENEFICIARY'S ACCOUNT.
2. (　) DOCUMENTS MUST BE PRESENTED WITHIN _____ DAYS AFTER DATE OF ISSUANCE OF THE TRANSPORT DOCUMENTS BUT WITHIN THE VALIDITY OF THIS CREDIT.
3. (　) THIRD PARTY AS SHIPPER IS NOT ACCEPTABLE, SHORT FORM/BLANK BACK B/L IS NOT ACCEPTABLE.
4. (　) ALL DOCUMENTS MUST BE FORWARDED IN_____.
5. (　) OTHER TERMS, IF ANY.

反面

开立国际信用证申请书

编号：_____年_____字_____号

致：中国银行股份有限公司_____浙江省_____行

现我司因业务需要，依据我司与贵行签署的编号为_____的开立国际信用证合同，向贵行申请开立信用证。由于此产生的权利义务，均按照前述协议及其附件/合同和本申请书的约定办理。

第一条　信用证的内容

信用证的内容见编号为_____的《开立信用证申请书》(英文格式)。

第二条　备付款项

我司将于信用证约定的付款日或贵行要求的其他日期(以日期较前者为准)前_____个银行工作日内将备付款项足额存入我司在贵行开立的账户(账号：_____)，以用于信用证项下对外付款。

第三条　垫款利率和计息

对人民币垫款，从垫款之日起，按万分之五的比例按日计收利息。

对外币垫款，从垫款之日起，在当期1年期固定贷款利率_____的基础上加收_____%计收利息。

第四条　费用

我司将按时向贵行支付因叙做本申请书项下业务而产生的相关费用，该费用的计收依据、标准和方式等按贵行有关规定执行。

我司将通过以下第_____种方式支付上述费用：

1. 在贵行通知后_____个银行工作日内通过_____支付。

2. 授权贵行直接从我司账户(账号：_____)中扣收。

3. 其他方式：_____。

对于提交此申请书时不能预见、在信用证开出后发生的应由我司承担的费用(包括受益人拒绝承担的银行费用)，我司将以与上述相同的方式向贵行支付。

第五条　担保(备注：据实作选择性填写，不适用条款需删除)

1. 本申请书项下债务的担保方式为：

□ 本申请书属于_____与贵行签订的编号为_____的□《最高额保证合同》/□《最高额抵押合同》/□《最高额质押合同》项下的主合同，由其提供最高额担保。

□ 本申请书属于_____与贵行签订的编号为_____的□《最高额保证合同》/□《最高额抵押合同》/□《最高额质押合同》项下的主合同；此外，由_____提供_____担保，……，并签订相应的担保合同，若提供保证金质押则按本条第2款的约定办理。其中：由该_____担保合同所对应的债务金额不在前述最高额担保合同之主债务范围内，其余债务金额在其主债务范围内。

□ 由_____提供_____担保，……，并签订相应的担保合同。若提供保证金质押，则按本条第2款的约定办理。

□ (其他担保方式)_____。

2. 依前款约定提供保证金质押的，按下列方式办理：

□ 出质人为第三人，由贵行与该出质人另行签订保证金质押合同。

☐ 本申请书属于我司与贵行签署的编号为＿＿＿＿＿＿＿＿＿＿＿＿＿＿＿的《保证金质押总协议》项下的主合同，由该协议提供保证金质押，并提交相应的《保证金质押确认书》或不再提交《保证金质押确认书》而直接按下述约定办理：

1)　保证金金额为：(币种)＿＿＿＿＿＿＿＿＿；(大写)＿＿＿＿＿＿＿＿＿＿＿；

(小写)＿＿＿＿＿＿＿＿＿＿＿＿＿。

2)　我司通过以下方式交付上述保证金：

☐ 在本申请书生效之日起＿＿＿个银行工作日内，通过＿＿＿＿＿＿＿＿＿＿＿＿＿将保证金划入/存入我司在贵行开立的保证金账户(账号：＿＿＿＿＿＿＿＿＿＿＿＿＿＿＿)。

☐ 授权贵行从我司在贵行开立的人民币账户(账号：＿＿＿＿＿＿＿＿＿＿＿＿＿＿＿)/外币账户(账号：＿＿＿＿＿＿＿＿＿＿＿＿＿＿＿＿＿)直接将保证金划入我司在贵行开立的保证金账户(账号：＿＿＿＿＿＿＿＿＿＿＿＿＿)。

☐ 我司在贵行办理的业务编号为＿＿＿＿＿＿＿＿＿＿＿＿的业务项下存入的保证金的担保责任经贵行确认已经解除，授权贵行直接从账号为＿＿＿＿＿＿＿＿＿＿＿＿＿＿的账户向我司在贵行开立的保证金账户(账号为：＿＿＿＿＿＿＿＿＿＿＿＿＿)中划入保证金。

☐ (其他方式)＿＿＿＿＿＿＿＿＿＿＿＿＿＿＿＿＿＿＿＿＿＿＿。

3)　如上述保证金的担保责任经贵行确认已解除，请贵行按以下方式返还：

☐ 退入我司在＿＿＿＿＿＿＿＿＿＿＿开立的账户(账号为：＿＿＿＿＿＿＿＿＿＿)。

☐ 按其存入的路径返还。

☐ 届时按我司的书面指示返还。

☐ (其他方式)：＿＿＿＿＿＿＿＿＿＿＿＿＿＿＿＿＿＿＿＿＿。

3. 若我司或担保人发生贵行认为可能影响其履约能力的事件，或担保合同变为无效、被撤销或解除，或我司、担保人财务状况恶化或涉入重大诉讼或仲裁案件，或因其他原因而可能影响其履约能力，或担保人在担保合同或与贵行之间的其他合同项下发生违约，或担保物贬值、毁损、灭失、被查封，致使担保价值减弱或丧失时，贵行有权要求，且我司有义务提供新的担保、更换保证人等以担保本申请书项下债务。

申请人(预留我行公章与财务章)：＿＿＿＿＿＿＿＿＿＿＿＿＿＿＿

有权签字人：＿＿＿＿＿＿＿＿

＿＿＿＿＿年＿＿＿月＿＿＿日

银行意见：＿＿＿＿＿＿＿＿＿＿＿＿＿＿＿

有权签字人/经办人：＿＿＿＿＿＿＿＿

＿＿＿＿＿年＿＿＿月＿＿＿日

示样 4-2　不可撤销跟单信用证——给受益人的通知

中国银行股份有限公司

BANK OF CHINA LIMITED　　　　　　　　　　　　　PO1065001546

信 用 证 通 知 书

NOTIFICATION OF DOCUMENTARY CREDIT

DATE:

TO: 受益人(BENEFICIARY)		WHEN CORRESPONDING	通知编号：
		PLEASE QUOTE OUR REF. NO.	
ISSUING BANK 开证行：		TRANSMITTED TO US THROUGH 转递行：	
L/C NO. 信用证号：	DATED 开证日期：	AMOUNT 金额：	EXPIRY PLACE 有效地：
EXPIRY DATE 效期：	TENOR 期限：	CHARGE 未付费用：	CHARGE BY 费用承担人：
RECEIVED VIA 来证方式：	AVAILABLE 是否生效：	TEST/SIGN 印押是否相符：	CONFIRM 我行是否保兑：

DEAR SIRS,敬启者

WE HAVE PLEASURE IN ADVISING YOU THAT WE HAVE RECEIVED FROM THE A/M BANK A(N) **LETTER OF CREDIT,** CONTENTS OF WHICH ARE AS PER ATTACHED SHEET(S).

THIS ADVICE AND THE ATTACHED SHEET(S) MUST ACCOMPANY THE RELATIVE DOCUMENTS WHEN PRESENTED FOR NEGOTIATION.

REMARKS:

PLEASE NOTE THAT THIS ADVICE DOES NOT CONSITITUTE OUR CONFIRMATION OF ABOVE L/C NOR DOES IT CONVEY ANY ENGAGEMENT OR OBLIGATION ON OUR PART.

THIS L/C CONSISTS OF　　SHEET(S), INCLUDING THE COVERING LETTER AND ATTACHMENT(S).

IF YOU FIND ANY TERMS AND CONDITIONS IN THE L/C WHICH YOU ARE UNABLE TO COMPLY WITH AND OR ANY ERROR(S), IT IS SUGGESTED THAT YOU CONTACT APPLICANT DIRECTLY FOR NECESSARY AMENDMENT(S) SO AS TO AVOID ANY DIFFICULTIES WHICH MAY ARISE WHEN DOCUMENTS ARE PRESENTED.

THIS L/C IS ADVISED SUBJECT TO ICC UCP PUBLICATION NO. 600.

BANK OF CHINA ZHEJIANG BRANCH

ADDRESS:

电话：

传真：

YOURS FAITHFULLY

FOR **BANK OF CHINA**

示样 4-3 不可撤销跟单信用证修改通知书

中国银行股份有限公司 BANK OF CHINA LIMITED

信 用 证 修 改 通 知 书

NOTIFICATION OF AMENDMENT

DATE:

TO: 受益人(BENEFICIARY)		WHEN CORRESPONDING	
		通知编号:	
		PLEASE QUOTE OUR REF. NO.	
ISSUING BANK 开证行		TRANSMITTED TO US THROUGH 转递行	
L/C NO. 信用证号:	DATED 开证日期:	AMOUNT 金额:	EXPIRY PLACE 有效地:
EXPIRY DATE 效期:	TENOR 期限:	CHARGE 未付费用:	CHARGE BY 费用承担人:
RECEIVED VIA 来证方式:	AVAILABLE 是否生效:	TEST/SIGN 印押是否相符:	CONFIRM 我行是否保兑:
AMEND NO.修改次数:	DATE 修改日期:	INCREASE AMT 增额:	DECREASE AMT 减额:

DEAR SIRS,

   WE HAVE PLEASURE IN ADVISING THAT YOU WE HAVE RECEIVED FROM THE A/M BANK A(N) **AMENDMENT TO THE CAPTIONED L/C,** CONTENTS OF WHICH ARE AS PER ATTACHED SHEET(S).

   THIS AMENDMENT SHOULD BE ATTACHED TO THE CAPTIONED L/C ADVISED BY US, OTHERWISE, THE BENEFICIARY WILL BE RESPONSIBLE FOR ANY CONSEQUENCES ARISING THEREFROM.

REMARKS:

   PLEASE NOTE THAT THIS ADVICE DOES NOT CONSITITUTE OUR CONFIRMATION OF ABOVE L/C NOR DOES IT CONVEY ANY ENGAGEMENT OR OBLIGATION ON OUR PART.

   PLEASE NOTE THAT THE L/C NO. HAS BEEN CHANGED.

   THIS AMENDMENT CONSISTS OF SHEET(S), INCLUDING THE COVERING LETTER AND ATTACHMENT(S).

   KINDLY TAKE NOTE THAT PARTIAL ACCEPTANCE OF THE AMENDMENT IS NOT ALLOWED.

   THIS AMENDMENT IS ADVISED SUBJECT TO ICC UCP PUBLICATION NO. 600.

   BANK OF CHINA ZHEJIANG BRANCH

   ADDRESS:

   电话:

   传真:

                                    YOURS FAITHFULLY
                                    FOR **BANK OF CHINA**

示样 4-4　不可撤销跟单信用证——给通知行的通知

IRREVOCABLE DOCUMENTARY CREDIT(ADVICE FOR THE ADVISING BANK)

NAME OF ISSUING BANK:	IRREVOCABLE DOCUMENTARY CREDIT	NUMBER
PLACE AND DATE OF ISSUE:	EXPIRY DATE AND PLACE FOR PRESENTATION OF DOCUMENTS\EXPIRY DATE:	
APPLICANT:	PLACE FOR PRESENTATION:	
	BENEFICIARY:	
ADVISING BANK: REFERENCE NO. :	AMOUNT:	
PARTIAL SHIPMENTS ☐ ALLOWED ☐ NOT ALLOWED	CREDIT AVAILABLE WITH ☐BY PAYMENT AT SIGHT	
TRANSSHIPMENT ☐ ALLOWED ☐ NOT ALLOWED	☐BY DEFERRED PAYMENT AT:	
☐INSURANCE COVERED BY BUYERS	☐BY ACCEPTANCE OF DRAFTS AT: ☐BY NEGOTIATION	
SHIPMENTS AS DEFINED IN UCP600 ARTICLE 46 FROM: FOR TRANSPORTATION TO: NOT LATER THAN:	AGAINST THE DOCUMENTS DETAILED HEREIN: ☐AND BENEFICIARY'S DRAFT(S) DRAWN ON:	

DOCUMENTS TO BE PRESENTED WITHIN ☐DAYS AFTER THE DATE OF SHIPMENT BUT WITHIN THE VALIDITY OF CREDIT.

WE HEREBY ISSUE THE IRREVOCABLE DOCUMENTARY CREDIT AS DETAILED ABOVE. IT IS SUBJECT TO UCP600.WE REQUEST YOU TO ADVISE THE BENEFICIARY:
☐WITHOUT ADDING YOUR CONFIRMATION
☐ADDING YOUR CONFIRMATION
☐ADDING YOUR CONFIRMATION IF REQUESTED BY THE BENEFICIARY
BANK TO BANK INSTRUCTIONS:

THIS DOCUMENT CONSISTS OF ☐ SIGNED PAGES
_____
NAME AND SIGNATURE OF THE ISSUING BANK

2．开证申请书的内容

开证申请书的内容如下所述。

(1) 信用证性质，如不可撤销的信用证、可转让的信用证。

(2) 信用证号码，开证行的信用证编号。

(3) 开证地点和日期。

(4) 信用证的到期地点和到期日。如"110302 IN CHINA"，表明该信用证于 2011 年 3 月 2 日在中国交单到期。

(5) 申请人的名称和地址，一般是买卖合同的买方。如买方是中间商，申请人可以是最终买方。

(6) 受益人的名称和地址，一般是买卖合同的卖方。

(7) 通知行，最好指定卖方所在地的银行为通知行。

(8) 信用证金额。金额应用大写与小写表示。如金额前加上"ABOUT"、"APPROXIMATELY"等词语时则允许有不超过 10%的增减幅度。同时，使用国际标准化组织制定的货币代号如 USD、GBP 等来表示货币种类。

(9) 被指定银行、信用证种类、汇票、付款期限、付款人等。

对受益人来讲，信用证最好规定在出口地有被指定银行。被指定银行可以是信用证的付款行、承兑行、议付行。此栏要填写指定银行的名称与地址。如填写"ANY BANK AT_____(CITY) OR IN_____(COUNTRY)"，则该证是自由兑付的信用证。如通知行是被指定银行，则将通知行名称写在此处，不要写"YOU OR YOUR BANK"，因其含义随格式不同而改变。

信用证种类要在小方格(口)内加注"X"来选择：即期付款、延期付款、承兑、议付。

汇票栏(AND BENEFICIARY'S DRAFTS DRAWN ON)的填写：如选择承兑，则要求受益人出票，在此小方格(口)内加注"X"；采用即期付款或议付方式，可要求有汇票或不用汇票，如要汇票，在此小方格(口)内加注"X"。

付款人(DRAWEE)栏，信用证下一般应填银行，不可填写开证申请人。

付款期限栏。即期付款，可填写"X"；远期付款，则注明具体的付款期限，如"30 DAYS"。

(10) 分批装运。在"允许"或"不允许"小方格(口)内加注"X"。

(11) 转运。仅在适合时方可在"允许"或"不允许"小方格(口)内加注"X"。

(12) 投保。仅在信用证要求提交保险单据，而且申请人表示他已经或将要为货物投保时，方可在小方格(口)内加注"X"。

(13) 起运港、目的港、装运期。一般填写"FROM_____FOR TRANSPORTATION TO_____NOT LATER THAN_____"。填写时应避免使用缩写和模糊用语，要注明装运国家。如货物从一个内陆国家或内陆发运地点出运，不应该规定从一个海港装运。在信用证中规定一个货物到达的日期是不正确的。

(14) 对货物或服务的描述。要简短通俗，不要罗列过多细节。

(15) 规定的单据。单据顺序一般为商业发票、运输单据、保险单据、其他单据。要明确表明单据名称及正副本份数。除运输单据、保险单据、商业发票以外，最好表明出单人名称、单据措辞及内容等。

运输单据分普通的和特定的。

- 运输单据(普通的)。海运提单正面必须注明承运人或多式运输经营人的名称；若使用指定国籍或国旗的船只运输，信用证应规定用什么单据来表示符合哪项条件，不应列有非单据化条件；避免规定"快船装运"或"班轮条件装运"；银行不接受不清洁的运输单据。如不采用海洋运输，则不能规定运输单据带有"清洁已装船"批注。

- 运输单据(特定的)。例如：多式运输单据、联运提单、海运单、租船合约提单、航空运输单据、公路/铁路/内河运输单据、邮政收据等。

(16) 交单期限。按照 UCP600，信用证必须规定一个交单的截止日。规定的承付或议付的截止日将被视为交单的截止日。同时，受益人也必须在不迟于运输单据规定的发运日后 21 个日历日内交单。

(17) 对通知行的指示。仅用于"致通知行的通知书"，如要求其对信用证加具保兑。

(18) 偿付指示。开证行表明何时、以何种方式偿付被指定指行。

(19) 信用证开立的页数。

(20) 开证行有权签字人的签名。

3. 信用证修改通知书的内容

信用证修改通知书的内容如下所述。

(1) 被修改的信用证的号码。

(2) 修改日期。

(3) 开证日期和地址。

(4) 被修改的信用证的申请人。

(5) 受益人。

(6) 通知银行。

(7) 中间空白部分，用于缮制修改内容。

(8) 开证行有权签字人的签名。

(9) 通知行指示，通知行将本行修改通知书的内容加以注释。

【案例4-2】买卖合同、开证申请书与对应信用证实例

(1) 买卖双方签订的售货合同样本

售货确认书 SALES CONFIRMATION		编号 NO.:	NA55578
		日期 DATE:	OCT. 29, 2008
		地点 PLACE:	HANGZHOU, CHINA

卖方(THE SELLERS):

HANGZHOU TENGLONG WEAVING CO., LTD.

买方 THE BUYERS:

NANCY FABRICS INC, 5 STREET NO. 43 AVENUE 5, HAMBURG , GERMANY

ORIGINAL

买卖双方同意以下列条款达成交易:

THIS UNDERSIGNED SELLERS AND BUYERS HAVE AGREED TO CLOSE THE FOLLOWING TRANSACTION ACCORDING TO THE TERMS AND CONDITIONS STIPULATED BELOW:

1. 品名及规格 COMMODITY & SPECIFICATION	2. 数量 QUANTITY	3. 单价及价格条款 UNIT PRICE & TRADE TERMS	4. 金额 AMOUNT
UPHOLSTERY FABRICS PATTERN NO. 11011 PLAIN, PATTERN NO. 11012 CHECK, PATTERN NO. 11013 STRIPE, PATTERN NO. 11014 JACQUARDS EACH PATTERN 5000 MTRS	20000 MTRS	CIF HAMBURG @USD2.70/MTR	USD54,000.00
TOTAL VALUE: SAY U.S. DOLLARS FIFTY FOUR THOUSAND ONLY.			USD54,000.00
5. 包装和唛头 (PACKING & SHIPPING MARKS)	ONE PIECE WITH ROLL PACKING, PIECE LENGTH 50(±5)MTRS		
6. 装运期及运输方式 TIME OF SHIPMENT & MEANS OF TRANSPORTATION	SEAFREIGHT, ON/BEFORE DEC. 15, 2008	7. 装运港和目的地 PORT OF LOADING & DESTINATION	FROM SHANGHAI TO HAMBURG

8. 保险 INSURANCE: CIF TO BE EFFECTED BY THE SELLERS AT 110% OF INVOICE VALUE COVERING ALL RISKS AND WAR RISKS AS PER CHINA INSURANCE CLAUSES (C.I.C) DATED 1/1/1981.

9. 付款方式

TERMS OF PAYMENT: BY 100% IRREVOCABLE L/C TO BE AVAILABLE BY SIGHT DRAFT, REACHING THE SELLERS 45 DAYS BEFORE SHIPMENT, REMAINING VALID FOR NEGOTIATION IN CHINA FOR FURTHER 15 DAYS AFTER THE PRESCRIBED TIME OF SHIPMENT, ALLOWING TRANSSHIPMENT & PARTIAL SHIPMENT.

合同(续)

10. 仲裁 ARBITRATION: ALL DISPUTES ARISING FROM THE EXECUTION OF, OR IN CONNECTION WITH THIS CONTRACT, SHALL BE SETTLED AMICABLY THROUGH FRIENDLY NEGOTIATION. IN CASE NO SETTLEMENT CAN BE REACHED THROUGH NEGOTIATION, THE CASE SHALL THEN BE SUBMITTED TO THE FOREIGN ECONOMIC & TRADE ARBITRATION COMMISSION OF THE CHINA COUNCIL FOR THE PROMOTION OF INTERNATIONAL TRADE, BEIJING, FOR ARBITRATION IN ACCORDANCE WITH ITS PROVISIONAL RULES OF PROCEDURE. THE ARBITRATION AWARD IS FINAL AND BINDING UPON BOTH PARTIES.

11. 一般条款 GENERAL TERMS

(1)REASONABLE TOLERANCE IN QUALITY, WEIGHT, MEASUREMENTS, DESIGNS AND COLORS IS ALLOWED, FOR WHICH NO CLAIMS WILL BE ENTERED.

(2)BUYERS ARE TO ASSUME FULL RESPONSIBILITIES FOR ANY CONSEQUENCES ARISING FROM: (A) THE USE OF PACKING, DESIGNS OR BRAND PATTERN MADE TO ORDER; (B)LATE SUBMISSION OF SPECIFICATION OR ANY DETAILS NECESSARY FOR THE EXECUTION OF THIS SALES CONFIRMATION; (C)LATE ESTABLISHMENT OF L/C; (D) LATE AMENDMENT TO L/C INCONSISTENT WITH THE PROVISIONS OF THIS SALES CONFIRMATION.

(3)SELLERS ARE NOT RESPONSIBLE FOR LATE OR NON-DELIVERY IN THE EVENT OF FORCE MAJEURE OR ANY CONTINGENCES BEYOND SELLER'S CONTROL.

(4)CLAIMS, IF ANY, CONCERNING THE GOODS SHIPPED SHOULD BE FILED WITHIN 30 DAYS AFTER ARRIVAL AT DESTINATION.

(5)BUYERS SHOULD SIGN ONE COPY OF THIS SALES CONFIRMATION AND RETURN IT TO SELLERS WITHIN 10 DAYS AFTER RECEIPT. IF NOTHING IS PROPOSED TO THE CONTRARY WITHIN THAT TIME, THIS SALES CONFIRMATION WILL BE EFFECTIVE. SALES CONFIRMATION, ISSUED ON THE STRENGTH OF BUYERS' ORDER OR EARLIER CONFIRMATION, IS EFFECTIVE IMMEDIATELY ON ITS ISSUANCE, AND SUBJECT TO NEITHER MODIFICATION NOR CANCELLATION, UNLESS AGREED UPON BOTH PARTIES.

(6)5% MORE OR LESS FOR EACH SHIPMENT IS ALLOWED.

THE BUYER: NANCY FABRICS INC.	THE SELLER: HANGZHOU TENGLONG
SIGNED	WEAVING CO., LTD.
	SIGNED

(2) 进口商填制的开证申请书

IRREVOCABLE DOCUMENTARY CREDIT APPLICATION	
TO: BANK OF CHINA LTD., ZHEJIANG BRANCH	DATE: 081031
□ISSUE BY AIRMAIL	CREDIT NO.: 50000585(注：银行审核后填入)
□ISSUE BY EXPRESS DELIVERY	DATE AND PLACE OF EXPIRY: 081230 IN CHINA
□WITH BRIEF ADVICE BY TELETRANSMISSION	
☒ ISSUE BY TELETRANSMISSION (WHICH SHALL BE THE OPERATIVE INSTRUMENT)	
APPLICANT:	BENEFICIARY (FULL NAME AND ADDRESS):

开证申请书(续)

NANCY FABRICS INC, 5 STREET NO. 43 AVENUE 5, HAMBURG, GERMANY		HANGZHOU TENGLONG WEAVING CO., LTD. #198 JIANSHE NO. 1 ROAD, XIAOSHAN ECONOMIC & TECHNOLOGICAL DEVELOPMENT ZONE, HANGZHOU, CHINA
ADVISING BANK: BANK OF CHINA LTD., ZHEJIANG BRANCH NO. 189 YANAN ROAD, HANGZHOU 310006, ZHEJIANG PROVINCE, CHINA		AMOUNT: USD54, 000.00 (TOTAL AMOUNT SAY U.S. DOLLARS FIFTY FOUR THOUSAND ONLY)
PARTIAL SHIPMENTS ☒ ALLOWED ☐NOT ALLOWED	TRANSSHIPMENT ☒ ALLOWED ☐NOT ALLOWED	CREDIT AVAILABLE WITH <u>ISSUING BANK</u> BY ☒ SIGHT PAYMENT ☐ACCEPTANCE ☐NEGOTIATION ☐DEFERRED PAYMENT AT
LOADING ON BOARD/DISPATCH/TAKING IN CHARGE AT/FROM: SHANGHAI, CHINA NOT LATER THAN: DEC. 15, 2008 FOR TRANSPORT TO: HAMBURG, GERMANY TRADE TERMS: ☐FOB ☐CFR ☒ CIF ☐OR OTHER TERMS		AGAINST THE DOCUMENTS DETAILED HEREIN ☐AND BENEFICIARY'S DRAFT(S) FOR <u>100 </u>% OF INVOICE VALUE AT <u>XX DAYS</u> AFTER SIGHT DRAWN ON <u>THE ISSUING BANK</u>

DOCUMENTS REQUIRED: (MARKED WITH X)

1. (X) SIGNED COMMERCIAL INVOICE IN 3 COPIES INDICATING L/C NO._____AND CONTRACT NO. _____.

2. (X) FULL SET OF CLEAN ON BOARD BILLS OF LADING MADE OUT TO ORDER OF THE ISSUING BANK, MARKED "FREIGHT [ ] TO COLLECT / [X] PREPAID" [   ] SHOWING FREIGHT AMOUNT NOTIFYING APPLICANT.

(   )AIRWAY BILLS/CARGO RECEIPT/COPY OF RAILWAY BILLS ISSUED BY   SHOWING "FREIGHT [ ] TO COLLECT/[   ] PREPAID" [   ] INDICATING FREIGHT AMOUNT AND CONSIGNED TO_____.

3. (X) INSURANCE POLICY/CERTIFICATE IN 2 COPIES FOR 110% OF THE INVOICE VALUE SHOWING CLAIMS PAYABLE IN DESTINATION IN CURRENCY OF THE DRAFT, BLANK ENDORSED, COVERING ICC(A) AND WAR RISKS AND SRCC RISKS.

4. (X) PACKING LIST/WEIGHT MEMO IN 3 COPIES INDICATING QUANTITY, GROSS AND WEIGHTS OF EACH PACKAGE.

5. ( ) CERTIFICATE OF QUANTITY/WEIGHT IN_____COPIES ISSUED BY _____.

6. ( ) CERTIFICATE OF QUALITY IN_____COPIES ISSUED BY [ ] MANUFACTURER/[   ] PUBLIC RECOGNIZED SURVEYOR_____.

7. (X)CERTIFICATE OF ORIGIN GSP FORM A IN_____COPIES ISSUED BY _____.

8. (X) BENEFICIARY'S CERTIFIED COPY OF FAX / TELEX DISPATCHED TO THE APPLICANT WITHIN 48 HOURS AFTER SHIPMENT ADVISING OF VESSEL, DATE OF SHIPMENT, NAME, QUANTITY, WEIGHT AND VALUE OF GOODS.

OTHER DOCUMENTS, IF ANY

DESCRIPTION OF GOODS:

UPHOLSTERY FABRICS 20,000 MTRS AT USD2.70/MTR   TOTAL AMOUNT USD54,000.00

PACKING: ROLL

ADDITIONAL INSTRUCTIONS:

1. (X) ALL BANKING CHARGES OUTSIDE THE OPENING BANK ARE FOR BENEFICIARY'S ACCOUNT.

2. (X) DOCUMENTS MUST BE PRESENTED WITHIN 21 DAYS AFTER DATE OF ISSUANCE OF THE TRANSPORT DOCUMENTS BUT WITHIN THE VALIDITY OF THIS CREDIT.

3. ( ) THIRD PARTY AS SHIPPER IS NOT ACCEPTABLE, SHORT FORM/BLANK BACK B/L IS NOT ACCEPTABLE.

4. (X) ALL DOCUMENTS MUST BE FORWARDED IN ENGLISH.

5. ( ) OTHER TERMS, IF ANY

(3) 开证行开出的信用证样本

FORM OF DOC. CREDIT: IRREVOCABLE

CREDIT NUMBER: 50000585

DATE OF ISSUE: 081102

EXPIRY: DATE: 081230 PLACE: CHINA

OPENING BANK: REPUBLIC NATIONAL BANK OF GERMANY, HAMBURG BRANCH

APPLICANT: NANCY FABRICS INC, 5 STREET NO. 43 AVENUE 5, HAMBURG, GERMANY

BENEFICIARY: HANGZHOU TENGLONG WEAVING CO., LTD., #198 JIANSHE NO. 1 ROAD, XIAOSHAN ECONOMIC & TECHNOLOGICAL DEVELOPMENT ZONE, HANGZHOU, 311215, CHINA

AMOUNT: CURRENCY: USD   AMOUNT: 54,000.00 ABOUT

VAILABLE WITH/BY: DRAFT(S) AT SIGHT BY PAYMENT

DRAWEE TO: REPUBLIC NATIONAL BANK OF GERMANY, HAMBURG BRANCH

PARTIAL SHIPMENTS: PARTIAL SHIPMENTS ALLOWED

TRANSSHIPMENT: TRANSSHIPMENT ALLOWED

LOADING IN CHARGE: SHANGHAI, CHINA

FOR TRANSPORT TO: HAMBURG, GERMANY

LATEST DATE OF SHIP.: 081215

DESCRIPT. OF GOODS: UPHOLSTERY FABRICS 20,000 MTRS AT USD2.70/MTR CIF HAMBURG,
GERMANY TOTAL AMOUNT USD54,000.00   PACKING: ROLL

DOCUMENTS REQUIRED :

+SIGNED COMMERCIAL INVOICE IN TRIPLICATE

+DETAILED PACKING LIST IN TRIPLICATE

+GSP FORM A

+3/3 SET NEGOTIABLE CLEAN ON BOARD OCEAN BILLS OF LADING CONSIGNED TO ORDER OF REPUBLIC NATIONAL BANK OF GERMANY, HAMBURG BRANCH NOTIFYING APPLICANT AND MARKED FREIGHT PREPAID.

+INSURANCE POLICY IN DUPLICATE COVERING AT LEAST 110% OF COMMERCIAL VALUE WITH CLAIM PAYABLE IN HAMBURG IN EUR AGAINST ICC(A) AND WAR RISKS AND SRCC RISKS.

ADDITIONAL REQUIREMENTS:

+ 5% MORE OR LESS ON QUANTITY AND AMOUNT ARE ACCEPTABLE.

+ DRAFTS ARE TO BE MARKED DRAWN UNDER REPUBLIC NATIONAL BANK OF GERMANY, HAMBERG BRANCH AND BEARING CREDIT NUMBER AND THE ISSUING DATE.

+ BENEFICIARY SHOULD BE CERTIFYING ON THE INVOICE AND B/L INDICATING THAT THE GOODS ARE COMPLYING WITH THE S/C CONTRACT NO. NA55578.

+ A DISCRIPANCY FEE OF USD 50.00 WILL BE DEDUCTED FROM THE PROCEEDS OF ANY DRAWING PRESENTED WITH DISCRIPANCIES.

+ IT IS A CONDITION OF THIS CREDIT THAT ALL DOCUMENTS ARE TO FORWARDED IN ONE COMPLETE SET MAILING TO REPUBLIC NATIONAL BANK OF GERMANY, HAMBURG BRANCH.

+ UPON RECEIPT OF DRAFTS AND ALL DOCUMENTS ACCOMPANIED IN CONFORMITY WITH THE TERMS AND CONDITIONS OF THIS CREDIT, WE WILL REMIT PROCEEDS TO YOUR

信用证(续)

ACCOUNT AS PER YOUR INSTRUCTION.

DETAILS OF EXCHARGES: ALL CHARGES OUTSIDE THE ISSUING BANK ARE FOR THE ACCOUNT OF THE BENEFICIARY.

PRESENTATION PERIOD: DOCUMENTS MUST BE PRESENTED WITHIN 21 DAYS FROM SHIPMENT DATE BUT WITHIN CREDIT VALIDITY.

CONFIRMATION: WITHOUT

ADVISE THROUGH: BKCHCNBJ910

BANK OF CHINA LTD., ZHEJIANG NO. 189 YANAN ROAD, HANGZHOU 310006, ZHEJIANG PROVINCE, CHINA

TRAILER: THIS CREDIT IS SUBJECT TO ICC PUBLICATION NO. 600 (2007 REVISION)

三、信用证当事人

信用证业务所涉及的基本当事人为两个：开证行和受益人。除此以外，还可能出现申请人、保兑行、通知行、被指定银行、转让行和偿付行等。

(一)申请人

信用证的开证申请人(APPLICANT)通常是进口商。申请人受两个合同的约束：一是与出口商所签订的进出口贸易合同，二是开证申请书。

作为进口商，必须根据合同内容，在合理的时间内开证。信用证的内容必须服从合同的内容。只有"证、同一致"，出口商才有可能在履行合同义务的同时获得信用证项下的金额。若信用证内容与合同不符，受益人提出修改，开证申请人有义务对信用证进行必要修改。但如果提出的修改不符合合同，没有必须修改的义务。总之，开证申请人的权利和义务如下。

(1) 合理指示开证。申请人在申请书上的措辞必须明确(CERTAIN)、简洁(CONCISE)、前后一致(CONSISTENCE)。按合同规定向银行交押金，要求开证(与合同相符)。

(2) 提供开证担保。开证行为了避免风险通常要求申请人提供一定形式的担保，如现金、动产或不动产，也可以是第三者提供的保证。现金保证就是开证押金，押金可为信用证金额的0～100%，开证押金的多少与申请人的资信状况直接相关。

(3) 及时赎单付款。开证行只是付款代理人，而申请人是承担付款责任的委托人。在交单相符的情况下，开证行履行其付款义务后，进口商应及时偿付货款并向开证行赎单。在赎单前进口商有权检验单据，如果发现交单不符，有权拒付。履行付款后，有权在适当的地点对货物进行检验，如发现货物品质或数量与信用证规定不符，进口商无权要求开证行赔付。进口商有权根据过失的责任，在信用证外向卖方提出索赔或退货。如属于运输或保险公司的责任范围，有权向运输和保险部门索赔。

(二)开证行

开证行(ISSUING BANK)受 3 个合同的约束：①与申请人之间的付款代理合同；②与受益人之间的信用证；③与通知行或议付行之间的代理协议。开证行是信用证业务中最重要的一方，开证行的信誉、业务经验是其他当事人参与信用证业务与否的主要考虑依据。

(1) 根据申请书的内容，按照 UCP600 要求开证。开证行按照开证申请人的指示行事，按 UCP600 处理业务。若信用证含有某些条件而未列明提交与之相符的单据，银行将认为未加列此条件，且对此不予理会。据此，开证行在开证时必须将申请人在申请书上所列的全部条款加以单据化。单据成为信用证的主要内容，是申请人对受益人行为进行约束的工具。受益人通过提交单据，证明自己已经履行了合同项下的义务。单据也是受益人支配信用证金额，获取货款的依据。

(2) 取得质押的权利。开证行与申请人是两个独立的"法人"关系，双方的权利和义务通过开证申请书的内容来确定。开证行接受了申请人的开证申请后，即承担了开证责任和由此引起的风险，有权向开证申请人收取手续费和预收押金。如市场和开证人资信发生变化，有权随时要求开证申请人补交押金，直到 100%为止。进口商被通知付款赎单，若无能力付款，开证行可以取得对货物的质押权，或自由处理货物以抵偿自己的垫款。对于不足部分，开证行有权向进口商追索。同时，收取的押金不能用于充抵申请人的其他债务而取消开证。

(3) 付款责任。开证行仅基于单据本身确定其是否在表面上构成相符交单。相符交单是指与信用证条款、ISBP 一致的交单。只要交单相符，开证行必须承付。开证行开出信用证后不能以开证申请人无付款能力、未交付押金或手续费、有欺诈行为等为借口而表示对信用证不再负责。

开证行验单付款后无追索权，除非在某些特殊情况下，即当付款足以构成"误付"(如金额付错)时，才可例外。在议付行采用电报索偿时，单到开证行后发现与信用证不符，有权追回已付的款项；对议付行所收下的错误单据可行使拒付的权利；对邮递过程中遗失、延误的单据，享有不负任何责任的权利。

【案例4-3】信用证伪造单据诈骗案

1. 案例介绍

我国某进口公司 A 与外国客商 B 签订了一份合同，采用承兑信用证结算。在信用证有效期内，被指定银行寄来了全套单据。开证行审单后没有发现任何不符点，于是通知 A 付款赎单，要求其在合理时间内办理相应付款手续。A经多方打听，认为B很有可能欺诈。因此，再三拖延，不予以办理相应付款手续，反而要求开证行予以拒付。在被指定银行的强烈合理要求下，开证行要求A同意付款。A尽管有所顾虑，但仍然办理了付款手续，开证行付款。A凭提单到目的港提取货物后，发现货物与信用证项下严重不符，只好提请仲裁，但最终未收回全部货款。

2. 案例分析

本案例的进口商发现了欺诈行为，却无法在合理期限内找到证据，保障自己的权益，使货款脱离了自己的控制，最终陷入纷繁复杂的法律纠纷当中。受益人伪造单据进行欺诈，最主要的方式就是利用信用证。信用证一经开出，开证行就必须负起交单相符项下的付款责任。作为进出口公司，应当紧密配合开证行、被指定银行等当事人，最大化己方信息，最小化己方风险。进口方一旦发现欺诈行为而交单相符的情况下，可以先在合理的时间内申请法院禁付令，禁止开证行对外拒付。在禁付令的有效期内，迅速查明欺诈事实，从而避免开证行最终对外支付，保障自己的权益。

(三)受益人

受益人(BENEFICIARY)一般是出口商或中间商，是接受信用证并享受其利益的一方。受益人受两个合同的约束：与开证申请人之间的贸易合同和与开证行之间的信用证。

受益人在收到信用证后，应以"证同一致"为原则仔细核对。如发现信用证与合同不符，有权要求修改。如修改后仍不符，且足以造成不能接受，有权拒绝受证，甚至单方撤销合同，并提出索赔。

受益人权利的兑现是以提交相符单据为前提。受益人应在信用证规定的装运期限内装运货物；按信用证条款规定缮制各种单据；在信用证有效期内向被指定银行或开证行、保兑行(如有的话)交单。只要做到交单相符，就有取得货款的权利。当然，如要求收款后不被申请人追索，还需要做到单货一致、单同一致。

受益人交单后，如遇开证行对相符单据拒付，有权向开证行提出质问并要求赔偿损失；如交单不符，可以在交单截止日到来前及时更改单据；如开证申请人和开证行一起倒闭，有权行使留置权、扣货并行使停运权。行使这些权利后，有权出售货物给他人，但必须通知进口商，如在合理时间内进口商未能付款或答复，才能售货给他人，但易腐品除外。如果开证行无支付的意愿或能力，出口商就可以向进口商直接交单要求付款，即使开证申请人已交押金，遭受了损失，也不影响受益人的权利；如果是保兑信用证，开证行倒闭可向保兑行要求付款，保兑行也倒闭了，可向开证申请人要求付款。

(四)通知行

信用证及其任何修改可以经由通知行(ADVISING BANK)通知受益人。非保兑行的通知行通知信用证及修改时不承担承付或议付的责任。通知行通知信用证或修改的行为表示其已确信信用证或修改的表面真实性，而且其通知准确地反映了其收到的信用证或修改的条款。在 UCP600 中增加了"第二通知行"的概念。通知行可以通过另一银行(第二通知行)向受益人通知信用证及修改。第二通知行通知信用证或修改的行为表明其已确信收到的通知的表面真实性，并且其通知准确地反映了收到的信用证或修改的条款。经由通知行或第二通知行通知信用证的银行必须经由同一银行通知其后的任何修改。

如一银行被要求通知信用证或修改，但其决定不予通知，则应毫不延误地告知自其处收到信用证、修改或通知的银行。

如一银行被要求通知信用证或修改而其不能确信信用证或修改的表面真实性，则应毫不延误地通知看似从其处收到指示的银行。如果通知行或第二通知行决定仍然通知信用证或修改，则应告知受益人或第二通知行其不能确信信用证、修改或通知的表面真实性。

当然，作为通知行，有权向开证行收取通知信用证或修改的手续费，但无义务对受益人进行议付或承付货款。如果通知行接受了担任议付或承付或保兑行的责任后，他便承担了通知行、被指定银行或保兑行的职责，同时也产生了其职责所应承担的权利和义务。值得注意的是保兑行的议付是无追索权的，而被指定银行的议付是有追索权的。

(五)保兑行

开证行可以授权(或要求)通知行或者其他银行对信用证加以保兑(ADD CONFIRMATION)。若该银行同意保兑，即为保兑行(CONFIRMING BANK)。

保兑信用证下的受益人可获得开证行和保兑行的双重独立付款保证：①当受益人向保兑行提交单据时，在交单相符的情况下，就构成保兑行在开证行之外的确定付款承诺，承担与开证行相同的付款责任。②保兑行付款后，只能向开证行索偿。若开证行无能力或无理拒付，则保兑行无权向受益人或者被指定银行追索。③无论开证行发生什么变化，保兑行都不能片面撤销其保兑责任。④在审单时发现单证不符，有权要求受益人在一定期限内改单或拒付。

UCP600 规定，被授权加具保兑的银行有权不予照办，但是必须毫不迟疑地通知开证行。为降低潜在风险，被授权加具保兑的银行一般对开证行的资信状况以及信用证的条款要加以严格的审查，然后才能决定是否加以保兑，除非两个银行之间的代理协议有硬性规定。

【案例 4-4】保兑信用证增加金额及展期后引起的纠纷案

1. 案例介绍

某银行于 2008 年 3 月 1 日开出一份信用证，金额为 3 万美元，有效期到 2008 年 5 月 31 日，通知行应开证行要求保兑了信用证。2008 年 4 月 15 日信用证金额增加了 20 万美元，有效期延展至 2008 年 8 月 31 日。试问：该保兑行是否必须对增加金额及展期的信用证进行保兑？如果保兑行不愿再加保兑，该保兑行应如何行事？

2. 案例分析

一银行是否同意加具保兑的请求是国际商会无法规定的，保兑通常是两家银行间的协议。虽然一家银行可能愿意保兑 3 个月期的 3 万美元的信用证，但它可能不愿保兑 6 个月期 23 万美元的信用证。这种拒绝保兑的权利由 UCP600 第 10 条 b 款规定，即保兑行可以选择将修改通知受益人而不对其加具保兑，但保兑行须毫不迟疑地告知开证行，并在其给受益人的通知中告知受益人。

(六)被指定银行

信用证必须规定其是以即期付款、延期付款、承兑还是议付的方式兑用。按照 UCP600，信用证业务当事人根据不同的信用证种类，可能出现付款行、承兑行和议付行。开证行可以授权另一家银行或指定自己成为付款行、承兑行和议付行。

按照 UCP600，为简便及统一付款及承兑信用证下银行责任的描述，引入了"HONOR"(承付)的概念。付款和承兑信用证项下被指定银行的行为描述为"HONOR"(承付)，而议付信用证项下被指定银行的行为描述为"NEGOTIATION"(议付)。

被指定银行(NOMINATED BANK)是指信用证可在其处兑用的银行，如信用证可在任一银行兑用，则任一银行均为被指定银行。被指定银行可以接受开证行的委托和指示，对受益人提交的相符交单予以承付或议付。

承付是指：①如果信用证为即期付款信用证，则即期付款。②如果信用证为延期付款信用证，则承诺延期付款并承诺在到期日付款。③如果信用证为承兑信用证，则承兑受益人开出的汇票并在汇票到期日付款。

议付是指被指定银行在相符交单下，在其应获偿付的银行工作日当天或之前向受益人预付或者同意预付款项，从而购买汇票(其付款人为被指定银行以外的其他银行)及(或)单据的行为。

被指定银行承付或议付相符交单并将单据转给开证行或保兑行(如有的话)之后，开证行或保兑行即承担偿付该被指定银行的责任。对承兑或延期付款信用证下相符交单金额的偿付应在到期日办理,无论被指定银行是否在到期日之前预付或购买了单据。开证行或保兑行偿付被指定银行的责任独立于开证行或保兑行对受益人的责任。

但是,如果被指定银行因交单不符被开证行或保兑行拒付,则承付信用证下的被指定银行对受益人无追索权,而议付信用证下的被指定银行对受益人有追索权。

如开证行开出信用证后指定一家出口地银行为被指定银行,这种信用证对出口商相对有利,而对进口商不利。在交单相符条件下,无论被指定银行是否在到期日之前预付或购买了单据,开证行或保兑行即承担偿付该被指定银行的责任。在欺诈例外项下,被指定银行作为善意的汇票持票人或正当持票人,对开证行或保兑行享有不受其他权益约束的请求权,被指定银行当事人是被保护的,也可视为出口商也被保护了。

【案例4-5】受益人拒绝向议付行退款欺诈案

1. 案例介绍

香港某开证行开出一笔27万美元的信用证,购买30 000件棉制女衬衣,CIF成交。信用证为自由议付信用证(CREDIT AVAILABLE WITH ANY BANK BY NEGOTIATION)并规定有软条款 "INSPECTION CERTIFICATE ISSUED BY MR. XXX (PASSPORT NO. XXX) WHOSE SIGNATURE MUST BE IN CONFORMITY WITH THE RECORDED HELD IN THE ISSUING BANK" (中国商检局签发的产地证,申请人应在检验证书上会签,其签字应与在开证行预留的签字样本一致)。

国内A企业收到信用证后,向中间商支付了25万人民币的质量保证金。货物生产完毕后,A企业在信用证规定的最迟装运期限前15天,与中间商联系装运事宜。A企业派人前来检验并出具了检验证书。A企业自己联系船公司,支付运费,并将30 000件服装运往香港。然后,A企业备齐了该信用证项下的全套单据向同市的B银行交单议付。B银行在没有确定检验证书签字人签字是否与开证行留存的签字样本是否一致的情况下,向A企业办理了议付。单据到达香港后,开证行因检验证书签字不一致原因拒付并退单。后经多方联系,中间商避而不见,开证申请人明确表示拒收货物。B银行随后向A企业追索,后者拒绝退款。B银行向法院起诉,法院冻结A企业账户余额30万元进入法庭审理。因此,本案的议付行和受益人都遭受了严重损失。B银行的27万美元垫款追回几乎已无可能,受益人A企业损失了25万质量保证金。货物到香港后,因无人提取,已产生大量的仓储费,并有可能被拍卖。

2. 案例分析

本案的要点有三个:①本案起因是出口企业风险意识薄弱,对支付保证金的无理要求没有引起足够的警惕;②对于信用证中的软条款没有表示异议;③被指定银行审单不严。

支付保证金的做法与国际贸易惯例不符。如买方担忧卖方的履约能力，可以要求卖方开具履约保函，而非缴纳保证金，更不应该将保证金汇给中间商。

本案中银企双方纠纷由诈骗引起。信用证业务中的银企双方都应增强防范意识，提高防诈骗能力。本案诈骗特点：①涉案金额大。②开证行没有在开立信用证时将签字样本寄给通知行转交受益人。即使开证申请人指派的检验人员在检验证书上签字，其签字也与留存样本不同。③开证人不是签约人。开证人与中间商联合欺诈，开出了软条款信用证。

对被指定银行来说，在审核单据时，应要求开证行将签字样本传真过来，以便核对。

(七)偿付行

开证行若授权另一家银行代为偿付被指定银行、保兑行(均称为索偿行)的索偿时，则该银行为偿付行(REIMBURSING BANK)。偿付行一般是信用证结算货币清算中心的联行或者代理行，主要是为了头寸调拨的便利。

开证行应及时通知偿付行，一般做法是将信用证副本抄送偿付行或给偿付行下达偿付授权书(REIMBURSING AUTHORIZATION)。如开证行通知不及时，偿付行则不负责任。偿付银行的费用由开证行承担，除非信用证有相反规定。偿付行相当于开证行的出纳行，单据正确与否并不构成其偿付的依据，因此索偿行不需向偿付行提供与信用证条款相符的证明，而只是向偿付行发出索偿书即可。若偿付行不能偿付，开证行并不能解除其自行偿付的义务；若偿付行未能在首次索偿时给予偿付，开证行应当对索偿行的利息负责。因此，在指定偿付行的情况下，索偿行一方面向偿付行邮寄索偿书，另一方面向开证行寄单，开证行若收到与信用证不符的单据，有权向索偿行追回已经偿付的款项，但开证行不得向偿付行追索。

四、跟单信用证的基本流程

(一)开证申请人申请开证

买卖双方在合同中约定采用信用证结算时，通常由买方向其所在地的一家银行提出开证申请，填写并提交开证申请书。开证申请书是申请人和开证行之间的法律文件，也是开立信用证的依据，其内容的完整性、明确性非常重要。开证指示就是指开证申请书，经申请人和银行签字后方能生效。开证申请书一般包括两部分内容。

(1) 正面是信用证的内容。信用证内容应该完全按照贸易合同的内容进行填写，合同是信用证的基础，是申请人申请开证和受益人审证的依据。实务中很多案例的发生都是由于合同条款订得不好而引起纠纷或使一方抓到了违约的把柄。

(2) 背面是申请人对开证行的申明，是进口商和开证行之间的法律契约，用以明确申请人与开证行之间的权责。为了减少资金方面的风险，大多数开证行都要求申请人在申请开证时交纳一部分开证押金。背面主要内容有：①明确申请人应及时偿还开证行的义务；②明确表示同意开证行根据 UCP600 的免责条款免除义务；③申请人同意在付款前将货物的所有权转让给开证行；④申请人承诺支付信用证项下的各项费用；⑤申请人明确遵循 UCP600 的开证要求。

(二)进口地银行开立信用证

1. 开证前的审查和检验

开证银行在接受申请人的开证申请书之前，开证行要进行开证前的审查和检验，严格把关，谨慎开立信用证，其目的是为了降低潜在的风险。一般过程如下。①审查开证申请书与开证担保书。②审查开证申请人的资信状况、目前的经营状况、财务状况以及经济实力和过去是否有不良的信用记录。③查验进口开证应当提供的有效证件。各国对进口商品有不同的管理条例。在我国，开证申请人应提供贸易项下的进口付汇核销证明；对实行进口配额管理或者特定产品进口管理的货物，申请人应当持进口许可证或者特定商品进口登记证明；对实行自动登记制的货物，申请人持相应的登记文件即可。④落实开证保证金。

2. 开立信用证

开证行以信开或电开方式将信用证的内容发送给出口商所在地的联行或代理行(通知行)，通过它们通知或转递信用证给受益人。由于现代通信科技的发展，全电开已成为主要的信用证传递方式，信开和简电开方式已很少使用了。全电开(FULL CABLE)是以电讯方式(TELEX 或 SWIFT)发出内容完整的信用证，是有效的信用证正本。SWIFT 的信用证格式为 MT700 和 MT701。与信开相比，SWIFT 信用证省略了保证条款，但加注密押，系统自动核对密押无误后，SWIFT 信用证才生效。除非特别规定，SWIFT 信用证从 2007 年 7 月 1 日起受 UCP600 约束。

3. 开立信用证修改书

银行凭修改申请书缮制信用证修改通知书，一般用 SWIFT 方式通过同一通知行通知。修改通知书副本按修改日期依次依附于信用证上留存备查。

(三)出口地银行通知或转递信用证

1. 通知信用证

通知行收到信用证核对密押无误后，按自己的通知书格式照录全文，通知受益人。如信用证以受益人为收件人，寄给出口地银行后，银行核对印鉴无误后，将原证交还受益人，这时候银行成为转递行(TRANSMITTING BANK)。

2. 通知加保信用证

如开证行要求通知行对信用证加具保兑，由于保兑行的责任同开证行，应邀保兑的通知行应注意避免风险，例如：只对开证行资信良好和有一定资金实力的信用证加保；对信用证中无对受益人收款不利的条款加具保兑等。

3. 通知修改书

信用证的修改书仍由通知行通知。如受益人接受，修改书生效；若受益人拒绝接受，则修改书无效，信用证仍以原条款为准。

(四)出口商审证发货并提交单据

1. 审证

为了保证受益人(出口商)同时完成信用证以及贸易合同项下的义务，受益人在审证时，必须严格根据合同审证，消除信用证交单时的潜在风险。随着信用证业务被广大企业所了解，我国的通知行已基本不需要审核信用证了。信用证由出口企业自行审核。出口企业审核信用证时主要判断信用证条款是否与合同一致，审核的项目一般包括如下内容。

(1) 信用证是否属通知行正式通知的有效信用证。

(2) 审核信用证的种类。

(3) 审核信用证是否加具保兑。审核信用证由哪一家银行保兑以及保兑费由谁承担是审核信用证的内容之一。一般来说，信用证由第三方银行加以保兑，其可靠程度比一般信用证高。但资信优良的开证行开出的信用证不需要保兑。

(4) 审核开证申请人和受益人。由于开证申请人的名称或地址经常会与进口商在进出口合同上显示的名称或地址不一样，因此要仔细审核开证申请人的名称和地址，以防错发错运货物。

(5) 审核信用证的支付货币和金额。信用证的金额和支付的货币种类应与合同一致，总金额的大小写数字必须一致。如果合同订有溢短装条款，那么信用证金额还应包括溢短装部分的金额。来证采用的支付货币种类如果与合同规定的货币不一致，应按银行外汇牌价折算成合同货币，在不低于或相当于原合同货币总金额时才可接受。

(6) 审核付款期限和有关货物的内容描述。审核付款期限是否与合同一致或者可接受。审核信用证有关货物的内容描述，如来证中的有关品名、质量、规格、数量、包装、单价、金额、装运港、卸货港、目的地、保险等是否与合同规定一致；有无附加特殊条款及保留条款；是否需要提供客户检验证明；商业发票是否要求证实或有进口国的领事签证等。这些条款必须仔细审核，视具体情况判断是否接受或提请修改。

(7) 审核信用证的到期地点。所有信用证均需规定到期日、到期地点与交单地点。所谓到期日，是交单的最后期限。所谓到期地点，是在效期内交单有效的地点。到期地点、到期时间与信用证的兑用银行，即交单有效银行所在地必须匹配。UCP600 规定："THE PLACE OF THE BANK WITH WHICH THE CREDIT IS AVAILABLE IS THE PLACE FOR PRESENTATION(信用证兑用的银行地点就是交单地点)。"即信用证规定在哪个银行兑用有效，就应把单据交到那个银行；在任何银行兑用有效的信用证，任何银行的地址都可作为交单地址。开证银行地址之外的交单地址为开证行地址之外的附加地址。但是，即使规定在开证行地址之外的地址交单，交到开证行也是可以的，以便与"在被指定行有效的信用证同样在开证行有效"的规定相匹配。按照 UCP600，信用证最好不要规定限制在开证行兑用有效，如信用证限制在开证行兑用，则出口地就没有被指定银行，而受益人不得不向非指定银行交单。在这种情况下，单据如果在寄单银行与开证行或保兑行之间遗失，开证行或保兑行没有付款责任(根据 UCP600 第 35 条相关规定推定)。

(8) 审核装运期，转船、分批装运条款和有效期。装运期是对货物装运时间的规定，原则上必须与合同一致。如果信用证到达太晚而不能按期装运，应及时电请国外进口商展延装运期限；如由于生产或船期等原因造成不能在装运期内按期装运，也可以与进口商友好协商延期装运。一般情况下，买方不愿意允许其进口的货物转船。审核有关条款时，应注意它是否与合同的规定一致。如果信用证规定允许转船，还应注意在允许转船的内容后面有无加列特殊限制或要求，例如：指定转运地点、船名或船公司。对这些限制或要求应考虑是否有把握控制，如不能，则应及时通知对方改证。信用证中如规定分批、定期、定量装运，那么在审核来证时，应注意每批装运的时间是否留有合适的间隔。按照国际惯例，对于分批装运的信用证，若任何一批未按期装运，则信用证中的该批和以后各批均视作失败，所以审证时要认真对待。信用证的有效期限与装运期限应有一定的合理间隔，以便在货物装运后有足够的时间进行制单和办理结汇。有些信用证的有效期与装运期规定在同一天，这种信用证称为"双到期信用证"，这种规定不完全合理，出口商应预先按照生产完工日期，结合船期情况、制单时间和银行必要的议付工作日等具体情况判断是否要求对方修改信用证。

(9) 审核信用证付款方式和提交的单据。银行的付款方式有四种：即期付款、延期付款、承兑或议付。所有的信用证都必须清楚地表明付款属于哪一类。同时，要仔细审核来证要求提供的单据种类、份数及填制要求等，如发现不适当的要求或规定，应酌情做出适当处理。

(10) 审核信用证上印就的其他条款和特殊条款。信用证上有许多印就的内容，特别是在信用证空白处或边缘处加注的字句和戳记应特别注意，这些内容往往是信用证内容的重要补充或修改，稍不注意就可能造成事故或损失。对于信用证上的特殊要求条款，如不能做到或认为不合理要及时提出修改。

【案例4-6】信用证"暂不生效"条款案

1. 案例介绍

某意大利银行开出的信用证规定,该证只有在收到意方进口许可证的通知后方能生效,而这种生效还需经开证申请人的授权(THIS CREDIT IS NOT OPERATIVE, IT WILL BECOME OPERATIVE AS SOON AS THE APPLICANT OBTAINS THE ITALIAN IMPORT LICENSE, WE SHALL ADVISE YOU OF THE RECEIPT OF IMPORT LICENSE AFTER WHICH DATE THE CREDIT WILL BECOME VALID)。

2. 案例分析

该证虽标有不可撤销信用证的字样,但其在实际运作中却与可撤销信用证毫无不同。因为开证申请人(进口商)自始至终都控制着整笔交易,而受益人(出口商)则完全处于被动地位。比较典型的带有未生效条款的软条款信用证通常还可以用几个"不"字来概括,即开证行不通知生效,不发修改书,开证人不出具证书或收据,不来验货,不通知船公司船名等,并常常伴有要求出口商提前支付 5%甚至更高履约金的字样。其中有不少是在证外合同中早就规定好了的。因为信用证不生效,即无法出运货物,而一旦这期间货物的国际市场价格下跌或有其他对申请人(进口商)不利的因素,申请人就会趁机拒发生效通知,使信用证无法生效,从而最终使受益人不能及时提交完整的出口单据给议付行寄单索汇,也使开证行自行免除跟单信用证项下的付款责任。而期间那些 5%甚至更高的履约金及佣金早已落入中介人或开证申请人囊中,此时,作为出口公司则既遭受了损失,又吃了哑巴亏。

尽管 UCP600 规定信用证是不可撤销的,但现实中存在着一些戴着"不可撤销帽子"的信用证,该类信用证中附有一些软条款(SOFT CLAUSES)。这种带软条款的信用证事实上就是开证行可以随时随地自行免责的信用证。

2. 受益人装运货物、制单并交单

受益人在审证无误后,可按期出运,签发跟单汇票(如需要),并备齐信用证所要求的全套单据,在信用证规定的交单截止日前,连同信用证一并送交保兑行、开证行或信用证指定的银行以获得付款。本环节应特别注意交单期限与单据质量。

(五)银行审单付款并向开证行寄单索汇

1. 银行审单、寄单

银行必须合理、小心地审核一切单据,以确定其表面是否符合信用证条款和条件的要

求,确定信用证规定的单据表面上符合信用证条款要求的依据是 UCP600 第 14 条。若单据存在不符点,银行可以要求受益人修改单据,无法修改的,银行应该电提或者表提不符点。所谓电提是银行审单后,向开证行电告不符点,单据保留在银行,要求开证行接洽申请人并回复申请人是否接受不符单据。若申请人接受不符点,则银行可履行议付并寄单和按信用证规定索偿。所谓表提不符点,是指银行寄单时在面函(COVER LETTER OR BILL OF PURCHASE)上申明不符点,要求开证行联系申请人并回复是否接受不符点并付款赎单。若申请人接受不符点,则银行按面函上付款指示付款或回复寄单行按信用证规定索偿。寄单面函是银行寄单时应当缮制的寄单索汇面函,在上面说明单据份数、索偿金额、费用,以及指示开证行或偿付行如何付款。

2. 银行付款、议付或者承兑

信用证项下的支付可以是付款、议付或者承兑,对应的指定银行可以是付款行、议付行或者承兑行。

(1) 受益人如向指定的保兑行或者付款行交单,后者需要审单,单据相符后,对受益人付款。该银行付款后对受益人无追索权。

(2) 受益人向议付行交单,无论是开证行指定的或是受益人自己指定的,受益人得到的只是凭单据抵押的银行融资或垫款。议付行对受益人的垫付有追索权,开证行若拒付,议付行可以向受益人追索。

(3) 受益人向指定的承兑银行交单。承兑行承兑后将已获承兑的汇票退回受益人。开证行一般会指定自己或者出口地某银行为承兑行。汇票到期,承兑行无追索权付款,但为了保证受益人利益,不管谁承兑,开证行都承担到期付款的责任。

3. 索偿

开证行若指定偿付行,指定银行应当一方面把单据寄交开证行,一方面直接向偿付行索偿。若未指定偿付行,所指定银行可以将单据一次或分次寄开证行并同时向开证行索偿。

信用证规定的索偿方式一般为四类:单到付款、主动借记、授权借记和向偿付行索偿。

(1) 单到付款是指议付行向开证行寄单、索偿,开证行审单无误后付款(UPON RECEIPT OF THE DOCUMENTS IN COMPLIANCE WITH CREDIT TERMS, WE SHALL CREDIT YOUR ACCOUNT WITH US OR WE SHALL REMIT THE PROCEEDS TO THE BANK NAMED BY YOU)。

(2) 主动借记是指开证行或其总行在议付行开立账户。信用证规定,议付后可立即借记其账户(YOU ARE AUTHORIZED TO DEBIT OUR ACCOUNT WITH YOUR BEIJING HEAD OFFICE UNDER ADVICE TO US)。

(3) 授权借记是指开证行在议付行虽然开立账户,但信用证规定,必须在开证行收到正确单据后，再授权议付行借记其账户(UPON RECEIPT OF THE SHIPPING DOCUMENTS IN COMPLIANCE WITH THE TERMS OF L/C，WE SHALL AUTHORIZE BANK OF CHINA BEIJING HEAD OFFICE TO DEBIT OUR ACCOUNT WITH THEM)。

(4) 向偿付行索偿是指开证行指定第三家银行为偿付行，偿付行一般在开证货币的发行国。信用证议付后，议付行向开证行寄单的同时，向偿付行索偿(IN REIMBURSEMENT OF YOUR NEGOTIATION UNDER THIS CREDIT，PLEASE DRAWN ON OUR ACCOUNT WITH THE ABC BANK)。

(六)开证行审单、偿付

开证行根据信用证条款全面审核保兑行或被指定银行寄来的单据后，根据本信用证适用的最新惯例(UCP LATEST VERSION，现为 UCP600)判定是否交单相符。交单相符，即可将款项偿付保兑行或被指定银行；若交单不符，在规定的期限内，开证行有权拒绝接受不符单据，拒绝对外支付信用证金额，如装运期超期的信用证。

审单必须合理谨慎。开证行经审单无误后应立即承付：如果信用证为即期付款信用证，则即期付款；如果信用证为延期付款信用证，则承诺延期付款并承诺在到期日付款；如果信用证为承兑信用证，则承兑受益人开出的汇票并在汇票到期日付款。UCP600 规定的银行审单时间为"收到单据的次日起算最长不超过 5 个银行工作日"(A MAXIMUM OF FIVE BANKING DAYS FOLLOWING THE DAY OF PRESENTATION)。当开证行确定交单不符后，可以拒绝付款，也可以自行决定联系申请人放弃不符点，但也必须在收到单据的次日起算最长不超过 5 个银行工作日内提出来。当开证行决定拒绝付款，必须给予交单人一份单独的拒付通知，该通知必须申明：①开证银行拒绝承付；②开证银行拒绝承付所依据的每一个不符点；③银行留存单据听候交单人的进一步指示，或者开证行留存单据直到其从申请人处接到放弃不符点的通知并同意接受该放弃，或者同意接受对不符点的放弃前从交单人处收到其进一步指示，或者银行将退回单据，或者银行将按之前从交单人处获得的指示办理；④拒付通知必须以电讯方式，如不可能，则以其他快捷方式，在不迟于自交单日起 5 个银行工作日结束前发出；⑤开证行按照以上要求发出拒付通知后，可以在任何时候将单据退还给交单人；⑥如开证行未能按照以上要求发出拒付通知，则无权宣称交单不符；⑦开证银行拒绝承付，并按照以上要求发出拒付通知后，有权要求返还已偿付的款项及利息。开证行拒付应一次性提出每个不符点，不可分期提出，不得以不正当的理由苛求交单人提交的单据。

(七)申请人付款赎单

开证行受单偿付后，应立即通知申请人付款赎单。开证申请人在接到开证行付款赎单的通知书后，应在付款前对单据予以审核，在确定单据无误后，应尽快向银行付清所有应付款项，以赎回全套单据，凭提单提货。若提出的货物与单据不符，则对开证行无要求赔偿的权利。如果审单有问题，进口商应向开证行说明拒付理由，但不得以货物的质量问题为由要求银行予以赔偿。开证申请人拒付后，开证行自己承担损失，对已偿付的款项，无追索的权利。

第二节　信用证种类概述

一、不可撤销信用证

按照 UCP600，信用证是不可撤销的，即使未如此说明。按照 UCP600，信用证一经开立，开证行即受约束。同时，UCP600 规定，除可转让信用证的某些特定情况外，未经开证行、保兑行(如有的话)及受益人同意，信用证既不得修改，也不得撤回。开证行自发出修改之时起，即不可撤销地受其约束。

二、保兑信用证和不保兑信用证

保兑信用证是指保兑行在开证行承诺之外做出承付或议付相符交单的确定承诺的信用证。否则，就是不保兑的信用证。保兑行根据开证行的授权或要求对信用证加具保兑，并自对信用证加具保兑之时起不可撤销地承担承付或议付的责任。如果开证行授权或要求一银行对信用证加具保兑，其可不予照办，但必须毫不延误地告知开证行。这样一来，该证也是不保兑的信用证。保兑行可将其保兑扩展至修改，并自通知该修改之时，即不可撤销地受其约束。但是，保兑行可以选择将修改通知受益人时而不对修改加具保兑。若想如此，其必须毫不延误地将此告知开证行，并在给受益人的通知中告知受益人。

实务中，如开证行授权或要求通知行对信用证加具保兑，则通知行在通知信用证时在通知面函上的"保兑"(CONFIRMATION)栏注明"是"(YES)，表明该证是保兑的信用证。如通知行不愿意保兑信用证或其修改，除毫不延误地通知开证行外，其在通知信用证或修改时，在通知面函上的"保兑"(CONFIRMATION)栏注明"非"(NO)，并在信用证或修改书上加注通知行签章，并注明"不保兑"(NON-CONFIRMATION)。另外，UCP600 规定信用证在转让时应反映原证的保兑情况(THE TRANSFERRED CREDIT MUST ACCURATELY REFLECT THE TERMS AND CONDITIONS OF THE CREDIT INCLUDING CONFIRMATION, IF ANY, OF THE ORIGINAL CREDIT)。对保兑行来说，只要规定的单据提交给保兑行，并且构成相符交单，保兑行必须履行以下责任。

(1) 承付，如果信用证为以下情形之一：①信用证由保兑行即期付款、延期付款或承

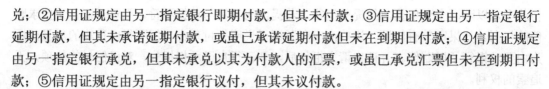

兑；②信用证规定由另一指定银行即期付款，但其未付款；③信用证规定由另一指定银行延期付款，但其未承诺延期付款，或虽已承诺延期付款但未在到期日付款；④信用证规定由另一指定银行承兑，但其未承兑以其为付款人的汇票，或虽已承兑汇票但未在到期日付款；⑤信用证规定由另一指定银行议付，但其未议付款。

(2) 无追索权议付，如果信用证规定由保兑行进行议付。保兑行在承付受益人、被指定银行的相符交单后，将单据转给开证行收款。如开证行拒付，保兑行就有风险。保兑行只有在很好地掌握开证行资信状况的情况下才能做出加保的选择。

从受益人方面考虑，保兑信用证有双重付款保证，对受益人最为有利。但是只要开证行的资信良好，能够承担付款责任，就无加保的需要。开证行一般不轻易对自己开立的信用证要求第三者加保，除非开证行认为本身资信不佳或无付款的能力。

三、即期付款、延期付款、承兑与议付信用证

UCP600 具有四种基本类型的信用证：即期付款信用证、延期付款信用证、承兑信用证或议付信用证。

(一)即期付款信用证

即期付款信用证(CREDIT AT SIGHT PAYMENT)可由开证行付款，也可由被指定银行付款，其条款一般为"本信用证可以在开证行(或被指定银行)即期付款兑用有效"(THIS CREDIT IS AVAILABLE WITH ISSUING BANK(OR XXX) BY PAYMENT AT SIGHT)。可以要求开立汇票，也可以不要求汇票。有无汇票在付款时间上基本无区别。但是，如无汇票，受益人不能凭以贴现，进口商、开证行也不能利用汇票上的不符点进行拒付。如要出票，受益人将在单据之外多了一层票据上的付款保护。

即期付款信用证项下，如有被指定银行，受益人可以向被指定银行提交单据，也可以直接向开证行进行交单。只要交单相符，开证行或被指定银行就要承付受益人款项，并且不能向受益人进行追索。

同是即期付款信用证，单到开证行付款的信用证与单到出口地被指定银行付款的信用证相比，对出口商来说，前者收款比较慢。因此，在出口商所在地有被指定银行的信用证对出口商比较有利。被指定银行承付受益人款项后，向开证行寄单索偿或按照规定的方法索偿。若开证行判定交单不符，则被指定银行应退款给开证行，自行承担风险。

(二)承兑信用证

承兑信用证(CREDIT BY ACCEPTANCE)是远期信用证的一种，受益人要开立汇票。开证行在开立承兑信用证时，可以规定由自己承兑汇票，也可以规定由被指定银行承兑汇

票。开证行或被指定银行对受益人开立的远期汇票一经承兑，信用证项下的不可撤销的付款责任就上升到票据上的无条件付款责任。承兑前，银行对受益人的权利和义务以信用证为准。承兑后，汇票和单据相分离，银行成为汇票的承兑人，即票据法规定的主债务人，对出票人、背书人、持票人承担保证付款的责任。即便出现了欺诈等纠纷，汇票的承兑人也不能拒付，因为该汇票的持票人作为善意的持票人或正当持票人可以得到票据法的保护。承兑后的汇票可以退回出票人，但大部分由承兑行保管，承兑人向受益人发出承兑通知书。若承兑行不是开证行，则承兑行向开证行寄单索汇。受益人如需要资金融通，可以要求承兑行将承兑汇票寄回，以便其拿到票据市场上进行贴现，也可采用福费廷的方式无追索权地卖出该票据，取得扣除利息后的净额，支付的贴息就是融资的成本。因而，承兑信用证对出口商比较有利，而对进口商则不利。

如承兑信用证在出口地有被指定银行，受益人可以选择向被指定银行或开证行直接交单，但建议受益人向被指定银行交单，以防单据在受益人向开证行邮寄的途中遗失。对开证行来说，被指定银行承付相符交单并将单据转给开证行后，开证行即承担偿付该被指定银行的责任，对远期信用证相符交单金额的偿付应在到期日办理，无论被指定银行是否在到期日前预付或购买了单据。开证行偿付被指定银行的责任独立于开证行对受益人的责任。如果被指定银行未承兑以其为付款人的汇票，或虽承兑了汇票，但未在到期日付款，只要交单相符，开证行必须承付。

为避免印花税，出现了没有汇票的远期付款信用证。实际上，即便是即期付款或议付的信用证也越来越少地运用汇票了。受益人可根据具体情况，要求申请人开立带有汇票的信用证。

按照 UCP600，单据在被指定银行与开证行/保兑行之间或开证行与保兑行之间遗失，开证行或保兑行必须付款。但在实践中，开证行要受益人提交单据副本以审核交单是否相符，而延误付款的利息由开证行承担。

实务中，承兑信用证的开立基于以下两种情况：①买卖双方签订远期销售合约，则买方申请开出一份远期付款的承兑信用证，称为卖方远期信用证。②买卖双方签订即期销售合约，但买方申请开出一份远期付款的信用证，但进口商承担即期付款的责任，银行承兑汇票的费用及贴现费用由开证申请人承担，称为买方承兑信用证或假远期信用证。其条款一般有：a. THE USANCE DRAFTS ARE PAYABLE ON A SIGHT-BASIS, DISCOUNT CHARGES AND ACCEPTANCE COMMISSION ARE FOR BUYER'S ACCOUNT(该远期信用证可以得到即期支付，贴现利息与承兑费用由买方承担)。b. DRAWEE BANK'S DISCOUNT OR INTEREST CHARGES, STAMP DUTY AND ACCEPTANCE COMMISSION ARE FOR ACCOUNT OF THE APPLICANT AND THEREFORE THE BENEFICIARY IS TO RECEIVE VALUE FOR TERM DRAFT AS IF DRAWN AT SIGHT (受票行的贴现或利息、印花税、承兑费用由开证申请人负担，因而受益人可以像即期汇票一样收取远期汇票的款项)。

假远期信用证与即期信用证相比，有共同点与不同点，具体见表4-1。

表4-1 假远期信用证与即期信用证的对比

项 目	假远期信用证	即期信用证
相同点	对卖方即期支付票面金额	
不同点	①开出远期汇票	①开出即期汇票
	②须办理提示要求承兑和贴现的手续	②须办理提示要求付款的手续，但不需要办理承兑和贴现手续
	③贴现后，支付给卖方的款项=票面金额=净款+买方支付的贴现利息	③受票行即期支付票面金额给卖方
	④贴现人为正当持票人，对卖方已付款有追索权	④受票行对卖方已付款无追索权
	⑤买方在远期汇票到期日付款	⑤买方付款赎单

【案例4-7】即期付款合同开立远期信用证致损案

1. 案例介绍

我国出口企业A公司与新加坡B公司达成一笔出口合同，规定采用即期信用证结算。合同中支付条款为"TERMS OF PAYMENT: BY IRREVOCABLE LETTER OF CREDIT AVAILABLE BY SELLER'S DOCUMENTARY DRAFT AT SIGHT，TO BE VALID FOR NEGOTIATION IN CHINA WITHIN 15 DAYS AFTER DATE OF SHIPMENT. THE CREDIT MUST REACH THE SELLER 30 DAYS BEFORE THE CONTRACTED MONTH OF SHIPMENT"(付款条件为不可撤销信用证，凭卖方即期跟单汇票于装运日后15日内在中国议付到期。信用证必须于合同规定的装运月前30天开到卖方)。

A公司按时收到B公司通过银行开来的信用证，但审核后发现该证实际为远期信用证。证中有条款如下："WE HEREBY INFORM YOU THAT WE HAVE OPENED OUR IRREVOCABLE CREDIT IN YOUR FAVOUR WITH AVAILABLE BY ACCEPTANCE AGAINST YOUR DRAFTS AT 120 DAYS AFTER SIGHT DRAWN ON XXX BANK"(我行特此通知你方，我行已开立以你方为受益人的不可撤销信用证，凭你方出具的以XXX银行为受票人的见票后120天付款的汇票承兑)。A公司要求B公司进行修改，并告知必须在信用证修改后才装运货物。

7天后，A公司收到了信用证修改书，条款为"根据本信用证项下的汇票可按即期办理，由我行负责贴现，其他条款不变"。

A公司认为信用证项下开具的远期汇票可按即期办理，前面顾虑的问题已不存在，随即装运了货物，并向银行交单。但A公司收账时发现，入账金额比发票金额少5000多美元。经查，原来是信用证按规定扣除了贴现利息和相关费用。A公司与B公司进行几番交涉，而B公司一再拒绝补齐金额。

2. 案例分析

本案的进口方擅自违反合同规定而将付款条件进行了修改，出口方提出修改是正确的，但其未对修改书的内容进行仔细的斟酌，最终导致支付贴现利息。该修改仅仅表明了该120天承兑信用证可以得到即期支付，但未表明贴现利息由谁承担。开证行办理贴现当然要收取贴现利息和费用。其实，本案的信用证修改函如将条款改为"THE USANCE DRAFTS ARE PAYABLE ON A SIGHT-BASIS, DISCOUNT CHARGES AND ACCEPTANCE COMMISSION ARE FOR BUYER'S ACCOUNT"，就能在信用证中明确贴现利息由买方承担。因此，作为出口商要注意远期信用证与假远期信用证以及汇票之间的关系。

(三)延期付款信用证

延期付款信用证(CREDIT BY DEFERRED PAYMENT)是远期信用证的一种，但是受益人不需要开立汇票。延期付款信用证可规定开证行延期付款，也可以规定由被指定银行延期付款。因为没有汇票，受益人无法在信用证外获得票据法的保护，只能受信用证的保护。如需要资金融通，也无法持承兑汇票到票据市场上进行贴现。因而，延期付款信用证对进口商比较有利，而对出口商则不利。

延期付款的信用证下，受益人交单，只要交单相符，被指定银行或开证行就必须承付。对受益人而言，若被指定银行是保兑行，则收款有直接的保证，到期不管被指定银行是否收到款项，都要保证向受益人付款。如是不保兑的信用证，被指定银行不构成确定的付款承诺，最终由开证行承担到期付款的责任，但是受益人还是缺乏直接的收款保证。因此受益人为了收款顺利，更倾向于接受延期付款加保兑的信用证。

(四)议付信用证

UCP600的"议付"可分解如下：第一，"议付"是指"买入"，受益人最终的款项不可能是100%的，因为议付行要先扣除利息；第二，"买入"的"对象"是汇票及/或单据；第三，"汇票付款人"是被指定银行以外的银行，一般是开证行；第四，"买入者"是被指定银行；第五，"买入前提"是交单相符；第六，"买入方式"是预付或同意预付给受益人；第七，"买入时间"是在开证行必须偿付被指定银行款项的银行工作日当天或之前；第八，隐含"远期议付"的做法。UCP600关于开证行责任的规定为第7条B款："信用证规定由被指定银行议付而其未议付。"

议付信用证开立的初衷是使受益人在市场上可选择低利息。"议付"用的是议付行自己的资金，利息由受益人承担，因此规定议付行有追索权。议付信用证可以规定要开立汇票，也可以规定不要汇票。如不要汇票，则买入的仅是单据；如要汇票，则被指定银行将同时买入汇票和单据。议付有追索权，除非议付银行同时是保兑行。除非信用证规定由开证行办理，否则议付信用证应授权一家银行议付。议付信用证可分为以下几类。

(1) 限制议付信用证(RESTRICTED NEGOTIATION CREDIT)，即只准许被指定银行议付的信用证。例如，THIS CREDIT IS AVAILABLE WITH ADVISING BANK BY NEGOTIATION(此信用证在通知行议付有效)。限制议付信用证的有效地点一般规定在被指定银行所在地。受益人可以在交单截止日前选择向开证行或被指定银行交单，最好不要向非指定银行交单。

(2) 自由议付信用证(FREELY NEGOTIATION CREDIT)，指任何银行均可议付的信用证。任何银行均是被指定银行，出口商交单方便。其条款一般为："THIS CREDIT IS AVAILABLE WITH ANY BANK BY NEGOTIATION" (此信用证在任何银行议付有效)。同时，信用证中有开证行的保证付款文句："WE HEREBY AGREE WITH THE DRAWERS, ENDORSERS AND BONA FIDE HOLDERS OF DRAFTS DRAWN UNDER AND IN COMPLIANCE WITH THE TERMS OF THIS CREDIT THAT SUCH DRAFTS WILL BE DULY HONORED ON DUE PRESENTATION OF THE DRAWEES IF NEGOTIATED ON OR BEFORE THE EXPIRATION DATE OR PRESENTED TO THE DRAWEES TOGETHER WITH THIS LETTER ON OR BEFORE THAT DATE" (我行向出票人、背书人、善意持票人保证，凭此信用证开出的与信用证条款相符的，于到期日或之前议付的，或者于到期日或之前连同信用证直接向付款人提示的汇票，在向我行提示时我行将及时予以承付)。

(3) 不可议付信用证(STRAIGHT CREDIT)，即开证行本身为付款人的信用证。受益人需将单据直接寄给开证行，不能交其他银行议付，开证行只对受益人负责，有效地点在开证行所在地，所有单据必须在有效期内到达开证行。开证行议付或付款后，对出票人无追索权。其条款一般为："WE HEREBY ENGAGE WITH YOU (BENEFICIARY)THAT ALL DRAFTS AND DOCUMENTS VERTIFIED IN COMPLIANCE WITH THE TERMS OF THIS CREDIT WILL BE DULY HONORED ON DELIVERY AND PRESENTATION TO US" (我方向你受益人做出保证，当所有的汇票与单据被证实已交付和向我行提示，并与信用证条款相符，我行将及时予以承付)。

【案例4-8】信用证限制议付案

1. 案例介绍

2009年8月14日，受益人B公司向P银行提交一套出口单据，P银行经审核后发现由 I 银行开出的信用证限制在 N 银行议付，8 月 15 日在 N 银行所在地到期。P 银行在信用证限制 N 银行议付的情况下，应 B 公司要求，在当天以寄单行的身份把单据寄往开证行。不久开证行来电拒付，其理由是单据限制在 N 银行议付，并且信用证有效期已过。

P 银行认为其并未对信用证议付，只是在受益人的要求下，以寄单行的身份，将单据直接寄往开证行。同时指出，信用证在中国到期，寄单行所提示的单据并未超过信用证效期。P 银行要求受益人向开证申请人做工作。最终开证行支付了货款。

2. 案例分析

本案争议的焦点是受益人将单据交到非信用证规定的限制议付行是否构成与信用证不符。根据 UCP600 第 15 条规定，如果符合信用证要求的单据被提交到开证行，就构成开证行确定的承付责任。本案例中，P 银行将单据直接寄开证行，只要交单相符，开证行就应当履行其付款责任。对于信用证限制议付，非指定银行可否寄单的问题，实务中有不同的看法。有些银行认为，受益人的利益是第一位的，受益人有权选择自己满意的银行。只要交单相符，开证行就应该付款，而不应过问是否由指定银行交单，也就是说这种限制是没有意义的。但也有银行认为，单据应提示给受益人的往来银行，由该往来银行负责审查后，再向被指定的限制议付行交单。事实上，按照 UCP600 的规定，只要受益人将符合信用证要求的单据在有效期内提交到开证行，受益人未从指定的议付行获得议付，不影响开证行的付款责任，也不构成与信用证条款的不符。

四、国内信用证

国内信用证只适用于国内企业之间商品交易产生的货款结算，并且只能用于转款结算，不得支取现金。国内信用证的操作办法具体见中国人民银行 1997 年 7 月 16 日发布的国内信用证结算办法(银发〔1997〕265 号)。国内信用证的内容参见示样 4-5。

示样 4-5　国内信用证

中国银行
国内信用证寄单通知书

寄单日期：
我行编号：

委托收款行/议付行：　　　　　　　　发至：　　　　银行
地址：　　　　　　　　　　　　　　开证行名称：
邮编：　　电传：　　　　　　　　　地址：
电话：　　传真：　　　　　　　　　邮编：
　　　　　　　　　　　　　　　　　电话：　电传：　传真：　电话：

现将　　　　　号信用证项下单据寄贵行，发票号＿＿＿＿＿＿共　　　　份，　我行对受益人

□已议付　☒未议付

受益人名称：＿＿＿＿＿＿＿＿　开户银行及账号：

开证申请人名称：

付款期限　　例如：货物收据签　　到期日　　　　　　　单据金额
　　　　　　发后 180 天

　　　　　　　　　　　　　　　　　　　　　　　　　　　应收金额

议付费　　　　　邮费　　　　电报费　　　委托收款验单手续费

　　　　　　　　　　　　　　　　　　　　　　　　　　费用总计

　　　　　　　　　　　　　　　　　　　　　　　　　　索赔金额

单据种类及份数：

增值税专用发票　　　提单/铁路　邮政收据　　货物收据/出库单　保险单　装箱单　　　　其他
　　　　　　　　　　/航空运单

委托收款凭证及有关通知书＿＿＿＿＿＿份，　请根据随附委托收款结算凭证偿付。

付款方式：电划

寄单方式：一次寄单　　□平邮　□快邮

以上款项请通过电子联行划入我行，并注明我行编号

备注：

注：本通知书一式两联，第一联寄开证行，第二联留存。

　　　　　　　　　　　　　　　　　　　　　　　寄单行签章

国内信用证

信用证号码：

致：

开证日期：

申	全　称		受	全　称
请	详细地址		益	详细地址
人	账　号		人	账　号
	开户行			开户行

开证金额　　　　　　　(小写)

　　　　　　　　　　　(大写)

有效时间及有效地点：

通知行名称：

付款方式：

分批装运：　　　　　　　　　转运：

货物运输起止地：

最迟装运日期：

合同编号：

货物描述：　　品名　　　　　　数量(吨)　　　　　单价(元/吨)　　　金额(元)

总金额：　　　　　(含税)

受益人应提供的单据：例如
1.税务部门统一印制/监制的正本增值税发票(包括发票联合抵扣联)，发票注明信用证号码及合同号码，并注明开票人为信用证受益人，受票人为信用证申请人。
2.由申请人出具的正本货物收据，显示收货人为申请人。

其他款项：
1.单据必须自货物收据签发日起＿＿＿日内提交。(不能晚于信用证有效期)
2.开证行以外的所有银行费用由受益人承担。
3.增值税发票出具日期、发货日期早于信用证开立日期不接受。
4.增值税专用发票必须是原始正本。影印件、传真件不接受，即使注明正本字样。
5.如果提交了单证不符的单据，我行将在付款时扣除　　　元人民币的不符点费。
6.信用证项下的所有单据和一份全套单据的复印件须一次性以快邮方式寄＿＿＿＿＿＿＿银行。如未将全套单据的复印件交我行，我行将扣除＿＿＿＿＿元人民币。
7.本信用证限制有中国银行股份有限公司或中信银行议付。
本信用证依据中国人民银行《国内信用证结算办法》和申请人的开证申请书开立。本信用证为不可撤销、不可转让信用证。我行保证在收到单证严格符合的单据后在上述付款期限到期日履行付款责任。

开证行：

YOURS FAITHFULLY

THE DOCUMENTS CONSISTS OF 1 SIGNED PAGE(S)

五、预支信用证

　　预支信用证(ANTICIPATORY CREDIT)是准许受益人在装货交单前支取全部或部分货款的信用证。其条款一般有：

　　WE (ISSUING BANK) HEREBY AUTHORIZE YOU(ADVISING BANK)AT YOUR DISCRETION TO GRANT TO THE BENEFICIARY AN ADVANCE OR ADVANCE TO THE EXTENT OF XXX (VALUE), ANY INTEREST ACCRUED THEREON SHOULD BE CHARGED TO HIM FROM THE DATE OF EACH ADVANCE TO THE DATE OF REPAYMENT AT THE CURRENT RATE OF INTEREST IN XXX(MAINLY, EXPORTATION PLACE). THE PROCEEDS OF ANY DRAFT NEGOTIATED UNDER THIS CREDIT MAY AT YOUR DISCRETION BE APPLIED BY YOU IN THE REPAYMENT TO YOU OF THE WHOLE OR ANY PART OF SUCH ADVANCE TOGETHER WITH INTEREST AS AFORESAID.

　　IN CONSIDERATION OF YOUR BANK MAKING SUCH ADVANCE TO THE BENEFICIARY WHO WILL EVENTUALLY FAIL TO EFFECT SHIPMENT COVERED BY THE CREDIT, WE GUARANTEE REPAYMENT AND UNDERTAKE TO PAY YOU ON

DEMAND ANY SUM OWING BY THE BENEFICIARY IN RESPECT OF SUCH ADVANCE TOGETHER WITH INTEREST THEREON.

预支信用证一般是由进口商要求开证行在信用证上加列预支条款。开证行授权出口地银行(一般为通知行或保兑行)作议付,受益人提交单据前开立光票支取全部或部分货款。待受益人交单后,被指定银行从货款金额中扣除已预支的款项和利息,受益人获得款项的净额。银行预支后要求受益人将信用证正本交出,以控制受益人必须向该行交单。若受益人不装运货物或不向其交单,垫款的被指定银行可向开证行提出还款要求,开证行保证偿还其垫款,并立即向申请人追索款项。预支信用证实际上是进口商利用开证行的信用对出口商进行融资。

六、循环信用证

信用证的部分或全部金额被使用后可以恢复到原金额再被利用的信用证称为循环信用证(REVOLVING CREDIT)。与一般信用证相比,它多一个循环系统,条款一般为"THE AMOUNT OF THIS LETTER OF CREDIT USD100,000 IS REVOLVING ON A MONTHLY BASIS FOR THE FIRST TIME IN XX,FOR THE LAST TIME IN XX, MAXIMUM AMOUNT PAYABLE UNDER THIS CREDIT USD800,000"(此份 10 万美元信用证的金额,可以按月循环使用,第一次使用时间为_____,最后一次使用时间为_____,信用证最大金额可累计为 80 万美元)。

进出口双方若签订长期的销售合约,需要均衡地分批装运货物,为了节省开证手续费和保证金,进口商可以申请开立循环信用证。循环信用证通常以时间或金额为循环基础。

1. 按时间循环的信用证

受益人在一定时间内支取信用证规定的金额后,在下次一定时间内仍可支取的信用证。按时间循环的信用证根据每期信用证余额处理方式的不同,分为不可累积循环信用证(NON-CUMULATIVE REVOLVING CREDIT)和可累积循环信用证(CUMULATIVE REVOLVING CREDIT)。

不可累积是指受益人在规定的循环期限内可支取的信用证有余额,但该余额不可转移到下一期使用,如"THE AMOUNT OF THIS CREDIT IS REVOLVING ON A MONTHLY NON-CUMULATIVE BASIS FOR SIX TIMES COMMENDING MAY 18, 200X"(此信用证从 5 月 18 日起循环)。

可累积是指受益人上一期未使用完的信用证余额,可以转移到下一期使用。

2．按金额循环的信用证

按金额循环的信用证是指在信用证金额议付后，仍恢复原金额，可以再次支取，直到用完规定金额的信用证。条款一般表示为"AMOUNT OF THIS CREDIT USD100,000, REVOLVING 5 TIMES TO MAXIMUM USD600,000"。按恢复金额方式的不同，按金额循环的信用证又分为以下几类。

(1) 自动循环信用证(AUTOMATIC REVOLVING CREDIT)。受益人按照规定期限装运、交单、支取信用证金额后，不需要等待开证行通知，信用证金额自动恢复到原金额。条款如"THE AMOUNT OF THIS CREDIT USD400,000 SHALL BE RENEWABLE AUTOMATICALLY TWICE AFTER DATE OF PAYMENT, THUS MAKING AN AGGREGATE AMOUNT OF USD800,000"。

(2) 半自动循环信用证(SEMI-AUTOMATIC REVOLVING CREDIT)。受益人按照规定期限装运、交单、支取信用证金额后，在一定时间内开证行未提出终止循环的通知，信用证金额自动恢复到原金额，条款如"SHOULD THE ISSUING BANK NOT ADVISE STOPPING RENEWAL WITHIN 7 DAYS AFTER EACH NEGOTIATION, THE UNUSED BALANCE OF THIS CREDIT SHALL BE INCREASED TO THE ORIGINAL AMOUNT ON THE 8TH DAY AFTER EACH NEGOTIATION"。

(3) 被动循环信用证(NON-AUTOMATIC REVOLVING CREDIT)。受益人每次支取信用证金额后，需等待开证行的通知，只有在收到开证行的通知后信用证才恢复到原金额，以供再次支取，如"THE AMOUNT OF THIS CREDIT SHALL BE RENEWABLE AFTER EACH NEGOTIATION ONLY UPON RECEIPT OF ISSUING BANK'S NOTICE STATING THAT THE CREDIT MIGHT BE RENEWABLE"。

七、可转让信用证

UCP600 第 38 条定义了可转让信用证："可转让信用证系指特别注明'可转让'(TRANSFERABLE)字样的信用证。"可转让信用证(TRANSFERABLE CREDIT)可应受益人(第一受益人)的要求转为全部或部分由另一受益人(第二受益人)兑用。转让行系指办理信用证转让的指定银行，或当信用证规定可在任一银行兑用时，开证行如此授权并实际办理转让的银行。开证行也可担任转让行。已转让信用证指由转让行转为可由第二受益人兑用的信用证。

UCP600 简化了可转让信用证的概念，增加了开证行可担任转让行的规定。在可转让信用证项下，只要信用证允许部分支款或部分发运，信用证可以分部分地转让给数名第二受益人。已转让信用证不得应第二受益人的要求转让给任何其后受益人，第一受益人不视为其后受益人。任何转让要求须说明是否允许及在任何条件下允许将修改通知第二受益人。已转让信用证须明确说明该项条件。如果信用证转让给数名第二受益人，其中一名或多名受益人对信用证修改的拒绝并不影响其他第二受益人接受修改。对接受者而言，该已转让信用证即被相应修改。而对拒绝修改的第二受益人而言，该信用证未被修改。已转让信用证应准确转载原证条款，包括保兑(如有的话)，但下列项目除外：信用证金额、规定的任何单价、截止日、交单期限或最迟发运日或发运期间。这些项目任何一项或全部均可减少或缩短；必须投保的保险比例可以增加，以达到原信用证或本惯例规定的保险金额。转让行可用第一受益人的名称替换原证中的开证申请人名称。如果原证特别要求开证申请人的名称应在除发票以外的任何单据中出现时，已转让信用证必须反映该项要求。第一受益人有权以自己的发票和汇票(如有的话)替换第二受益人的发票和汇票，其金额不得超过原信用证金额。经过替换后，第一受益人可在原信用证项下支取自己的发票与第二受益人的发票间的差价(如有的话)。如果第一受益人应提交其自己的发票和汇票(如有的话)，但未能在第一次要求时照办，或第一受益人提交的发票导致了第二受益人的交单中存在不符点，而其未能在第一次要求时修正，转让行有权将从第二受益人处收到的单据照交开证行，并不再对第一受益人承担责任。在要求转让时，第一受益人可以要求在信用证转让后的兑用地点，在原信用证的截止日之前(包括截止日)对第二受益人承付或议付。第二受益人或代表第二受益人的交单必须交给转让行。

八、对背信用证

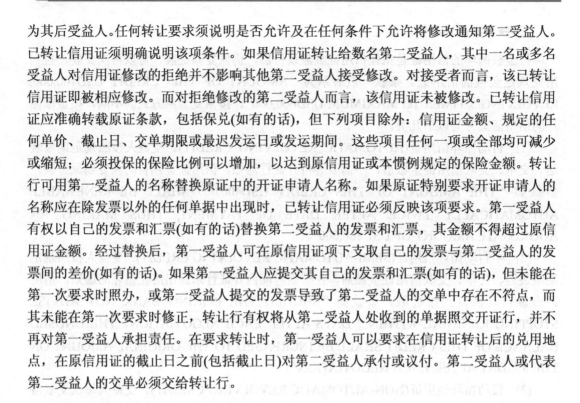

对背信用证(BACK TO BACK CREDIT)是指信用证的受益人以该证为保证，要求一家银行开立以实际供货商为受益人的信用证，其使用背景是因为中间商或代理商的存在。由于进口商开立的信用证是不可转让的，因此受益人以该证作保证，要求该证的通知行或其他银行在该证的基础上开立一张以本地的或第三国的实际供货商为受益人的新证，又称从属信用证。中间商开立对背信用证，可以原证项下收到的货款来支付对背信用证开证行垫付的资金，从而无须向实际供货商直接支付货款。

对背信用证使用程序如下所述：①原证受益人申请开立对背信用证。②开立对背信用证。开证行要求中间商交出原证作为开证保证，因为原证是原开证行承诺付款的保证。对背信用证必须以此承诺作为开立新证的依据，否则银行有权拒绝开立对背信用证。同时，新证开证行可能要求中间商交付其他形式的担保，以防止存在的风险。对背信用证条款与原证基本相同，但变动如下：a. 第一受益人为新证开证申请人；b. 以实际供货商为受益人；c. 开证行是原证的通知行或其他出口地银行；d. 信用证金额及单价，比原证小，差额为中间商利润；e. 装期与效期提前，交单期缩短。③通知对背信用证，一般通过受益人所在地银行。④实际供货商交单，向对背信用证的通知行交单。⑤中间商换发票和汇票。⑥向原证的开证行索偿。

对背信用证和可转让信用证均适用于中间贸易，是中间商利用信用证方式进行融资的手段，但性质不同。两者的比较见表4-2。

表4-2　对背信用证和可转让信用证的比较

对背信用证	可转让信用证
对背信用证的开立，并非原始信用证申请人和开证行的意旨，而是受益人的意旨，申请人和开证行与对背信用证无关	可转让信用证的开立，是原始信用证申请人的意旨并获得开证行的同意，在信用证性质前加列"TRANSFERABLE"字样
凭原始信用证开立对背信用证，两证同时存在	可转让信用证的全部或部分权利转让出去，该证就失去那部分金额的存在
对背信用证的受益人得不到原始信用证的付款保证	可转让信用证的第二受益人可得到开证行的付款保证
开立对背信用证的银行即为该证的开证行	转让行按照第一受益人的指示开立变更条款的新的可转让信用证，并通知第二受益人。该转让行地位不变，仍然是转让行

九、对开信用证

对开信用证(RECIPROCAL CREDIT)是易货贸易的一种支付方式。实务中为防止对方只享受权利不履行义务而要求对方开立对开信用证，第一张信用证的受益人就是第二张信用证的申请人，第一张信用证的通知行往往是第二张信用证的开证行，反之亦然。后开的称为"回证"，与第一证金额大致相等，其条款一般表示为"THIS CREDIT IS RECIPROCAL CREDIT AGAINST XX BANK CREDIT NO. XX FAVORING XX COVERING SHIPMENT OF XX"。

对开信用证一般规定生效条款，主要有两种不同的生效方式。

1. 同时生效

第一证开立后暂不生效，待对方开来回证后，经受益人同意后，再通知对方银行生效，即两证同时生效，条款一般为"THIS CREDIT SHALL NOT BE AVAILABLE UNLESS AND UNTIL THE RECIPROCAL CREDIT IS ESTABLISHED BY XX BANK IN FAVOUR OF XX FOR A SUM OF XX COVERING SHIPMENT FROM XX TO XX. THE RECIPROCAL CREDIT IN EFFECT SHALL ADVISE BY TELEX FROM XX BANK TO BENEFICIARY"。

2．分别生效

各证开立后立即生效。第一证开立后不以回证的开立和接受为条件而是立即生效，回证另开。或者第一证受益人在交单议付时，附一担保书，保证在若干时间内开立以第一证申请人为受益人的回证。但在这种情况下，第一证的申请人存在风险。补偿贸易，来料加工，进口机器设备、原料等一般是远期付款方式，而出口成品一般即期付款。条款一般为"THIS CREDIT IS AVAILABLE BY DRAFT DRAWN ON US AT 180 DAYS AFTER BILL OF LADING DATE. PAYMENT WILL BE EFFECTED BY US ON MATURITY OF THE DRAFT AGAINST THE ABOVE-MENTIONED DOCUMENTS AND OUR RECEIPT OF THE CREDIT OPENER'S ADVICE STATING THAT A RECIPROCAL CREDIT IN FAVOUR OF APPLICANT ISSUED BY XX BANK FOR ACCOUNT OF BENEFICIARY AVAILABLE BY SIGHT DRAFT HAS BEEN RECEIVED BY AND FOUND ACCEPTABLE TO THEM"。

另外，按有无汇票和偿还方式的不同可分为凭单付款信用证和电索条款信用证。

第三节　与信用证结算方式相关的其他案例

(一)空运方式下的信用证风险防范

1．案例介绍

我某出口公司A与印度B公司达成总金额为6万美元的羊绒出口合同,合同规定空运,贸易条件为"CPT NEW DELHI AS PER INCOTERMS 2010"，采用信用证结算。合同签订后，B公司按期开来信用证。A公司收到信用证后，按规定空运了货物，并将单据办理了议付手续。国内银行将有关单据寄到开证行后不久收到了开证行的拒付通知书，理由是"AWB W/O SHOWING THE TEL NO. AND FAX NO. OF CONSIGNEE"(航空运单上未显示收货人的电话和传真号码)。A公司立即联系B公司要求对方付款赎单，而国内议付银行也向开证行发出SWIFT，申明该不符点不成立，要求对方按照UCP600规定及时履行付款义务。但进口方和开证行对此均置之不理。在此情况下，A公司立即联系空运承运人，要求其扣留货物，但其在新德里的货运代理告知该批货物已被收货人提走。最终，出口方不得不同意对方降价20%的要求作为最终获得付款的代价。

2．案例分析

本案例的关键在于空运方式下的物权问题。由于航空运单不是物权凭证，进口方向开证行付款赎单前就收到了到货通知单，从而凭以提货。因此，空运方式下采用信用证结算，对出口方来说是不保险的。实务中，不可避免地会采用空运，出口商可采用以下措施来防范空运方式下的信用证风险。

(1) 争取与其他结算方式结合，如采用预付和信用证结合，以分散风险。

(2) 严格审查开证行的资信状况，以免开证行恶意挑剔单据，使买方不付款而提货，必要情况下可要求信用证加保。

(3) 严查进口商的资信情况，以便核定其销售信用额度。

(4) 投保出口信用险。如果可能因国外进口商的商业风险和政治风险而给本国出口商造成收不到货款的损失，则可投保该险获得保障。

(5) 谨慎制单，做到单证严格一致。在单据方面不给对方以可乘之机，并与议付银行积极配合。

(6) 因航空运单不能做成"指定抬头"，因此可要求信用证将航空运单的收货人做成是开证行。这样一来，航空公司通知开证行提货，而开证行如想拒付就不敢将货物在进口商付款前放给进口商。

(7) 与航空承运人及其目的地代理保持密切联系。一旦觉察到任何变故，立即要求航空公司保留货物，或将货物退回，或变更目的地，或变更收货人。

(8) 如果货物金额太大，可要求分批交货。

(二)信用证改做托收案例

1. 案例介绍

2月10日C银行受理B公司一笔D/P AT SIGHT托收业务。根据国际商会《跟单托收统一惯例》，C银行于当日处理完毕后向代收行R银行香港分行寄单托收。2月20日，C银行收到R银行的收单回执。同时，C银行被B公司告知：上述托收单据系为可转让信用证项下的单据。R银行为该转让信用证项下的通知行和转让行，出票人B公司系本笔转让信用证的第二受益人，受票人系第一受益人。之所以采用D/P AT SIGHT托收方式是因为单据中出现了不符点，受票人即第一受益人因款项问题无法赎单。因此，R银行无法根据信用证条款将更换后的单据寄至开证行索汇。后经C银行与R银行多次联系，确认了可转让信用证改作托收的事实，并要求R银行将上述托收按信用证办理。如不予以办理，则要求R银行香港分行将所有单据退回。3月22日，C银行收到R银行香港分行的SWIFT来电：根据你行授权，我行已将更换后的单据寄给开证行要求付款。收到开证行付来的款项，我行将按照你行付款指示付款给你行。3月25日，C银行全额收汇，本笔业务结束。

2. 案例分析

本案的要点是第二受益人在单据不符情况下，将可转让信用证结算方式改作即期付款交单方式向转让行托收是否妥当。以即期付款交单方式(D/P AT SIGHT)托收，代收行必须在受票人付清票款之后，才能将货运单据交给受票人，而在转让信用证项下，转让行在收到第二受益人通过银行寄来的单据之后，通知第一受益人更换必要的单据，然后将更换后的单据寄给开证行索汇。需要特别指出的是，第一受益人在更换单据时一般不需要履行付款责任，而只有在转让行从开证行处获得货款后，才对第二受益人付款。

本案例中，出口商将转让信用证项下交单改成托收是欠妥的。如果第二受益人将不符单据以即期付款交单方式向转让行托收，转让行(代收行)就无法将单据更换后提示给开证行。第一受益人也不会向转让行(代收行)赎单(因为第一受益人通常为中间商)。因而，造成款项难以收回。在转让信用证业务中，通常情况下，转让行只有在收到开证行支付的款项后才会付款给第二受益人银行。因此，即使单据含有不符点，第二受益人还是应该将单据提交给转让行，由转让行向开证行托收为妥。应该说，在使用可转让信用证的情况下，对于信用证的第二受益人来说，存在的风险相当大，或者说，第二受益人在信用证项下受到的保护非常弱，与D/P并无多大差别。

(三) "客检证" 条款欺诈案

1. 案例介绍

12 月 25 日，我国 A 银行收到日本 B 银行的即期不可撤销的信用证，金额为 134 400 美元，申请人为日本的 D 公司，受益人为我国的一个外贸公司属下的食品加工企业 C。银行收到信用证后认真审查了该证，发现有一软条款 "INSPECTION CERTIFICATE ISSUED BY MR. ZHANG OF D COMPANY IN TWO COPIES"。A 银行工作人员在通知受益人时，指出了该软条款，提醒受益人注意。受益人称该张先生现长驻其公司，未提出异议。后 C 公司在信用证有效期内分为两次发货，并提交规定单据到 A 银行议付。第一次议付时间是次年 1 月 29 日，金额为 26 880.00 美元，该次准时收回货款，问题出在第二次议付上。第二次议付时间是 2 月 5 日，议付金额为 107 520 美元，因该证有偿付行，议付行及时收到了押汇款。可时隔几日开证行发电至议付行称该单据有不符点，"检验证书上签字系伪造"，拒付单证并要求退回已收到的偿付行的款项。同时，申请人 D 公司派人来到 A 银行，称他们收到的为空箱，根本没有货。A 银行意识到问题的严重性，经研究做出决定：首先要保证资金安全，收到的款项不能退回。根据 UCP600 第 34 条 "银行对任何单据的形式、充分性、准确性、内容真实性、虚假性或法律效力，或对单据中规定或附加的一般或特殊条件，概不负责" 的规定同开证行据理力争，毫不退让。经过交涉，使开证行最终在 3 月 15 日同意付款。

2. 案例分析

我国 A 银行工作人员在通知受益人时，已经指出了该信用证中的软条款，而 C 公司接受了这种绵里藏针的"软条款"，从而使出口商承担很大的收汇风险。在实务中，如果要求签字式样须与开证行的留样相符，进口商可以在开证行留张三的印鉴而派李四去签单，这样，如果行情看涨时他可以签发检验证，万一行情下跌，可以利用"印鉴不符"拒付。我国的 C 公司盲目接受"软条款"信用证，造成收汇的困难。A 银行对客户 C 公司的资信和生产能力不够了解。在处理纠纷的过程中，A 银行了解到，该公司确实存在一定的欺诈现象。首先，货物质量存在问题；其次，货物短装，虽未超过 UCP600 规定标准，却未相应减少货款，而是依照信用证金额足额索汇；最后，C 公司不配合银行工作，迫于无奈才说出事情真相。银行给客户做出口押汇，要对客户的资信状况有充分的了解，落实还款保障。从本案例看，A 银行业务人员忽略了这根本的一点。从该笔信用证本身的两次议付看，颇有可疑之处。这其中有三个时间、三个金额的比较：收到信用证的时间为 12 月 25 日，金额为 134 400 美元；第一次议付时间为 1 月 29 日，金额为 26 880.00 美元；第二次议付时间为 2 月 5 日，金额为 107 520 美元。假设该公司从收到信用证开始备货，那么出第一批货用了近 35 天，而短短的 6 天后，又备齐了整整 4 倍于第一批的货，因此，货物存在质量和短装问题也就不奇怪了。当然，就本案的进口公司 D 来说，其做法有欠妥当。第一，如其真正需要货物，最好请一个有资格、有权威的独立于贸易双方的第三方专业检验机构来进行公正的检验，其指派专人检验的做法不够稳妥，因为此人工作的勤勉态度直接关系到进口商的自身利益。本案中，该检验人员有可能未检验第二批货物，C 公司伪造了其签发的检验证书，也有可能他接受了 C 企业的贿赂，在检验证书上故意签字不符。第二，D 公司自行跑到 A 银行进行交涉的做法也违背了 UCP600 第 5 条的规定，即"银行处理的是单据，而不是单据可能涉及的货物、服务或履约行为"。因此，外国 D 公司的做法欠妥。

本 章 小 结

本章主要阐述了信用证的性质、作用及其基本内容，信用证业务中的当事人及其权利与义务，信用证业务的流程以及信用证的种类，并结合案例讲解了各环节应注意的事项。

信用证是银行有条件的付款承诺，其支付条件是交单相符。交单相符包括单证一致和单单一致。信用证是抽象的单据化业务，并且独立于贸易合同，信用证的独立性和抽象性堪称信用证大厦的两块基石。调整信用证业务的国际惯例是 UCP600(2007 年 7 月 1 日正式生效)。在学习中，要注意理解与掌握 UCP600 在某些条款方面的具体规定。

复习思考题

1. UCP600 关于信用证、承付、议付、第二通知行、保兑行和被指定银行的定义是什么？

2. 信用证的内容有哪些？该如何填写？

3. 信用证业务的基本流程是怎样的？

4. 按照 UCP600，可转让信用证该如何转让？

5. 按照 UCP600，保兑行、开证行、被指定银行在交单相符的情况下，该如何付款？在交单不符的情况下，该如何拒付？

第五章

银行保函与备用信用证

学习目标： 掌握银行保函的定义、作用、种类和银行保函的基本内容及保函项下银行的付款责任；掌握运用保函和备用信用证时应注意的事项；了解银行保函与基础合同的关系、银行保函的开立方式和业务流程以及保函项下索赔与理赔的流程；了解备用信用证与银行保函、跟单信用证之间的异同。

关键概念： 银行保函、见索即付保函、直接担保、间接担保、备用信用证

第一节 银行保函基本知识

一、银行保函的定义、作用及当事人

(一)银行保函的定义

在国际经济交易(贸易、借贷、租赁、投资等)中，由于交易双方往往分处不同的国家和地区，致使交易具有复杂性和风险性，交易双方不满足于对方在合同中做出的有关承诺，而是进一步要求由第三方对合同的履行及其他有关事项提供额外的保证，因而产生了对跨国担保业务的需求。商业银行因有雄厚的资金和较强的经营能力，常常应客户的要求充当这种担保人，担保成为银行的经常性业务。在国际经济交易中，银行担保普遍以保函的形式出现。保函(GUARANTEE)的称谓还有很多，如担保(BOND)、保证书(SURETY GUARANTEE)、付款承诺(PAYMENT UNDERTAKING)等。

银行保函(BANKER'S LETTER OF GUARANTEE，L/G)是指银行以自身信誉担保，应其客户(委托人)的要求或应其他人(指示方)的指示而开立的保证文件，它就委托人关于某一基础合同的债务或责任向第三方当事人(债权人或受益人)做出保证，如委托人未能履行合同规定的义务，则由银行向第三方当事人做出赔偿。银行从事担保业务的规模可以不受资产负债比率及各项管理规定的制约，并可以增加业务收入，因为担保业务只构成银行的或有负债(CONTINGENT LIABILITY)，属于不列入资产负债表的表外项目(OFF BALANCE SHEET ITEM)。在担保业务中，银行可以通过反担保或收取抵押品等形式事先进行有效的风险抵补。基础合同(UNDERLYING CONTRACT)一旦违约，银行能有效控制风险和减少

损失。

【案例5-1】中行吉林省分行保函营销业务成功案例

2006年上半年，中行吉林省分行通过全面的市场调研和积极的客户营销，争取到长春轨道客车股份有限公司承揽的首都机场工程直线和北京地铁二号线两个项目下的全部保函业务，保函金额总计4.5亿元人民币，直接为该行带来业务收入60万元人民币。

(二)银行保函的作用

银行保函适用于高风险、比较复杂的结算方式，更适用于任何经济交易，为承担风险的一方提供保障。银行作为担保人，由于委托人未履行全部或部分义务或违约、过失而承担的付款(或赔款)责任，有第一性的偿付责任和第二性的偿付责任之分。

(1) 第二性的偿付责任 (SECOND OBLIGATION)，又称为从属的偿付责任 (ACCESSORY OBLIGATION)，即担保人的偿付责任从属于或依附于委托人在基础合同项下的责任和义务。如果委托人已履行基础合同项下的责任和义务，或根据交易合同条款，经授权机构裁决，业已解除了交易合同项下的责任和义务，担保人也随之免除了对受益人的偿付责任。

(2) 第一性的偿付责任 (PRIMARY OBLIGATION)，又称为独立的付款承诺 (INDEPENDENT UNDERTAKING OF PAYMENT)，即担保人的偿付责任独立于委托人在基础合同项下的责任和义务。只要保函规定的偿付条件已经具备，担保人就应偿付受益人的索偿。至于委托人是否未履行基础合同项下的责任和义务，是否已被合法地解除了该项责任和义务，担保行不负责任。

2010年7月1日，国际商会(ICC)发布的新版《见索即付保函统一规则》(URDG758)正式实施，这是ICC针对1992年开始实施的URDG458的首次修订。URDG758是继UCP600之后的又一重要国际惯例，突出了见索即付保函的独立性和单据化特征，更加强调保函业务的"先赔付、再争论"的理念，从而在全球商界、企业界和金融界确立了共同遵从的国际惯例，已先后得到了国际咨询工程师联合会(FIDIC)、世界银行、联合国国际贸易法委员会等机构的支持和承认。2010年7月，我国国家外汇管理局发布了《关于境内机构对外担保管理问题的通知》，梳理并澄清了保函业务实践中需要明确的诸多技术性和操作性问题，同时通过强化事后核查机制，简化了管理程序。

(三)银行保函涉及的当事人

1. 基本当事人

银行保函具有三个基本当事人。

(1) 委托人(PRINCIPAL)或称为投保人(APPLICANT)，是指向银行提出申请并委托银行开立保函的当事人。

(2) 受益人(BENEFICIARY)，即基础合同的债权人，接受保函并有权按保函规定向担保银行提出索赔的当事人。受益人是基础合同中与委托人相对的当事人。

(3) 担保人(GUARANTOR)，即开立保函的银行。

2. 可能涉及的相关当事人

(1) 通知行(ADVISING BANK)，也称为传递行(TRANSMITTING BANK)。因担保行与受益人分处两地，该银行受担保行之托将保函代为传递或通知保函。其主要职责是负责审核保函的真伪，严格按照担保行的要求和指示及时通知受益人。

通知行对于保函项下的赔付不承担任何责任。发生索赔时，除可代受益人向担保行转交索赔文件或其他书面单据外，并不受理任何索赔。

(2) 保兑行(CONFIRMING BANK)。应担保行的要求，保兑行以其自身卓著的信誉在担保行已经做出的支付承诺之外另行附加保证，承诺一旦发生担保行无故拒付或无力支付的情况，由其代为履行付款责任。受益人有两种选择。一是选择由国际性大银行或本国银行对原保函加具保兑。这样，一份保函具有两个保证人。二是要求本国银行另开保函，则出现反担保行。

(3) 反担保行(COUNTER GUARANTOR)。委托人求助于本国银行的支持，要求本国银行委托其在受益人所在地的往来银行出具保函，并同时做出在受托行遭到索赔时立即予以偿付的承诺。接受申请人委托而发出开立保函委托指示的银行就称为反担保行，而受益人所在地的受托行成为实际上的担保行。

二、银行保函的开立方式、基本内容和业务流程

(一)银行保函的开立方式

1. 直接担保

直接担保，又称直开，是指担保银行应委托人的申请，径向受益人开立保函，并凭此直接向受益人承担责任的一种方式。按保函开立后是否通过通知行转交，分为直交或转交。

直交是指担保银行开立保函后将其直接寄交或带交受益人，转交是担保行请受益人当地银行作为通知行将保函代为转交给受益人。

2. 间接担保

间接担保，又称转开。委托人所在地的银行应其客户的请求，根据标书或合同的有关

规定以及受益人所在国的惯常做法及法律要求，以提供反担保的形式来委托另一家银行(通常为受益人所在地的银行，即担保行)代其出具保函，并由后者向受益人承担付款责任的一种方式。在转开的情况下，与受益人构成担保合同关系的是受益人所在地的担保行，反担保行只是与担保行构成委托担保关系。受益人在申请人发生违约的情况下，只能向担保行请求赔付，而无权越过担保行直接向反担保行请求赔付。反担保行仅就反担保向担保行负责，而不向受益人承担任何直接责任。

(二)银行保函的格式和内容

保函格式(FORM OF GUARANTEE)即保函的文字条款，它体现保函项下担保人所承担的责任和义务以及责任范围的大小。不同的格式反映着担保人在某一担保类别下不同的风险程度和不同的赔付或付款承诺。银行保函的内容应该清晰、准确，避免过多的细节。保函必须具备以下八大要素。

(1) 各方当事人的名称和地址，包括委托人或申请人、受益人、担保行、通知行。

(2) 要求开立保函的基础合同内容，如有关的交易合同、协议的编号或标书的编号，日期，或供应货物的名称、数量，工程项目名称等。

(3) 保函的编号、开立日期、有效日期及保函的种类、保函的金额和货币名称。保函的有效期，即自生效日至到期日的期限，包括保函的生效期限与失效期限或失效事件。生效期限：投标保函，开立之日起生效；预付款保函，收到款项之日起生效。失效事件如施工完毕、验收合格、交货结束等事件。

(4) 承诺条款又称为责任条款，表明担保行在何种条件下，凭受益人提交的何种单据、证件负责向受益人付款。

(5) 索偿条件，一般应规定单据化条款。

(6) 索偿办法，指受益人向担保行提出索偿的方式(如信索或电索)和路线(是否通过通知行)等。

(7) 减额条款。保函应明确规定，在某一特定日期或在向担保人提示保函规定的某种单据后，保函金额可以减少某一特定金额或可事先决定的金额。

(8) 其他条款。包括与保函有关的保兑、修改、撤销及仲裁等内容。

上述八项内容连贯起来，即可构成一份内容完整的保函。

(三)银行保函的业务流程

在保函有效期内，银行在该笔担保项下承担一种或有负债，直到保函效期届满为止。银行保函的业务流程如下。

1. 申请人申请出保

申请人填写开立保函申请书，或与担保行签订委托担保协议，提交一定的保证金或以其他形式的反担保作为抵押，提交有关的业务参考文件(如标书、合同、契约、协议等)。保函申请书的内容具体见示样 5-1。

示样 5-1　开立保函/备用信用证申请书

编号：　　年　　字　　号

现我公司因业务需要，依据我公司与贵行签署的＿＿＿＿年＿＿＿＿字＿＿＿＿号《授信额度协议》及附件，向贵行申请开立保函/备用信用证。开立保函/备用信用证而产生的权利义务，均按照前述协议、附件和本申请书的约定办理。

第一条　保函/备用信用证内容

我公司向贵行申请按下列要素开立保函/备用信用证。

1. 保函/备用信用证申请人名称和地址(中英文)：＿＿＿＿＿＿＿＿＿＿

2. 货物/项目描述：

3. 工程和项目名称/协议/合同/标书编号：

4. 工程项目/协议/合同币种及金额：

5. 保函/备用信用证币种及金额：

6. 保函/备用信用证有效期：自保函/备用信用证开出之日＿＿＿＿到＿＿＿＿为止。

7. 保函/备用信用证类别：

8. 保函/备用信用证开立方式：(1)由贵行信开；(2)由贵行电开。

9. 保函/备用信用证递交方式：

    (1) 由贵行交我公司代交受益人。

    (2) 由贵行委托＿＿＿＿＿＿＿＿银行(英文全称)通知受益人。

    (3) 由贵行开出后委托＿＿＿＿＿＿＿＿银行(英文全称)转开交受益人。

    (4) 由贵行开出后委托＿＿＿＿＿＿＿＿＿银行(英文全称)转开交我公司代理机构代交受益人，我公司代理机构的名称和地址＿＿＿＿＿＿＿＿＿。

    (5) 由贵行直接邮寄给受益人。

10. 保函/备用信用证受益人名称和地址(英文)＿＿＿＿＿＿＿＿＿＿＿＿

11. ＿＿＿＿＿＿＿＿＿＿＿＿＿＿＿＿＿＿＿＿＿＿＿＿＿＿＿

12. ＿＿＿＿＿＿＿＿＿＿＿＿＿＿＿＿＿＿＿＿＿＿＿＿＿＿＿

示样 5-1 （续）

第二条 支付备付金

我公司将于保函/备用信用证约定的付款日或贵行要求的日期(以日期较前者为准)前_____个银行工作日内通过以下第_____种方式向贵行支付本笔业务下的备付金。备付金数额按贵行规定执行。

1. 通过_____向贵行支付本笔业务的应付款项。

2. 请从我公司在贵行开立的人民币账户（账号_____)/外币账户（账号_____)中直接划收本笔业务下的应付款项。

3. _____

第三条 保证金的交纳及金额(本条为选择性条款，双方的选择是：1. 适用；2. 不适用)

我公司将通过以下第_____种方式向贵行交纳保证金。

1. 在贵行接受此申请书后_____个银行工作日内主动通过_____将本笔业务的保证金划入我公司在贵行开立的保证金账户(账号_____)/外币账户(账号_____)。

2. 请从我公司在贵行开立的人民币账户(账号_____)/外币账户(账号_____)中直接划收本笔业务下的保证金。

3. _____

第四条 费用

我公司将通过以下第_____种方式向贵行交纳本笔业务下的费用。

1. 在贵行接受此申请书后____个银行工作日内主动通过_____向贵行交纳本笔业务下的费用。

2. 请从我公司在贵行开立的人民币账户(账号____)/外币账户(账号_____)中直接划收本笔业务下的费用。

3. _____

申请人：   银行意见：

授权签字人：   授权签字人：

_____年____月____日   _____年____月____日

地点：   地点：

缮制保函申请书应注意以下事项。

(1) 仔细阅读合同的有关条款，根据合同的具体要求，填报申请书，核算保函的金额大小以及有效期的长短，做到准确无误，一丝不苟。

(2) 根据合同或标书的具体规定以及国外受益人所在国的传统习惯及法律要求，并结合费用多寡的因素，选择对自己最有利且能为受益人接受的开立方式。

(3) 保函的开立方式确定后，还要对诸如转递行、背书行、保兑行、转开行这些国外受托银行进行严格遴选。

委托人申请开立保函的目的是为了巩固其履行合同的责任与承诺，同时向开立保函的银行保证，在银行凭保函做出赔付后，对银行做出足额补偿。

2. 担保行签发保函

担保银行对担保品(COLLATERAL)和反担保措施要进行审查。

(1) 审查是否有其他银行或金融机构，有资金实力的商业团体、企业、公司或其他经济实体出具的反担保函。

(2) 审查是否有申请人自己或他人的不动产抵押(MORTGAGE)或动产抵押(HYPOTHECATION)。

(3) 审查申请人在担保行的账户头寸以及担保行给予申请人的授信额度抵押等。

(4) 对基础合同项目的可行性进行评估以及对效益进行审查。

(5) 对保函申请书及委托担保协议进行审查。保函内容的审查要着重围绕八大基本要素展开，审查保函内容是否完备，是否与合同内容相一致。

【案例 5-2】保函业务中的欺诈条款

保函业务在实践中发生的诈骗案很多。欺诈人在订立条款时挖空心思做文章，以创造索赔机会。以某价值 100 万美元的来料加工合同为例，境外来料方以保证来料加工后返销为由，要求国内加工方提交 12 万美元的履约保函，在条款中订立由来料方检验加工样品，合格后再加工生产，如果加工方未按规定的时间发货，在任何情况下，担保人都保证赔款。加工方在审核条款后发现以上条款存在很大漏洞，首先，如果来料方检验加工样品延误了发货期怎么办？其次，如果检验结果发生争议由哪方判定？很明显，这样的条款，是对加工方设置了陷阱，增加了担保银行的风险。

3. 保函项下的索赔和理赔

按照 URDG 的规定，担保行独立承担第一性的偿付责任。根据受益人提交的符合保函规定的索赔文件，向受益人做出不超过保函金额的赔偿。根据保函开立的方式，保函项下的索赔有三种形式：①受益人凭保函进行索赔。受益人在索赔时提出赔偿要求，也可以提出"赔偿或展期"(COMPENSATION OR EXTENSION)的要求。②担保人根据反担保协议向反担保人索赔。③反担保人向委托人索赔。

担保行做出赔付后，取得代位求偿权(SUBROGATION)，即可取代债权人向委托人或其提供的反担保人索取赔偿。

4. 保函的撤销

保函在下列情况下予以撤销：因到期而失效；合同完结，受益人退回保函正本；受益人签署文件，明确放弃保函项下的一切权利而撤销；保函项下担保余额已全部支付。

URDG 规定，只要保函未到期，担保将继续存在。随着保函在以上四种情况下的撤销，担保行的担保职责即告解除，保函业务随之宣告结束。但要注意约旦、巴基斯坦、泰国等国的法律规定，保函到期后的规定时间内(如 3 年、5 年、60 年不等)，只要受益人提出赔偿，担保人仍有义务受理并付款。

三、银行保函的种类

银行保函按其应用范围划分，可分为出口类保函、进口类保函、对销贸易类保函与其他类保函。

(一)出口类保函

出口类保函是指银行应出口方申请向进口方开出的保函，如由商品或劳务的提供者和工程的承包方委托开立的保函。

1. 投标保函

投标保函(TENDER GUARANTEE OR BID BOND)(见示样 5-2)保证投标人在其报价有效期内不撤标、不改标、不更改原报价条件。一旦中标，则按招标文件的规定在一定期限内与招标方签订合同并提交履约保函。该保函于开标日后一定天数截止有效。若投标人日后有违法行为，担保银行将立即向招标人赔付一定金额的款项作为补偿。如果投标人落选，且未有违约行为发生，招标人将退回投标保函，以供银行解除担保责任。

2. 履约保函

履约保函(PERFORMANCE GUARANTEE OR PERFORMANCE BOND)是担保银行应委托人(即供货方或劳务承包方)的请求而向受益人(购买方或业主)开立的一种保证文件，保证委托人忠实地履行商品或劳务合同，按时、按质、按量地交运货物或完成所承包的工程。履约保函(见示样 5-3)失效有两种情况：①交货完毕或施工完毕即告失效，②在交货或施工结束后再加一段规定的时期才失效。

3. 预付款保函

预付款保函(ADVANCED PAYMENT GUARANTEE)即还款保函(REPAYMENT GUARANTEE)，在买卖合同中为定金保函(DOWN PAYMENT GUARANTEE)。预付款保函(见示样 5-4 和示样 5-5)是银行同意卖方或承包商的申请出具的一种书面承诺。一旦委托人未能履约或未能全部履约，担保行将在收到买主或业主所提出的索赔后向其返还预付等额款项，或相当于合约尚未履行部分相应比例的预付金款项。该保函一般自委托人收到受益人应支付的足额预付款项时生效，失效有以下情况：①在交货或施工完毕时，预付款全部转化为委托人的营业收入，保函项下无款可回，该保函自动失效；②规定减额条款，即随工程进度或交货情况而"自动、按比例地"进行扣减，直至减至款项为零时，保函自动失效。

示样5-2　投标保函

TENDER GUARANTEE OR BID SECURITY

TO:_____ (BENEFICIARY)　　　　　　　ISSUING DATE:_____

BIDDING SECURITY FOR BID NO._____

FOR SUPPLY OF_____

　　THIS GUARANTEE IS HEREBY ISSUED TO SERVE AS A BID SECURITY OF _____(NAME OF BIDDER) (HEREINAFTER CALLED THE "BIDDER") FOR INVITATION FOR BID (BID NO._____)FOR SUPPLY OF_____(DESCRIPTION OF GOODS) TO_____(NAME OF THE BUYER).

　　_____(NAME OF ISSUING BANK)HEREBY UNCONDITIONALLY AND IRREVOCABLY GUARANTEES AND BINDS ITSELF, ITS SUCCESSORS AND ASSIGNEES TO PAY YOU IMMEDIATELY WITHOUT RECOURSE, THE SUM OF_____(AMOUNT IN WORD) UPON RECEIPT OF YOUR WRITTEN NOTIFICATION STATING ANY OF THE FOLLOWING:

　　(A) THE BIDDER HAS WITHDRAWN HIS BID AFTER THE TIME AND DATE OF THE BID AND BEFORE THE EXPIRATION OF ITS VALIDITY PERIOD; OR

　　(B) THE BIDDER HAS FAILED TO ENTER INTO CONTRACT WITH YOU WITHIN THIRTY(30)CALENDAR DAYS AFTER THE NOTIFICATION OF CONTRACT AWARD; OR

　　(C) THE BIDDER HAS FAILED TO ESTABLISH ACCEPTABLE PERFORMANCE SECURITY WITHIN THIRTY(30) CALENDAR DAYS AFTER THE NOTIFICATION OF CONTRACT AWARD.

　　IT IS FULLY UNDERSTOOD THAT THIS GUARANTEE TAKES AFFECT FROM THE DATE OF THE BID OPENING AND SHALL REMAIN VALID FOR A PERIOD OF _____CALENDAR DAYS THEREAFTER, AND DURING THE PERIOD OF ANY EXTENSION THEREOF THAT MAY BE AGREED UPON BETWEEN YOU AND THE BIDDER WITH NOTICE TO US, UNLESS SOONER TERMINATED AND OR RELEASED BY YOU.

ISSUING BANK:_____

SIGNED BY:_____

(PRINTED NAME AND DESIGNATION OF OFFICIAL

AUTHORIZED TO SIGN ON BEHALF OF ISSUING BANK

OFFICIAL SEAL:_____

示样 5-3　履约保函

PERFORMANCE GUARANTEE OR PERFORMANCE BOND FOR SUPPLY OF_____

TO:_____ (BENEFICIARY)　　　　　ISSUING DATE:_____

PERFORMANCE BOND NO.: _____

DEAR SIRS:

　　THIS BOND IS HEREBY ISSUED AS THE PERFORMANCE BOND OF _____ (APPLICANT) (HEREINAFTER CALLED THE "SUPPLIER") FOR SUPPLY OF_____(DESCRIPTION OF GOODS) UNDER CONTRACT NO._____ TO _____(NAME OF THE BENEFICIARY).

　　THE _____(NAME OF THE GUARANTOR) HEREBY IRREVOCABLY GUARANTEES ITSELF, ITS SUCCESSORS AND ASSIGNEES TO PAY YOU UP TO THE AMOUNT OF _____(AMOUNT OF THE GUARANTEED VALUE) REPRESENTING _____PERCENT OF THE CONTRACT PRICE AND ACCORDINGLY COVENANTS AND AGREES AS FOLLOWS:

　　(A) ON THE SUPPLIER'S FAILURE OF FAITHFUL PERFORMANCE OF THE CONTRACT (HEREINAFTER CALLED THE FAILURE OF PERFORMANCE),WE SHALL IMMEDIATELY, ON YOUR DEMAND IN A WRITTEN NOTIFICATION STATING THE EFFECT OF THE FAILURE OF PERFORMANCE BY THE SUPPLIER, PAY YOU SUCH AMOUNT OR AMOUNTS AS REQUIRED BY YOU NOT EXCEEDING _____(THE GUARANTEED AMOUNT)IN THE MANNER SPECIFIED IN THE SAID STATEMENT.

　　(B) THE COVENANTS HEREIN CONTAINED CONSTITUTE IRREVOCABLE AND DIRECT OBLIGATION OF THE GUARANTOR, NO ALTERNATION IN THE TERMS OF THE CONTRACT TO BE PERFORMED THEREUNDER AND NO ALLOWANCE OF TIME BY YOU OR ANY OTHER ACT OR OMISSION BY YOU, WHICH BUT FOR THIS PROVISION MIGHT EXONERATE OR DISCHARGE, THE BANK SHALL IN ANY WAY RELEASE THE GUARANTOR FROM ANY LIABILITY HEREUNDER.

　　(C) THIS PERFORMANCE BOND SHALL BECOME EFFECTIVE FROM ISSUING DATE AND SHALL REMAIN VALID UNTIL_____(THE DATE OF EXPIRY). UPON EXPIRY, PLEASE RETURN THIS BOND TO US FOR CANCELLATION.

　　　　　　　　　　　　　　　　　　　　　　　FOR_____

　　　　　　　　　　　　　　　　　　　　　　　SIGNATURE_____

示样 5-4　预付款保函

ADVANCE PAYMENT GUARANTEE FOR SUPPLY OF_____

TO:_____ (BENEFICIARY)　　　ISSUING DATE:_____

　　　　　　　　　　　　　　　　　　GUARANTEE NO.:_____

DEAR SIRS:

　　THIS GUARANTEE IS HEREBY ISSUED AS THE ADVANCE PAYMENT GUARANTEE OF _____(APPLICANT) (HEREINAFTER CALLED THE "SUPPLIER")　FOR _____(THE NAME OF THE CONTRACT AND ITS NUMBER) TO _____(NAME OF THE BENEFICIARY) (HEREINAFTER CALLED THE "BUYER").

　　WHEREAS THE BUYER HAS AGREED TO ADVANCE TO THE SUPPLIER AN AMOUNT OF ____(SAY_____ONLY), WHEREAS THE BUYER HAS REQUIRED THE SUPPLIER TO FURNISH A GUARANTEE WITH AN AMOUNT EQUAL TO THE ABOVE SAID ADVANCE PAYMENT FOR PERFORMANCE OF HIS OBLIGATION UNDER THE CONTRACT, THE _____(THE NAME OF THE GUARANTOR) , AT THE REQUEST OF THE SUPPLIER AND IN CONSIDERATION OF THE BUYER'S AGREEING TO MAKE THE ABOVE SAID ADVANCE TO THE SUPPLIER, HAS AGREED TO FURNISH THE ABOVE REQUIRED GUARANTEE.

　　NOW, THEREFORE , THE GUARANTOR HEREBY GUARANTEES THAT THE SUPPLIER SHALL UTILIZE THE ABOVE SAID ADVANCE FOR THE PURPOSE OF THE CONTRACT AND IF HE FAILS AND COMMITS DEFAULT IN FULFILLMENT OF ANY OF HIS OBLIGATION FOR WHICH THE ADVANCE PAYMENT IS MADE, IT SHALL ENTITLE THE BUYER TO BE PAID NOT EXCEEDING THE ABOVE MENTIONED AMOUNT.

　　AGAINST DEMAND IN WRITING OF ANY DEFAULT, WHICH THE GUARANTOR SHOULD BE GIVEN BY THE BUYER STATING THAT THE SUPPLIER HAS FAILED TO FULFILL ITS OBLIGATIONS TO THE BUYER, AND UPON SUCH FIRST DEMAND PAYMENT SHALL BE MADE BY THE GUARANTOR'S OBLIGATION UNDER THIS GUARANTEE SHALL NOT IN ANY CASE EXCEEDING THE SUM OF_____(SAY _____ONLY).

　　THIS GUARANTEE SHALL BECOME EFFECTIVE FROM THE DATE OF RECEIPT OF THE ABOVE SAID ADVANCE BY THE SUPPLIER AND VALID UNTIL_____(THE DATE OF EXPIRY). UPON EXPIRY, PLEASE RETURN THIS GUARANTEE TO US FOR CANCELLATION.

　　　　　　　　　　　　　　　　　FOR_____

　　　　　　　　　　　　　　　　　SIGNATURE_____

示样 5-5 直开转交以 SWIFT 方式开立的预付款保函

GUARANTEE/STANDBY LETTER OF CREDIT

SEQUENCE OF TOTAL	*27:	1/1
TRN	*20:	9876345
FURTHER IDENT.	*23:	ISSUE
DATE	30:	090409
APPLICABLE RULES:	*40C:	OTHER/
DETAILS OF GUARANT.	*77C:	

WE ASK YOU TO ADVICE OUR FOLLOWING ADVANCE PAYMENT GUARANTEE TO THE BENEFICIARY WITHOUT ANY OBLIGATION ON YOUR SIDE.

ZHEJIANG DONGDONG CABLE CO. LTD.   SOUTH VILLAGE INDUSTRIAL ZONE LINAN, P. R. CHINA

ADVANCE PAYMENT GUARANTEE NO. 9876345

WE ARE INFORMED THAT YOU AS BUYERS AND ROSIN MACHINE GMBH, AUSTRIA, AS SELLERS HAVE CONCLUDED THE CONTRACT NO. 09-CTRE05-0403 FOR DELIVERY OF ONE UNIT WELDING AND CORRUGATING MACHINE AT A TOTAL VALUE OF EUR390.000,00.

ACCORDING TO THE TERMS OF THE A. M. CONTRACT YOU WILL MAKE AN ADVANCE PAYMENT, WHICH POSSIBLE REPAYMENT SHALL BE SECURED BY A BANK GUARANTEE.

THIS BEING STATED, WE, BY ORDER OF OUR A. M. CUSTOMER, IRREVOCABLY UNDERTAKE TO PAY TO YOU WITHOUT EXAMING THE UNDERLYING LEGAL SITUATION AND WAIVING ALL RIGHTS OR OBJECTION AND DEFENSE ANY AMOUNT YOU MAY CLAIM UP TO, ——BUT NOT EXCEEDING THE TOTAL AMOUNT OF

EUR78.000,00 (BEING 20 PERCENT OF CONTRACT VALUE)
(IN WORDS: EURO SEVENTY EIGHT THOUSAND 00/00)

PAYMENT(S): CASH PAYMENT EXCLUDED, WILL BE EFFECTED WITHIN 8 BUSINESS DAYS (ON WHICH BANKS ARE OPEN FOR BUSINESS IN AUSTRIA) UPON RECEIPT OF YOUR FIRST WRITTEN DEMAND TO AN ACCOUNT TO BE INDICATED TO US. YOUR DEMAND FOR PAYMENT MUST INCLUDE THE FOLLOWING DECLARATION: WE HEREWITH CONFIRM THAT THE SELLERS HAVE FAILED TO FULFILL THEIR DELIVERY OBLIGATION ARISING OUT OF THE CONTRACT.

FOR PURPOSE OF IDENTIFICATION YOUR DEMAND FOR PAYMENT HAS TO BE PRESENTED BY WAY OF A FIRST RATE BANK CONFIRMING THAT THE DEMAND FOR PAYMENT HAS BEEN DULY SIGNED.

THIS GUARANTEE WILL ONLY ENTER INTO FORCE UPON RECEIPT OF THE ADVANCE PAYMENT AMOUNT OF EUR 78.000,00 FREE OF CHARGES AND ONLY IF EFFECTED ON THE ACCOUNT NO. 00000-002626 (IBAN: AT88 20815 00000002626, BIC:STSPAT2G) OF OUR CUSTOMER HELD WITH US, QUOTING OUR GUARANTEE NO. 9876345, UNTIL APRIL 15, 2009, AT THE LATEST AND AFTER OPENING OF AN IRREVOCABLE LETTER OF CREDIT IN THE AMOUNT OF EUR312.000,00, ACCEPTANCE BY THE SELLERS UNTIL JULY 09, 2009, AT THE LATEST (ISSUED DIRECTLY TO STSPAT2G) INCL. TERMS AND CONDITIONS AS PER CONTRACT.

LATEST DATE OF SHIPMENT UNDER THIS CONTRACT IS OCTOBER 09, 2009 EXW SELLER'S ADDRESS. CONSEQUENTLY CLAIMS UNDER THIS GUARANTEE WILL NOT BE HONORED BEFORE OCTOBER 10, 2009.

OUR OBLIGATIONS UNDER THIS GUARANTEE WILL TERMINATE UPON RETURN TO US OF THE ORIGINAL LETTER OF GUARANTEE OR AFTER PRSENTATION OF A PHOTOCOPY OF THE RELEVANT TRANSPORT DOCUMENT CMR AND INVOICE (PRO RATA IN CASE OF PARTSHIPMENT) BY MESSRS ROSIN MACHINE GMBH, AUSTRIA. BUT IN ANY EVENT ON OCTOBER 16, 2009. UP TO THE END OF WHICH DATE YOUR WRITTEN DEMAND FOR PAYMENT—FAX TRANSMISSION EXCLUDED—MUST HAVE REACHED US AT OUR COUNTERS.

IN THE EVENT THAT THIS DAY SHOULD NOT BE A BANK BUSINESS DAY IN AUSTRIA, THE WRITTEN DEMAND FOR PAYMENT SHALL BE RECEIVED BY US THE END OF THE PREVIOUS BANK BUSINESS DAY AT THE LATEST.

IN CASE OF PARTIAL DRAWING(S) OUR OBLIGATION UNDER THIS GUARANTEE SHALL BE REDUCED ACCORING TO THE PAID AMOUNT(S).

ANY ASSIGNMENT OF RIGHTS OUT OF THIS GUARANTEE IS SUBJECT TO OUR PRIOR WRITTEN CONSENT, THE APPLICANT HAS ASSIGNED TO US ANY AND ALL CLAIMS FOR THE RETURN OF ANY PAYMENTS MADE UNDER THIS GUARANTEE. IN THE EVENT THAT ANY AMOUNT SHOULD BE RETURNED AFTER THE GUARANTEE HAS BEEN INVOKED AND PAYMENT HAS BEEN MADE BY US, SUCH AMOUNTS SHALL BE PAID BACK SOLELY AND EXCLUSIVELY TO US.

THIS GUARANTEE IS SUBJECT TO AUSTRIA LAW.

FOR ANY DISPUTES ARISING OUT OF THIS GUARANTEE THE COMPETENT COURTS IN GRAZ HAVING SUBJECT MATTER JURISDICTION SHALL BE THE EXCLUSIVE PLACE OF JURISDICTION. ALL CHARGES ARISING OUTSIDE OF OUR INSTITUTION ARE FOR YOUR ACCOUNT.

KIND REGARDS
STEIERMAERKISCHE BANK UND SPARKASSEN AG GRA Z/AUSTRIA
INT. DIV./B. SEYER-DORNER

4. 质量保函和维修保函

质量保函(QUALITY GUARANTEE)和维修保函(MAINTENANCE GUARANTEE)是大型工程机械设备等资本物资的进出口贸易或劳务承包交易项下的委托人(卖方或承包方)申请开立的以买方或业主为受益人的期限一般为一年(自交货或施工完毕之日起),担保货物或工程质量符合合同要求的保函。

【案例5-3】中行厦门分行成功开立网上支付关税保函

2006年,中行厦门分行积极努力,成功获准成为厦门关区唯一试点开办的"先放后税"业务银行,并在2006年6月顺利为戴尔(中国)有限公司开立了第一笔金额达7 000万元的网上支付关税保函。

(二)进口类保函

进口类保函是由商品或劳务的购买者、工程项目的业主委托银行开立的以基础合同的相对方为受益人的银行保函。

1. 付款保函

在大型资本货物交易或工程承包业务项下，付款保函(PAYMENT GUARANTEE)(见示样5-6)可作为保证买方或业主按工程进度支付款项的保证文件。

示样5-6　付款保函

PAYMENT GUARANTEE FOR SUPPLY OF_____

TO:_____(NAME OF SELLER)　　　　ISSUING DATE:_____

RE: OUR IRREVOCABLE LETTER OF GUARANTEE NO._____

DEAR SIRS:

WITH REFERENCE TO CONTRACT NO. _____ FOR A TOTAL VALUE OF _____SIGNED BETWEEN YOU (HEREINAFTER REFERRED TO AS "THE SELLER")AND _____(HEREINAFTER REFERRED TO AS "THE BUYER")CONCERNING THE BUYER'S PURCHASE FROM THE SELLER OF_____(NAME OF THE GOODS), WE AT THE REQUEST OF THE BUYER, OPEN OUR IRREVOCABLE LETTER OF GUARANTEE NO._____ IN FAVOUR OF THE SELLER TO THE EXTENT OF _____COVERING 100% OF THE TOTAL VALUE OF THE CONTRACT AND UNDERTAKE THAT PAYMENT WILL BE EFFECTED BY THE BUYER AS FOLLOWS:

1. 90% OF THE TOTAL CONTRACT PRICE, VIZ_____ SHALL BE PAID BY THE BUYER AFTER HIS HAVING RECEIVED FROM THE SELLER THE FOLLOWING DOCUMENTS AND HAVING FOUND THEM IN ORDER.

2. 5% OF THE TOTAL CONTRACT PRICE, VIZ_____ SHALL BE PAID BY THE BUYER AFTER HIS HAVING RECEIVED FROM THE SELLER_____(SUCH AS ONE CERTIFICATE OF ACCEPTANCE OF THE CONTRACT PLANT).

3. 5% OF THE TOTAL CONTRACT PRICE, VIZ_____ SHALL BE PAID BY THE BUYER AFTER EXPIRY OF THE GUARANTEE PERIOD OF _____(SUCH AS CONTRACT PLANT)AND HIS HAVING RECEIVED FROM THE SELLER_____(SUCH AS ONE CERTIFICATE OF EXPIRY OF THE GUARANTEE PERIOD).

IN CONNECTION WITH THE ABOVE, WE UNDERTAKE THAT IF THE BUYER FAILS TO PAY WHOLLY OR PARTIALLY WE WILL WITHIN 3 DAYS AFTER RECEIPT OF THE SELLER'S WRITTEN DEMAND PAY THE SELLER RELATIVE AMOUNT PLUS SIMPLE INTEREST AT THE RATE OF 7% PER ANNUM FOR DELAYED PAYMENT, WHICH THE BUYER IS LIABLE UNDER THE CONTRACT, PROVIDED THAT BUYER IS UNABLE TO SUBMIT ANY PROOF THAT THE DOCUMENTS PRESENTED BY THE SELLER ARE NOT IN CONFORMITY WITH THE STIPULATION OF THE CONTRACT. OUR LIABILITY UNDER THIS LETTER OF GUARANTEE SHALL DIMINISH PROPORTIONALLY WITH THE PERCENTAGE OF AMOUNT PAID BY THE BUYER. THE LETTER OF GUARANTEE SHALL BECOME EFFECTIVE ON THE DATE OF ISSUE AND SHALL AUTOMATICALLY BECOME NULL AND VOID AFTER PAYMENT MADE AS ABOVE STATED.

　　　　　　　　　　　　　　　FOR_____

　　　　　　　　　　　　　　　SIGNATURE_____

---

2. 留置金保函

留置金保函(RETENTION MONEY GUARANTEE)是业主或买方以现金滞留的形式对承包方或供货方在项目和合同维修期间应负的维修责任所采取的一种制约手段。

3. 提货保函

提货保函(SHIPPING GUARANTEE)是进口商向银行申请开立的以船公司为受益人，要求船公司允许进口商不凭正本提单提货的保函。船公司由此产生的一切费用、责任、风险，银行保证进行赔偿，而且担保行保证一旦收到卖方寄来的正本提单或遗失的提单后，将及时把它交给船公司从而换回提货保函而注销。

4. 费用保付保函

费用保付保函(PAYMENT GUARANTEE FOR COMMISSION OR ANY OTHER CHARGES)，主要针对一些特殊的合同和协议项下的价款支付，如中间商佣金的保付、寄售项下货款的保付、机场起降费的保付等。

(三)对销贸易类保函和其他类保函

对销贸易类保函有补偿贸易保函(COMPENSATION GUARANTEE)、来料加工保函(PROCESSING GUARANTEE)和来件装配保函(ASSEMBLY GUARANTEE)等。

其他类保函有借款保函(LOAN GUARANTEE OR SECURITY FOR A CREDIT LINE)、关税保付保函(DUTY PAYMENT GUARANTEE)、租赁保函(LEASING GUARANTEE)和保释金保函(BAIL GUARANTEE OR BAIL BOND)等。

第二节　备用信用证基本知识

一、备用信用证的概念与特点

(一)备用信用证的概念

备用信用证起源于美国，根据《美国联邦银行法》，在美国的商业银行不得开出保函。商业银行被禁止参与担保业务。为满足客户提出的担保需求，美国银行开立了实际上是保函性质的备用信用证，并在美国及美国以外的国家有了较快的发展。

根据美联储管理委员会的定义，备用信用证是一种能为受益人提供下列担保或类似安排的信用证：①偿还债务人的借款或预支给债务人的款项；②支付由债务人所承担的负债；

③对债务人不履行契约而付款。

(A STANDBY LETTER OF CREDIT IS ANY LETTER OF CREDIT, OR SIMILAR ARRANGEMENT HOWEVER NAMED OR DESCRIBED, WHICH REPRESENTS AN OBLIGATION TO THE BENEFICIARY ON THE PART OF THE ISSUER:

(A) TO REPAY MONEY BORROWED BY OR ADVANCED TO OR FOR THE ACCOUNT OF THE ACCOUNT PARTY OR

(B) TO MAKE PAYMENT ON ACCOUNT OF ANY INDEBTEDNESS UNDERTAKEN BY THE ACCOUNT PARTY OR

(C) TO MAKE PAYMENT ON ACCOUNT OF ANY DEFAULT BY THE ACCOUNT PARTY IN THE PERFORMANCE OF AN OBLIGATION.)

(二)备用信用证的特点

UCP600 规定其可适用的范围包括跟单信用证和备用信用证，而《见索即付统一规则》(URDG)则申明：备用信用证在技术上可属本规则范围之内，开立者如为方便起见，也可规定适用本规则。由此可见，备用信用证既具有信用证的特点，也具有保函的特点。可以说，备用信用证是一种具有保函性质的信用证。

1999 年 1 月 1 日生效的《国际备用证惯例》(INTERNATIONAL STANDBY PRACTICES 1998，国际商会第 590 号出版物，简称 ISP98)第 1、第 11 条 B 款解释：本规则中的"备用信用证"是指本规则试图加以适用的独立承诺。1995 年 12 月 11 日颁布的并于 2000 年 1 月 1 日正式实施的《独立保函和备用信用证联合公约》(UNITED NATIONS CONVENTION ON INDEPENDENT GUARANTEES AND STANDBY LETTERS OF CREDIT)第 2 条规定："承诺是独立的承担责任，在国际惯例中被认为是独立保函或是备用信用证。"

备用信用证的独立承诺体现了三个特点：①备用信用证是一个独立的文件；②开证行承担第一性付款责任；③受益人提交的单据如符合该证的条款和条件，则应付款给受益人。

由于备用信用证只在申请人不能履约时才有支付作用，如果申请人履约就无需支付，因此其往往备而不用。

二、备用信用证、跟单信用证、银行保函三者的异同

备用信用证现已发展成为一种全面的金融工具，其适用范围比违约付款型的独立性保函和跟单信用证更广。

(一)银行保函与备用信用证的异同

银行保函与备用信用证的具体对比见表 5-1。

表 5-1　银行保函与备用信用证的异同

项　目	银行保函	备用信用证
相同点	①从定义上看，法律当事人基本相同 ②从应用上看，都可以提供担保 ③从性质上看，都具有第一性、独立性、单据化等特点	
不同点	①保函有从属性保函与独立性保函之分，传统保函是从属性的，属于第二性的付款责任，而独立性保函属于第一性的付款责任，属单据化业务，与基础合约无关 ②保函适用的国际惯例影响较小	①独立性、自足性、单据化，与基础合约无关 ②有统一的国际惯例，而且国际惯例有深远的影响，当事人在执行过程中受国际惯例的制约

(二)独立性银行保函与跟单信用证的异同

从根本上说，独立性保函与跟单信用证有许多相似之处。

(1) 抽象的付款承诺。只要受益人未表示拒绝，保函一旦开立该承诺即具有约束力。

(2) 独立于基础交易。

(3) 独立于委托人与担保人之间的契约关系。

(4) 单据化业务。

(5) 索款须与保函或信用证条款一致。

(6) 银行对单据的审核仅限于表面相符。

(7) 银行责任仅限于诚信与合理的谨慎，对于其不能控制的行为不负责任。

(8) 反担保函独立于保函。

当然，独立性保函与跟单信用证也有许多不同之处。

(1) 适用的惯例不同。

(2) 作用不同。保函的主要作用是担保，其项下担保银行承担的是一种或有付款责任；而跟单信用证主要用于货款或劳务费的结算，一经开立，其付款责任必然存在。

(3) 单据不同。保函项下需要提交申请人违约的证明文件，而跟单信用证主要采用商业单据。

(三)备用信用证与跟单信用证的异同

开立备用信用证是为了支持一项基于贷款或合约或预付款到期、履行或违约后的支付义务，或其他不确定的事件发生或不发生所产生的支付义务的履行。开立跟单信用证是为了支持基于运交货物或提供服务而产生的支付义务的履行。备用信用证和跟单信用证都是在不同情况下订立的独立承诺。

备用信用证可被认为是具有信用证形式的银行保函。与跟单信用证相比，备用信用证的适用范围更广。备用信用证有违约付款型和直接付款型之分，而跟单信用证无此种分类。

1. 违约付款型备用信用证

20 世纪 80 至 90 年代，人们把备用信用证与独立保函等同看待。如果因为申请人违反合同造成受益人损失，开证行从备用信用证金额中赔付受益人，简称违约付款。

该时期的备用信用证具体种类有履约备用信用证(PERFORMANCE STANDBY L/C)(见示样 5-7)、投标保证金备用信用证(TENDER BOND/BID BOND STANDBY L/C)和预付款备用信用证(ADVANCE PAYMENT STANDBY L/C)。接着，出现了反担保备用信用证(COUNTER STANDBY L/C)(支持反担保备用信用证受益人开立单独备用信用证或其他承诺书)和保险备用信用证(INSURANCE STANDBY L/C)(支持申请人的保险或再保险)。

违约付款型备用信用证与跟单信用证相比，其不同点如下：①跟单信用证在受益人正面履行交货时开证行予以付款，而备用信用证是在申请人发生负面违约或遇到负面事务发生时开证行予以付款；②跟单信用证每笔必须付款，备用信用证带有预备性质，不是每笔必须付款；③跟单信用证适用于货款结算，备用信用证适用于非贸易的宽广领域，仅有少量预付备用证用于贸易结算；④跟单信用证的单据比较复杂，备用信用证的单据比较简单。

2. 直接付款型备用信用证

直接付款型备用信用证，保证一项基本付款义务，开证行到期付款但不涉及是否违约。具体类型包括：①融资备用信用证(FINANCIAL STANDBY L/C)。融资备用信用证从违约付款型发展为直接付款型。备用证保证到期日不涉及借款人是否违约或者履约，全部由开证行直接支付给贷款行，借款人在到期日还款给开证行，从而偿付开证行的垫付，而且每证必须付款。②直接付款备用信用证(DIRECT PAY STANDBY L/C)。③商业备用信用证(COMMERCIAL STANDBY L/C)(见示样 5-8 和示样 5-9)。商业备用信用证类似于跟单信用证，两者异同点对比见表 5-2。

示样 5-7　融资备用信用证

THE SANWA BANK LIMITED

电话(TEL):021-58793818　　　　　　传真(FAX):58793816, 58793817

电挂(CABLE): SANWA BANK SHANGHAI　　　电传(TELEX): 337182 SASH CN

DATE: JAN. 18, 2009

TO: BANK OF CHINA LTD., TIANJIN BRANCH CREDIT BUSINESS DEPT.

ADDRESS:80 JIEFANG, RD TIANJIN, CHINA

FROM: THE SANWA BANK LIMITED, SHANGHAI BRANCH

ADDRESS: 16TH FLOOR MARINE TOWER NO. 1 PUDONG AVENUE, SHANGHAI, CHINA

OUR REF.: 695/470/5302

STANDBY LETTER OF CREDIT NO. 695/470/5302

WITH REFERENCE TO THE LOAN AGREEMENT ("AGREEMENT") DATED AND SIGNED ON JAN. 18, 2009 BY YOURSELVES TIANJIN SUNSHINE PLASTIC CO. LTD. ("TJSUN") AND BANK OF CHINA LTD., TIANJIN BRANCH("BOCTJ"),WE HEREBY OPEN OUR IRREVOCABLE STANDBY LETTER OF CREDIT NO. 695/470/5302 IN YOUR FAVOUR FOR ACCOUNT OF "TJSUN" FOR A SUM OR SUMS NOT EXCEEDING A TOTAL AMOUNT OF USD320,000.00 AVAILABLE BY YOUR DRAFTS DRAWN ON OURSELVES AT SIGHT FOR 100 PERCENT OF STATEMENT VALUE TO BE ACCOMPANIED BY THE FOLLOWING DOCUMENTS:

SIGNED STATEMENT IN DUPLICATE ISSUED BY YOU CERTIFYING THAT THE AMOUNT DRAWN HEREUNDER REPRESENTS AND COVERS THE UNPAID BALANCE OF INDEBTEDNESS DUE TO YOURSELVES BY "TJSUN" UNDER "AGREEMENT".

ALL DRAFTS DRAWN HEREUNDER MUST BE MARKED "DRAWN UNDER THE SANWA BANK LTD., SHANGHAI BRANCH IRREVOCABLE STANDBY LETTER OF CREDIT NO. 695/470/5302 DATED ON JAN. 18, 2009".

THIS CREDIT IS AVAILABLE AS FROM JAN. 18, 2009.

WE ENGAGE WITH DRAWERS THAT SUCH DRAFTS DRAWN UNDER AND IN COMPLIANCE WITH TERMS OF THIS CREDIT SHALL BE DULY HONORED ON DUE PRESENTATION AND DELIVERY OF THE DOCUMENTS AS SPECIFIED ABOVE IF RPESENTED TO US FOR PAYMENT ON OR BEFORE DEC. 30, 2009.

THIS STANDBY LETTER OF CREDIT IS SUBJECT TO UCP600.

　　　　　　　　　　　　　　　　　　FOR THE SANWA BANK LIMITED

　　　　　　　　　　　　　　　　　　SIGNATURE

表 5-2　商业备用信用证与跟单信用证的对比

项　目	商业备用信用证	跟单信用证
共同点	①都是独立的支付文件 ②开证行承担第一性付款责任 ③凭规定的单据符合信用证条款而付款 ④每笔信用证均需付款	
不同点	①卖方直接寄送正本货运单据给买方 ②单据比较简单 ③审单简单，不审核单单是否一致 ④受益人交单遇到银行拒付的可能性小 ⑤申请人先取货后付款，处于有利地位 ⑥银行不掌握物权单据，开证行付款责任很重，面临申请人不及时偿付或无力偿付的风险，需要与申请人订立能够控制其偿付的协议 ⑦适用 ISP98 和 UCP600 ⑧申请人可以较早检查出受益人是否伪造单据	①卖方向银行提示单据，经银行转交买方 ②单据比较复杂 ③审单复杂，单单不一致是单据的不符点 ④受益人交单遇到银行拒付的可能性很大 ⑤申请人向开证行付款赎单，而即期信用证要求先付款后取货 ⑥银行掌握物权单据，可以作为开证行的抵押品 ⑦适用 UCP600 ⑧申请人不能较早检查出受益人是否伪造单据

示样 5-8　商业备用信用证 1

ISSUE OF A STANDBY CREDIT

SEQUENCE OF TOTAL	27 :	1/2
FORM OF DOC. CREDIT	40A:	IRREVOCABLE STANDBY
DOC. CREDIT NUMBER	20 :	LIKG0815930
DATE OF ISSUE	31C:	081105
APPLICABLE RULES	40E:	UCP LATEST VERSION
EXPIRY	31D:	DATE 090401 PLACE BUDAPEST
APPLICANT	50 :	777 UPDATE KFT 99881 BUDAPEST FEHERVART UT 98. HUNGARY
BENEFICIARY	59:	ZHEJIANG KASHA INDUSTRIAL CO., LTD., LINAN ECONOMIC DEVELOPMENT ZONE, LINAN, ZHEJIANG, CHINA
AMOUNT	32B:	CURRENCY EUR AMOUNT 126.280,00
AVAILABLE WITH/BY	41D:	MKB BANK ZRT BUDAPEST BY PAYMENT
PARTIAL SHIPMENTS	43P:	NOT ALLOWED
TRANSHIPMENT	43T:	NOT ALLOWED

PORT OF LOADING	44E:	SHANGHAI PORT, CHINA
PORT OF DISCHARGE	44F:	ANY EUROPEAN PORT
FINAL DESTINATION	44B:	BUDAPEST
LATEST DATE OF SHIP	44D:	081201
DESCRIPT. OF GOODS	45A:	TWISTED PAIR TELEPHONE CABLE ACCORDING TO SPECIFICATION …FOB SHANGHAI
DOCUMENTS REQUIRED	46A:	1) BENEFICIARY'S DECLARATION DULY STAMPED AND SIGNED IN 1 ORIGINAL CONFIRMING THAT THEY FULFILLED THEIR SHIPMENT OBLIGATION BUT APPLICANT DID NOT EFFECT PAYMENT YET HOWEVER MATURITY DATE WAS 45 DAYS AFTER BILL OF LADING DATE I.E. /EXACT DATE/

2) COPY OF UNPAID COMMERCIAL INVOICE DULY STAMPED AND SIGNED.

3) NOT NEGOTIABLE COPY OF ORIGINAL CLEAN ON BOARD BILL OF LADING MADE OUT TO ORDER BLANK ENDORSED EVIDENCING SHIPMENT FROM SHANGHAI THROUGH ANY EUROPEAN PORT TO BUDAPEST AND NOTIFY APPLICANT SHOWING FREIGHT PAYABLE AT DESTINATION.

4) CERTIFICATE OF ORIGIN IN COPY OR PHOTOCOPY.

5) WEIGHT LIST IN COPY OR PHOTOCOPY.

6) PACKING LIST IN COPY OR PHOTOCOPY.

| ADDITIONAL COND. | 47B: | 1)THIS STANDBY LETTER OF CREDIT IS SUBJECT TO ICC PUBL. 600 REV. 2007. |

2)PARTIAL DRAWING ARE NOT ALLOWED.

3)DOCUMENT PRESENTING BANK HAS TO CONFIRM AUTHENTICITY OF SIGNATURES APPEARING ON BENEFICIARY'S CERTIFICATE.

4)ALL DOCUMENTS HAVE TO BEAR THE RELATIVE CONTRACT NUMBER AND STANDBY LETTER OF CREDIT NUMBER.

5)REQUEST OF PAYMENT UNDER THIS STANDBY LETTER OF CREDIT CANNOT BE MADE EARLIER THAN 10 DAYS AFTER MATURITY DATE I.E. 55 DAYS AFTER SHIPMENT DATE.

6)WITH ANY PAYMENT EFFECTED UNDER THIS STANDBY LETTER OF CREDIT OUR ENGAGEMENT WILL BE REDUCED PRORATA.

7)PLEASE FORWARD DOCUMENTS TO THE FOLLOWING ADDRESS: MKB BANK ZRT. 1056 BUDAPEST ,VACI U.38, HUNGARY.

DETAILS OF CHARGES	71B:	ALL BANKING CHARGES OUTSIDE OF HUNGARY ARE FOR BENEFICIARY'S ACCOUNT PLUS OUR SWIFT CHARGES SUBJECT TO DOC. HANDLING AND PAYMENT.
CONFIRMATION	49:	CONFIRM
INSTRUCTION	78:	AFTER RECEIPT OF COMPLYING PRESENTATION WE SHALL EFFECT PAYMENT AS PER YOUR INSTRUCTION.

TRAILER>

示样 5-9 商业备用信用证 2

COMMERCIAL STANDBY LETTER OF CREDIT

ISSUING BANK: _____

TO: _____(BENEFICIARY, OR SELLER)

DATE:_____

DEAR SIRS:

WE HEREBY ISSUE OUR IRREVOCABLE STANDBY LETTER OF CREDIT NO. ____ BY ORDER OF_____(APPLICANT) FOR AN AMOUNT OF_____(VALUE IN FIGURE AND IN WORD) WHICH EXPIRES AT OUR COUNTERS ON_____(EXPIRY DATE).

THIS CREDIT IS AVAILABLE BY PAYMENT AGAINST PRESENTATION TO US OF THE FOLLOWING DOCUMENTS:

(A) YOUR SIGHT DRAFT DRAWN ON ISSUING BANK FOR THE AMOUNT OF YOUR DRAWING.

(B) YOUR CERTIFICATE STATING THAT YOU HAVE MADE SHIPMENT OF THE REQUIRED GOODS AND HAVE SUPPLIED THE REQUIRED DOCUMENTS TO THE BUYERS (APPLICANT)AND HAVE NOT BEEN PAID WITHIN 30 DAYS OF THE INVOICE DATE.

PARTIAL DRAWING ARE ALLOWED.

ALL CHARGES UNDER THIS STANDBY LETTER OF CREDIT ARE FOR ACCOUNT OF THE BENEFICIARY.

EXCEPT WHERE OTHERWISE EXPRESSLY STATED, THIS STANDBY LETTER OF CREDIT IS SUBJECT TO THE UNIFORM CUSTOMS AND PRACTICE FOR DOCUMENTARY CREDIT(1993 REVISION, ICC PUBLICATION NO. 500). PLEASE QUOTE OUR REFERENCE NUMBER ON ANY CORRESPONDENCE.

YOUR FAITHFULLY
ISSUING BANK'S NAME AND SIGNATURE

第三节　与银行保函和备用信用证相关的案例

一、与银行保函相关的案例

(一)条款过于严格的履约保函

1. 案例介绍

我国文具生产企业 A 公司，参与非洲某国教育部(以下为保函受益人)的委托文具招标后收到了中标通知书。A 公司向我国某银行(以下为担保银行)申请开立履约保函。担保行审核中标通知书及有关资料后,建议保函申请人(A 公司)联系受益人(B 公司)进行以下修改:

(1) 原标书规定的保函金额为合同金额的20%，比例过高，建议降到10%以下。

(2) 原标书、合同规定允许分批装运，建议在保函中加列允许保函金额随申请人履约情况按照比例予以递减。

(3) 原标书规定中标方接到中标通知书以后就出具银行保函，同时与买方签订合同。买方根据合同开立延期付款信用证。担保行建议A公司与招标方(买方)商议，先将合同签订下来，并在买方开来信用证后，再按照买方要求开立履约保函。

买方(保函受益人)先于保函的开立与买卖合同的签订，开来了两笔信用证。我国A公司也申请对外开立了履约银行保函。A公司按照合同正常出货，然后，向担保银行提出撤销保函。担保银行致电对方银行，要求确认保函失效并解除担保行的责任。但没过几天，收到对方银行的来电，申明保函受益人已经递交正式文件，申明保函申请人违约，并要求赔付全部保函金额，并要求担保行偿付。经了解得知，因A公司的第二批货物到港晚了两天，为对方提供了索赔的理由。为了维护信誉，担保行不得不对外赔付，并最终向A公司(保函申请人)追索。

2. 案例分析

本案的关键在于A公司与对方签订的合同条款过于严苛，从而造成保函受益人有机会利用保函索赔。本案的教训总结如下：

(1) 选择投标前，应详细了解标书的条款，做好心理准备。对于一些不利、过于苛刻的条款要多注意。对于投标而言，投标方无法参与中标条款、履约保函的文件制作。

(2) 履约保函金额不宜过高，一般为5%~10%。如果过高，会刺激受益人发生商业欺诈。

(3) 保函应规定金额递减条款，否则稍有违约会带来巨大损失。

(4) 我国对外开立保函要慎重，因为保函是受益人欺诈的主要工具。即便对方不想欺诈，但可提出索赔的要求。

(二)借款保函赔付案

1. 案例介绍

开证行A银行于1993年4月为B公司的2 000万港元借款出具担保函，受益人为C银行，期限9个月，利率12%。由于B公司投资房地产失误，大量资金沉淀难以回笼，导致该公司负债累累，已名存实亡，保函还款期满后仍未能依约还款。1995年3月，C银行向当地中级人民法院起诉B公司和A银行。经当地中级人民法院《民事调解书》裁定：B公司应在1995年4月30日前将其债权1100万港元收回并偿还给C银行，余款在1995年12月底还清，如不能履行，由A银行承担代偿责任。1995年5月底，B公司只归还了6 371 222.79港元，仍欠本金13 628 777.21港元及利息12 482 130.22港元未还。鉴于此，当地中级人民法院执行庭多次上门要求A银行履行担保责任，否则将采取强制措施，查封

A银行资产。而该笔担保的反担保单位D酒店，只剩下一个空壳公司，难以履行反担保责任。A银行为维护自己的声誉，避免更大的影响，在经过周密分析后，就此问题提出两种处理意见。第一种，新增贷款给B公司偿还借款。根据该企业目前的情况，已严重资不抵债，企业名存实亡，所欠A银行贷款本息在信贷资产中列为损失类，被列为"六个一批"企业。所以，这种方法的可行性极低。第二种，使用"167"科目暂付款偿还。采取这种方法暂时解决燃眉之急后，A银行将积极与当地政府共同协商，要求其追回该企业欠款后，首先偿付A银行该笔暂付款。目前情况下，该方法基本可行。

2. 案例分析

在本案例中，A银行对保函申请人和反担保人两方面的风险都未能有效控制，最终造成损失。因此，对外开具保函的银行应在确保资金安全的情况下，积极而谨慎地开展这一业务，一方面有利于企业进行融资，提高竞争能力，另一方面，应充分认识到对外开立保函尤其是融资类保函的风险性。因为一旦申请人违约，担保行将承担付款责任或连带责任，一旦发生经济纠纷，涉及诉讼时，将造成严重的资金损失而面临巨大的金融风险。担保行在开立保函前，必须认真审查和了解申请人及反担保人的商业信用，按严格的信贷程序进行审查。保函开立后，应对申请人和反担保人进行及时的监控，一旦出现信用问题，应及时采取积极措施以规避和减少风险。应将对外担保业务纳入信贷管理，只对符合信贷审查要求、信誉和经济效益良好的企业出具保函，且必须以真实的合同为依据，申请开具保函的企业必须在开证行存有足够的保证金或担保足额有效的反担保。

(三)银行保函失效受损案

1. 案例介绍

1993年1月，我国F公司(以下简称买方)受用户委托向J国W公司订购精密仪器一套，价值150万美元，交货期为次年3月份。买方订购的仪器技术较先进，需经巴黎统筹委员会(COCOMM)批准方能出口。合同规定，支付方式为：签约一个月后凭卖方银行出具的保函支付20%，系合同定金；凭买方开出的信用证支付70%；凭买方在安装调试后出具的验收报告支付最后的10%。关于卖方银行出具的保函效期，买卖双方经过多次商谈，最后同意如下："THIS LETTER OF GUARANTEE IS IN ANY EVENT TO BECOME NULL AND VOID ON THE END OF APRIL, 1994, UNLESS WE SHALL HAVE IN THE MEANTIME AGREED TO EXTEND SUCH EXPIRY DATE."据此，该保函到1994年4月底即交货期后一个月失效。

合同执行情况如下：1993年2月，卖方银行出具保函；3月初，买方审核无误，支付

20%定金计30万美元；7月，卖方按合同规定向巴黎统筹委员会提出申请出口许可证；11月，买方开出了银行信用证；1994年1月，卖方通知货已备妥，请买方告知订舱情况；买方通知卖方，因厂房尚未竣工，要求推迟到4月底发运；卖方确认同意，买方做L/C变更，交货期延至4月份；2月，卖方电告，因手续等原因，出口许可尚未得到批准，要求买方速邮寄最终用户用途担保；3月初，卖方电告，货物被对方海关扣留，买方速寄最终用户用途担保；4月，卖方电告，因手续等原因无法及时装运，要求延迟到5月装运，买方同意，并相应修改L/C装运期，L/C有效期延迟到6月21日；6月初，W公司宣布破产，当地法院指定财产清查委员会进行清算，全部资产被冻结，对此，买方一无所知。

7月，B公司来华通知，W公司被拍卖并已被B公司买进，B公司负责W公司合同履约等事项。为此，买方立即通知银行拒付议付单据，经查此时L/C及银行保函均已失效。买卖双方就20%定金进行协商，买方要求卖方协助追回20%定金。B公司坚持认为因拍卖过程中未得到该笔款项，不承担义务。买方则坚持己见，双方僵持不下。后因用户用货紧急，双方商定协议如下："THE BUYER SHALL INCREASE THE RETURNED DOWN PAYMENT AMOUNTING TO XXX INTO THE NEWLY OPENED L/C UPON GETTING THE REFUNDED DOWN PAYMENT FROM THE XX BANK"(买方一旦从XX银行得到上述款项，该款项将追加到新开立的信用证金额中)。在此情况下，买方同意签订。双方签订了合同变更协议，即供货方由W公司变为B公司，合同其他条款照旧。与此同时，买方急告使馆商务处，并与W公司所在国驻华使馆联系，追索20%定金。

9月，由于对W公司所在国破产法等不甚了解，几经周折，买方将追索对象转向财产清算委员会，要求将买方列入债权人，但该委员会迟迟不予答复。

11月，该委员会在买方多番催促下，同意将买方列入普通债权人，而非第一债权人。为此，买方一边聘请律师，以求协助，另一方面与其驻华使馆联系，寻求帮助。在得到有关部门同意后，迅速派出以买方、银行、律师、用户四方组成的索款小组去J国索款，拟定索款对象为：①财产清算委员会；②J国国家银行；③B公司。索款途径为：派员交涉；请求银行协助；通过使馆做工作；诉诸法律。

向财产清算委员会索款的理由是在买方向其提出要求后，其将买方列为普通债权人。如未得到财产清算委员会的许可，J国国家银行不会将款项退回买方。同时，该合同货物已在码头，委员会将该笔货物拍卖给B公司，实际上该笔货物20%的所有权应属于买方，交涉过程中，该委员会不得不承认没有通知买方是其工作不够完善，买方可以上诉，但买方了解后得知，虽然可上诉，但按J国诉讼法规定，向法院上诉要聘请当地律师，而W公司财产已按债权人顺序拍卖完毕，该委员会并无偿付能力，即使胜诉，意义也不大。同时，该委员会是法院指定的代理人，其会受到法院的保护，向其索款基本无望。

向J国国家银行索款的理由是：L/C与L/G均通过该银行。尽管在我方得知W公司破产时我方开立的信用证仍然有效(失效期为 1994 年 6 月 21 日),在此期间,该行未向买方提供 W 公司的任何情况,对此,该行承认未及时将 W 公司的财务资信通知买方有一定的责任,但其称该责任为非法定责任,强调 L/C 的延期不代表 L/G 有效期的相应延展,L/G 的担保期是该行对该货物预付款承担责任的界限,该行认定 L/G 有效期已过,不再负有任何退款的责任,买方向该行索款无法律依据。

向 B 公司索款的理由是 B 公司在拍卖中买进了 W 公司,并承担继续履约的责任,而该货物的所有权中事实上已包括买进买方 20%的预付款,但 B 公司认为是按 100%的货价向财产清算委员会买进的,在变更合同的供货方时,又未订明双方索款责任,买方未将索款作为变更合同的充决条件,因此,向 B 公司索款理由亦难成立。

2. 案例分析

(1) 本案中的财产清算委员会及 J 国国家银行,均分别承认其工作有不够完善之处,有一定责任,等等,但事实上他们均拒不承担付款责任。因为,前者是法院指定的从事该破产公司清算事宜的机构,既不负经济责任,又无款项可以分配;后者则以其所开保函的有效期为其承担法律责任的界限,有效期已过,再无付款责任可言。而买方,则对有关法律方面的重要事项未能切实掌握,对卖方宣告破产一无所知,以致失去了依法向清算委员会申请的有利时机。对用户申请开立的保函有效期缺乏监控。在买方一再延长自己所开信用证的到期日时,未相应地要求买方延长其通过银行所开保函的有效期,而在当时只是举手之劳。由此可见,在进出口企业中,加强有关人员的法律意识,向他们宣传法律知识十分必要。此外,设置内部的法律部门或专职法律人员,规定其职责和办事制度,也应提上议事日程。

(2) 在合同变更时,本来可能将索款与合同变更捆在一起,如 B 公司不答应向 J 国家银行或财产清算委员会索款的条件,买方可不同意变更合同。尽管并没有把握使 B 公司就范,但毕竟是买方可能由被动转为主动的一次机会,然而由于用户急于要货,买方未能坚持下去。

(3) 买方对 J 国法律不熟悉,在获悉 W 公司倒闭后除了通知买方银行拒付外,不知如何着手索款。买方通过各种渠道打听款项在何处,确定索款对象花了大量时间,丧失了宝贵的时间。

(4) 买方对卖方资信变化的了解不及时。本案合同交货期较长,因此对外商资信应经常了解,不仅应在合同签订前了解,在合同执行过程中也应经常跟踪。

二、与备用信用证相关的案例

(一)备用信用证索赔失败的教训

1. 案例介绍

1995 年 5 月，国内 A 公司与美国 B 公司签订合同进口一笔货物。A 公司先通过 C 银行向美国 D 银行开出一张不可撤销的跟单信用证，金额为 100 万美元，有效期至 1995 年 8 月 30 日，以 B 公司为受益人。由于货物数量大，金额大，为防止 B 公司不履约而造成损失，A 公司在开证前，要求 B 公司开出一份以 A 公司为受益人的备用信用证，信用证金额为 2 万美元。该备用信用证中规定：THIS CREDIT IS AVAILABLE BY BENEFICIARY'S DRAFT DRAWN ON OURSELVES AT SIGHT WHEN ACCOMPANIED BY THE FOLLOWING DOCUMENTS STATING THAT THE APPLICANT HAS FAILED TO FULFILL THE OBLIGATIONS UNDER THE CONTRACT NO. XXX (本信用证凭受益人开具的以开证行为付款人的即期汇票，并随附开证申请人未按第 XXX 号合同履行的证明可以得到支付)。同时，该备用信用证还规定：THIS CREDIT IS NOT OPERATIVE UNLESS BENEFICIARY OPEN AN IRREVOCABLE LETTER OF CREDIT FOR USD1000,000.00 IN FAVOUR OF APPLICANT UNDER CONTRACT NO. XXX AND WILL BE EXPIRED ON AUG. 30, 1995 WITHIN 14 DAYS AFTER ADVISING BANK RECEIPT OF THIS L/C AND SUCH L/C MUST BE ADVISED THROUGH US AND RESTRICTED TO US FOR NEGOTIATION(本证生效的条件是受益人开出一份位于合同号 XXX 项下的以本证申请人为受益人的金额为 100 万美元的不可撤销信用证，本证有效期为 1995 年 8 月 30 日，并且必须于通知行收到信用证之日起 14 天之内开出，本证应由我行通知并限制在我行议付)。

我 A 公司对外开证时，并没有通知 C 银行在信用证中加列"限制在 D 银行议付"条款。在合同执行过程中，A 公司发现 B 公司有违约行为。在找出充分证据后，C 银行应 A 公司要求使用该备用信用证，向 D 银行寄出索赔单据，金额为 2 万美元。

不几日，D 银行来电称，不接受 C 银行提交的单据和索赔，理由是 C 银行开出的信用证未写明限制在 D 银行议付，C 银行将情况告知了 A 公司。

在备用信用证交涉期间，C 银行收到 D 银行寄来的跟单信用证项下单据一套，金额为 978 989.90 美元。C 银行审核单据后，发现有许多实质性不符点，C 银行向 D 银行发出拒付通知。后经买卖双方协商，B 公司同意减价处理，此案了结。

2．案例分析

(1) 这是一起备用信用证与跟单信用证结合使用的案例。本案中 A 公司采用备用信用证索赔失败的关键在于 A 公司对外开证时未加列"限制在 D 银行议付"条款。如果加列该条款，B 公司一旦违约，A 公司就能收回 2 万美元违约金。这时候，B 公司的单据有实质性不符点，那么 A 公司就更能掌握主动权。本案中，如果 B 公司的单据与信用证相符，那么 C 银行将不得不对外支付，因为 A 公司对外开立的信用证是正常的信用证，未加列任何限制性生效的条款。

(2) 应该提醒的是，本案中未提及备用信用证的有效期。一般情况下，备用证的有效期应当晚于跟单证的有效期，以防备用证的申请人(跟单证的受益人)不履约时，有充足的时间向备用证的开证行索赔。

(3) 本案中备用证是作为担保形式出现的，在实际中应用很少。在使用过程中，首先应该像跟单信用证一样，认真审核开证行的印押是否一致，以确定其真伪。备用信用证都是不可撤销的，有效地点一般应规定在受益人所在地，并要在其有效期内交单。

(二)利用伪造的备用信用证诈骗银行资金案

1．案例介绍

2000 年 6 月 26 日，某省 I 银行通过电传接收到由其总行转发的，据称是美国 M 银行开来的金额为 500 万美元、期限自 2000 年 6 月 21 日至 2001 年 6 月 21 日、申请人(借款人)为某省 F 市 H 公司、受益人(贷款银行)为某省 I 银行辖属的 F 市分行的一份备用信用证，该证格式规范、条款清晰，主要用于 H 公司向 F 银行申请外汇担保项下的人民币贷款之用。由于该证没有密押，I 银行无法确认该备用信用证的表面真实性，因此于当天下午以 MT799 格式，通过 SWIFT 系统向美国 M 银行发出查询书，要求其通过 SWIFT 系统对该证进行确认。6 月 27 日，I 银行又通过电传接收到据称从美国 M 银行发来的金额为 500 万美元的加押电传，经 I 银行核实，密押相符，但电传报文内容不完整、措辞含糊，且未直接回答某省 I 银行提出的查询内容。为了对受益人(贷款银行)负责，I 银行又于当天中午第二次通过 SWIFT 系统以 MT999 格式要求美国 M 银行再一次确认该备用信用证的真伪并要求一定通过 SWIFT 格式回复。经过两天的等待，6 月 30 日早上 I 银行收到美国 M 银行通过 SWIFT 系统以 MT799 格式的回复。该回复声称该证不是美国 M 银行所开，系伪造的备用信用证，而且美国 M 银行所引用的备用信用证参考号和受益人有误。

为了对申请人(借款人)负责，I 银行又于当天继续通过 SWIFT 以 MT799 格式向美国 M 银行发出第三次查询，以进一步明确该备用信用证的真伪以及美国 M 银行的回复中参考号和受益人引用是否有误。经过近一个星期的等待，未见美国 M 银行的答复，I 银行又于 7

月 7 日通过 SWIFT 以 MT799 格式第四次发出查询，要求美国 M 银行尽快答复。7 月 10 日，I 银行收到美国 M 银行通过 SWIFT 以 MT799 格式发来的查询回复，明确答复该备用信用证系伪造的。至此，I 银行成功地堵截了一起伪造备用信用证的行动，并及时制止了一起拟以伪造的备用信用证申请人民币贷款的金融诈骗活动。

2. 案例分析

本案的关键在于如何合理谨慎地审核所通知的信用证的表面真实性。在本案例中，M 银行的第一次电传没有密押，第二次电传有密押，且相符，但内容不完整，没有正面回复 I 银行的查询，I 银行并没有简单地认为第一次电传格式规范、条款清晰，第二次电传密押相符，而由此确定该备用信用证的表面真实性。而通知行仅通知而不审核信用证的表面真实性，会使受益人遭受莫大风险而最终损害银行的信用。

本 章 小 结

本章阐述了银行保函的定义、作用、涉及的当事人，保函与基础合同的关系，银行保函的基本内容、开立方式和业务流程，并介绍了银行保函的种类，通过案例分析了银行保函业务在条款签订、银行保函与信用证等结算方式结合使用时应注意的事项。银行保函使用范围较广，适合比较复杂的贸易结算。

备用信用证可以称为具有信用证性质的银行保函。备用信用证具有担保或融资性质。它是单据化业务。本章阐述了备用信用证的起源，介绍了备用证的种类，分析了备用证、跟单信用证、银行保函三者的异同点，并结合相关案例分析了运用备用信用证应注意的问题。

复习思考题

1. 简述银行保函的概念及其与基础合同之间的关系。反担保函在什么情况下可能出现？
2. 银行保函的基本种类有哪些？
3. 备用信用证的概念是什么？其适用的国际惯例有哪些？
4. 备用信用证的种类有哪些？
5. 试对比备用信用证、银行保函、跟单信用证之间的异同点。

第六章

国际结算相关的单据

学习目标：掌握商业发票、海运提单、保险单、原产地证书等单据制作的具体要求，并能根据一份具体的信用证来判定所要提交的单据和条件，并与具体单据内容衔接；了解 UCP600 关于单据的要求。

关键概念：基本单据、附属单据、商业单据、运输单据、保险单据、官方单据、商业发票、装箱单、海运提单、航空运单、保险单、一般原产地证、FORM A、FORM E、检验证书

第一节　单据的种类

国际贸易中的单据种类很多，按其作用不同可分为两大类：基本单据和附属单据。基本单据(BASIC DOCUMENTS)是指交易中不可缺少的单据，如在 FOB 和 CFR 价格条件下，出口商需要提供商业发票和运输单据，而在 CIF 价格条件下，则需加上保险单据。附属单据(ADDITIONAL DOCUMENTS)是进口商根据进口地当局的规定或货物的不同特点等要求出口商特别提供的单据，如海关发票、领事发票、产地证、卫生证书及附属于商业发票的单据，如包装单、尺码单、检验证等。按照单据的性质，可将单据分为商业单据、运输单据、保险单据和官方单据。

世界上不同国家对进口单据的要求不相统一。有些国家对发票、产地证书的种类及内容的要求也不一致，例如：要求提供证实发票、领事发票、海关发票，产地证书必须加签"未再加工"证明、领事认证等。又如：据墨西哥政府的规定，对列入反倾销商品清单的鞋、玩具和服装，出口墨西哥时要出具墨西哥规定格式的原产地证书，并须经墨西哥驻华使馆的认证才有效。

(一)商业单据

商业单据主要是指描述商品品质或证明其状况的单据，包括发票、装箱单及其他需要出口商、船公司出具的函抄等。

1. 发票

发票(INVOICE)一般指商业发票(COMMERCIAL INVOICE)。商业发票(见示样 6-1、示样 6-2 和示样 6-3)是卖方在装运货物后开立的凭以向买方索取货款的价目清单和货物状况总说明。商业发票在全部单据中起核心作用，其他单据均须参照它来缮制，在内容上不得与发票的记载相矛盾。

示样 6-1　空白商业发票 1

<table>
<tr><td colspan="5" align="center">浙江省国兴进出口有限公司
ZHEJIANG ZITIC IMPORT & EXPORT CO.，LTD.
8F ZITIC BUILDING, NO. 519-521 YANAN ROAD, HANGZHOU, CHINA
TEL:　　　　　　　　　　　　　　　　FAX:</td></tr>
<tr><td colspan="5" align="center">COMMERCIAL INVOICE</td></tr>
<tr><td colspan="2" rowspan="4">TO:</td><td colspan="3">INVOICE NO.:</td></tr>
<tr><td colspan="3">INVOICE DATE:</td></tr>
<tr><td colspan="3">S/C NO.:</td></tr>
<tr><td colspan="3">S/C DATE:</td></tr>
<tr><td colspan="2">FROM:</td><td colspan="3">TO:</td></tr>
<tr><td colspan="2">LETTER OF CREDIT NO.:</td><td colspan="3">ISSUED BY:</td></tr>
<tr><td>MARKS & NUMBERS</td><td>NUMBER AND KIND OF PACKAGE; DESCRIPTION OF GOODS</td><td>QUANTITY</td><td>UNIT PRICE</td><td>AMOUNT</td></tr>
<tr><td></td><td></td><td></td><td></td><td></td></tr>
</table>

示样 6-2　空白商业发票 2

ISSUER:			商业发票 COMMERCIAL INVOICE		
TO:					
TRANSPORT DETAILS:			NO. :	DATE:	
			S/C NO. :	L/C NO. :	
			TERMS OF PAYMENT:		
MARKS & NUMBERS	NUMBER AND KIND OF PACKAGE; DESCRIPTION OF GOODS		QUANTITY	UNIT PRICE	AMOUNT
	TOTAL:				

示样 6-3　空白形式发票

浙江省国兴进出口有限公司

ZHEJIANG ZITIC IMPORT AND EXPORT CO., LTD.

ROOM 819, ZITIC BUILDING, NO. 519-521 YANAN ROAD, HANGZHOU 310006, P. R. CHINA

TEL: 0571-85069118　　FAX: 85069871

PROFORMA INVOICE

TO:		INVOICE NO.:	
		INVOICE DATE:	
		S/C NO.:	
		S/C DATE:	

TERM OF PAYMENT:	
PORT TO LOADING:	
PORT OF DESTINATION:	
TIME OF DELIVERY:	
INSURANCE:	
VALIDITY:	

MARKS AND NUMBERS	NUMBER AND KIND OF PACKAGE; DESCRIPTION OF GOODS	QUANTITY	UNIT PRICE	AMOUNT

SAY TOTAL:	
BENEFICIARY:	
ADVISING BANK:	
NEGOTIATING BANK:	

我国进出口商品报关与报检要求的发票一般采用商业发票即可。但是，世界上许多国家对进出口货物申报所需发票内容及形式的规定不尽相同。出口企业制单时，应按照进口地的实际需要，根据信用证或进口商的具体要求提供正确的发票种类及内容。例如：某些国外来证中规定提交"INVOICE"(发票)、"SHIPPING INVOICE"(装运发票)、"TRADE INVOICE"(贸易发票)，其内容一律可按商业发票掌握；如要求发票的形式为详细发票(DETAILED INVOICE)、证实发票(VERIFIED INVOICE)、收妥发票(RECEIPT INVOICE)、厂商发票(MANUFACTURERS INVOICE)、形式发票(PROFORMA INVOICE)、样品发票(SAMPLE INVOICE)、领事发票(CONSULAR INVOICE)、海关发票(CUSTOMS INVOICE)等，则发票的名称不能有误，并要符合其特定规范和要求。有些国家规定，如发票形式与内容不符合进口国海关的规定，进口货物将不能成功办理进口清关。

商业发票作为国际贸易中卖方必须向买方提供的主要单据，其作用主要表现在以下几个方面：①核对卖方履约情况是否符合合同规定。②买卖双方记账及核算的依据。③进出口报验，办理产地证、许可证、出口交单的必备与核心单据。④报关、交税的计算依据。发票中载明的价值和有关货物的说明是海关凭以核定税款的依据，也是出口地验关放行、进口地迅速清关提货的凭证之一。⑤在不用汇票结算的业务中，发票代替汇票作为付款的依据。⑥发票还可作为海关数字统计、保险索赔的价值证明，补充确定交易细节等的主要凭证。

2. 装箱单

装箱单(PACKING LIST)(见示样 6-4)用以表明包装货物的名称、规格、数量、唛头、箱号、件数、重量及包装情况，是商业发票的附属单据。它是进口地海关验货、公证行检验、进口商核对货物时的依据之一，用以了解包装件号在内的具体内容和包装情况。对于从我国出口的货物，装箱单是出口货物报关、商检和货款议付的必备单据之一。当信用证条款要求提供详细装箱单时，应提供尽可能详细的内容，描述每件包装的细节，包括商品的货号、色号、尺寸搭配、毛净重及包装的尺码等。不同商品有不同形式的装箱单，除标明"装箱单"(PACKING LIST)外，常用的还有：重量单(WEIGHT LIST)、尺码单(MEASUREMENT LIST)、包装说明(PACKING SPECIFICATION)、详细装箱单(DETAILED PACKING LIST)、包装提要(PACKING SUMMARY)、重量证书(WEIGHT CERTIFICATE)、磅码单(WEIGHT MEMO)、花色搭配单(ASSORTMENT LIST)等。

示样 6-4　空白装箱单/重量单

ISSUER:						
		装箱单/重量单 PACKING LIST/WEIGHT LIST				
TO:		INVOICE NO.:	DATE:			
MARKS & NUMBERS	NUMBER AND KIND OF PACKAGE; DESCRIPTION OF GOODS	QUANTITY	PACKAGE	G.W.	N.W.	MEAS.

3. 其他商业单据

(1) 装船通知(SHIPPING ADVICE)。出口商在货物装运之后，向进口商发出报告装货情况的通知。如采用 FOB 或 CFR 贸易条件成交，出口商必须先以电讯方式通知进口商，以便进口商及时办理保险手续。

(2) 受益人证明(BENEFICIARY'S CERTIFICATE)。在以信用证交易时，出口商根据信用证的要求，出具已经履行合同义务的证明。

(3) 电抄本(TELEX/CABLE/FAX COPY)。它用于证明出口商已经按进口商要求或其他有关要求发出有关电文。

(4) 船公司证明(SHIPPING COMPANY'S CERTIFICATE)。由船公司出具的用来证明船籍、船龄、航程等的单据。

(5) 船长收据(CAPTAIN'S RECEIPT)。进口商为了防止单据迟于货物到达或出于其他原因，要求出口商随船带交一套正本或副本单据或某种单证。出口商将单据交给船长后，船长出具收据，这就是船长收据。收据注明了收到的单据种类、份数，并声明单据将于到达目的港后径交指定人。

(6) 中性单据(NEUTRAL DOCUMENT)。进口商有时要求单据上不写出口商的名称。其目的是为了他可以通过让购单据售出货物，而不致把原始人暴露给他的买主。这种不写明出口商名称的单据叫中性单据。其实中性单据本身并不是一种单据，而只是把某种单据中性化了(NEUTRALIZED)。提单、保险单据、装箱单、商检证书等都可以做成中性单据。

(7) 装船证明——SHIPMENT CERTIFICATE(TEXTILE PRODUCTS)。装船证明适用于无配额的纺织品类，只做一般性的控制，在我国则由中华人民共和国商务部签发。

(二)运输单据

运输单据是证明货物载运情况的单据。当出口商将货物交给承运人办理装运时，承运人签发给出口商的证明文件，表明货物已发运或已装上运输工具或已接受监管。

1. 海运提单

海洋运输是最主要的运输方式，其运输单据可以签发海运提单(BILL OF LADING, B/L)或海运单据(SEAWAY BILL)。海运提单(见示样 6-5)是物权凭证(少数情况下例外)，而海运单据不是物权凭证。海运提单是由承运人或其代理人根据运输合同签发给托运人的，表明接受特定的货物或货物已装上船并将经海洋运至目的地交给收货人的收据和物权凭证。收货人在目的港提取货物时，必须提交正本提单。若运输货物在途中受到损失，海运提单也是货主向船公司或保险公司提出索赔的依据之一。

海运提单有许多不同的分类方法。例如，按照货物是否已装船，可分为已装船提单和备运提单；按照运输方式，可划分为直达提单、转船提单和联运提单；按照提单收货人抬头的不同，可分为记名提单、不记名提单和指示提单；按照提单有无承运人批注，可分为清洁提单和不清洁提单；按提单形式的完整性，可分为全式提单和简式提单；按提单到达收货人手中的时间，可分为一般提单、过期提单、倒签提单和预借提单；按使用船只的不同，可分为班轮提单和租船提单；按承运人身份的不同，可分为承运人提单和运输行提单；按在装运港是否付运费划分，可分为运费到付提单和运费已付提单。另外，提单还有集装箱提单(CONTAINER B/L)和舱面提单(ON DECK B/L)等。

示样 6-5　海运提单

1. SHIPPER INSERT NAME, ADDRESS AND PHONE	B/L NO.

中远集装箱运输有限公司
COSCO CONTAINER LINES
TLX: 33057 COSCO CN
FAX: +86(021) 6545 8984

ORIGINAL

2. CONSIGNEE INSERT NAME, ADDRESS AND PHONE	

3. NOTIFY PARTY INSERT NAME, ADDRESS AND PHONE (IT IS AGREED THAT NO RESPONSIBILITY SHALL ATTACH TO THE CARRIER OR HIS AGENTS FOR FAILURE TO NOTIFY.)	

PORT-TO-PORT OR COMBINED TRANSPORT BILL OF LADING RECEIVED IN EXTERNAL APPARENT GOOD ORDER AND CONDITION EXCEPT AS OTHER-WISE NOTED. THE TOTAL NUMBER OF PACKAGES OR UNITS STUFFED IN THE CONTAINER, THE DESCRIPTION OF THE GOODS AND THE WEIGHTS SHOWN IN THIS BILL OF LADING ARE FURNISHED BY THE MERCHANTS, AND WHICH THE CARRIER HAS NO REASONABLE MEANS OF CHECKING AND IS NOT A PART OF THIS BILL OF LADING CONTRACT. THE CARRIER HAS ISSUED THE NUMBER OF BILLS OF LADING STATED BELOW, ALL OF THIS TENOR AND DATE, ONE OF THE ORIGINAL BILLS OF LADING MUST BE SURRENDERED AND ENDORSED OR SIGNED AGAINST THE DELIVERY OF THE SHIPMENT AND WHEREUPON ANY OTHER ORIGINAL BILLS OF LADING SHALL BE VOID. THE MERCHANTS AGREE TO BE BOUND BY THE TERMS AND CONDITIONS OF THIS BILL OF LADING AS IF EACH HAD PERSONALLY SIGNED THIS BILL OF LADING. SEE CLAUSE 4 ON THE BACK OF THIS BILL OF LADING (TERMS CONTINUED ON THE BACK HEREOF, PLEASE READ CAREFULLY). *APPLICABLE ONLY WHEN DOCUMENT USED AS A COMBINED TRANSPORT BILL OF LADING.

4. COMBINED TRANSPORT *PRE-CARRIAGE BY	5. COMBINED TRANSPORT * PLACE OF RECEIPT

6. OCEAN VESSEL VOY. NO.	7. PORT OF LOADING

8. PORT OF DISCHARGE	9. COMBINED TRANSPORT * PLACE OF DELIVERY

MARKS & NUMBERS. CONTAINER / SEAL NO.	NO. OF CONTAINERS OR PACKAGES	DESCRIPTION OF GOODS (IF DANGEROUS GOODS, SEE CLAUSE 20)	GROSS WEIGHT KGS	MEASUREMENT CBM

10. TOTAL NUMBER OF CONTAINERS AND/OR PACKAGES (IN WORDS)

SUBJECT TO CLAUSE 7 LIMITATION

11. FREIGHT & CHARGES DECLARED VALUE CHARGE	REVENUE	RATE	PER	PREPAID	COLLECT

EX. RATE:	PREPAID AT	PAYABLE AT	DATE AND PLACE OF ISSUE
	TOTAL PREPAID	NO. OF ORIGINAL B(S)/L	SIGNED FOR THE CARRIER
DATE	BY		

2. 航空运单

航空运单(AIRWAY BILL，AWB)(见示样 6-6)是承运人与托运人之间签订的运输契约，也是承运人或其代理人签发的货物收据，还可作为核收运费的依据和海关查验放行的基本单据。航空运单不具有物权凭证的性质，不能转让，也不能做成指示性抬头。

3. 铁路运单

铁路运输可分为国际铁路联运和国内铁路运输，国内铁路运输签发的铁路运单(RAILWAY BILL)和国际铁路联运签发的多式联运单据在格式和内容上有所不同，但都只是运输契约的证明和货物收据，不是物权凭证，同航空运单一样，一律记名，不得转让。由于国内铁路运单不能作为对外结汇的凭证，我国出口港澳签发的是承运货物收据(CARGO RECEIPT)，它是物权凭证。

4. 公路运单

公路运单(ROADWAY BILL)是利用汽车运输时，由承运人或代理人签发的，作为收到货物的收据和运输合同的证明。汽车运输主要用于货物的集港和疏港运输、边境公路的过境运输等，具有灵活、简便、快捷、直达的特点，能深入偏远的地区，但运量有限，费用较高。

5. 邮包收据和快邮收据

邮包收据和快邮收据(POST/PARCEL RECEIPT AND COURIER RECEIPT)是货物采取邮包运输方式邮寄时，邮局或快递公司出具的货物收据或邮寄证明。邮包收据和快邮收据一律做成记名抬头，只能由指定收件人领取，它只是邮件收据和合同证明，不是物权凭证，不能转让。

6. 多式联运单据

多式联运是随集装箱运输的推广而发展起来的一种综合运输方式。签发多式联运单据(MULTIMODAL TRANSPORT DOCUMENT)的人叫联运经营人，他一般不掌握运输工具，一方面以承运人身份向货主揽货，另一方面又以托运人的身份向实际承运人托运。对托运人来说，他是总承运人，负责完成全程运输并负责赔偿货物在运输过程中发生的灭失和损坏。联合运输单据可以概括如下：①一张单据。即全程运输只要一份运输单据。②一人签发。即单据只需由多式联运经营人签发，而不需每个承运人签发。③一个多式联运航程。尽管使用几种运输工具，但只作为一个航程对待。④一人负责整个航程的完成。即联合运输经营人负责自收货地到交货地的运输。⑤一人负责灭失与损坏。即由联合运输经营人负责在运输过程中的灭失与损坏。

示样 6-6　航空运单

SHIPPER'S NAME AND ADDRESS	NOT NEGOTIABLE AIRWAY BILL
	ISSUED BY BEIJING KINTE WORLD EXPRESS CO., LTD.
CONSIGNEE'S NAME AND ADDRESS	IT IS AGREED THAT THE GOODS DESCRIBED HEREIN ARE ACCEPTED IN APPARENT GOOD ORDER AND CONDITION (EXCEPT AS NOTED) FOR CARRIAGE SUBJECT TO THE CONDITIONS OF CONTRACT ON THE REVERSE HEREOF, ALL GOODS MAY BE CARRIED BY ANY OTHER MEANS, INCLUDING ROAD OR ANY OTHER CARRIER UNLESS SPECIFIC CONTRARY INSTRUCTIONS ARE GIVEN HEREON BY THE SHIPPER. THE SHIPPER'S ATTENTION IS DRAWN TO THE NOTICE CONCERNING CARRIER'S LIMITATION OF LIABILITY. SHIPPER MAY INCREASE SUCH LIMITATION OF LIABILITY BY DECLARING A HIGHER VALUE OF CARRIAGE AND PAYING A SUPPLEMENTAL CHARGE IF REQUIRED.
ISSUING CARRIER'S AGENT NAME AND CITY	

AGENTS IATA CODE	ACCOUNT NO.	

AIRPORT OF DEPARTURE(ADDRESS OF FIRST CARRIER) AND REQUESTED ROUTING				ACCOUNTING INFORMATION				

TO	BY FIRST CARRIER	TO	BY	TO	BY	CURRENCY	DECLARED VALUE FOR CARRIAGE	DECLARED VALUE FOR CUSTOMS
AIRPORT OF DESTINATION			FLIGHT/ DATE	AMOUNT OF INSURANCE	INSURANCE—IF CARRIER OFFERS INSURANCE AND SUCH INSURANCE IS REQUESTED IN ACCORDANCE WITH THE CONDITIONS THEREOF, INDICATE AMOUNT TO BE INSURED IN FIGURES IN BOX MARKED "AMOUNT OF INSURANCE"			
PREPAID WEIGHT CHARGE COLLECT				OTHER CHARGES				
VALUATION CHARGE								
TAX								
TOTAL OTHER CHARGES DUE AGENT				SHIPPER CERTIFIES THAT THE PARTICULARS ON THE FACE HEREOF ARE CORRECT AND THAT INSOFAR AS ANY PART OF THE CONSIGNMENT CONTAINS DANGEROUS GOODS, SUCH PART IS PROPERLY DESCRIBED BY NAME AND IS IN PROPER CONDITION.				
TOTAL OTHER CHARGES DUE CARRIER								
TOTAL PREPAID				FOR CARRIAGE BY AIR ACCORDING TO THE APPLICABLE DANGEROUS GOODS REGULATIONS.				
				SIGNATURE OF SHIPPER OR HIS AGENT				
				EXECUTED ON____ AT_____ SIGNATURE OF ISSUING CARRIER OR AS AGENT				
CURRENCY CONVERSION RATES								
FOR CARRIER'S USE ONLY AT DESTINATION				TOTAL COLLECT CHARGES			AIRWAY BILL NUMBER	
HANDLING INFORMATION								

NO. OF PIECES	GROSS WEIGHT	RATE CLASS	CHARGEABLE WEIGHT	RATE/ CHARGE	TOTAL	NATURE AND QUANTITY OF GOODS

多式联运单据分为可转让的和不可转让的。前者像提单一样做成指示式，通过背书交付来完成转让手续；后者必须列明收货人，收货人不能转让单据。

(三)保险单据

国际贸易结算中经常涉及的保险单据主要有保险单(见示样 6-7)、保险凭证和联合凭证。

示样6-7 保险单

中国人民保险公司杭州市分公司

THE PEOPLE'S INSURANCE COMPANY OF CHINA

PICC

HANGZHOU BRANCH

总公司设于北京 一九四九年创立

HEAD OFFICE BEIJING ESTABLISHED IN 1949

货物运输保险单
CARGO TRANSPORTATION INSURANCE POLICY

发票号(INVOICE NO.):

合同号(CONTRACT NO.):   保单号次
                                                          POLICY NO.:

信用证号(L/C NO):

被保险人(INSURED):

中国人民保险公司(以下简称本公司)根据被保险人的要求，由被保险人向本公司缴付约定的保险费，按照本保险单承保险别和背面所载条款与下列特款承保下述货物运输保险，特立本保险单。

THIS POLICY OF INSURANCE WITNESSES THAT THE PEOPLE'S INSURANCE COMPANY OF CHINA (HEREINAFTER CALLED "THE COMPANY")AT THE REQUEST OF THE INSURED AND IN CONSIDERATION OF THE AGREED PREMIUM PAID TO THE COMPANY BY THE INSURED, UNDERTAKES TO INSURE THE UNDERMENTIONED GOODS IN TRANSPORTATION SUBJECT TO THE CONDITIONS OF THIS POLICY AS PER THE CLAUSES PRINTED OVERLEAF AND OTHER SPECIAL CLAUSES ATTACHED HEREON.

标 记 MARKS&NO.S	包装及数量 QUANTITY	保险货物项目 DESCRIPTION OF GOODS	保险金额 AMOUNT INSURED

总保险金额 TOTAL
AMOUNT INSURED:

保费：　　　　　　　　　启运日期　　　　　　　　　　装载运输工具：
PREMIUM: **AS ARRANGED** DATE OF COMMENCEMENT:　　　　　PER CONVEYANCE:

自　　　　　　　　　　　经　　　　　　　　　　　　　　至
FROM:　　　　　　　　　　VIA　　　　　　　　　　　　　TO

承保险别：
CONDITIONS:

所保货物，如发生保险单项下可能引起索赔的损失或损坏，应立即通知本公司下述代理人查勘。如有索赔，应向本公司提交保单正本(本保险单共有 份正本)及有关文件。如一份正本已用于索赔，其余正本自动失效。

　　IN THE EVENT OF LOSS OR DAMAGE WHICH MAY RESULT IN A CLAIM UNDER THIS POLICY, IMMEDIATE NOTICE MUST BE GIVEN TO THE COMPANY'S AGENT AS MENTIONED HEREUNDER. CLAIMS, IF ANY, ONE OF THE ORIGINAL POLICY WHICH HAS BEEN ISSUED IN TOGETHER WITH THE RELEVENT DOCUMENTS SHALL BE SURRENDERED TO THE COMPANY. IF ONE OF THE ORIGINAL POLICY HAS BEEN ACCOMPLISHED, THE OTHERS TO BE VOID.　　　　　　　　　　　　　　　　　　　　　　ORIGINAL(S)

中国人民保险公司杭州市分公司
THE PEOPLE'S INSURANCE COMPANY OF CHINA
HANGZHOU BRANCH
AUTHORIZED SIGNATURE

地址(ADD.) 中国杭州体育场路 27 号人保大厦 17-18 楼
ADD.:17-18, FLOORS PICC BUILDING, NO. 27, TIYUCHANG ROAD, HANGZHOU, CHINA　　电话(TEL): (0571)85284216
邮编(POST CODE): 310004　　传真(FAX): (0571)85284217

保险单(INSURANCE POLICY)俗称"大保单"，是保险人与被保险人之间建立保险契约关系的正式凭证，也是保险索赔与理赔的依据。保险单除具有基本内容之外，还附有保险契约的全部条款，对保险人和被保险人的权利义务做了详尽规定，是完整的承保形式保险凭证。

保险凭证(INSURANCE CERTIFICATE)是保险公司表示已接受保险的一种证明文件，是一种比较简单的保险单据，又称"小保单"。它只包括保险单据的基本内容，但不附有保险条款的全文，保险人和被保险人的权利义务以正式的条款为准。在效力方面，保险凭证与保险单是相同的。

信用证要求出具保险凭证而非保险单时，银行也可接受保险单。但是，信用证要求出具保险单时，银行不能接受保险凭证，因为它缺乏完整的独立性。联合凭证(RISK NOTE)，又叫联合发票，是一种比保险凭证更简单的单据。它只是在出口商的商业发票上加章注明承保的金额、险别及编号，而不单独出具保险单据。

(四)官方单据

有些国家的政府根据法令或需要对进出口货物所要求的必须缴验的单证统称为官方单据或政府单据。它主要包括进、出口许可证，海关发票，领事发票，产地证，黑名单证书及商品检验证书等。

1. 原产地证明书

原产地证明书(CERTIFICATE OF ORIGIN)，简称产地证，用于证明交易货物的生产地或制造地，并作为进口国给予出口国配额或优惠关税待遇的凭证。在交易双方商定以产地作为商品品质标准时，也是交货品质的证明。

产地证根据不同情况可以有不同的出具人。在买方信用证上未作具体要求时，银行可以接受任何机构签发的原产地证明书，包括由出口商自己签发的原产地证明书。有时，进口商为了保证产地证的客观性和证明效力，在信用证中规定，应由主管当局出具产地证。所谓主管当局是指政府授权的具有公证资格的机构。按国际商业习惯，商会和商品检验机构均被视为主管当局。

原产地证明书按照其不同的用途分为以下四类：①普遍优惠制原产地证明书(GENERALIZED SYSTEM OF PREFERENCES，GSP)，简称普惠制证明书、GSP证明书或FORM A证明书，用于证明某产品可以享受普惠制给惠国的普惠制关税待遇。普惠制关税待遇是发达国家对发展中国家向其出口的货物，尤其是制成品与半制成品，普遍给予的一种关税优惠待遇的制度，简称普惠制。②非优惠原产地证明书，又称一般原产地证明书或简称 C/O 证明书，主要用于证明某产品可以享受 WTO 最惠国关税待遇。③区域经济集团互惠原产地证明书，用于证明某产品可以享受区域贸易安排优惠关税待遇。例如：中国—东盟自贸区的原产地证明书属于区域经济集团互惠原产地证明书，专用于证明中国—东盟自贸区产品享受自贸区优惠关税待遇。④专用原产地证明书，用于某些国际组织或国家对烟草、纺织品等特定产品的规定。

1) 普惠制原产地证明书(FORM A)的申请

截至 2008 年，给予我国普惠制待遇的国家一共有 38 个，分别是欧盟 27 国(即法国、德国、意大利、荷兰、比利时、卢森堡、丹麦、爱尔兰、英国、希腊、西班牙、葡萄牙、奥地利、芬兰、瑞典、马耳他、塞浦路斯、波兰、匈牙利、捷克、斯洛伐克、斯洛文尼亚、爱沙尼亚、拉脱维亚、立陶宛、罗马尼亚和保加利亚)、土耳其、日本、挪威、新西兰、瑞士、澳大利亚、加拿大、俄罗斯、白俄罗斯、乌克兰和哈萨克斯坦。普惠制原产地证明书申请单位领证时需要提交如下资料：①《原产地证明书申请书》(见示样 6-8)一份。②《普惠制原产地证明书》(FORM A)(见示样 6-9)一套，要求英文缮制。③正式出口商业发票正本一份，如发票内容不全，另附装箱单。注意：发票和装箱单要盖章，内容不得涂改。④含有进口成分的产品，必须提交《产品成本明细单》(见示样 6-10)。⑤复出口日本的来料加工产品或进料加工产品需提交《从日本进口原料证明书》。⑥签证机构需要的其他单据。⑦签证费 40 元。

2) 一般原产地证明书(C/O)/加工装配证明书/转口证明书的办理

一般原产地证明书(见示样 6-11)在国际上通常是由各国商会等中介机构签发，我国由中国贸促会(CCPIT)/中国国际商会(CCOIC)和国家出入境检验检疫局(CCIQ)签发，其中，贸促会/国际商会属于民间机构性质，出入境检验检疫局属于官方机构性质。如信用证未对签发人做出规定，也可以由出口商自行签发。

示样 6-8　出入境检验检疫局原产地证明书申请书

原产地证明书申请书

申请单位及注册号码(盖章)：　　　　　　　　　　证书号：

申请人郑重声明：

本人是被正式授权代表单位申请办理原产地证明书和签署本申请书的。

本人所提供原产地证明书及所付单据内容正确无误，如发现弄虚作假，冒充证书所列货物，擅改证书，自愿接受签证机关的处罚及负法律责任。现将有关情况申报如下：

生产单位			生产单位联系人电话		
中文品名	H.S.编码	数(重)量	FOB 值(美元)		产品进口成分*
商业发票号			商品 FOB 总值(以美元计)		

贸易方式(请在相应的"□"内处打勾)

□一般贸易	□灵活贸易	□零售贸易	□展卖贸易	□其他贸易方式
中转国/地区		最终销售国	拟出口日期	

申请证书(单)类型：(请在相应的"□"内处打勾)

1.□《普惠制原产地证明书》

2.□《<亚太贸易协定>原产地证明书》

3.□《<中国—东盟自由贸易区>优惠原产地证明书》

4.□《<中国与巴基斯坦优惠贸易安排>优惠原产地证明书》

5.□《输欧盟农产品原产地证明书》(输欧盟蘑菇罐头原产地证明书)

6.□《烟草真实性证书》

7.□《中华人民共和国出口货物原产地证明书》

8.□《加工装配证明书》

9.□《转口证明书》

10.□《原产地异常调查结果单》

11.□其他原产地证明书(请列明

　　　　　　　　　　　　　　　　　　　　　　　　)

备注：	申报员(签名)：　　　　电话(手机)：
	日期：　　年　　月　　日

现提交出口商业发票副本一份，原产地证书一套，以及其他附件　　份，请予审核签证。

*注："产品进口成分"栏是指产品含进口成分的情况，如果该产品不含进口成分，则填 0%，若含进口成分，则此栏填进口成分占产品出厂价的百分比。

示样 6-9 普惠制原产地证明书(FORM A)

ORIGINAL

1. GOODS CONSIGNED FROM (EXPORTER'S BUSINESS NAME, ADDRESS, COUNTRY)	REFEREN CE NO. **GENERALIZED SYSTEM OF PREFERENCES** **CERTIFICATE OF ORIGIN** (COMBINED DECLARATION AND CERTIFICATE)
2. GOODS CONSIGNED TO (CONSIGNEE'S NAME, ADDRESS, COUNTRY)	**FORM A** ISSUED IN **THE PEOPLE'S REPUBLIC OF CHINA** (COUNTRY) SEE NOTES OVERLEAF
3. MEANS OF TRANSPORT AND ROUTE (AS FAR AS KNOWN)	4. FOR OFFICIAL USE

5. ITEM NUMBER	6. MARKS AND NUMBERS OF PACKAGES	7. NUMBER AND KIND OF PACKAGES; DESCRIPTION OF GOODS	8. ORIGIN CRITERION (SEE NOTES OVERLEAF)	9. GROSS WEIGHT OR OTHER QUANTITY	10. NUMBER AND DATE OF INVOICES

11. CERTIFICATION IT IS HEREBY CERTIFIED, ON THE BASIS OF CONTROL CARRIED OUT, THAT THE DECLARATION BY THE EXPORTER IS CORRECT.	12. DECLARATION BY THE EXPORTER THE UNDERSIGNED HEREBY DECLARES THAT THE ABOVE DETAILS AND STATEMENTS ARE CORRECT, THAT ALL THE GOODS WERE PRODUCED IN **CHINA** (COUNTRY) AND THAT THEY COMPLY WITH THE ORIGIN REQUIREMENTS SPECIFIED FOR THOSE GOODS IN THE GENERALIZED SYSTEM OF PREFERENCES FOR GOODS EXPORTED TO
------------------------------------ PLACE AND DATE, SIGNATURE AND STAMP OF CERTIFYING AUTHORITY	------------------------------------ PLACE AND DATE, SIGNATURE AND STAMP OF AUTHORIZED SIGNATORY

示样 6-10　产品成本明细单

产品成本明细单

(每张表填一种商品，附上原材料发票复印件)

申请单位注册编号：　　　　　　　　　填写人：　　　填写日期：　年　月　日

申请单位		联系人		联系电话		
生产企业		联系人		联系电话		
品名(中英文)						
产品型号		H.S.编码		产品计算单位	货币单位	

产品所用原辅料、零部件名称	H.S.编码(国产原料 H.S.编码免填)	原料原产地(进口的注明国别；国产的注明地区)	原料计算单位	原料单价	单位用料(每件或每公斤等单位产品所用原料)	原料价值(单价×单位用料)(人民币)	
						国产	进口
填不下请加附页							
原料价值合计(人民币)							
加工费		成本价(国产、进口原料价值+加工费)(人民币)					
成品出厂价(人民币)		进口及来源地不明的原料价值占成品出厂价的百分比					
加工工序							

注：三资企业的成品出厂价按合同上的出厂价填写；三来一补企业的成品出厂价等于原料价值+加工费。

例：夹克衫原辅料为面料、里料、松紧带、拉链和商标。面料的原料价值＝单价 50(元/米)×每件用料 1.3 米＝65 元

示样 6-11 一般原产地证明书

ORIGINAL

1. EXPORTER	CERTIFICATE NO.
2. CONSIGNEE	**CERTIFICATE OF ORIGIN OF** **THE PEOPLE'S REPUBLIC OF CHINA**
3. MEANS OF TRANSPORT AND ROUTE	5. FOR CERTIFYING AUTHORITY USE ONLY
4. COUNTRY / REGION OF DESTINATION	

6. MARKS AND NUMBERS	7. NUMBER AND KIND OF PACKAGES; DESCRIPTION OF GOODS	8. H.S. CODE	9. QUANTITY	10. NUMBER AND DATE OF INVOICES

11. DECLARATION BY THE EXPORTER THE UNDERSIGNED HEREBY DECLARES THAT THE ABOVE DETAILS AND STATEMENTS ARE CORRECT, THAT ALL THE GOODS WERE PRODUCED IN CHINA AND THAT THEY COMPLY WITH THE RULES OF ORIGIN OF THE PEOPLE'S REPUBLIC OF CHINA.	12. CERTIFICATION IT IS HEREBY CERTIFIED THAT THE DECLARATION BY THE EXPORTER IS CORRECT.
-- PLACE AND DATE, SIGNATURE AND STAMP OF AUTHORIZED SIGNATORY	-- PLACE AND DATE, SIGNATURE AND STAMP OF CERTIFYING AUTHORITY

对于一般原产地证明书，申请单位可以到当地的贸促会/国际商会或出入境检验检疫局办理。申领原产地证有两种方式：一是申领人员到贸促会或出入境检验检疫局专门办理原产地证的柜台办理，二是网上申领。依据《中华人民共和国出口货物原产地规则》及我国有关法律、法规，贸促会/国际商会除对外签发《中华人民共和国出口货物原产地证明书》外，还可以签发《加工装配证明书》和《转口证明书》。

如申领《一般原产地证明书》，则申请单位在领证时需要提交的资料如下：①《原产地证明书申请书》一份。如向出入境检验检疫局申领，填写出入境检验检疫局印制的申请书格式；如向贸促会申领，填写《中华人民共和国出口货物原产地证明书/加工装配证明书申请书》(见示样 6-12)。②《一般原产地证明书》(C/O)一套(一式四份)，要用英文缮制。③正式出口商业发票正本一份，如发票内容不全，另附装箱单。注意：发票和装箱单的内容不得手写和涂改，并应注明包装、数量、毛重或另附装箱单或重量单。实行产地证电子签证后，申请单位应一并提供企业端软件生成的发票。④含有进口成分的产品，必须提交《产品成本明细单》。⑤签证机构需要的其他单据，如信用证、合同、提单及报关单等。⑥一定的签证费用。

如申领《加工装配证明书》，则申请单位在领证时需要提交的资料如下：①《中华人民共和国出口货物原产地证明书/加工装配证明书申请书》一份；②出口商业发票一份；③《含进口成分产品加工工序成本明细单》；④缮制好的《加工装配证明书》一式四份。

如申领《转口证明书》，则申请单位在领证时需要提交的资料如下：①《转口证明书申请书》一份；②进口货物原产国的原产地证明书、进口发票、进口报关单或进口提单复印件；③出口合同、出口报关单和出口商业发票；④缮制好的《转口证明书》一式四份。

3) 区域经济集团互惠原产地证明书

区域经济集团互惠原产地证明书是具有法律效力的在协定成员国之间就特定产品享受互惠减免关税待遇的官方凭证。我国目前现有的区域经济集团互惠原产地证明书主要有：①《<亚太贸易协定>原产地证明书》(FORM B)；②《<中国—东盟自由贸易区>优惠原产地证明书》(FORM E)；③《<中国与巴基斯坦优惠贸易安排>优惠原产地证明书》；④ 香港原产地证明书、澳门原产地证明书等；⑤《中国—智利原产地证明书》(FORM F)。

示样 6-12　贸促会一般原产地证明书申请书

中华人民共和国出口货物
原产地证明书/加工装配证明书申请书

企业名称：　　　　　　　　　　　　证书号：

企业注册号：　　　　　　　　　　　审单号：

申请人郑重声明：

　　本人被正式授权代表本企业办理和签署本申请书。本申请书及《中华人民共和国出口货物原产地证明书/加工装配证明书》所列内容正确无误，如发现弄虚作假，冒充证书所列货物，擅改证书，本人愿按《中华人民共和国出口货物原产地规则》的有关规定接受处罚并承担法律责任，现将有关情况申报如下：

商品名称(中英文)			HS编码		
商品FOB总值(以美元计)			最终目的国/地区		
拟出运日期		发票号		转口国/地区	
贸易方式和企业性质(请在适用处划"√")					
一 般 贸 易		灵 活 贸 易		其 他 贸 易	
中资企业	外资企业	中资企业	外资企业	中资企业	外资企业
数量或重量：		是否含有进口成分：是(　) 否(　)			
证书种类(划"√")			一般原产地		加工装配证
该批货物实际生产企业					

现提交中国出口货物商业发票副本一份，《中华人民共和国出口货物原产地证明书/加工装配证明书》一正三副及其他附件　　份，请予审核签证。

申请单位盖章：

　　　　　　　　　　　　　　　　　申领人(签名)：

　　　　　　　　　　　　　　　　　电话：

　　　　　　　　　　　　　　　　　日期　　年　　月　　日

注：1. 灵活贸易包括：来料加工、补偿贸易、进料加工贸易。

　　2. 外资企业指所有含有外资的企业。

　　3. 其他贸易指一般贸易和灵活贸易以外的贸易，如展卖、易货、租凭等贸易方式。

退证原因：

(1) 《<亚太贸易协定>原产地证书》(FORM B)。《亚太贸易协定》的前身是《曼谷协定》。《曼谷协定》签订于 1975 年，是在联合国亚太经济社会委员会(简称亚太经社会)主持下，在发展中国家之间达成的一项优惠贸易安排，现有成员国为中国、孟加拉国、印度、老挝、韩国和斯里兰卡。2005 年 11 月 2 日，在北京举行的《曼谷协定》第一届部长级理事会上，各成员国代表通过新协定文本，决定将《曼谷协定》更名为《亚太贸易协定》，并在各成员国完成国内法律审批程序后，实施第三轮关税减让谈判结果，降税幅度从 5%到 100%不等。《曼谷协定》原产地标准如表 6-1 所示。

表 6-1 《曼谷协定》原产地标准

原产地标准	填入"原产地标准"栏的内容
(1)完全获得产品	"X"
(2)符合增值标准的产品	单一国家成分的百分比，例如 40%
(3)符合累计增值标准的产品	中国—东盟累计成分的百分比，例如 40%
(4)符合产品特定原产地标准的产品	"产品特定原产地标准"

可以签发《<亚太贸易协定>原产地证明书》的国家有韩国、斯里兰卡和印度，证书样本参见示样 6-13。享受关税减让优惠的货物必须符合以下条件：①属于《亚太贸易协定》进口成员国关税减让优惠产品清单的范围。②符合《亚太贸易协定》原产地规则。同批货物中的每项商品均要符合该规则。③符合《亚太贸易协定》原产地规则中的直接运输条款规定。一般情况下，货物必须按照第五条的规定从出口国直接运输到进口国。

(2) 《<中国—东盟自由贸易区>优惠原产地证明书》(FORM E)。自 2004 年 1 月 1 日起，凡出口到东盟的农产品(H.S.第 1～8 章)凭借检验检疫机构签发的《<中国—东盟自由贸易区>优惠原产地证明书》(见示样 6-14)可以享受关税优惠待遇。可以签发《<中国—东盟自由贸易区>优惠原产地证明书》的国家有 10 个：文莱、柬埔寨、印尼、老挝、马来西亚、缅甸、菲律宾、新加坡、泰国和越南。申请 FORM E 时需要提交的资料如下：①《原产地证明书申请书》一份。②缮制完毕的《<中国—东盟自由贸易区>优惠原产地证明书》一套。由一份正本及三份无碳副本组成，正本为米黄色，副本为浅绿色。证书的正本和第二副本应由出口人提供给进口人以供其在进口国通关时使用；第一副本应由出口的缔约方签证机构留底；第三副本由出口人留存。产品通关后，进口的缔约方海关在第二副本第四栏上批注并在合理的期限内将第二副本返还出口缔约方的签证机构。③正式出口商业发票正本一份，如发票内容不全，另附装箱单。注意：发票和装箱单要盖章，内容不得涂改。④含有进口成分的产品，必须提交《产品成本明细单》。⑤签证机构需要的其他单据。⑥签证费 40 元。

示样 6-13 <亚太贸易协定>原产地证明书

Asia-Pacific Trade Agreement

(Combined declaration and certificate)

1.Goods consigned from: (Exporter's business name, address, country)	Reference No. Issued in .... (Country)
2. Goods consigned to: (Consignee's name, address, country)	3. For Official use
4. Means of transport and route:	

5. Tariff item number	6. Marks and number of packages	7. Number and kind of packages/description of goods	8. Origin criterion (see notes overleaf)	9. Gross weight or other quantity	10. Number and date of invoices

11. Declaration by the exporter :	12. Certificate
The undersigned hereby declares that the above details and statements are correct: that all the goods were produced in .... (Country) and that they comply with the origin requirements specified for these goods in the Asia-Pacific Trade Agreement for goods exported to .... (Importing Country) .... Place and date, signature of	It is hereby certified on the basis of control carried out, that the declaration by the exporter is correct. .... Place and date, signature and Stamp of Certifying Authority

示样6-14　FORM E

1. GOODS CONSIGNED FROM (EXPORTER'S NAME, ADDRESS, COUNTRY)			REFERENCE NO.		
			ASEAN-CHINA FREE TRADE AREA PREFERENTIAL TARIFF		
			CERTIFICATE OF ORIGIN		
2. GOODS CONSIGNED TO (CONSIGNEE'S NAME, ADDRESS, COUNTRY)			(COMBINED DECLARATION AND CERTIFICATE)		
			FORM E		
			ISSUED IN THE PEOPLE'S REPUBLIC OF CHINA		
			(COUNTRY)		
3. MEANS OF TRANSPORT AND ROUTE (AS FAR AS KNOWN)			4. FOR OFFCIAL USE		
5. ITEM NUMBER	6. MARKS AND NUMBERS OF PACKAGES	7. NUMBER AND TYPE OF PACKAGES; DESCRIPTION OF GOODS(INCLUDING QUANTITY WHERE APPROPRIATE AND HS NUMBER OF THE IMPORTING COUNTRY)	8. ORIGIN CRITERION (SEE NOTES OVERLEAF)	9. GROSS WEIGHT OR OTHER QUANTITY AND VALUE(FOB)	10. NUMBER AND DATE OF INVOICES
11. DECLARATION BY THE EXPORTER THE UNDERSIGNED HEREBY DECLARES THAT THE ABOVE DETAILS AND STATEMENT ARE CORRECT, THAT ALL THE GOODS WERE PRODUCED IN _____(COUNTRY) AND THAT THEY COMPLY WITH THE ORIGIN REQUIREMENT SPECIFIED FOR THESE GOODS IN THE ASEAN-CHINA FREE TRADE AREA PREFERENTIAL TARIFF FOR THE GOODS EXPORTED TO _____(IMPORTING COUNTRY) _____ PLACE AND DATE, SIGNATURE OF AUTHORISED SIGNATORY			12. CERTIFICATION IT IS HEREBY CERTIFIED ON THE BASIS OF CONTROL CARRIED OUT, THAT THE DECLARATION BY THE EXPORTER IS CORRECT. _____ PLACE AND DATE, SIGNATURE OF AUTHORISED SIGNATORY		

(3) 《<中国与巴基斯坦优惠贸易安排>优惠原产地证明书》。《<中国与巴基斯坦优惠贸易安排>优惠原产地证明书》暂时使用普惠制原产地证明书(FORM A)，除第 8 栏外，其余各栏填法与 FORM A 相同。

(4) 香港原产地证明书和澳门原产地证明书。根据《内地与香港关于建立更紧密经贸关系的安排》和《内地与澳门关于建立更紧密经贸关系的安排》，就实行零关税的原产香港、澳门的货物向内地出口前，应由出口人或生产企业按规定向香港、澳门经济局申领原产地证明书。

(5) 《中国—智利原产地证明书》(FORM F)。2006 年 10 月，我国与拉美国家签署的第一个自由贸易协定——《中国—智利自由贸易协定》正式实施。智利对原产于我国的 5 891 种产品，以及中国对原产于智利的 2 806 种产品的关税同时降为零。进口商凭一份《中国—智利原产地证明书》，就可享受智利进口关税减免。

4) 专用原产地证明书

专用原产地证明书是国际组织和国家根据政策和贸易措施的特殊需要，针对某一特殊行业的特定产品规定的原产地证明书，例如：

(1) 协定国家纺织品(配额)产地证明书。对于协定国家出口纺织品，许多产品需要办理(配额)产地证明书。如对欧盟出口某些纺织品，需要同时办理输欧纺织品原产地证明书(CERTIFICATE OF ORIGIN TEXTILE PRODUCT)和纺织品出口许可证(EXPORT LICENSE FOR TEXTILES PRODUCT)，两证是进口国海关控制配额的依据。在我国，纺织品产地证和出口许可证由地方外经贸委(厅)颁发。GSP 产地证是取得关税优惠，而纺织品产地证是取得配额证明。

(2) 对美国出口的商品原产地声明书。凡属对美国出口的配额商品，如纺织品等，应由出口商填写原产地声明书，其有三种格式。①格式 A：单一国家声明书(SINGLE COUNTRY DECLARATION)，声明商品产地只有一个国家。②格式 B：多国家产地声明书(MULTIPLE COUNTRY DECLARATION)，声明商品的原材料是由两个或两个以上国家生产的。③格式 C：非多种纤维纺织品声明书，亦称否定声明书(NEGATIVE DECLARATION)，凡纺织品的主要价值或主要重量属于麻或丝的原料或含羊毛量不超过 17%，则可填用此格式，以说明该类商品为非配额产品。

(3) 金伯利进程国际证书。2003 年 1 月 1 日起在中华人民共和国实施《金伯利进程国际证书制度》，将金伯利进程毛坯钻石国际证书制度规定的毛坯钻石列入我国《实施检验检疫的进出境商品目录》，归类在 H.S.编码 7102.10、7102.21、7102.31 项下的毛坯钻石，属于《中华人民共和国货物进出口管理条例》中限制进出口的货物，其进出口仅限于"金伯利进程"成员国之间进行，以履行我国的国际义务，制止"冲突钻石"非法交易，维护非洲地区的和平与稳定。

《金伯利进程国际证书制度》的39个成员国为(含1个区域性经济集团)：安哥拉、澳大利亚、博茨瓦纳、巴西、布基纳法索、加拿大、科特迪瓦、中非共和国、中国、刚果民主共和国、欧洲共同体、加蓬、加纳、几内亚、印度、以色列、韩国、莱索托、毛里求斯、墨西哥、纳米比亚、挪威、菲律宾、俄罗斯联邦、塞拉里昂、南非、斯威士兰、瑞士、坦桑尼亚、泰国、乌克兰、阿拉伯联合酋长国、美国、津巴布韦、塞浦路斯、日本、马耳他、斯里兰卡和越南。

其他专用产地证明书种类有：手工制品原产地证，证明货物的加工和制造是全人工的而非机械生产的一种证明；濒危动植物原产地证，证明加工成货物的动物或植物来自饲养的而非野生的濒危动植物(或在数量限制以内)；输往欧盟蘑菇罐头原产地证明书和烟草真实性证明书等。

5) 南非原产地声明——格式DA59

据南非海关与关税委员会订立的《海关与关税规则》规定：自1994年11月1日后运往南非的附表2项下的货物必须出具"南非原产地声明——格式DA59(DECLARATION OF ORIGIN FORM DA59)"。中国贸促会作为国际上承认的商会，接受南非中国问题研究中心的委托，代其向需要出具此种产地证的公司发放DA59格式的产地证，并对该产地证进行认证。需要办理"南非原产地声明——格式DA59"的产品范围为H.S.编码下的下列产品：480920，481620，551311，551321，551331，551341，610711，610821，610910，630260，700529，820110，820120，820130，845121，848220，848250，9401，9403，2823，291529，291550，292429和320610。

2. 商品检验证书

检验证书(INSPECTION CERTIFICATE)是各种进出口商品检验证书、鉴定证书和其他证明书的统称。检验证书一般由国家指定的检验机构出具，也可根据不同情况，由出口企业或生产企业自行出具。检验证书的出具必须注意以下事项：①出证机构检验的货物名称和检验项目必须符合信用证的规定。②注意检验证书的有效期，一般货物为60天，新鲜果蔬类为2~3个星期。货物务必在有效期内出运，如超过期限，应重新报验。

在国际贸易中，检验证书是有关各方履行契约义务、处理争议，索赔和仲裁、诉讼举证的有效证件，也是海关验放、征收关税和优惠减免关税的必要证明，具有重要的法律地位。目前我国检验检疫机构签发的检验证书种类主要有品质检验证书、重量或数量检验证书、包装检验证书、兽医检验证书、卫生/健康证书、消毒检验证书、熏蒸证书、残损检验证书、温度检验证书、船舱检验证书、货载衡量检验证书、价值证明书、生丝品级及公量检验证书、舱口检视证书、监视装/卸载证书、舱口封识证书、油温空距证书、集装箱监装/拆证书、集装箱租箱交货检验证书、租船交船剩水/油重量鉴定证书等。

上述各种检验证书,尽管类别不一,但作用是基本相同的,主要表现在下列几个方面:①作为证明卖方所交货物的品质、重量(数量)、包装以及卫生条件等是否符合合同规定的依据;②作为买方对品质、重量、包装等条件提出异议,拒收货物、要求索赔、解决争议的凭证;③作为卖方向银行议付货款的单据之一;④作为海关验关放行的凭证。

3.黑名单证明

黑名单证明(BLACKLIST CERTIFICATE)(见示样 6-15)是一个国家与其他国家政治关系恶化、紧张,或某国处于战争状态时,要求对一些事项进行的证明,例如:①货物产地不属于某特定国家;②有关各方(制造商、银行、保险公司、船公司等)不属于黑名单之列,例如船公司黑名单;③装货船只或飞机不停靠此类国家港口,悬挂此类国家的旗帜。但是,许多国家的有关机构特别是商会抵制提供此项证书。

示样6-15　BLACKLIST CERTIFICATE

FRANK MIDDLE INTERNATIONAL TRADE CORP. 00/00 CAMOMILE STREET
LONDON EC8A 9HB

TO WHOM IT MAY CONCERN

THE S.S. NURMAHAL IS NOT SCHEDULED OR INTENDED TO CALL AT ANY ISRAELI PORTS WHILE ON HER PRESENT VOYAGE. WE ARE ADVISED BY HER OWNERS THAT THIS VESSEL IS NOT ISRAELI OWNED. TO THE BEST FOR OUR KNOWLEDGE AND BELIEF THIS VESSEL IS NOT INCLUDED IN THE ARABIAN BOYCOTT OF ISRAEL BLACKLIST.

FOR FRANK MIDDLE INTERNATIONAL TRADE CORP.
LOADING BROKERS.
(SIGNATURE)

4.进口许可证

进口许可证(IMPORT LICENSE)是国家有关当局批准的商品可以进口的证明文件。国家对某些商品禁止进口或控制进口时,常规定没有进口许可证不得进口。其内容包括证号、进口商品的国别,货物的名称、数量、金额及有效期限等。其作用一是限制某种商品的进口,以保护民族经济;二是作为海关入境的凭证;三是进口国银行开立信用证的依据。

5.出口许可证

出口许可证(EXPORT LICENSE)是国家对实行出口许可证管理的商品批准其出口的法律文件,是海关监管验放出口货物的依据。凡实行出口许可证管理的商品(规定免领的除外),各类出口企业应在商品出口前按规定在指定的发证机关申领出口许可证,海关凭出口许可证接受申报。所谓配额许可证管理即实行配额与许可证配合使用,出口企业在取得配额后再申请出口许可证(如输美纺织品许可证)。根据我国《对外贸易法》的规定，我国出口许可证管理实行非自动出口许可证与自动出口许可证分类管理办法。

第二节　UCP600 关于单据的有关规定

UCP600 第 5 条规定：银行处理的是单据，而不是单据可能涉及的货物、服务或履约行为。由于单据比较繁杂，信用证纠纷大都与单据有关。在具体介绍单据制作与审核单据的技术之前，有必要先对 UCP600 的相关规定进行确切的了解，以作为确定制单与审单标准的基本参照。

一、关于条件单据化的规定

信用证付款的条件是提交与信用证规定相符的单据。因此，信用证要注明必须提交的单据种类。这条原则是赋予开证申请人和开证行的义务。一是要求其开证指示和信用证指示(包括修改)应完整明确，明确规定需提交的单据种类或名称以及根据需要注明单据的份数。二是要求条件单据化。按照 UCP600 第 14 条 h 款："如果信用证含有一项条件，但未规定用以表明该条件得到满足的单据，银行将视为未作规定并不予理会。"例如，如果在信用证中有"受益人必须在装船后两天内将装船细节电告开证申请人"字样，则信用证中应明确要求受益人提交通知装船细节的电传副本，作为受益人已履约的条件之一。

按照 UCP600 第 14 条 g 款："提交的非信用证所要求的单据将不予理会，并可被退回给交单人。"因此表明银行仅与信用证中规定的单据有关系，没有责任去审核受益人交来的额外单据。

二、关于单据签发人的规定

UCP600 第 3 条规定："用诸如'第一流的'、'著名的'、'合格的'、'独立的'、'正式的'、'有资格的'等词语描述信用证项下单据的出单人时，允许除受益人之外的任何人出具该单据。"规定这条原则的目的是因为在信用证业务中，银行对单据的审核只能从单据表面确认是否与信用证条件相符，而不能由其凭主观想象来判断与条件是否一致。因此，"第一流的"、"著名的"、"合格的"、"独立的"等这类限定词语出现在信用证条款中时，银行可不予考虑。

三、关于单据正、副本与签字的规定

(一)关于单据正、副本的规定

关于单据"正本"的概念，UCP600 第 17 条的 a、b、c 款规定："a. 信用证规定的每一种单据须至少提交一份正本。b. 银行应将任何带有看似出单人的原始签名、标记、印戳或标签的单据视为正本单据，除非单据本身表明其非正本。c. 除非单据本身另有说明，在以下情况下，银行也将其视为正本单据：I. 单据看似由出单人手写、打字、穿孔或盖章；II. 单据看似使用出单人的原始信纸出具；III. 单据申明其为正本单据，除非该声明看似不适用于提交的单据。"

关于单据"副本"的概念，UCP600 第 17 条的 d 款规定："如果信用证要求提交单据的副本，提交正本或副本均可。"

单据正副本与单据份数的表述也有关。UCP600 第 17 条的 e 款明确指出："如果信用证使用诸如'一式两份'(in duplicate)、'两份'(in two fold)、'两套'(in two copies) 等用语要求提交多份单据，则提交至少一份正本，其余份数可以副本来满足，除非单据本身另有说明。"这里的"单据本身另有说明"是指像提单那样已注明正本签发份数的单据。也就是说，如果单据上注明了正本份数为"3"，就必须提交全套正本单据，而不能只交一份正本而其余两份以副本替代。

(二)关于单据签字的规定

单据上的签字主要有两个作用：一是作为区别真伪的手段，二是明确出单人的责任。至于签字的方式，UCP600 第 3 条规定："单据签字可用手签、摹样签字、穿孔签字、印戳、符号或任何机械或电子的证实方式为之。诸如单据须履行法定手续、签证、证明等类似要求，可由单据上任何看似满足该要求的签字、标记、印戳或标签来满足。"而 UCP600 第 18 条 a (iv)款规定："商业发票无须签名。"

四、关于单据出单日的规定

一般来说，所有的单据都应有出单日期。按照信用证的特点，交运货物、取得代表物权或证明货物已发运时都必须缮制与之有关的单据。因此，一般情况下，受益人所提交单据的签发日期要比信用证的开证日期晚。但是，国际贸易方式较多，转售、三角贸易也是常见的，在这种情况下，往往会出现信用证开立之前，运输单据、产地证、检验证等有关单据已签发的可能。因此，关于单据的出单日，UCP600 规定："除非信用证另有规定，银行将接受出单日期早于信用证日期的单据，但该单据必须在信用证和本惯例规定的期限内

提交。"根据这一规定,接受出单日早于信用证开证日期的单据的条件是单据必须在信用证的有效期内提交,并且不得晚于信用证规定的装运期后必须交单的特定期限。如果信用证未规定交单的特定期限,则单据的提交不得超过装运日后 21 天。

五、关于交单日及交单方法的规定

UCP600 第 6 条的 d 款、第 29 条的 a 款规定:"信用证必须规定一个交单的截止日。规定的承付或议付的截止日期将被视为交单的截止日;可在其处兑用信用证的银行所在地即为交单地点。可在任一银行兑用的信用证其交单地点为任一银行所在地。除规定的交单地点外,开证行所在地也是交单地点。受益人或者代表受益人的交单应在截止日当天或之前完成,除非信用证的截止日或最迟交单日适逢接受交单的银行非因 UCP600 第 36 条所述原因而歇业,则截止日或最迟交单日视何者使用,将顺延至其重新开业的第一个银行工作日。如果在顺延后的第一个银行工作日交单,指定银行必须在其致开证行或保兑行的面函中声明交单是在根据第 29 条 a 款顺延的期限内提交的。"

UCP600 第 36 条的规定为"不可抗力"条款:"银行对由于天灾、暴动、骚乱、叛乱、战争、恐怖主义行为或任何罢工、停工或其无法控制的任何其他原因导致的营业中断的后果,概不负责。当银行恢复营业时,对于在营业中断期间已逾期的信用证,不再进行承付或议付。"另外,UCP600 第 33 条规定:"银行在其营业时间外无接受交单的义务。"

第三节 单 据 制 作

一、商业发票的制作

1. 商业发票的具体内容

国际上对商业发票的内容与格式并没有统一的规定。通常而言,商业发票的内容可以分为首文(HEADING)、本文(BODY)和结文(COMPLEMENTARY CLAUSE)三个部分。

首文部分有发票名称、发票开立人的名称与地址、发票号码、合同号码、发票开立的地点与日期、装运货物的船名、装运港、卸货港、收货人的名称、信用证号码等。

本文部分包括运输标志(SHIPPING MARK)、货物的描述及数量、规格、包装、单价、总金额、毛重与净重以及价格条件等。

结文部分的内容主要是开立人的签字与盖章。UCP600 第 18 条规定:"商业发票必须看似由受益人出具;必须出具成以申请人为抬头,但在被转让信用证中可用第一受益人的名称替换原证中的开证申请人名称。"

2．商业发票的具体制作

1)　发票名称

在采用信用证付款方式时，如信用证要求递交"发票"(INVOICE)，但对发票种类未做进一步定义，则提交的任何形式的发票都可以接受，如商业发票(COMMERCIAL INVOICE)、海关发票(CUSTOMS INVOICE)、税务发票(TAX INVOICE)、签证发票(CERTIFIED INVOICE)、领事发票(CONSULAR INVOICE)等。但是，出口商递交"临时发票"、"预开发票"或类似的发票是不可接受的，除非信用证另有授权。当信用证要求提交商业发票时，标为"发票"的单据可以接受，但最好是递交商业发票。

2)　出单人

发票顶端应有醒目的出单人名址，包括联系电话、电传、电挂、传真(见示样 6-1)。出单人一般为信用证的受益人(出口商)，他们往往采用自己设计的发票或函头(HEADING)形式。出单人在发票上还可用"ISSUER"、"SHIPPER"、"SELLER"、"SHIPPED BY"等类似名称来表示。在采用非信用证结算时，出单人填出口商(卖方)；采用信用证结算时，一般填受益人；在被转让信用证项下，以第二受益人作为出单人。

值得注意的是，按照 UCP600 第 14 条"单据审核标准"的规定，当信用证受益人和申请人的地址出现在任何规定的单据中时，无须与信用证或其他规定单据中所载相同，但必须与信用证中规定的相应地址同在一国。联络细节(传真、电话、电子邮件及类似细节)作为受益人和申请人地址的一部分时将被不予理会。但是，如果申请人的地址和联络细节为运输单据上的收货人或通知方细节的一部分时，应与信用证规定的相同。

3)　抬头人

(1)　发票抬头人前通常印有"TO"、"SOLD TO MESSRS"、"FOR ACCOUNT AND RISK OF MESSRS"、"CONSIGNED TO"等。实际业务中，此处一般填写买卖合同中的买方的名称与地址。

(2)　大多数信用证对发票抬头都不作说明，只有少数信用证在发票条款中指定抬头人。若信用证无具体规定，发票抬头人应填开证申请人或收货人的名址，但不同于提单收货人。

(3)　若信用证中有指定抬头人，则按来证制单。若信用证规定以第三方为发票抬头人，如"ALL DOCUMENTS INCLUDING INVOICES MUST BE IN THE NAME OF DEEP 2ST.S.D P. O. BOX 101 LAS PALMAS CANARY ISLANDS"，则应照打该指定抬头人"DEEP 2ST.S.D P. O. BOX 101 LAS PALMAS CANARY ISLANDS"，这表明该证的开证申请人仅为中间商，并非真实买主。

(4)　如银行代替某公司申请开证(转开信用证)，例如信用证规定开证申请人为"THE

BANK OF TOKYO LTD., TOKYO A/C ESG CO. LTD., TOKYO"，则发票抬头应打"ESG CO. LTD.，TOKYO"。若开证申请人栏只有银行名称而无公司名称，如"THE BANK OF TOKYO LTD.，TOKYO"，则只能以该银行为抬头人。

(5) 开证申请人若是两个公司，如"APPLICANT: ABC CO. FOR ACCOUNT OF EFG CO. LTD."，这说明前一公司是中间商，后一公司为实际买方，此时发票抬头应将两公司名称照打。

(6) 信用证规定"AT REQUEST OF XXX BANK"，同时规定"BY ORDER OF ABC CO. LTD. FOR ACCOUNT OF EFG CO. LTD."，则不打银行，只打"ABC CO. LTD. FOR ACCOUNT OF EFG CO. LTD."。

(7) 有时信用证特别规定了收货人名称，则发票应以该收货人为抬头人。如信用证规定："APPLICANT: AHM CO. LTD., PARIS; INVOICE TO BE MADE OUT IN THE NAME OF KS CO. LTD., PARIS"，则发票抬头应打后者"KS CO. LTD., PARIS"。如信用证规定开证申请人为"KS CO. LTD., NEW YORK"，但又规定发票抬头注明"KS CO. LTD., NEW YORK ON BEHALF OF ID CO. LTD., NEW YORK"，则发票抬头应全部照打。

4) 出票地址和日期

出票地址(PLACE)为出口商所在地；如采用信用证结算，则为受益人所在地，通常也是议付行所在地。出票日期，即发票签发日期(DATE)不宜过早，一般不应晚于提单日期，但对背信用证或可转让信用证除外。如果发票日期晚于提单日期，则其一定不能晚于议付日和汇票日。

5) 发票编号

发票编号(INVOICE NO.)是出单人开出发票的顺序号，一般按出口报关单号码编制，便于查对。在我国一些地区为使结汇不致混乱，通常使用银行编制的统一编号。在中国银行办理出口业务的公司，信用证项下使用 BP 号，托收项下使用 OC 号。每年年底，中国银行将发给各出口公司下一年度的业务编号。

6) 合同号与信用证号

合同是一笔业务的基础，内容比较完善的发票应包括合同号(CONTRACT NO.)，如同一发票内显示几个合同的货物，则这几个合同号都应注明，特别是在采用非信用证结算的情况下。如果采用信用证结算，信用证是出具发票的依据，因此发票中应注明信用证号码(L/C NO.)。如果信用证无特殊规定或没有开证行的授权，两个或两个以上信用证项下货物不能合并在同一份发票反映，所以一份发票内只能注明一个信用证号。但如系转让或转开信用证，则中转的编号亦可加注。

如果信用证中没有规定合同号，合同号可以不在发票上注明。如果信用证上有合同号，则合同号应严格按信用证规定(如"THIS L/C IS OPENED AS PER CONTRACT NO. XXX")

填制。

7) 起讫地点(FROM... TO...)、运输方式及运输工具

可参照提单填制。有些发票省略了该栏目。

8) 唛头

唛头(SHIPPING MARK)一般填在"SHIPPING MARKS & NUMBERS"的下方。有些发票没有规定唛头栏，则其通常置于发票中心内容的左上方。如果唛头过多，应加附页。在发票该栏处加注"SEE ATTACHED SHEET"或"AS PER ATTACHED SHEET"，以提示有附页，同时在附页上注明发票号，亦可将附页贴在发票上并加骑缝章。如采用信用证结算，但其对唛头有特别的规定，则应按信用证内容填制。如果信用证规定有两个或两个以上的唛头，制单时可将其组合成一个唛头，以少占位置或简化手续。组合时可以用加斜线、加逗号或错行的办法来完成。以同样的办法，亦可将一个大唛头分成几个小唛头。例如：

MARKS：STYLE NO. 095

STYLE NO. 097

可写成：STYLE NO. 095/097   或 STYLE NO. 095，097   或 STYLE NO. 095

097

如果混唛过多，可直接在单据上注明"MIXED DESCRIPTION"(混唛)，而不注唛头。

9) 包装种类、件数及货物描述

包装种类、件数及货物(NUMBER AND KIND OF PACKAGES; DESCRIPTION OF GOODS)的描述应与信用证中的描述一致。

填写货物名称时应注意：如果证中列明的货物较多，又冠有统称，制单时在具体品名上面应照来证打统称；如果来证规定多种货名，如"STONEWARE/PORCELAIN WARE"，制单应根据实际发货情况标注，不能盲目照抄；如果证中关于货物的描述使用了法文或德文等多种语种，制单时应照打，必要时后面可加括号用英文注释；信用证没有规定的内容，发票上应尽量少作说明。如果信用证没有规定详细品质与规格，必要时可按合同加注一些说明，但不能与信用证内容相抵触，以防国外银行故意挑剔或拒付；如信用证中规定了商品的品质机动幅度，如出口鱼粉，规定"PROTEIN：55-65%"，则发票应按此规定范围注明蛋白质含量。若此范围是对卖方装运货物的标准限度，如出口煤炭，发热量可规定为每公斤6800大卡以上，而实际出口货物可能为每公斤7000大卡以上，此时应按检验证书的实际检测结果在发票上如实反映；如信用证在货名之后注有"AS PER CONTRACT NO. XXX"，"AS PER ORDER NO. XXX"，"AS PER PROFORMA INVOICE NO. XXX"，"AS PER SAMPLE"等有关发货依据的字样，发票中应照抄或有所体现，如"ALL OTHER DETAILS AS PER CONTRACT NO. XXX"。

填写包装件数时应注意：包装与重量说明不是发票的主要内容。凡经包装装运的货物

如没有装箱单或重量单，则发票上最好有包装件数条款，如"100 SETS"和"500 MTS"等。该内容应按实际装运情况和信用证有关规定填写，并注明包装件数的合计数。如有两种以上包装单位，发票应全部给予注明，并以"PACKAGE"为单位注明合计数；如果以托盘装运，发票应注明包装数量及托盘数量，两者缺一不可；如果交易货物为散装货，可注明"IN BULK"字样，但不注亦可；如采用"坚固木箱装"不应只打"木箱装"；"适合海运的纸箱装"不应只打"纸箱装"；凡是以重量计量或计价的，都应详细注明毛、净重；若有装箱单或重量单，发票上可不再反映包装件数和重量，如要反映，注明包装件数及总重量即可。

10) 数量

数量(QUANTITY)内容的填制包括实际装运数量和计量单位，其中计量单位必须与价格条款计量单位一致。填制时应注意：发票中数量的填制一定要能反映货物的实际装运数量。有时，因受客观条件的制约，如装船时因舱容不够或集装箱容量有限而少装一部分货物或为充分占用空间或舱位而适当增加货量均可造成实际发运量与预计发运量的出入。制单时务必注意单货一致；当货物有不同的品种或类别时，应注明每一品种类别的货量；对按公量计价的货物，应排除不符合标准的成分，算出和表明标准重量；对按重量计价的货物，如合同规定了水分含量等指标，货物的计价重量应以此为标准进行调整，并在发票上一一予以说明。如出口煤炭 300 吨，合同规定的水分含量标准为 10%，实际含量为 11%，发票上可说明"TOTAL SHIPPING WEIGHT: 300M/T，INSPECTED ACTUAL MOISTURE: 11%，OVER 1% DEDUCTED: 3M/T，CALCULATED WEIGHT: 297M/T"。有时根据信用证规定或实际业务需要，一批货物可分制几套单据，每套单据可缮制一份或多份发票，发票的货量总和应等于该批货物的总货量；制单时应根据信用证的要求把握好货量的伸缩幅度。如信用证允许分批，又规定一定的增减幅度，则每批货物按相同的增减幅度掌握；如货量允许一定的增减幅度，所发货物又包含有不同的品种，则每个品种应按相同的增减幅度掌握。当证中未明确规定数量增减幅度时，货物的增减幅度情况可为：以"把"、"打"、"套"、"件"、"桶"等计数的货物不能增减数量；以重量(如公吨)计数的货物，可增减数量的 5%；数量前后加"ABOUT"的货物，可增减数量的 10%。

11) 价格

价格是发票的关键内容，包括单价(UNIT PRICE)与金额(AMOUNT)两个栏目。单价包括计价货币、计价单位、单位数额和价格术语四个部分，如"USD34.50 PER PC CIF LONDON"。目前大多数信用证对单价的表示分散且不规范，或根本没有规定，制单时一定要注意，防止遗漏，要与信用证或合同保持一致。商业发票上的计价货币必须与信用证的货币相同；计价单位一般应与货物的计量单位保持一致，若遇不一致的情形，如石油以公吨计数，但按桶计价，则应先将货量折算成与计价单位相同的货量来表示，再乘以单价，得出总值；价格术语一般在总值栏内单独列出，它是发票最为重要的项目之一，直接关系到交易双方的责任与风险，也是海关核定关税、统计进出口货物的依据，因此不可遗漏。填制时应注意：如果信用证中只规定了笼统的港口名称，如"FOB CHINESE PORT"，则发票内应根据实际打具体港口名称，如"FOB DALIAN"，对重名港口，还应加注国名。如果经修改改变了原定的起运港或目的港，但对价格条件未涉及，则价格条件后的港口名称可不变。如这种修改引起受益人的额外支出，经与开证人交涉，可加在发票金额内同货款一并收取。有时合同规定 FOB 或 CFR 价，但开证人委托受益人代办运输或保险，来证可能改为 CFR 或 CIF 价，同时规定由此引起的额外支出可在证下或超证支取，则依信用证缮制发票时可同时将运、保费与货款加在一起算收。

有些单价还包括佣金或折扣。若涉及佣金和折扣，缮制发票时应注意：若信用证中没有扣佣规定，但信用证金额为扣佣后净额，为保证单证一致，发票应反映扣佣全过程。在下列几种情况下，发票上不应反映扣佣过程：证中未提及佣金，汇票金额规定为发票金额的___%(一般为95%以上)；证中要求受益人出具佣金单，汇票金额与减佣后的发票金额相等；证中规定银行在议付时应扣除佣金；合同规定佣金，但证中未含佣金额，且未提及佣金(先收后付)；代理人佣金不应在发票内反映。

总额应为发票上列明的单价与数量的乘积。对于单价因规格不同而不同的商品(如出口冻虾仁，每一品种规格不同而单价不同)，缮制发票时须清楚、明白地将数字表达出来，每一品种的金额要作一累计，最后发票的总金额也应作一总计。总额一般用大、小写表示，以防发生涂改小写数字等舞弊现象。大、小写金额应相等，且不能超过信用证金额。如果来证规定，额外费用可在证下或超证支取，受益人应将这些费用与货款加在一起在发票上反映。如 L/C 规定"EXTRA CHARGE SUCH AS FREIGHT SURCHARGES, CONGESTION SURCHARGES, INSURANCE PREMIUM, OPTION CHARGES IF ANY MAY BE DRAWN UNDER THIS CREDIT OR IN EXCESS OF CREDIT VALUE"，则发票总额可做成：

PROCEEDS	USD15,672.00
PLUS FREIGHT SURCHARGE	USD300.00
OPTION CHARGE	USD200.00
INSURANCE PREMIUM	USD450.00
TOTAL AMOUNT	USD16,622.50

如果发票金额超支，按指定行事的被指定银行、保兑行(如有的话)或开证行可以接受该发票，但不允许该银行对超过信用证金额的部分做承付或者议付。因此，超出信用证的部分金额可另做托收。如来证金额为"USD2,955.00，货款为 USD3,150.00"，发票应做成：

PROCEEDS	USD3,150.00
LESS EXCESSIVE VALUE FOR COLLECTION	USD195.00
NET AMOUNT	USD2,955.00

当计价货币为 JPY(日元)等时，货币金额不要小数，小数以下辅币应四舍五入。

12) 细节条款

根据信用证的要求，发票有时须加注某些细节条款或特殊条款。常见细节内容有：①信用证号或合同号(L/C NO. OR CONTRACT NO.)；②形式发票号(PROFORMA INVOICE NO.)；③订单号(ORDER NO./INDENT NO.)；④海关税则号(CUSTOMS TARIFF NO.)；⑤银行注册号(BANK REGISTRATION NO.)；⑥外汇批准号(EXCHANGE PERMIT NO.)；⑦进口许可证号(IMPORT LICENSE NO.)；⑧注明"任何条件下进口"，如"IMPORT UNDER W.E.S."或"IMPORT UNDER O.G.L."；⑨加注厂商或生产厂商的名址(NAME AND ADDRESS OF MANUFACTURER OR PRODUCER)。对证中规定应批注的细节内容，受益人应据实加注在发票货物描述下面。

13) 特殊条款

对证中有关特殊条款的规定，发票上应照打或灵活反映。常见的特殊条款有：①有些来证要求注明产地，并附价值声明，如发票上可注"WE HEREBY CERTIFY/ STATES/ DECLARE THAT(或 THIS IS TO CERTIFY THAT)THE GOODS ARE OF CHINESE ORIGIN AND THAT THE VALUE IN REAL, AUTHENTIC AND IN CONFORMITY WITH OUR RECORDS"。②有些来证要求证明发票所列货物、单价等是真实正确的，且是唯一的发票。例如"WE HEREBY CERTIFY THAT THIS INVOICE IS IN ALL RESPECTS CORRECT AND TRUE BOTH REGARDING TO THE PRICES AND DESCRIPTION OF THE GOODS STATED THEREIN, AND ONLY ONE ISSUED BY US FOR THE GOOD"。③受政治因素、民族因素的影响，有的来证要求出口商声明货物中不含以色列原料，货物或集装箱包装上不带以色列的六角星标记。对此，可作以下声明："WE HEREBY DECLARE THAT THE PRODUCTS STATED IN THE INVOICE DO NOT CONTAIN ANY ISRAELI MATERIALS, AND THAT THE GOODS OR CONTAINER ARE NOT BEARING HEXAGON STAR"。若来证主要受益人声明在以色列没有投资，则发票上可注"WE HEREBY CERTIFY THAT OUR COMPANY IS A STATE ENTERPRISE AND HAS NO RELATIONS WHATSOEVER WITH ISRAEL"。④有些国家(如澳大利亚)规定，可在发票上加注"发展中国家声明"条款，声明进口商品为发展中国家自产产品，以此作为取得普惠制的依据，这种发票的作用相当于FORM A。例如加注以下声明"I DECLARE THAT FINAL PROCESS OF MANUFACTURE

OF THE GOODS FOR WHICH SPECIAL RATES ARE CLAIMED HAS BEEN PERFORMED IN THE PEOPLE'S REPUBLIC OF CHINA AND THAT NOT LESS THAN ONE-HALF OF THE FACTORY OR WORKS COST OF THE GOODS IS REPRESENTED BY THE VALUE OF LABOR OR MATERIALS OR OF LABOR AND MATERIALS OF THE PEOPLE'S REPUBLIC OF CHINA AND AUSTRALIA".

14) 签章

根据 UCP600 规定，发票无需签字，但须表明是由受益人出具的发票。在实践中，发票一般由出票人加具正式签章。若信用证要求"MANUALLY SIGNED"，则必须手签，盖章位置通常在发票的右下角，若信用证规定须由贸促会等机构证实，则证实机构的签章应在发票的左下角。一般只需在第一联由证实机构签章(SIGNATURE)；如果客户要求，也可在数联签章。

15) 发票的份数

若来证将发票分成正副本，则所有正本发票上应盖"ORIGINAL"字样；若为电脑制单，也可直接在发票上打出"ORIGINAL"字样；如份数显示"IN DUPLICATE/2 COPIES"(一式两份)、"IN TRIPLICATE/3 COPIES"(一式三份)，则出口商向银行交单的发票至少一份是正本，也可以全部交纳正本。

16) 其他项目

发票下端通常印有"有错当查"(E. & O. E.)字句，这种字句并非发票的必要项目，它是发货人的预先声明，表示万一发生错误或遗漏，可以更正。

3. 从信用证条款谈发票的制作

1)　有关发票名称、号码、出票日和装运日的问题

(1) 发票名称和号码必须与信用证规定的一致。例如"SPECIAL U.S. CUSTOMS INVOICES FORM 5515 SHOWING CIFC 5% NEW YORK FOR EACH ITEM IN 3 COPIES"(美国专用海关发票格式 5515 三份，必须显示每项货物的 CIFC 5% 纽约价格)。按照本条款，出口商应提交美国格式 5515 的海关发票，而不是一般的发票。特别注意的是当来证中不要求出具汇票时，发票上加注"DRAWN UNDER L/C NO. XXX DATED ON D/M/Y"。

(2) 出票日和装运日必须合乎来证要求。例如"WE ISSUE AN IRREVOCABLE AND TRANSFERABLE DOCUMENT CREDIT NO. 3300/93/005 DATED 20 JAN. 1999, VALIDITY APRIL 12, 1999, SHIPMET AT THE LATEST MARCH 31, 1999"(不可撤销信用证号码 3300/93/005，该证的开立日期为 1999 年 1 月 20 日，有效日期为 1999 年 4 月 12 日，最迟装运日期为 1999 年 3 月 31 日)。对该条款，在制作发票时一般要求：发票的出单日期应晚于开证日期(这样做，绝对不会错)，发票上的装运日期应显示实际装运日期，最晚为 1999

年3月31日(包括提单等单据上的装运日期均必须满足本要求，而且要单单一致)。

2) 有关发票抬头人、受益人/运输方式及目的港的问题

(1) 发票上的抬头人和受益人名称必须符合信用证的规定。除非信用证另有规定，商业发票一般均由信用证指定的受益人开立，且必须做成以信用证的申请人为抬头。例如：BENEFICIARIES SIGNED COMMERCIAL INVOICE IN FOUR COPIES ISSUED IN THE NAME OF ABOU ZEID TRADING EST/BERRUT-LEBANON(受益人签署的商业发票四份，以"ABOU ZEID TRADING EST/BERRUT-LEBANON"的名义开立)。

(2) 发票上的运输方式和目的港必须与来证要求和提单显示一致。发票上的运输方式包括陆运、海运或空运方式，即采用车、船、飞机等运输工具将货物运往指定地点。它往往包括双程运输，首程为当地车(PRECARRIAGE BY)或船(LOCAL VESSEL)，次程为远洋船(OCEAN VESSEL)，两者之间可用符号"/"连接起来。例如：SHIPMENT FROM ANY CHINESE PORT TO PORT SAID PUBLIC FREE ZONE IN TRANSIT BY EAGLE LINE INTO CONTAINER(从任何中国港口装运到塞得港公共自由区，由"EAGLE LINE"负责运输，采用集装箱运输)。

3) 有关货物描述、唛头/价格条件和金额的问题

(1) 发票的货名描述和唛头必须和信用证要求一致。信用证对发票上货物描述的要求是非常严格的，不允许有任何偏差。不仅商品名称要与来证要求一致，而且有关的品质、规格、包装情况也要符合其规定，不能随意变更。不同的条款对唛头有不同的要求，应首先准确理解来证对唛头的要求，然后在发票上正确地显示出来。例如，COVERING CHINESE WHITE ANGARA RABBIT HAIR, ABT 3000 KILOGRAMS SECOND GRADE GUANGXI ORIGIN AT USD18.50/KG, ABT 1000 KILOGRAMS THRID GRADE GUANGXI ORIGIN AT USD17.00/KG, ABT 1000 KGS OFF GRADE GUANGXI ORIGIN AT USD13.00/KG CIFC5 BREMEN(中国安哥拉兔毛，二等品约3000公斤，广西产，18.50美元/公斤；三等品约1000公斤，广西产，17.00美元/公斤；等外品约1000公斤，广西产，13.00美元/公斤；价格条款为CIFC5 BREMEN)。

(2) 价格条件和金额必须合乎来证规定。发票金额受限于信用证金额，但信用证一般规定有5%的减幅。例如，UNIT PRICE USD44.00/MT FOB ST BEIHAI SHIPMENT FROM NINGBO, CHINA TO KOREAN PORT(单价每公吨44美元，价格条款为FOB北海，包括平舱和理舱，从中国宁波港装运到韩国港口)。

4) 有关使用文字/份数/签署和证实等其他问题

(1) 发票使用的文字和份数必须与信用证要求一致。例如：ALL DOCUMENTS REQUIRED FOR NEGOTIATION IN TRIPLICATE AND SHOULD BE MADE OUT IN ENGLISH(所有议付单据必须提交一式三份并用英文制作)。

(2) 签署和证实必须符合信用证的规定。发票签署是指在发票上签名或盖章，而证实则是指由有关机构(如商会或贸促会等)在发票上做某些陈述，并正式签署，或仅对发票所述盖章确认。签署和证实在发票中具有重要意义，不可掉以轻心。例如：MANUALLY SIGNED INVOICE IN DUPLICATE CERTIFYING GOODS OF CHINESE ORIGIN(手签商业发票一式两份，并在发票上证明中国制作)。

(3) 增减比例(或溢短装)及分批装运必须与来证要求相符。如信用证条款中有"约/近似/大约"字样，则实际装运的数量有10%的增减。如以包装单位或个数计算，不允许增减。一般情况允许有 5%的增减。例如：5% MORE OR LESS IN QUANTITY AND VALUE ACCEPTABLE(数量与金额允许5%的增减)。

二、装箱单的制作

装箱单可以不填制号码和日期。如若填制，一般采用发票号码和发票日期。毛、净重应列明每件包装的毛重和净重，总的毛重和净重数字必须与发票和运输单据、产地证、出口许可证的数字相符。装箱单上一般应列明内包装情况(INNER PACKING)，例如，"每件装一胶袋，每打装一盒，每20打装一箱"，则须注明"PACKING EACH PIECE IN A POLY BAG, ONE DOZEN IN A CARDBOARD BOX AND THEN 20 DOZENS IN A CARTON"。如果采用信用证结算，并且信用证规定要列明的，则必须在单据中充分表示出来。如信用证要求提供重量单、尺码单等其他形式的装箱单据，提供单据的名称应与信用证内规定名称一致，其内容既要包括包装的商品内容，也包括包装的种类和件数，每件包装的毛、净重和整批货物的毛、净总重量，每件外包装的尺码和总尺码(体积)。按海关、商检机构、信用证或客人的规定或要求提供相应的装箱单正副本份数。最好一次性缮制完整、正确。如果中途数量发生更改，要一并修改并保持统一。

制作装箱单时应注意：单据的名称应与信用证或合同要求一致，装箱单上的货物名称应与其他单据一致，包装情况、重量单等应与发票、提单一致，日期应不迟于发票日期(可以相同)，号码可为发票号码(除非信用证要求不显示)。

三、海运提单的制作

1. 海运提单的内容

不同船公司设计的提单格式和内容不尽相同。由于海运提单是物权凭证，直接牵涉各关系人的责任和权益，所以要求内容尽可能详尽、明确，以避免或减少纠纷。完整的提单包括正面关于商品装运情况的记载和背面印就的运输条款。

1) 提单的正面内容

提单正面记载的内容可分为三部分：①由托运人提供的部分，包括托运人、收货人和被通知方的名称和地址、提单号码、船名、装运港和目的港、货物名称和描述、装船件数、毛重、体积、运输标志、包装方式、全套正本提单份数等；②由承运人或代理人填写的部分，包括运费交付情况、签发日期与地点、船公司的签章、船长或其代理人的签章等；③承运人或其代理人指定的部分，这是承运人对接受委托承运货物的若干代契约型的声明文字，主要包括装船条款、内容不知悉条款、承认接受条款和签署条款。

2) 提单的背面内容

提单背面印就的运输条款规定了承运人的义务、权利和责任的豁免，是承运人与托运人双方处理争议时的依据。根据 UCP600 规定，银行不审核这些条款。出口企业必须严格、谨慎地审核提单的内容。提单也是银行重点审核和决定是否接受的重要单据。根据 UCP600 第 20 条的规定，银行接受海运提单的条件如下。①表明承运人名称，并由下列人员签署：承运人或其具名代理人，或者船长或其具名代理人。承运人、船长或代理人的任何签字必须表明其承运人、船长或代理人的身份。代理人的任何签字必须表明其系代表承运人还是船长签字。②通过以下方式表明货物已在信用证规定的装货港装上具名船只：预先印就的文字，或已装船批注注明货物的装运日期。③注明信用证规定的装货港和卸货港。④全套正本提单。⑤银行审核内容以提单表面为限。银行不审核承运条款和条件的内容。⑥没有注明受租船合同的约束及(或)注明承运船只仅以风帆为动力。⑦其他方面都符合信用证的规定。

2. 海运提单的具体制作

(1) 托运人(SHIPPER)。一般即为出口商，也即信用证的受益人。如果开证申请人为了贸易上的需要，在信用证中要求做成以第三者为托运人也可照办，例如请货运代理做托运人。

(2) 收货人(CONSIGNEE)。该栏又称提单抬头，应严格按信用证规定制作。如以托收方式结算，则一般做成指示式抬头，即写成 "TO ORDER" 或 "TO THE ORDER OF SHIPPER" 字样。不可做成以买方为抬头的记名提单或以买方为指示人的提单，以免过早转移物权。

(3) 被通知方(NOTIFY PARTY)。这是货物到达目的港时船方发送到货通知的对象，通常为进口方或其代理人。但无论如何，应按信用证规定填写。如果信用证没有规定，则正本提单以不填为宜，但副本提单中仍应将进口方名称地址填明，以便承运人通知。

(4) 提单号码(B/L NO.)。提单上必须注明编号，以便核查，该号码与装货单(又称大副收据)或(集装箱)场站收据的号码是一致的。没有编号的提单无效。

(5) 船名及航次(NAME OF VESSEL &VOY. NO.)。填列所装船舶及航次。如中途转船，只填写第一程船名及航次。

(6)　装运港(PORT OF LOADING)和卸货港(PORT OF DISCHARGE)。应填写具体港口名称。卸货港如有重名,则应加注国名。卸货港如采取选择港方式,应全部列明,如为"伦敦/鹿特丹/汉堡",则在卸货港栏中填上"OPTION LONDON/ROTTERDAM/ HAMBURG"。收货人必须在船舶到达第一卸货港前在船公司规定时间内通知船方卸货港,否则船方可在其中任意一港卸货。选择港最多不得超过三个,且应在同一航线上,运费按最高者计收。如中途转船,卸货港即填写转船港名称,而目的港应填入"最终目的地"(FINAL DESTINATION)栏内。也可在卸货港内填上目的港,同时注明"在 XX 港转船"(W/T AT XX)。

(7)　唛头。与发票所列一致。

(8)　包装件数和种类(NUMBER AND KIND OF PACKAGES)与货物描述(DESCRIPTION OF GOODS)。按实际情况列明。一张提单有几种不同包装应分别列明,托盘和集装箱也可作为包装列填。裸装有捆、件,散装货应注明"IN BULK"。货物名称允许使用货物统称,但不得与信用证中货物的描述有抵触。危险品应写清化学名称,注明国际海上危险品运输规则号码(IMCO CODE PAGE)、联合国危规号码(UN CODE NO.)和危险品等级(CLASS NO.);冷藏货物注明所要求的温度。

(9)　毛重和尺码(GROSS WEIGHT & MEASUREMENT)。除信用证另有规定外,重量以千克或公吨为单位,体积以立方米为计算单位。

(10)　运费和费用(FREIGHT & CHARGES)。本栏只填运费支付情况。以 CFR 和 CIF 条件成交,应填写运费预付(FREIGHT PREPAID);以 FOB 条件成交,一般填写运费到付(FREIGHT COLLECT),除非买方委托发货人代付运费。程租船一般只写明"AS ARRANGED"(按照约定)。如信用证另有规定,按信用证规定填写。

(11)　正本提单份数(NUMBER OF ORIGINAL B(S)/L)。按信用证规定签发,并分别用大小写数字填写,如"(2)TWO"。如信用证中仅规定"全套"(FULL SET),习惯做两份正本,但一份正本亦可视为全套。

(12)　提单日期和签发地点。除备运提单外,提单日期均为装货完毕日期,不能迟于信用证规定的装运期。提单签发地点按装运地填列。如果船期晚于规定装运期,要求船方同意以担保函换取较早日期提单,这就是"倒签提单"(ANTI DATED B/L)。货未装上船就要求船方出具已装船提单,这就是"预借提单"(ADVANCED B/L),这种做法系国际航运界陋习,一旦暴露,可能造成对方索赔乃至拒收而导致巨大损失。

(13)　签署。海运提单表面应注明承运人名称,并由承运人或其具名代理人,或者船长或其具名代理人签署。签署人的任何签字必须表明其身份。代理人的任何签字必须表明其系代表承运人还是船长签字。

(14)其他。信用证要求在提单上加注的内容。如信用证规定"每份单据上均应显示信用证号码"、"提单需提供贸促会证明"等，必须按信用证规定处理。

3. 从信用证条款看海运提单的制作

(1) 提单的发货人/收货人/被通知方/签发人问题。提单的发货人一般为出口商或受益人。除非信用证另有规定，银行将接受表明受益人以外的第三者为发货人的运输单据，例如：FULL SET OF ORIGINAL AND 2 NON-NEGOTIABLE COPIES SHIPPED ON BOARD OCEAN BILLS OF LADING SHOWING BENEFICIARY AS SHIPPER MADE OUT TO ORDER AND BLANK ENDORSED MARKED "FREIGHT PREPAID" AND NOTIFY THE APPLICANT(全套正本和两份副本已装船海运提单，以受益人为托运人，做成指示抬头并加空白背书，通知开证申请人并标明运费预付)。

提单上的被通知方和签发人要与来证一致。如信用证未规定被通知方，则可以在正本上显示空白，副本上表明买方的名称地址。例如：FULL SET OF CLEAN ON BOARD OCEAN BILLS OF LADING MADE OUT TO THE ORDER OF PUSAN BANK MARKED "FREIGHT PREPAID" AND NOTIFY APPLICANT(全套清洁已装船海运提单做成凭"PUSAN BANK"指示抬头，标明运费预付，并通知开证人)。

(2) 提单上的运输工具/航行航线/装货港/卸货港问题。

① 运输工具和航行航线必须符合信用证规定。例如：GOODS MUST BE SHIPPED IN SEA WORTHY CONFERENCE VESSEL WHICH SHOULD BE ON APPROVED LIST OF THE LLOYD'S(货物必须由适合海运的班轮运输，该运输船只必须列入劳氏确认名单)。

② 装运港/卸货港(或目的地)应与来证一致。例如：BILLS OF LADING MUST SPECIFY THE NAME OF LOADING PORT: NINGBO AND DISCHARGING PORT: HAMBURG(提单必须特别注明装运港口为宁波和卸货港口为汉堡)。

(3) 分批装运/转运/集装箱/唛头问题。分批装运和转运必须符合合同和 UCP600 关于分批装运和转运的界定。例如"SHIPMENT TO BE EFFECTED IN TWO LOTS BY SEPARATE VESSELS WITH AN INTERVAL OF MINIMUM 40 DAYS BETWEEN THE SHIPMENT UNDER FULL SEPARATE SETS OF DOCUMENTS FOR EACH LOT"。集装箱和唛头应与来证一致，例如"FULL SET OF 3/3 ORIGINAL CLEAN ON BOARD OCEAN MARINE BILLS OF LADING MADE OUT TO SHIPPER'S ORDER AND ENDORSED IN BLANK AND MARKED "FREIGHT PREPAID" AND NOTIFY UNION MERCHANTS OVERSEAS LTD., LONDON, EVIDENCING SHIPMENT IN A CONTAINER STATING CONTAINER NUMBER ON LCL/FCL OR FCL/FCL TERMS"。

(4) 货物描述/计量单位/运输费用/运输代理问题。货物描述和计量单位必须合乎信用证要求，例如"COVERING SHIPMENT OF: EITHER MEI THANKG OR LONG ZHU OR

LIPAO SZE BRAND OF 5,000 M/TONS PORTLAND CEMENT 525"。运输费用和运输代理要与来证一致，例如"COMPLETE SET OF CLEAN ON BOARD MARINE BILLS OF LADING CONSIGNED TO ORDER AND BLANK ENDORSED AND MARKED "FREIGHT PREPAID" AND NOTIFY APPLICANT"。

(5) 装船标记/签单日期/签发份数/证明内容及其他问题。装船标记和签单日期必须符合信用证的规定，例如"IF AN ON BOARD NOTATION HAS BEEN ADDED TO THE BILL OF LADING THEN THIS MUST BE DATED AND SIGNED BY A FULL SIGNATORY OF THE CARRIER/MASTER OR NAMED AGENT ON BEHALF OF THE CARRIER/MASTER TOGETHER WITH THE APPROPRIATE STAMP"。签发份数和证明内容及其他事项也要和来证规定一致。签发份数包括所需要的正本提单份数和副本提单份数。证明内容是指信用证要求在提单上对某项内容加以证实的条款，例如"FULL SET CLEAN SHIPPED ON BOARD OCEAN BILLS OF LADING MADE OUT TO THE ORDER OF PERWIA HABIB BANK MALAYSIA BERHAD, NOTIFY BUYERS MARKED 'FREIGHT PREPAID'"。

四、保险单的制作

保险单的内容包括正反两面。反面是印就的保险条款，说明保险人与被保险人的权利义务。正面内容要由保险人根据每一笔保险的具体情况填写，主要有：保险人和被保险人的名称、保险标的、保险金额、保费和费率、运输工具的名称和开航日期、运输起止点、承包的险别、检验或理赔代理、赔付地点、出单日期和地点、保险人签字盖章、发票号码和保险单号码等。

不同保险公司出具的保险单据的内容大同小异，多以英国劳合社船货保险单(S.G. POLICY)为蓝本。保险合同的当事人有保险人、被保险人、保险经纪人、保险代理人、勘验人、赔付代理人等。中外保险公司都可以以自己名义签发保单并成为保险人，其代理人是保险经纪人，保险代理人代表货主；勘验人一般是进口地对货物损失进行查勘之人；赔付代理人指单据上载明的在目的地可以受理索赔的指定机构，应详细注明其地址和联系方式。

(一)保险单的具体内容及其制作

1. 被保险人

被保险人(INSURED)即保险单的抬头，正常情况下应是信用证的受益人。但如信用证规定保单为"TO ORDER OF XXX BANK"或"IN FAVOR OF XXX BANK"，应填写"受益人名称＋HELD TO ORDER OF XXX BANK"或"IN FAVOR OF XXX BANK"；如信用证要求所有单据以"XX"为抬头人，保单中应照录；如信用证要求中性抬头"THIRD PARTY"

或"IN NEUTRAL FORM"，可填写"TO WHOM IT MAY CONCERN"；如要求保单"MADE OUT TO ORDER AND ENDORSED IN BLANK"，填写"受益人名称+ TO ORDER"；信用证对保单无特殊规定或只要求"ENDORSED IN BLANK"或"IN ASSIGNABLE/NEGOTIABLE FORM"，填受益人名称。

2. 保险货物项目、唛头、包装及数量

这些内容应与发票和提单保持一致。

3. 保险金额

保险金额(AMOUNT INSURED)是所保险的货物发生损失时保险公司给予的最高赔偿限额，一般按 CIF/CIP 发票金额的 110%投保。加成如超出 10%，超过部分的保险费由买方承担的则可以办理。信用证项下的保单必须符合信用证规定，如发票价包含佣金和折扣，应先扣除折扣再加成投保，被保险人不可能获得超过实际损失的赔付。保险金额的大小写应一致，保额尾数通常要"进位取整"或"进一取整"，即不管小数部分数字是多少，一律舍去并在整数部分加"1"。

4. 保费和费率

通常事先印就"AS ARRANGED"(按约定)字样，除非信用证另有规定，两者在保单上可以不具体显示。保险费(PREMIUM)通常占货价的比例为 0.1%～0.3%左右。险别不同，费率(RATE)不一(水渍险的费率约相当于一切险的1/2，平安险的费率约相当于一切险的1/3)。

5. 运输方面的要求

开航日期(DATE OF COMMENCEMENT)通常填提单上的装运日，也可填"AS PER B/L"或"AS PER TRANSPORTATION DOCUMENTS"；起运地、目的地、装载工具(PER CONVEYANCE)的填写与提单上的操作相同。

6. 承保险别

承保险别(CONDITIONS)是保险单的核心内容，填写时应与信用证规定的条款、险别等要求严格一致；在信用证无规定或只规定"MARINE/FIRE/LOSS RISK"，"USUAL RISK"或"TRANSPORT RISK"等，可根据所买卖货物、交易双方、运输路线等情况投保 ALL RISKS、WA 或 WPA、FPA 三种基本险中的任何一种；如信用证中规定使用中国保险条款(CIC)、伦敦协会货物条款(ICC)或美国协会货物条款(AICC)，应按信用证规定投保、填制。所投保的险别除明确注明险别名称外，还应注明险别适用的文本及日期；某些货物的保单上可能出现 IOP(不考虑损失程度/无免赔率)的规定；目前许多合同或信用证都要求在基本险的基础上加保 WAR RISKS 和 SRCC(罢工、暴动、民变险)等附加险；集装箱或甲板货的

保单上可能会显示 JWOB(抛弃、浪击落海)险；货物运往偷盗现象严重的地区/港口的保单上频现 TPND(偷窃、提货不着险)。

7. 赔付地点

此栏按合同或信用证要求填制。如信用证中并未明确，一般将目的港/地作为赔付地点(CLAIM PAYABLE AT/IN)。

8. 日期

日期(DATE)指保单的签发日期。由于保险公司提供仓至仓(W/W)服务，所以出口方应在货物离开本国仓库前办结手续，保单的出单时间应是货物离开出口方仓库前或船舶开航前或运输工具开行前的日期。除另有规定，保单的签发日期必须在运输单据的签发日期之前。

9. 签章

由保险公司签字或盖章(AUTHORIZED SIGNATURE)以示保险单正式生效。单据的签发人必须是保险公司/承保人或他们的代理人，在保险经纪人的信笺上出具的保险单据，只要该保险单据是由保险公司或其代理人，或由承保人或其代理人签署的可以接受。UCP 规定除非信用证有特别授权，否则银行不接受由保险经纪人签发的暂保单。

10. 保单的背书

保单的背书分为空白背书(只注明被保险人名称)、记名背书(业务中使用较少)和记名指示背书(在保单背面打上"TO ORDER OF XXX"和被保险人的名称)三种。保单做成空白背书意味着被保险人或任何保单持有人在被保货物出险后享有向保险公司或其代理人索赔并得到合理的补偿的权利，做成记名背书则意味着保单的受让人在被保货物出险后享有向保险公司或其代理人索赔的权利。在货物出险时，只有同时掌握提单和保单才能真正地掌握货权。

11. 保单的份数

当信用证没有特别说明保单份数时，出口公司一般提交一套完整的保险单；如有具体份数要求，应按规定提交，注意提交单据的正(ORIGINAL)、副本(COPY)的不同要求。

12. 保单的其他规定

保单号码(POLICY NUMBER)由保险公司编制，投保及索赔币种以信用证规定为准，投保地点一般为装运港/地的名称，如信用证或合同对保单有特殊要求，也应在单据的适当位置加以明确。

(二)缮制保单的注意事项

(1) 保单和保险凭证的关系。两者同效，前者有背面条款，较常见。如要求前者，不可以提供后者；如要求后者，提供前者也不会有问题。

(2) 预约保险单多见于常有货物运输的公司或我国进口业务中，这样做的最大好处是防止漏保、方便客户和不必逐笔洽谈保险条件。

(3) FOB、CFR 条件下出口卖方代保问题。如保险费用有保障，卖方可以按信用证或合同规定予以代办。

(4) 避免业务中一律一切险的做法。应针对不同商品、按不同条款选择投保合适的险别。

(5) 保险责任起讫时间规定为 W/W 不意味着这期间发生的损失保险公司都会赔偿(按FOB 和 CFR 成交，装运前的风险由出口方负责)。

(6) 投保单可以中英文混合填写，保单必须以英文制作。

(三)信用证具体保险条款分析

(1) INSURANCE POLICIES/CERTIFICATE IN TWO FOLD PAYABLE TO THE ORDER OF COMMERCIAL BANK OF LONDON LTD. COVERING MARINE INSTITUTE CARGO CLAUSES A, INSTITUTE STRIKE CLAUSES CARGO, INSTITUTE WAR CLAUSES CARGO FOR INVOICE VALUE PLUS 10% INCLUDING WAREHOUSE TO WAREHOUSE UP TO THE FINAL DESTINATION AT SWEDEN, MARKED "PREMIUM PAID", SHOWING CLAIMS IF ANY, PAYABLE IN GERMANY, NAMING SETTLING AGENT IN GERMANY.

根据上述规定，制作保单时应做到：两份正本，被保险人填写为"受益人+HELD TO THE ORDER OF COMMERCIAL BANK OF LONDON LTD."，险别为协会货物 A 险、罢工险和战争险，保险金额为发票金额加成 10%，含到目的地瑞典的仓至仓条款，标明保费已付，索赔地点在德国，列明设在德国的赔付代理人。

(2) INSURANCE POLICIES/CERTIFICATE IN TRIPLICATE ENDORSED IN BLANK FOR 110% OF INVOICE VALUE COVERING ALL RISKS AND WAR RISKS AS PER CIC WITH CLAIMS PAYABLE AT SINGAPORE IN THE CURRENCY OF DRAFT (IRRESPECTIVE OF PERCENTAGE), INCLUDING 60 DAYS AFTER DISCHARGES OF THE GOODS AT PORT OF DESTINATION(OF AT STATION OF DESTINATION) SUBJECT TO CIC.

其意思是：保单或保险凭证三份，做成空白背书，按发票金额的 110%投保中国保险条款的一切险和战争险，按汇票所使用的货币在新加坡赔付(无免赔率)，并以中国保险条款为准确定承保期限在目的港卸船(或在目的地车站卸车)后 60 天为止。

(3) INSURANCE COVERED BY THE APPLICANT. ALL SHIPMENT UNDER THIS CREDIT MUST BE ADVISED BY THE BENEFICIARY AFTER SHIPMENT DIRECTLY TO PRAGATI INSURANCE LTD. JUBILEE ROAD BRANCH, CHITTAGONG, BANGLADESH AND APPLICANT ALSO TO US QUOTING OUR CREDIT NO. AND MARINE COVER NOTE NO. PIL/JBL/0102005 DATED AUG. 01, 2005, GIVING FULL DETAILS OF SHIPMENT AND COPY OF SUCH ADVICE MUST ACCOMPANY SHIPPING DOCUMENTS.

该信用证对保险单的要求是：申请人买保险。货装船后，受益人应发装船通知给 PRAGATI 保险公司(地址是孟加拉吉大港 JUBILEE 支路)、申请人和开证行。通知上标明信用证号码、2005 年 8 月 1 日签发的暂保单的号码 PIL/JBL/0102005 和详细的装船信息，装船通知副本要随整套单据一并交银行。

五、原产地证明书的制作及注意事项

(一)原产地证明书的填制

1. 普惠制原产地证明书(FORM A)的填制

证书号(REFERENCE NO.)：普惠制原产地证明书标题栏(右上角)，填上检验检疫机构编定的证书号。下面举例说明证书号编定规则。如证书号 ZJGA33121/050001，其中，ZJ 代表浙江，G 代表 FORM A，A33121 代表公司注册号，05 代表 2005 年，0001 代表企业流水号。

第 1 栏：出口商的名称、地址、国别。此栏出口商公司名称应与注册时相同。必须打上国名、地址，例如"ZHEJIANG NATIVE PRODUCTS & ANIMAL BY-PRODUCTS I/E CORP., NO. 368 NORTH ZHONGSHAN ROAD, HANGZHOU, CHINA"。

第 2 栏：收货人的名称、地址、国别。除欧盟 25 国和挪威外，此栏须填上给惠国最终收货人名称，不可填中间转口商的名称，此栏须打上国名。欧盟 25 国、挪威对此栏非强制性要求，若第 2 栏进口商国家和第 12 栏最终目的国都是欧盟国家，则可以与第 12 栏国家不同，也可以不填详细地址，只填上"TO ORDER"。

36 个给惠国及输入代码为：305 法国(FRANCE)、303 英国(UNITED KINGDOM)、306 爱尔兰(IRELAND)、304 德国(GERMANY)、302 丹麦(DENMARK)、307 意大利(ITALY)、301 比利时(BELGIUM)、309 荷兰(NETHERLANDS)、308 卢森堡(LUXEMBOURG)、310 希腊(GREECE)、312 西班牙(SPAIN)、311 葡萄牙(PORTUGAL)、315 奥地利(AUSTRIA)、330 瑞典(SWEDEN)、318 芬兰(FINLAND)、327 波兰(POLAND)、321 匈牙利(HUNGARY)、350 斯洛文尼亚(SLOVENIA REP.)、352 捷克(CZECH REP.)、353 斯洛伐

克(SLOVAK REP.)、334 爱沙尼亚(ESTONIA)、335 拉脱维亚(LATVIA)、336 立陶宛(LITHUANIA)、108 塞浦路斯(CYPRUS)、324 马耳他(MALTA)、137 土耳其(TURKEY)、331 瑞士(SWITZERLAND)、326 挪威(NORWAY)、116 日本(JAPAN)、601 澳大利亚(AUSTRALIA)、609 新西兰(NEW ZEALAND)、501 加拿大(CANADA)、344 俄罗斯(RUSSIA)、347 乌克兰(UKRAINE)、340 白俄罗斯(BYELORUSSIA)和 341 哈萨克斯坦(KAZAKHSTAN)。

第 3 栏：运输方式及路线(就所知道而言)。

① 一般应填上装货、到货地点(始运港、目的港)及运输方式(如海运、陆运、空运)。如 "FROM HANGZHOU TO SHANGHAI BY TRUCK, THENCE TRANSSHIPPED TO HAMBURG BY SEA"。

② 转运商品应加上转运港，如 "FROM SHANGHAI TO HAMBURG BY SEA VIA HONG KONG"。

③ 商品如果输往内陆给惠国(如瑞士、奥地利)，由于这些国家没有海岸，因此如系海运，都须经第三国，再转运至该国，填证时应注明，如 "BY VESSEL FROM SHANGSHAI TO HAMBURG, IN TRANSIT TO SWITZERLAND"。

第 4 栏：供官方使用。此栏由签证当局填写，正常情况下此栏空白。特殊情况下，签证当局在此栏加注。例如：①货物已出口，签证日期迟于出货日期，签发"后发"证书时，此栏盖上 "ISSUED RETROSPECTIVELY" 红色印章；②证书遗失、被盗或者损毁，签发"副本"证书时盖上 "DUPLICATE" 红色印章，并在此栏注明原证书的编号和签证日期，并声明原发证书作废，其文字是 "THIS CERTIFICATE IS IN REPLACEMENT OF CERTIFICATE OF ORIGIN NO....DATED...WHICH IS CANCELLED"。

注意：在录入后发证书时，请在申请书备注栏注明"申请后发"，否则计算机退回。

第 5 栏：商品顺序号。如同批出口货物有不同品种，则按不同品种分列"1"、"2"、"3"……，以此类推。单项商品，此栏填"1"。

第 6 栏：唛头及包装号。填具的唛头应与货物外包装上的唛头及发票的唛头一致。唛头不得出现中国以外的地区和国家制造的字样，也不能出现香港、澳门、台湾原产地字样，例如 "MADE IN TAIWAN" 和 "HONG KONG PRODUCTS"。如货物无唛头应填"N/M"；如唛头过多，此栏不够填则打上(SEE THE ATTACHMENT)，用附页填打所有唛头(附页的纸张要与原证书一样大小)，在右上角打上证书号，并由申请单位和签证当局授权签字人分别在附页末页的右下角和左下角手签、盖印。附页手签的笔迹、地点、日期均与证书第11、12栏相一致。

注意：有附页时，请在申请书备注栏注明"唛头见附页"，否则计算机退回。

第 7 栏：包装数量和种类及商品的描述。包装数量必须用英文和阿拉伯数字同时表示，例如"ONE HUNDRED AND FIFTY(150)CARTONS OF WORKING GLOVES"。

注意事项如下。①如果包装数量超过一千，则千与百单位之间不能有"AND"连词，否则计算机退回。例如"TWO THOUSAND ONE HUNDRED AND FIFTY (2150)CARTONS OF WORKING GLOVES"。②数量、品名要求在一页内打完，如果内容过长，则可以合并包装箱数，品名合并。例如"ONE HUNDRED AND FIFTY(150) CARTONS OF GLOVE, SCARF, TIE, CAP"。③包装必须打具体的包装种类，如"POLYWOVEN BAG"、"DRUM"、"PALLET"、"WOODEN CASE"等)，不能只填写"PACKAGE"。如果没有包装，应填写"NUDE CARGO"(裸装货)，"IN BULK"(散装货)，"HANGING GARMENTS"(挂装)。④商品名称必须具体填明(具体到能找到相对应的 4 位 H.S.编码)，不能笼统填"MACHINE"(机器)、"GARMENT"(服装)等。例如：玩具电扇应注明为"TOYS: ELECTRIC FANS"，不能只列"ELECTRIC FANS"(电扇)。⑤商品的商标、牌名(BRAND)及货号(ARTICLE NUMBER)一般可以不填。商品名称等项列完后，应在下一行加上表示结束的符号，以防止加填伪造内容。国外信用证有时要求填写合同、信用证号码等，可加填在此栏空白处。

第 8 栏：原产地标准。

完全原产品，不含任何非原产成分，出口到所有给惠国，填写"P"。

含有非原产成分的产品，出口到欧盟、挪威、瑞士和日本，填写"W"，其后加上出口产品的 H.S.编码，例如"W" 42.02。条件：①产品列入了上述给惠国的"加工清单"并符合其加工条件；②产品未列入"加工清单"，但产品生产过程中使用的非原产原材料和零部件经过充分的加工，产品的 H.S.编码不同于所用的原材料和零部件的 H.S.编码。

含有非原产成分的产品，出口到加拿大，填写"F"。条件：非原产成分的价值未超过产品出厂价的 40%。

含有非原产成分的产品，出口到俄罗斯、乌克兰、白俄罗斯、哈萨克斯坦、捷克、斯洛伐克六国，填写"Y"，其后加上非原产成分价值占该产品离岸价格的百分比，例如"Y" 38%。条件：非原产成分的价值未超过产品离岸价的 50%。

输往澳大利亚、新西兰的货物，此栏可以留空。

第 9 栏：毛重或其他数量。此栏应以商品的正常计量单位填，如"只"、"件"、"双"、"台"、"打"等，例如"3200 DOZ."或"6270 KGS"。以重量计算的则填毛重，只有净重的，填净重亦可，但要标上 N.W.(NET WEIGHT)。

第 10 栏：发票号码及日期。此栏不得留空。月份一律用英文(可用缩写)表示，例如"PHK50016 APR. 6, 2005"。此栏的日期必须按照正式商业发票填具，发票日期不得迟于出货日期。

第 11 栏：签证当局的证明。此栏填打签证机构的签证地点和日期，例如"HANGZHOU, CHINA, APR. 6, 2005"。检验检疫局签证人经审核后在此栏(正本)签名，盖签证印章。

注意：此栏日期不得早于发票日期(第 10 栏)和申报日期(第 12 栏)，而且应早于货物的出运日期(第 3 栏)。

第 12 栏：出口商的声明。进口国横线上填最终进口国，进口国必须与第 3 栏目的港的国别一致。另外，申请单位应授权专人在此栏手签，标上申报地点和日期，并加盖申请单位的中英文印章。手签人笔迹必须在检验检疫局注册登记，并保持相对稳定。此栏日期不得早于发票日期(第 10 栏)(最早是同日)。盖章时应避免覆盖进口国名称和手签人姓名。本证书一律不得涂改，证书不得加盖校对章。

2．一般原产地证明书(C/O)的制作

具体填制要求如下。

证书号栏：应在证书右上角填上检验检疫机构编定的证书号，不得留空，否则无效。

证书号编定规则以 ZJCA33121/050001 为例说明。其中：ZJ 代表浙江，C 代表 CO，A33121 代表公司注册号，05 代表 2005 年，0001 代表企业流水号。

第 1 栏：出口商的名称、地址、国别

此栏出口商公司名称应与注册时相同，必须打上国名、地址，例如：

ZHEJIANG NATIVE PRODUCTS & ANIMAL BY-PRODUCTS I/E CORP.

NO. 368 NORTH ZHONGSHAN ROAD, HANGZHOU, CHINA

第 2 栏：收货人的名称、地址、国别

应填写最终收货方的名称、详细地址及所在国家(地区)。但由于贸易的需要，信用证规定所有单证收货人一栏留空，在这种情况下，此栏应加注 "TO WHOM IT MAY CONCERN" 或 "TO ORDER"，但不得留空。若需要填写转口商名称时，可在收货人后面加填英文 VIA，然后再填写转口商的名称、地址、国别。例如：

ZHEJIANG NATIVE PRODUCTS & ANIMAL BY-PRODUCTS I/E CORP.

NO. 368 NORTH ZHONGSHAN ROAD, HANGZHOU, CHINA VIA HONG KONG MACHINERY CO. LTD.

第 3 栏：运输方式和路线

应填写从装货港到目的港的详细运输路线。如经转运，应注明转运地。例如 "FROM SHANGHAI TO HONG KONG ON APR. 6, 2005, THENCE TRANSSHIPPED TO ROTTERDAM BY VESSEL" 或 "FROM SHANGHAI TO ROTTERDAM BY VESSEL VIA HONG KONG"。

第 4 栏：目的国家/地区

应填写货物最终运抵港，一般与最终收货人和最终目的港国别一致，不得填写中间商国别。

第5栏：签证机构用栏

此栏为签证机构在签发后发证书、重发证书或加注其他声明时使用。证书申领单位应将此栏留空。

第6栏：运输标志

应按照出口发票上所列唛头填写完整图案、文字标记及包装号码，不可简单地填写"AS PER INVOICE NO....."(按照发票)或者"AS PER B/L NO....."(按照提单)。包装无唛头，应填写"N/M"或者"NO MARK"。

此栏不得留空。如唛头较多本栏填写不下，可填写(SEE THE ATTACHMENT)，用附页填打所有唛头(附页的纸张要与原证书一样大小)，在右上角打上证书号，并由申请单位和签证当局授权签字人分别在附页末页的右下角和左下角手签、盖印。附页手签的笔迹、地点、日期均与证书第11、12栏相一致。

注意：有附页时，请在申请书备注栏注明"唛头见附页"，否则计算机退回。

第7栏：包装数量和种类及商品描述

例如"ONE HUNDRED(100)CARTONS OF COLOUR TV SETS"，在英文表述后注明阿拉伯数字。注意：①如果包件数量超过一千，则千与百单位之间不能有连词"AND"，否则计算机退回，例如"TWO THOUSAND ONE HUNDRED AND FIFTY (2150)CARTONS OF WORKING GLOVES"。②数量、品名要求在一页内打完，如果内容过长，则可以合并包装箱数，品名合并，例如"ONE HUNDRED AND FIFTY (150)CARTONS OF GLOVES, SCARF, TIE, CAP"。③包装数量及种类要按具体单位填写，例如"POLYWOVEN BAG"，"DRUM"，"PALLET"，"WOODEN CASE"，不能只填写"PACKAGE"。如果没有包装，应填写"NUDE CARGO"(裸装货)，"IN BULK"(散装货)，"HANGING GARMENTS"(挂装)。④应填写具体商品名称(具体到能找到相对应的 4 位 H.S.编码)，例如"TENNIS RACKET"(网球拍)，不得用概括性表述，例如"SPORTING GOODS"(运动用品)、"FABRIC"(织物)等。⑤商品的商标、牌名(BRAND)及货号(ARTICLE NUMBER)一般可以不填。商品描述等项列完后，应在下一行加上表示结束的符号，以防止加填伪造内容。国外信用证有时要求填写合同、信用证号码等，可加填在此栏空白处。

第8栏：商品编码

此栏要求填写商品 H.S.编码。若同一份证书包含几种商品，则应将相应的 H.S.编码全部填写。此栏不得留空。

第9栏：量值

填写出口货物的量值并与商品的计量单位联用。如果填重量，应该以千克为单位，同时应该注明 N.W.或 G.W.。

第 10 栏：发票号码及日期

应按照申请出口货物的商业发票填写。此栏日期应早于或同于实际出口日期。此栏不得留空。

第 11 栏：出口方声明

此栏由申领单位已在签证机构注册的申领员签字并加盖单位的中英文印章，填写申领地点和日期。此栏日期不得早于发票日期。

第 12 栏：签证机构证明

由签证机构签字、盖章，并填写签证地点、日期。签发日期不得早于发票日期(第 10 栏)和申请日期(第 11 栏)。

3. FORM B 的制作

第 1 栏：货物出口人。注明出口人的全称、地址和国别。须与发票上的出口人名称一致。

第 2 栏：货物收货人。注明收货人的全称、地址和国别。该收货人名称必须与发票上的进口商名称一致。如果属于第三方贸易，应该注明"凭背书"字样。

第 3 栏：官方使用。由签发证书的机构填写。

第 4 栏：运输工具和线路。详细注明出口货物的运输工具和路线。如果信用证等单证未详细列明时，应注明"空运"或"海运"字样；如果货物运输途中经过第三国时，应当参照下例注明："空运，从老挝至印度途经曼谷"。

第 5 栏：税则号列。注明各项商品的 4 位 H.S.编码。

第 6 栏：包装唛头及编号。注明包装上的唛头及编号。应当与货物包装上的唛头及编号相一致。

第 7 栏：包装件数和种类及货物名称。出口货物的名称应当与发票上的名称相符。准确的货物名称有助于进口国海关快速清关。

第 8 栏：原产地标准。享受关税减让优惠的货物必须符合《亚太贸易协定》原产地规则第二条规定，是在出口成员国完全获得或者生产的；或者在出口成员国非完全获得或者生产的符合原产地规则第三条、第四条规定的。

① 完全获得或者生产的，在第 8 栏中填写字母 "A"。

② 非完全获得或者生产的，在第 8 栏中应当按照下列方式填写。

a. 如果符合第三条规定的原产地标准，则在第 8 栏中填写字母 "B"。在字母 "B"的后面填上使用非成员国原产或不明原产地的材料、零件或产物的总价值，以在船上交货价格(FOB 价格)中所占的百分比表示(如 "B 50%")。

b. 如果符合第四条规定的原产地标准，则在第 8 栏中填写字母 "C"。在字母 "C"的后面填上在出口成员国原产成分的累计总和，以占出口货物的成本加运费、保险费价格(CIF价格)的百分比表示(如"C 60%")。

c. 如果符合原产地规则第十条规定的特殊比例标准，则在第 8 栏中填写字母"D"。

第 9 栏：毛重或者其他数量。注明货物毛重或其他数量(如件数、千克)。

第 10 栏：发票编号及日期。注明发票编号及日期。随附发票上的日期不应当迟于原产地证书格式正式启用的日期。

第 11 栏：出口人声明。"出口人"是指发货人，该发货人可以是贸易商也可以是制造商。声明中应当注明原产国、进口国、地址和日期，且该栏目应当由公司授权人员签名。

第 12 栏：证明。本栏目由签证机构签章确认。

4. FORM E 的制作

签发《<中国—东盟自由贸易区>优惠原产地证明书》的国家和代码：105 文莱(BRUNEI)、107 柬埔寨(CAMBODIA)、112 印尼(INDONESIA)、119 老挝(LAOS)、122 马来西亚(MALAYSIA)、106 缅甸(MYANMAR)、129 菲律宾(PHILIPPINES)、132 新加坡 (SINGAPORE)、136 泰国(THAILAND)和 141 越南(VIETNAM)。给予关税优惠的商品为 H.S.编码中第 1～8 章的农副产品，该项下的产品享受零关税待遇。

证书号栏：证书标题栏(右上角)，填上检验检疫机构编定的证书号。

证书号编定规则以 ZJEA33121/050001 为例说明。其中：ZJ 代表浙江，E 代表《<中国—东盟自由贸易区>优惠原产地证明书》，A33121 代表公司注册号，05 代表 2005 年，0001 代表企业流水号。证书的第 1、2、3、5、6、9、10、11 栏内容和填制要求参见《普惠制原产地证明书》(FORM A)相应各栏的填制要求。

第 4 栏：官方使用。不论是否给予优惠待遇，进口成员国海关必须在第 4 栏做出相应的标注。

第 7 栏：货物名称和 H.S.编码。货物品名必须详细，以便验货的海关官员可以识别。生产商的名称及任何商标也应列明。H.S.编码为国际上协调统一的 H.S.编码，填 4 位数 H.S.编码。

第 8 栏：原产地标准。

- 货物为出口国完全生产的，不含任何非原产成分，填写"X"。
- 货物在出口成员国加工但并非完全生产，未使用原产地累计规则判断原产地标准的，填写该国家成分的百分比，例如 70%。
- 货物在出口成员国加工但并非完全生产，使用了原产地累计规则判断原产地标准的，填写中国—东盟累计成分的百分比，例如 40%。
- 货物符合产品的特定原产地标准的，填写"产品特定原产地标准"。

第 12 栏： 官方证明。

此栏填打签证机构的签证地点和日期。检验检疫局签证人员经审核后在此栏(正本)签名,盖签证印章。当申请单位申请后发证书时,需在此栏上加注"ISSUED RETROSPECTIVELY";当申请单位申请重发证书时,需在此栏上加注"CERTIFIED TRUE COPY"。证书应由下列颜色的一份正本及三份副本组成：

- 正本——米黄色,交给进口商。
- 第一副本——浅绿色,检验检疫机构留存。
- 第二副本——浅绿色,交给进口商,货物在进口国通关后交还检验检疫机构。
- 第三副本——浅绿色,出口商留存。

5. 《<中国与巴基斯坦优惠贸易安排>优惠原产地证明书》的制作

证书号栏： 证书标题栏(右上角),填上检验检疫机构编定的证书号。证书号编定规则以 ZJPA33121/050001 为例说明。其中：ZJ 代表浙江,P 代表《<中国与巴基斯坦优惠贸易安排>优惠原产地证明书》,A33121 代表公司注册号,05 代表 2005 年,0001 代表企业流水号。

签发《<中国与巴基斯坦优惠贸易安排>优惠原产地证明书》的国家与代码：127 巴基斯坦(PAKISTAN)。

《<中国与巴基斯坦优惠贸易安排>优惠原产地证明书》暂时使用普惠制原产地证明书(FORM A),除第 8 栏外,其余各栏填法与 FORM A 相同。第 8 栏的填制方法,应遵循下述原则。①完全原产或完全获得产品：在第 8 栏填写字母"A"。②对于非完全原产或完全获得产品,第 8 栏的填制方法如下：对于符合原产地标准的产品,第 8 栏应填写字母"B",字母 B 后还应填上非中国原产或产地不明的原材料、零部件占产品 FOB 总值的百分比(例如"B 50%")。

(二)申请签发产地证应注意的事项

1. 申请签发"后发证书"

原产地证原则上应在装运前签发。如越南海关原则上规定：外国原产地证正本应在装运之前或装运之时签发,有正当理由时,亦可在装运之日后签发,但必须由该发证机关在该原产地证正本上加盖注明"DELIVER A POSTERIORLI"或"ISSUED RETROSPECTIVELY"的印章后方可接受。为保障我国对越正常出口,中国贸促会要求对出运日后办理的出口到越南的原产地证统一在产地证第 5 栏加盖 ISSUED RETROSPECTIVELY("后补")印章。

由于非故意的疏忽或其他特殊原因,货物出运前未能及时申请签发产地证的,申请单位亦可在货物发出后申请签发后发证书。

签证机构通常不接受货物出运后才递交的原产地证申请。但如属特殊情况(例如并非申请单位过失),签证机构可接受迟交的申请书,并酌情办理补证。在此情况下,申请单位递交原产地证和申请书时,必须提交下列证明文件:解释迟交申请书原因的函件,商业发票及提单/报关单。申请人应在申请单上注明"申请后发",证书第 11 栏和第 12 栏应为实际申请日期和签发日期。

产地证签证通过网上申报。通过网络,将产地证传输到签证机构;企业待收到正确回执后,企业注册手签人带上有关单据、中英文印章(需盖"后发章"的,需附提单)到签证机构取证。签证机构在证书第 5 栏加注英文"ISSUED RETROSPECTIVELY"印章,取单时提交提单复印件。

2. 申请签发"更改证书"

申请单位要求更改已签发的证书内容时,必须按规定填写《中华人民共和国出口货物原产地证明书更改/重发申请书》,并同时退回原已签发的证书正本给签证机构注销。如证书已交银行,必须提供申请单位证明、解释原因及保证退回证书的具体时间的保证函等文件。申请单位要求更改已签发证书的内容时,应提交如下资料:

(1) 填写《重发或更改 FORM A/CO 证书申请书》一份。

(2) 打开原证书,在原证书号后加字母 R,第二次更改在原证书号后加 R2,以此类推。系统内填制《更改/重发申请书》,再选择更改证,重新发送。

(3) 重新提交正本出口商业发票和装箱单各一份。

(4) 退回原已签发的证书。

(5) 重新缴费。

3. 申请签发"重发证书"

如已签发的证书遗失或损毁,从签发之日起半年内,申请单位必须向签证机构书面申明理由和提供依据,填写《中华人民共和国出口货物原产地证明书更改/重发申请书》,经签证机构审查同意后重新办理申请手续。

签证机构在证书第 5 栏加注英文"THIS CERTIFICATE IS IN REPLACEMENT OF CERTIFICATE OF ORIGIN NO._____ DATED_____WHICH IS CANCELLED",证书第 11 栏和第 12 栏的日期应为重发证书的实际申请日期和签发日期。

如果证书遗失,申请单位申请重新签证的手续如下:

(1) 先在《国门时报》上做遗失声明。

(2) 填写《重发或更改 FORM A/CO 证书申请书》一份。

(3) 重新发送一份新证书,新的证书号应在原证书号后加字母 D,新证书的签证日期和申请日期应为实际的日期，发送时，应选择重发证。

(4) 重新提交正本出口商业发票和装箱单。

(5) 提交原证书的复印件或副本。

(6) 重新缴费。

第四节　国际贸易结算单据引发的案例

出口美国记名提单造成无单放货致损案

1. 案例介绍

原告 Z 公司出口一批水果罐头到美国，委托被告 LINK 货运代理有限公司(以下简称 LINK 公司)办理出口运输事宜。LINK 公司按照托运货物的内容签发了正本提单一式三份，托运人为 Z 公司，收货人为 M INC.，到货通知人为 KK SHIPPING CO.，装货港为宁波，卸货港为纽约，提单签发地为宁波。该提单抬头印制的公司名称为 "KK SHIPPING CO."，但其签章载明 "由 JASON LIN(即 LINK 公司法定代表人林某)代表 LINK 公司签发"。其背面条款第一条规定：本提单中的 "承运人"(CARRIER)指 "KK SHIPPING CO."。第二条规定：本提单有关承运人的权利义务将适用 1936 年《美国海上货物运输法》。货物于 3 月 31 日到达纽约港，后被收货人分两次提走，而 Z 公司则仍持有 LINK 公司签发的正本提单三份，原因是其未从与之订立合同的买方处收回货款，也未指示任何一方在未收回正本提单的情况下可以放货。原告 Z 公司于当年 12 月向上海海事法院起诉称被告 LINK 公司及 "KK SHIPPING CO." 被告在客户未付款赎单的情况下，擅自将这批货让客户提走，导致原告至今无法收回货款并造成无法退税的税款损失。请求法院判令二被告连带赔偿原告全部经济损失，包括银行利息并承担本案诉讼费用及原告的律师费用。

被告 LINK 公司辩称，根据本案中提单的背面条款，本案应适用 1936 年《美国海上货物运输法》。依据该美国法，承运人将货物交付给记名提单上记名的收货人即为合法交货，并不需要收回正本记名提单。即使根据中国法律，原告未收回货款也是由于其贸易上的原因，被告 LINK 公司将货物交付记名提单上记名的收货人，已履行其义务，并未违约。另外原告的所谓 "出口退税损失" 与被告无正本提单放货并无因果关系。而上海海事法院经审理认为，原告 Z 公司与被告 LINK 公司之间形成了国际海上货物运输合同关系，提单即为该海上货物运输合同的证明。虽然该提单抬头为买方 "M INC."，但该提单系被告 LINK 公司借用被告 "KK SHIPPING CO." 的格式提单而签发的。本案中海上货物运输合同作为承运人的一方是被告 LINK 公司，被告 "KK SHIPPING CO." 在该海上货物运输中的地位只是被告 LINK 公司在美国的放货代理。由于提单的背面条款第一条即将该种格式提单的承运人定为"KK SHIPPING CO."，而该提单所证明的海上货物运输合同的承运人是被告LINK 公司，所以其背面条款中第二条法律适用条款在本案中当然无效，本案不应适用该法律适用条款所指明的外国法律，而应当适用与本案有"最密切联系"的中华人民共和国法律。

根据《中华人民共和国海商法》的规定，提单是承运人保证据以交付货物的单证，提单中载明的向记名人交付货物，或者按照指示人的指示交付货物，或者向提单持有人交付货物的条款，构成承运人据以交付货物的保证。所以无论何种提单，承运人交付货物都必须凭正本提单，这也是提单本身所具有的性质；而承运人只有在见到、收回正本提单时才交付货物也早已成为国际航运惯例。如果承运人违反有关提单的这一规定，未收回正本提单而将运输货物交付给非提单持有人，它应当承担违约责任。

本案中被告 LINK 公司作为海上货物运输合同的承运人，基于海上货物运输合同而占有原告的出口货物，其向原告签发了三份正本提单，当货物运输到目的港后，不管是由于其本身的原因，还是由于其代理的原因，或由于其他人的原因，当原告持有全部正本提单向其请求返还货物时，它已无法履行交付货物的义务，则被告对于原告来说，已构成无正本提单错误交货，它应对原告承担违约责任，按照原告出口货物的实际价值赔偿原告的损失及其利息。

对于原告请求的出口退税损失，法院不予支持。因为出口退税是国家鼓励企业出口的一项税收优惠政策，与海上货物运输没有必然联系，因此原告未能从其买方处收汇致使无法办理出口退税，与被告 LINK 公司的违约行为没有因果关系。

被告"KK SHIPPING CO."与原告没有海上货物运输合同关系，对原告的损失不承担任何赔偿责任。依照《中华人民共和国海商法》第 71 条、第 55 条第 1、2 款的规定，上海海事法院判决被告 LINK 货运代理有限公司赔偿原告 Z 公司货款损失及相关利息，驳回原告 Z 公司对被告"KK SHIPPING CO."的诉讼请求。

2. 案例分析

本案例涉及的主要问题是应以哪国法律为依据来解决纠纷，以及当事人的责任确定。但首先要确定提单运输关系的当事人，以此决定法律的适用性问题。①海运提单上的承运人是谁？尽管本案提单抬头印制的公司名称为"KK SHIPPING CO."，但其签章载明由被告 LINK 公司法定代表人林某代表该公司签发，则被告 LINK 公司为本案提单运输合同中的承运人无疑。只不过是被告 LINK 公司借用了"KK SHIPPING CO."的格式提单而已，则本案无单放货的责任应由作为承运人的被告承担。②适用哪一国法律？尽管本案提单背面条款第二条规定，本提单有关承运人的权利义务将适用 1936 年《美国海上货物运输法》，但其背面条款第一条又规定，本提单的"承运人"是指"KK SHIPPING CO."，而"KK SHIPPING CO."并非本提单的当事人，则提单背面条款第二条即无适用的余地，即该法律适用条款无效，而应适用法院地法即我国法律来确定提单上当事人的责任。根据我国《海商法》第 269 条的规定，在合同当事人没有选择合同适用的法律的情况下，适用与合同有最密切联系的国家的法律。而本案的主要当事人均是我国的，货物是从我国出运的，相关的证据大都分布在我国，等等，都说明我国即是与该合同"有最密切联系的国家"，该合同纠纷应以我国法律为依据来解决。③责任如何确定？根据我国《海商法》的规定，提单是承运人保证据以交付货物的单证，提单中载明的向记名人交付货物，或者按照指示人的指示交付货物，或者向提单持有人交付货物的条款，构成承运人据以交付货物的保证。所以，在我国，无论何种提单，承运人交付货物都必须凭正本提单，这也是我国法律规定的提单本身所具有的性质。如果承运人违反了我国法律有关必须凭单交货的规定，未收回正本提单而将运输货物交付与非提单持有人，则它应当承担由此而产生的法律责任。④如若本案例中的 LINK 货运代理公司是用 "KK SHIPPING CO." 的提单格式签发提单，提单签署也由 "KK SHIPPING CO." 作为承运人签发，而非像本案中由 LINK 货运代理公司法定代表林某作为 "KK SHIPPING CO." 的代理签发，那么提单背面的第一、二条款适用，本案的原告 Z 公司要求被告赔偿的要求将被驳回，本案将依据美国法律判定。按照美国相关法律，记名提单不是物权凭证，承运人可以直接放货给提单载明的收货人。

本 章 小 结

国际贸易结算单据可分为商业单据、运输单据、保险单据和官方单据。商业单据主要包括发票、装箱单；运输单据的种类很多，本章主要介绍了海运提单的性质及其具体种类与内容；保险单据主要是保险单、保险凭证与联合凭证，本章也简单介绍了保险单的基本内容；官方单据主要是原产地证、许可证和检验证书等，本章详细介绍了原产地证的种类及其办理程序。结合 UCP600 规则，本章阐述了银行对结算单据在单据化条件、出单人资格、出单日、单据正副本、单据签字、交单期等方面的具体要求。通过案例，本章也相应介绍了出口企业在信用证项下审证、制单、条件单据化判定等方面应注意的事项。

复习思考题

1. 国际结算涉及的单据有哪些？分别具有什么样的作用？
2. UCP600 关于单据的要求有哪些规定？

第七章

跟单信用证项下单据的审核

学习目标：掌握 UCP600 的单据审核标准，学会判定相符交单和不符交单；掌握开证行和被指定银行拒付单据的做法及要求；熟悉银行审单方法和审单要点。

关键概念：审核标准、不符单据、拒付通知、审单方法

第一节　UCP600 的单据审核标准及相符交单与不符单据

一、单据审核标准

审单的目的是为了确定交单是否相符，而交单相符包括单证一致和单单一致。UCP600 将单据审核标准统一纳入其第 14 条规定。与 UCP500 相比，其单据审核标准更明确、宽松、务实，但却很难掌握。

1. 审单原则

按指定行事的被指定银行、保兑行(如有的话)或者开证行须审核交单，并仅基于单据本身确定其是否在表面上构成相符交单(UCP600 第 14 条 a 款)。审单的一个最重要的规则是"信用证的任何规定都必须执行"。

2. 审单时间

被指定银行、保兑行(如有的话)或者开证行各自有从收到交单的次日起算的至多 5 个银行工作日用以确定交单是否相符。这一期限不因交单日当天或之后信用证截止日或最迟交单日届至而受到缩减或影响(UCP600 第 14 条 b 款)。在信用证业务中，出口地的被指定银行、进口地的开证行都需要审核单据。如果有保兑行，若被指定银行或受益人向其交单，保兑行也要审核单据。

3. 交单时间

如果单据中包含一份或多份正本运输单据，则须由受益人或其代表在不迟于本惯例所指的发运日后的第 21 个日历日内交单，但是在任何时候下都不得迟于信用证的截止日

(UCP600 第 14 条 c 款)。

4. 单据种类审核

提交非信用证所要求的单据将不予理会，并可退还给交单人(UCP600 第 14 条 g 款)。如果信用证含有一项条件，但未规定用以表明该条件得到满足的单据，银行将视为未作规定而不予理会(UCP600 第 14 条 h 款)。

5. 单据内容审核

(1) 数据。单据中的数据，在与信用证、单据本身以及国际标准银行实务参照解读时，无须与该单据本身的数据、其他要求的单据或信用证中的数据等同一致，但不得矛盾(UCP600 第 14 条 d 款)。

(2) 货物描述。除商业发票外，其他单据中的货物、服务或履约行为的描述，如果有的话，可使用与信用证中的描述不矛盾的概括性用语(UCP600 第 14 条 e 款)。

(3) 地址。当受益人和申请人的地址出现在任何规定的单据中时，无须与信用证或其他规定单据所载相同，但必须与信用证中规定的相应地址同在一国；联络细节(电传、电话、电子邮件及类似细节)作为受益人和申请人地址的一部分时将被不予理会。然而，如果申请人的地址和联络细节为第 19、20、21、22、23、24 或 25 条规定的运输单据上的收货人或通知方细节的一部分时，应与信用证规定的相同(UCP600 第 14 条 j 款)。

(4) 出单人。如果信用证要求提交运输单据、保险单据或者商业发票之外的单据，却未规定出单人或其数据内容，则只要提交的单据内容看似满足所要求单据的功能，且其他方面符合第 14 条 d 款，银行将接受该单据(UCP600 第 14 条 a 款)；在任何单据中注明的托运人或发货人无须为信用证的受益人(UCP600 第 14 条 k 款)；运输单据可以由任何人出具，无须为承运人、船东、船长或租船人，只要其符合第 19、20、21、22、23 或 24 条的要求(UCP600 第 14 条 l 款)。

(5) 出单日期。单据日期可以早于信用证的开证日期，但不得晚于交单日期(UCP600 第 14 条 i 款)。

【案例 7-1】UCP600 标准宽松的"负效应"

被指定银行向保兑行香港 U 银行交单。为确保收汇安全，受益人缮制单据十分小心。然而，U 银行收到单据后竟然以下列理由拒付：Packing list showing invoice NO as 211Mo791162F1 I/O The number 211M0791162F1 shown on the invoice. U 银行的拒付大意是"发票上标注的号码中是数字"0"，而装箱单上显示的发票号码是英文字母"o"，被指定银行查阅单据留底，发现两个号码中的"0"几乎一样，根本没有数字"0"与字母"o"的明显区别。但是，即便一个是数字"0"，一个是字母"o"，根据 ISBP，打印错误只要不影响所在单词或句子的意思，并不构成不符点。然而，U 银行坚持拒付，并从开证行的付款中扣除 1500 美元作为自己的保兑费。显然，U 银行仅为收取费用而加具保兑，根本不打算承担保兑责任。在单据完全相符的情况下，以莫须有的不符点拒付，明显违背 UCP600 的原则。

然而，这种不顾 UCP600 的宽松标准而"硬"拒付的情况，不仅在外国开证行中司空见惯，在我国的一些银行也有出现。外国某杂志报道过我国一些开证行拒付时所提的不符点 "Documents showing beneficiary's name 'ABC Ltd' didn't exactly match the 'ABC Limited'in the L/C"。该文指出，中国的一些银行最近形成了一种挑剔单据的不良习惯，经常以一些琐碎的问题甚至是标点符号作为拒付的不符点。这种现象在中国蜂拥而起的中小商业银行中更为明显。相对于信誉而言，他们的业务人员由于开拓业务的压力更忠于自己的客户。(案例来源：《中国外汇》杂志 2011 年 1 月下半月刊)

二、UCP600 关于"相符交单"的规定

相符交单是指与信用证条款、UCP600 的相关适用条款以及与国际标准银行实务一致的交单。当开证行确定交单相符时，必须承付；当保兑行确定交单相符时，必须承付或议付并将单据转交给开证行；当被指定银行确定交单相符予以承付或议付后，必须将单据转交给保兑行(如有的话)或开证行。

【案例 7-2】开证行收单后拒不理睬

受益人通过交单银行向乌兹别克一家银行提交即期信用证下相符交单，开证行并未拒付。但半个月过去了，但开证行一直未付款。交单银行催收，开证行一直不予回应。之后一个多月，尽管交单银行分别向其部门经理、行长发电加大催收力度，但所有电报如石沉大海。两个月后，开证行终于付款，但对于迟付款不作任何解释。交单银行向其催收利息，开证行不予理睬。开证对相符交单置若罔闻，对交单银行的交涉、查询置之不理，是目前令交单行和受益人深感头痛的不良作风。这种视国际惯例如儿戏的做法，在金融危机期间外汇紧张的国家中表现尤其突出。(案例来源：《中国外汇》杂志 2011 年 1 月下半月刊)

三、UCP600 关于"不符单据、放弃及通知"的规定

当按照指定行事的被指定银行、保兑行(如有的话)或者开证行确定交单不符时，可以拒绝承付或者议付。他们各有从交单次日起的至多 5 个银行工作日用以确定交单是否相符。这一期限不因交单日当天或之后信用证截止日或最迟交单日届至而受到缩减或影响。

(1) 当开证行确定交单不符时，可以自行决定联系申请人放弃不符点。

(2) 当按照指定行事的被指定银行、保兑行(如有的话)或者开证行决定拒绝承付或者议付时，必须给予交单人一份单独的拒付通知(见示样 7-1 和示样 7-2)。

(3) 拒付通知必须申明：①银行拒绝承付或者议付。②银行拒绝承付或者议付所依据的每一个不符点。③ A)银行留存单据听候交单人的进一步指示；或者 B)开证行留存单据直到其从申请人处接到放弃不符点的通知并同意接受该放弃；或者其同意接受对不符点的放弃之前从交单人处收到进一步指示；或者 C)银行将退回单据；或者 D)银行将按之前从交单人处获得的指示处理。④拒付通知必须以电讯方式，如不可能，则以其他快捷方式，在不迟于自交单次日起第 5 个银行工作日结束前发出。⑤按照指定行事的被指定银行、保兑行(如有的话)或者开证行在按照上述 A)、B)发出通知之后，也可以在任何时候将单据退回交单人。⑥如果开证行、保兑行未能按照以上规定行事，则无权宣称交单不符。⑦当开证行拒绝承付或保兑行拒绝承付或议付，并且按照以上要求发出拒付通知后，有权要求返回已偿付的款项及利息。

示样 7-1　拒付通知 1

Eximbills Enterpriste Incoming Swift

Message Type: MT734

Send bank: CITIMYKLJOD

Recv Bank: BKCHCNBJ910

User Name: ZJ105002

Print Times: 1

Print date: 2011-04-28　　MIR: 110428CITIMYKLBJOD1012075654

ADVICE OF REFUSAL

:20:[Sender's TRN]6976600158/73401

:21:[Presenting Bank's Reference]BP2704411000049

:32A:[Date and Amount of Utilisation] 110427USD101251.20

:77J:[Discrepancies] PACKING LIST SHOWING PACKAGES 385 ROLLS

INCONSISTENT WITH INVOICE, B/LADING

+++MESSAGE 1/1+++

WE ARE HOLDING DOCUMENTS AS PER ARTICLE 16C(III)B OF UCP600

--END

示样 7-2 拒付通知 2

2011 MAR 29 16:35:38   **LOGICAL TERMINAL PB11**

MT S734   ADVICE OF REFUSAL   PAGE 00001

                                                                   FUNC ZJHQLARV

                                                                   UMR 50428183

MSGACK DWS7651 AUTH OK, KEY DIGEST, BKCHCNBJ SCBLCNSX RECORD

BASIC HEADER   F 01 BKCHANBJXXX   2003 494572

APPLICATION HEADER   0 734 1035 110328 SCBLCNXXXSHA 0351 210318 110328 1035 N

                          *STANDARD CHARTERED BANK (CHINA)

                          *LIMITED

                          *SHANGHAI

                          *(SHANGHAI BRANCH)

USER HEADER   SERVICE CODE   103：

                  BANK PRIORITY   113：

                  MSG USER REF.   108：0000075186

                  INFO. FROM CI   115：

SENDER'S TRN   *20 : 111153036085-A

PRESENT. BANK'S REF. *21 : BP9277779

DATE/CUR./AMOUNT   *32A : DATE 110325 CURRENCY USD AMOUNT 11,998.78

TOTAL AMOUNT CLAIM.*33B : DATE   CURRENCY USD AMOUNT 11,998.78

SEND. TO REC. INFO.   72 :   DOCS REFUSED DUE TO DISCREPANCIES.

                              APPLICANT CONTACTED AS PER ARTICLE 16C(III)

                              (B) OF UCP600

DISCREPANCIES   *77J: OUR REF.: 111153036085-A ISS 000

                              WE ADVICE HAVING OBSERVED THE FOLLOWING

                              DISCREPANCIES IN THE DOCUMENTS SUBMITTED

                              BY YOU:

                              1.B/L NOT SHOW FREIGHT PREPAID.

                              2.SHIP. CO. CERT. AND I/P SHOW VOYAGE NO. INCORRECT

                              ATTENTION INTERNATIONAL DEPARTMENT.

YOUR REFERENCE BP9277779 UNDER OUR REFERENCE
111153036085-A FOR USD 11,998.78
PLS KINDLY REPLY US WITHIN 2 DAYS AND CONFIRM YOUR
GOOD BANK HAS ENDORSED ON THE ORIGINAL L/C,
OTHERWISE WE WILL SEND A MESSAGE TO GET APPROVAL
FROM THE ISSUING BANK FOR AUTHORIZATION TO SEND
THE DOCUMENTS TO THEM WITHOUT ORIGINAL L/C
PRESENTED AND ENDORSED AT OUR COUNTER.
MEAWHILE,WE WILL HOLD THE DOCUMENTS AT YOUR
DISPOSAL.
IN VIEW OF THE ABOVE DISCREPANCIES, WE HEREBY
NOTIFY UNDER ARTICLE 16 OF UCP600, OF OUR REFUSAL TO
ACCEPT DOCUMENTS SUBMITTED BY YOURSELVES. WE
ARE HOLDING THE DOCUMENTS AT YOUR RISK AND
DISPOSAL. WITHOUT PREJUDICE TO THE ABOVE
DISCREPANCIES, WE HAVE NOTIFIED THE APPLICANT OF
THE ABOVE DISCREPANCIES AND REQUESTED THEM TO
ADVICE US OF THEIR DECISION TO ACCEPT OR REFUSE THE
DISCREPANCIES. IF WE HAVE NOT RECEIVED INSTRUCTIONS
TO THE CONTARY FROM YOU AND THE APPLICANT WAIVES
THE ABOVE DISCREPANCIES IN THE MANNER SPECIFIED BY
THE BANK, AND SUCH WAIVER BEING ACCEPTABLE TO US,
THE BANK WILL DELIVER THE DOCUMENTS TO THE
APPLICANT. PLS BE INFORMED THAT SATURDAY /SUNDAY
WILL NOT QUALIFY AS BANKING DAYS AS UNDERSTOOD BY
ARTICLE 2 OF UCP600 FOR OUR TRADE FINANCE/OPERATIONS.

DISPOSAL OF DOC.   *77B: /NOTIFY/

TRAILER   ORDER IS <MAC:> <PAC:><ENC:> <CHK:> <TNG:> <PDE:>

        MAC: 27337460

        CHK:75EDEBF06399

第二节　审单方法和单据审核要点

一、审单方法

银行收到交单人交来的单据和交单委托书(见示样 7-3)后，银行审单工作人员必须首先阅读信用证，看信用证上都要求哪些单据，是否全部如数收到，然后再逐字阅读信用证，看信用证上各项要求是否完全在单据上得到满足。同时，还要看单单之间是否一致，如果有的单据未交，或有的单据份数不足，或信用证上有些要求没有做到，或单单之间有不一致的地方，就把这些情况也即差错写下来。这些差错称为"不符点"(DISCREPANCY)。

有不符点的单据称为不符单据(DISCREPANT DOCUMENT)。银行可以拒绝接受不符单据。但是，不符点可以分为可改不符点和不可改不符点两种。例如缺一份发票，没有在单据上签字等差错，都属于可以修改的不符点。在日常处理中，银行一般都是退还交单方，请其改正。但如迟交单、逾装期这类情况，都属于不可改不符点。对于含有这类不符点的单据，指定银行可以拒受，但很多情况下都是保留议付或保留付款，有时凭受益人出具赔偿保证书或保函给予议付或付款。

审单顺序一般是先审汇票(如果有汇票的话)、发票，然后以发票为中心，依次审核发票的附属单据(如果有的话)、保险单据、运输单据等。发票审完以后，其他单据的内容可以根据方便，或与发票核对，或与信用证核对，最后是审核单单之间是否一致。

二、单据审核要点

1. 面函的审核

寄单面函是指定银行寄送给开证行凭以索偿的通知单，开证行收到面函后应该审核：①寄单面函是否交与本银行；②面函上是否有当前的日期；③面函及所附单据属于相关的信用证号码项下；④列举的单据均包含在内；⑤单据中的金额与面函提及金额一致；⑥交单银行(如有的话)是否为信用证项下的付款行、承兑行或议付行；⑦付款指示是否明确易懂；⑧是否提及有任何不符点，是否凭担保函或有保留地付款、承兑或议付。

示样 7-3　客户交单委托书

致：中国银行＿＿＿＿＿＿＿＿＿＿＿　　　　　　日期：　年　月　日

随附下列出口单据，信用证业务请按信用证使用的国际商会《跟单信用证统一惯例》(UCP600)办理，跟单托收业务请按国际商会《托收统一规则》(URC522)办理。

发票编号：＿＿＿＿＿＿　　　金额：＿＿＿＿　　　核销单编号：＿＿＿＿＿

单据	名称		汇票	发票	装箱单/重量单	产地证	FORM A	检验证	保险单	提单	空运单	陆运收据	货物收据	电抄	受益人证明	船公司证明	邮据	装船通知	传真报告		
	份数	正本																			
		副本																			
托收			代收行：										付款人：								
			【　】付款交单(D/P)										期限/到期日：								
			【　】承兑交单(D/A)																		
信用证			开证行：																		
			信用证号：										通知编号								

（　）请按照信用证规定支付佣金/折扣及费用，有关责任及费用均由我公司承担。

（　）无需验单，请向开证行/代收行寄单，我司承担一切责任。

（　）限制其他银行议付信用证。请直接向开证行寄单，我司承担一切责任。

（　）单据有下列不符点，请向开证行寄单，我司承担一切责任。

　　　　□ 迟交单　　　□ 逾装期　　　□ 逾效期　　　□ 其他

（　）此笔业务项下款项的性质为：

　　【　】贸易项下，请划入我司待核查出口收汇存款账户，

　　　　账号＿＿＿＿＿＿＿＿，开户行＿＿＿＿＿＿＿＿＿。

　　【　】非贸易项下(具体说明：＿＿＿＿＿＿＿)，请划入我司账户，

　　　　账号＿＿＿＿＿＿＿＿，开户行＿＿＿＿＿＿＿＿＿。

　　　　　　　　　　　　　　　　　　　　公司公章：

公司联系人：＿＿＿＿　　　手机：＿＿＿＿　　　固定电话：＿＿＿＿

中国银行＿＿＿＿＿＿＿＿＿＿分行(支行)	
联系人：	联系电话：

【案例7-3】开证行收单后诈称单据缺少

受益人注意到出口货物适逢国际市场价格大跌，为做到万无一失，与交单银行合作，在制单与审单时非常谨慎，在确保单据齐全、不存在任何不符点的情况下寄单给开证行。开证行收到单据后第5个工作日发来拒付通知，所提不符点是"缺少一份信用证要求的证明"，称如果受益人同意按照D/A托收处理，则申请人可以考虑接受单据。显然，拒付的原因是进口货物市场价格下跌，但开证行与申请人在信用证中找不到任何不符点，因此，便将上述证明抽出，以单据份数不符合信用证要求拒付。而信用证下的单据都是通过快递机构提交。交单行按信用证规定寄递单据，开证行收单的数量是否相符，全凭收单者的基本良心，UCP600与交单行对此无能为力。一些作风恶劣，置基本信誉不顾的开证行，正是利用此种交单死无对证，诈称交单不足，作为拒付相符交单的最后一招杀手锏，此点成为信用证业务的死穴。(案例来源：《中国外汇》杂志2011年1月下半月刊)

2. 汇票的审核

汇票是兑用信用证的凭证。信用证所需的汇票一般属于跟单汇票，随附的单据是汇票的附件。因此，汇票也必须符合信用证的规定。汇票审核要点如下：

(1) 信用证规定应记载"DRAWING CLAUSE"时，汇票上的开证行名称、信用证号码及开证日期等应与信用证规定相符。

(2) 出票人应是信用证的受益人。

(3) 受票人记载应符合信用证规定，不能以开证申请人作为受票人。即期付款的信用证如要求汇票，汇票付款人一般是被指定的付款行；承兑信用证的汇票付款人一般是被指定的承兑行。对于议付信用证，根据"议付"的定义："议付是指被指定银行在相符交单下，在其应获偿付的银行工作日当天或之前向受益人预付或者同意预付款项，从而购买汇票(其付款人为被指定银行以外的其他银行)及／或单据的行为。"因此，议付信用证的汇票付款人一定是议付行以外的一家银行，通常是开证行。

(4) 汇票金额应与商业发票所载金额相同，但信用证规定汇票金额为发票金额一定百分比的(如"DRAFT FOR 90% INVOICE VALUE")汇票除外。

(5) 汇票金额应不超过信用证可支取的金额。

(6) 汇票金额大小写必须一致，货币必须与信用证所规定的相符。

(7) 汇票期限应与信用证中的规定相符。

(8) 跟单汇票的出票日不能早于提单日和迟于信用证的有效期。

(9) 汇票要背书，它应能被正确背书，一般不能作限制性背书。

(10) 除非信用证授权，否则，不应开立"无追索权"的汇票。

3. 商业发票的审核

商业发票是全套单据的核心,银行在审核商业发票时应格外小心谨慎。

(1) UCP600第18条规定:除可转让信用证外,商业发票必须看似由受益人出具(MUST APPEAR TO HAVE BEEN ISSUED BY THE BENEFICIARY)。

(2) 商业发票必须做成以申请人为抬头,但在已转让信用证项下可用第一受益人的名称替换原证中的开证申请人名称。

(3) 商业发票的货币必须与信用证的货币相同且发票无须签名。但是,如果信用证要求商业发票被签字、公证人证实、合法化、证明等,应确保正确照办。即如果信用证要求签字的发票,则发票需要单独签字;如果信用证不要求签字的发票,则证明该发票不需签字和注明日期。

(4) 商业发票上的货物、服务或履约行为的描述应该与信用证中的描述一致。

(5) 商业发票的金额审核,依据以下几点综合判定:①按指定行事的被指定银行、保兑行(如有的话)或开证行可以接受金额大于信用证允许金额的商业发票,其决定对有关各方均有约束力,只要该银行对超过信用证金额的部分未作承付或者议付。②"约"(ABOUT)或"大约"(APPROXIMATELY)用于信用证金额或信用证规定的数量或单价时,应解释为允许有关金额或数量或单价有不超过10%的增减幅度。③在信用证未以包装单位件数或货物自身件数的方式规定货物数量时,货物数量允许有 5%的增减幅度,只要总支取金额不超过信用证金额。④如果信用证规定了货物数量,而该数量已全部发运,及如果信用证规定了单价,而该单价又未降低,或当以上第③条不适用时,则即使不允许部分装运,也允许支取的金额有 5%的减幅。若信用证规定有特定的增减幅度或使用以上第②条提到的用语限定数量,则该减幅不适用。

(6) 商业发票不要加注"临时的"(PROVISIONAL)、"形式的"(PROFORMA)或类似用语,除非信用证特别准许。

(7) 商业发票上的货物数量、重量、尺码、装运、包装、运费等数据与其他单据中的数据之间应不矛盾,但无须等同。信用证如无特殊规定,商业发票中不要列入仓租、佣金、电报费等额外费用。

(8) 如果信用证规定的单价含有"佣金"(COMMISSION),商业发票上应照样填写,不应以"折扣"(DISCOUNT)字样代替。如果信用证的单价规定有"现金折扣"(CASH DISCOUNT)字样,在商业发票上也应全名照打,不能只写"折扣"或"贸易的折扣"(TRADE DISCOUNT)等字样。

(9) 发票份数必须与信用证要求一致,包括份数及正本和副本。

4. 运输单据的审核

运输单据的审核是单据审核的重要内容之一。UCP600 规定的运输单据种类有联合运输单据，提单，不可转让的海运单，租船合同提单，空运单据，公路运输、铁路运输或内陆水运单据，快递收据、邮政收据或投邮证明，分别对应 UCP600 的第 19、20、21、22、23、24 和 25 条。以提单为例，说明运输单据的审核要点如下。其余运输单据的审核要点可参照提单审核要点与相应的 UCP600 条款的规定。

(1) 提单的名称、份数、签署应与信用证的规定相符。必须提交全套(FULL SET)正本运输单据，除非信用证另有规定。另外，提单无论名称如何，必须看似：①表明承运人名称并由以下人员签署：承运人或其具名代理人，或船长或其具名代理人。②承运人、船长或代理人的任何签字必须表明其承运人、船长或代理人的身份。③代理人的任何签字必须表明其系代表承运人还是船长签字。

(2) 提单日期。提单的出具日期将被视为发运日期，除非提单载有标明装运日期的已转船批注，此时已装船批注中显示的口期将被视为发运日期。

(3) 收货人。收货人的名称应符合信用证要求。对于不具有物权凭证性质的运输单据(如空运单据)，应在信用证中指定开证行为收货人；对具有物权凭证性质的运输单据(如提单)，可在信用证中要求将收货人做成空白抬头、空白背书(MADE OUT TO ORDER AND BLANK ENDORSED)或开证行指示抬头(MADE OUT TO THE ORDER OF ISSUING BANK)等。

(4) 运输工具。提单应通过以下方式表明货物已在信用证规定的装货港装上船只：预先印就的文字，或已装船批注注明货物的装运日期。如果提单载有"预期船只"或类似的关于船名的限定语，则需以已装船批注明确发运日期以及实际船名。

(5) 运输路线。提单必须表明货物从信用证规定的装货港发运至卸货港。如果提单没有表明信用证规定的装货港为装货港，或者其载有"预期的"或类似的关于装货港的限定语，则需以已装船批注表明信用证规定的装货港、发运日期以及实际船名。即使提单以事先印就的文字表明了货物已装载或装运于具名船只，本规定仍适用。

(6) 货物描述。货名描述可采用与信用证中的描述不矛盾的概括性用语，但唛头、数量、重量、运输路线、运输方式、收货人、通知人等记载应与信用证相符。

(7) 运输单据上的托运人或发货人无须为信用证的受益人，除非信用证有特别规定。

(8) 运输单据上的成交条件或有关运费的记载应与信用证和发票一致。如成交条件为 CIF、CFR、CPT、CIP，应注明"FREIGHT PREPAID OR PAID"，但不能注明"FREIGHT PAYABLE OR TO BE PAID"。

(9) 转运。转运是指在信用证规定的装货港到卸货港之间的运输过程中，将货物从一船卸下并再装上另一船的行为。提单可以表明货物将要或可能被转运，只要全程运输由同一提单涵盖。即使信用证禁止转运，注明将要或可能发生转运的提单仍可接受，只要其表明货物由集装箱、拖车或子船运输。

(10) 如果运输单据需要背书，受益人在交单时应确保它被适当地背书。例如，提单抬头为"TO ORDER OF SHIPPER"，"SHIPPER'S ORDER"或"TO ORDER"时，则运输单据的托运人应作空白背书，或作完全背书。

(11) 确保运输单据上没有能够使其"有瑕疵"或"不清洁"的条款。提单中申明承运人保留转运权利的条款将被不予理会。

5. 保险单据的审核

保险单据的审核要点如下。

(1) 保险单签发人：保险单据必须看似由保险公司或承保人或其代理人或代表出具并签署。代理人或代表的签字必须表明其系代表保险公司或承保人签字。

(2) 保险单份数：如果保险单据表明其以多份正本出具，所有正本须提交。

(3) 保险单种类：可以接受保险单代替预约保险项下的保险证明书或声明书，但暂保单将不被接受。如果信用证要求的是保险单，保险凭证或预保单项下的保险证明或保险声明就不能接受；如果信用证要求保险凭证或信用证明确要求预保单项下的保险证明或保险声明，保险单可作为替代；如果信用证没有明确种类，笼统地要求保险单据，则只要与信用证其他条件及统一惯例各项规定相符的单据都可受理。

(4) 投保日期：保险单据日期不得晚于发运日期，除非保险单据表明保险责任不迟于发运日有效。

(5) 保险金额：①保险单据必须表明投保金额并以与信用证相同的货币表示，除非信用证另有规定，否则保险单据的货币应与信用证的货币相同；②信用证对于投保金额为货物价值、发票金额或类似金额的某一比例的要求，将被视为对最低保额的要求；③如果信用证对投保金额未做规定，投保金额须至少为货物的 CIF 或 CIP 价格的 110%；④如果从单据中不能确定 CIF 或 CIP 价格，投保金额必须基于要求承付或议付的金额，或者基于发票上显示的货物总值来计算，两者中取金额较高者。

(6) 风险区间：保险单据须表明承保的风险区间至少涵盖从信用证规定的货物接管地或发运地开始到卸货地或最终目的地为止。

(7) 保险险别：保险单据的承保责任险别应与信用证的规定相符。如果信用证使用诸如"通常风险"或者"惯常风险"等含义不明确的用语，无论是否有漏保之风险，保险单据将被照常接受。当信用证规定投保"一切险"时，如保险单据载有任何"一切险"批注或条款，无论是否有"一切险"标题，将均被接受，即使其申明任何风险除外。

(8) 援引条款：保险单据可以援引任何除外条款。

(9) 免赔率：保险单据可以注明受免赔率或免赔额(减除额)约束。

(10) 保险单据上所记载的唛头、号码、船名、航程、装运地、卸货地、起运日期等，必须与运输单据所记载的不相矛盾，但无须严格等同。保险单据上填写的发票号码应与承保货物的商业发票号码一致，以体现不同单据间的关联性。

(11) 如果被保险人的名称不是保兑行、开证行或买方，应带有适当的背书。

(12) 保险单据上注明的赔款偿付地点，应按信用证的规定填写，如信用证未规定，应以货物运抵的目的地或其相邻地点作为赔付地点。如信用证要求赔付给某一指定公司，应在赔付地点之后加注。

6. 产地证的审核

产地证是证明货物原产地的文件。产地证的审核要点如下。

(1) 产地证应由信用证指定的机构签署。如果信用证规定由主管当局(COMPETENT AUTHORITY)出具产地证时，应由出入境检验检疫局、贸促会或国际商会签发正式的产地证明书。当然，如果信用证没有规定，则由受益人出具的单据也是可以接受的。

(2) 按照信用证要求，确保它已被签字、公证人证实、合法化、签证等。

(3) 确保产地证上面的进口商名称、唛头、货名、件数等资料与信用证条款相符，并与发票和其他单据一致。

(4) 确保产地证上记载的产地国家应符合信用证的要求。如果信用证规定产地国家，产地证上应予以注明；如果信用证规定产地为中国某地(如天津)，则产地证上应填写"天津，中国"，而不应只写"中国"。

(5) 除非信用证规定，否则应提供独立的产地证明，不要与其他单据联合使用。在信用证只要求证明商品的产地时，则可以在商业发票上加注："兹证明装运货物的原产地是中国"(WE HEREBY CERTIFY THAT THE GOODS SHIPPED ARE OF CHINESE ORIGIN)，这就是产地证明与商业发票的联合格式。但是，当信用证要求提供产地证明书时，就不能采用在商业发票上加注证明货物产地的联合格式，而要出具单独的产地证，并应签字，加注日期和正当地注明其名称。

(6) 产地证的签发日不得迟于提单日期，但是可以迟于发票日期。

7. 装箱单的审核

装箱单、重量单是商业发票内容的重要补充。货物到达目的港后，可用于海关检查和核对货物。

(1) 单据名称和份数应与信用证要求的一致。

(2) 不要与其他单据联合使用，除非信用证准许。

(3) 确保单据上记载的货物名称、规格、数量及唛头等资料与其他单据所记载的不相互矛盾。

(4) 数量、重量及尺码的小计与合计须与信用证、提单及发票所记载的内容不相互矛盾。

(5) 如信用证要求经签字的装箱单，则应由制单人签字。否则，装箱单无须签字。

8. 检验证书的审核

检验证书是商检机构对进出口商品进行检验鉴定后出具的证明文件，是国际贸易中不可缺少的重要凭证。

(1) 检验证书应由信用证规定的检验机构检验、出具。检验证书的签发机构一般为政府设立的商品检验机构或国际性的民间公证机构，如我国的出入境检验检疫局、瑞士通用鉴定公司(S.G.S.)等。

(2) 检验证书的名称应符合信用证的要求，并签字及注明日期。检验证书的出单日期应略早于提单日期，表明属于装运前检验。

(3) 检验证书的内容必须与发票或其他单据的记载不相矛盾，并符合信用证的规定。检验结果只要符合信用证的要求就算合格。

(4) 除非信用证准许，确保它没有包含关于货物、规格、品质包装等的不利的声明。

9. 各类函抄及附属单据的审核

UCP600 规定，如果信用证要求提交运输单据、保险单据或者商业发票以外的单据，却未规定出单人或其数据内容，则只要提交的单据内容看似满足所要求单据的功能，且与其他单据的数据不矛盾，银行将接受该单据。如果信用证要求该单据是作为"证明书"之用时，应确保该单据被签字。

第三节　信用证审单操作实例

仔细阅读下列信用证，并审核全套单据。说明：单据于 2011 年 6 月 8 日星期三提交，其中发票两份，保险单两份正本，无背书的正本提单三份。(案例来源：顾宏远. 国际贸易结算——实务操作与案例分析. 杭州：浙江大学出版社，2006.)

(一)信用证

SEQUENCE OF TOTAL	:27:	1/1
FORM OF DOCUMENTARY CREDIT	:40A:	IRREVOCABLE WITHOUT OUR CONFIRMATION
DOCUMENTARY CREDIT NUMBER	:20:	IM1JPU0002911
DATE OF ISSUE	:31C:	110505

APPLICABLE RULES	:40E:	UCP LATEST VERSION
EXPIRY	:31D:	110620 IN LIMA
ISSUING BANK	:52D:	BANK IN PERU, LIMA, PERU
APPLICANT	:50:	BUILDERS ,S.A., LIMA, PERU
BENEFICIARY	59:	HENRY CLYDE PRECISION PARTS
		ROCHESTER, NEW YORK
CURRENCY CODE, AMOUNT	:32B:	CURRENCY USD AMOUNT 6000.00
		(U.S. DOLLARS SIX THOUSAND ONLY)
PRECENTAGE CREDIT AMOUNT	:39A:	05/05
AVAILABLE WITH/BY	:41D:	WITH THE BANK OF NEW YORK, NEW YORK, N.Y.
		BY NEGOTIATION
DRAFTS AT…	:42C:	60 DAYS SIGHT
DRAWEE	:42A:	ADVISING BANK
PARTIAL SHIPMENT	:43P:	NOT ALLOWED
TRANSSHIPMENT	:43T:	ALLOWED
LOADING IN CHARGE	:44A:	NEW YORK
FOR TRANSPORT TO	:44B:	CALLAO
LATEST DATE OF SHIP.	:44C:	110605
DESCRIPT. OF GOODS	:45A:	TOOLS
DOCUMENTS REQUIRED	:46A:	

+SIGNED COMMERCIAL INVOICE IN TRIPLICATE

+CONSULAR INVOICE

+MARINE INSURANCE POLICY OR CERTIFICATE TO ORDER OF BUILDERS, S.A., COVERING MARINE AND WAR RISKS AND S.R. & C.C. LOSSES, IF ANY, PAYABLE IN LIMA, PERU, IN U.S. DOLLARS

+FULL SET OF CLEAN ON BOARD OCEAN BILL OF LADING MADE OUT TO ORDER OF ISSUING BANK , MARKED NOTIFY BUYERS AND "FREIGHT PREPAID"

ADDITIONAL CON.   :47A:

+ DRAFTS DRAWN MUST BE DESCRIBED WITH THE NUMBER AND DATE OF THIS L/C.

CONFIRMATION   :49:   WITHOUT

INSTRUCTIONS   :78:

+ DRAFTS AND DOCUMENTS TAKEN UP UNDER THIS CREDIT ARE TO BE FORWARDED IN ONE LOT TO BANK IN PERU, LIMA, PERU.

+UPON RECEIPT OF L/C CONFIRMATION DOCUMENTS COVER WILL BE SENT AT YOUR CONVENIENCE.

(二)单据

1. 汇票

(1) 汇票正面

EXCHANGE FOR USD6,000.00   NEW YORK   08 JUNE 2011

AT 30 DAYS   SIGHT OF THIS FIRST OF EXCHANGE (SECOND OF EXCHANGE) BEING UNPAID

TO THE ORDER OF THE BANK OF NEW YORK, NEW YORK, N.Y. THE SUM OF USD SIX
THOUSAND ONLY

DRAWN UNDER L/C NO.IM1JPU0002911 DATED ON 110505

TO: HENRY CLYDE PRECISION PARTS
                                                        ELEANOR PYE
                                                         MANAGER

(2) 汇票反面

HENRY CLYDE PRECISION PARTS
ELEANOR PYE
MANAGER

2. 商业发票

ISSUER: HENRY CLYDE PRECISION PARTS 42 SAFEWAY BLVD., ROCHESTER, NEW YORK	商业发票 COMMERCIAL INVOICE ORIGINAL		
TO: BUILDERS, S.A., LIMA, PERU	**NO. :** 9609	**DATE:** JUNE 03, 2011	
TRANSPORT DETAILS: FROM NEW YORK TO CALLAO BY SEA	**S/C NO. :**	**L/C NO. :** IM1JPU0002911	
	TERMS OF PAYMENT: L/C 60 DAYS BY PAYMENT		
MARKS & NUMBERS	NUMBER AND KIND OF PACKAGE; DESCRIPTION OF GOODS	QUANTITY	UNIT PRICE	AMOUNT
AIB 471	400 GRADE "B" #7 ROUTER BITS PACKED IN 25 CTNS	USD6,000.00 CIF CALLAO		
	TOTAL: AMOUNT SAY USD SIX THOUSAND ONLY			

HENRY CLYDE PRECISION PARTS
ELEANOR PYE
MANAGER

3. 保险单

XXX INSURANCE COMPANY

CARGO TRANSPORTATION INSURANCE POLICY

INVOICE NO.	9609	POLICY NO.	
CONTRACT NO.			
L/C NO.	IM1JPU0002911		
INSURED	HENRY CLYDE PRECISION PARTS		

THIS POLICY OF INSURANCE WITNESSES THAT XXX INSURANCE COMPANY (HEREINAFTER CALLED "THE COMPANY") AT THE REQUEST OF THE INSURED AND IN CONSIDERATION OF THE AGREED PREMIUM PAID TO THE COMPANY BY THE INSURED, UNDERTAKES TO INSURE THE UNDERMENTIONED GOODS IN TRANSPORTATION SUBJECT TO THE CONDITIONS OF THIS POLICY AS PER THE CLAUSES PRINTED OVERLEAF AND OTHER SPECIAL CLAUSES ATTACHED HEREON. IT IS HEREBY UNDERSTOOD AND AGREED THAT IN THE CASE OF THE LOSS, SUCH LOSS IS PAYABLE TO THE ORDER OF BANK IN PERU, LIMA, PERU, IN US DOLLARS.

MARKS& NUMBERS	QUANTITY	DESCRIPTION OF GOODS	AMOUNT INSURED
AIB 471	25 CARTONS	TOOLS	USD5,500.00

总保险金额 TOTAL AMOUNT INSURED	US DOLLARS FIVE THOUSAND FIVE HUNDRED ONLY					
PREMIUM	AS ARRANGED	DATE OF COMMENCEMENT	06 JUNE 2011	PER CONVEYANCE	S. S. TOM	
FROM	NEW YORK	VIA		TO	CALLAO，PERU	

CONDITIONS:
ALL RISKS INCLUDING S.R. & C.C. AND WAR RISKS

IN THE EVENTS OF LOSS OR DAMAGE WHICH MAY RESULT IN A CLAIM UNDER THIS POLICY, IMMEDIATE NOTICE MUST BE GIVEN TO THE COMPANY'S AGENT AS MENTIONED HEREUNDER. CLAIMS, IF ANY, ONE OF THE ORIGINAL POLICY WHICH HAS BEEN ISSUED IN TOGETHER WITH THE RELEVENT DOCUMENTS SHALL BE SURRENDERED TO THE COMPANY. IF ONE OF THE ORIGINAL POLICY HAS BEEN ACCOMPLISHED, THE OTHERS TO BE VOID. THE INSURANCE POLICY IS ISSUED IN TWO ORIGINALS.

| 2 | ORIGINAL(S) |

CLAIMS PAYABLE IN LIMA PERU IN USD	XXX INSURANCE COMPANY BROWN ELLEN
DATE: 07 JUNE 2011	
(ADD.):................NEW YORK	

4. 提单

1. SHIPPER INSERT NAME, ADDRESS AND PHONE HENRY CLYDE PRECISION PARTS ROCHESTER, NEW YORK				**A&P SHIPPING COMPANY LTD.**		
2. CONSIGNEE INSERT NAME, ADDRESS AND PHONE TO ORDER OF BANK IN PERU, LIMA, PERU				RECEIVED BY THE CARRIER FROM THE SHIPPER IN APPARENT GOOD ORDER AND CONDITION (UNLESS OTHERWISE NOTED HEREIN). THE TOTAL NUMBER OR QUANTITY OF CONTAINER OR OTHER		
3. NOTIFY PARTY INSERT NAME, ADDRESS AND PHONE BANK IN PERU, LIMA, PERU				IN WITNESS OF THE CONTRACT HEREIN CONTAINED THE NUMBER OF ORIGINALS STATED OPPOSITE HAS BEEN ISSUED, ONE OF WHICH BEING ACCOMPLISHED, THE OTHER(S) TO BE VOID. ORIGINAL		
4. COMBINED TRANSPORT * PRE-CARRIAGE BY	5. COMBINED TRANSPORT* PLACE OF RECEIPT				B/L NO.	0001
			6. OCEAN VESSEL VOY. NO.	SS ROSALIND		
			7. PORT OF LOADING	NEW YORK		
9. COMBINED TRANSPORT *	10. PLACE OF DELIVERY CALLAO		8. PORT OF DISCHARGE	CALLAO		
MARKS & NUMBERS CONTAINER / SEAL NO.	NO. OF CONTAINERS OR PACKAGES	DESCRIPTION OF GOODS (IF DANGEROUS GOODS, SEE CLAUSE 20)			GROSS WEIGHT KGS	MEASUREMENT
AIB 471	25 CTNS	TOOLS SHIPPED ON BOARD DATE: CIF CALLAO FREIGHT COLLECT			413 KGS	8.0 CBM
11. TOTAL NUMBER OF CONTAINERS AND/OR PACKAGES (IN WORDS): TOTAL TWENTY FIVE CARTONS ONLY						
SUBJECT TO CLAUSE 7 LIMITATION						
12. FREIGHT & CHARGES	REVENUE TONS	RATE	PER		PREPAID	COLLECT
COLLECT DECLARED VALUE CHARGE						
EX. RATE	PREPAID AT	PAYABLE AT	PLACE AND DATE OF ISSUE	NEW YORK, 06 JUNE 2011		
	TOTAL PREPAID	NO. OF ORIGINAL B(S)/L 3	A & P SHIPPING COMPANY LTD. GEORGE GATES AS MASTER			
DATE	BY					

(三)单据审核结果

(1) 汇票的空白背书人应是 "THE BANK OF NEW YORK, NEW YORK, N.Y.", 而非 "HENRY CLYDE PRECISION PARTS"。

(2) 汇票是 30 天远期, 而信用证规定是 60 天远期。

(3) 汇票未注明付款银行(BANK IN PERU, LIMA, PERU)。

(4) 商业发票货物栏 "400 GRADE 'B' #7 ROUTER BITS PACKED IN 25 CARTONS" 与信用证规定 "TOOLS" 不符。

(5) 保险单据未做成 "BUILDERS, S.A." 的抬头。

(6) 漏交领事发票。

(7) 提单上通知人为 "BANK IN PERU", 而信用证要求是 "BUYERS"。

(8) 提单上没有装船批注。

(9) 提单未注明 "FREIGHT PREPAID" (运费已付), 而是填写了 "COLLECT" (到付)。

(10) 保险金额少于发票金额。

(11) 提单上船名与保险单上船名不符。

(12) 保险单签发日期晚于提单签发日期。

第四节 跟单信用证项下交单不符拒付的相关案例

信用证是有条件的付款承诺, 即交单相符付款。交单不符是指信用证项下所提交的单据表面上有一处或多处不符合信用证条款。按照 UCP600 第 16 条 a、b 款规定, "当按照指定行事的被指定银行、保兑行(如有的话)或者开证行确认交单不符时, 可以拒绝承付或议付。当开证行确定交单不符时, 可以自行决定联系申请人放弃不符点"。因此, 交单不符会导致出口商的风险增加。

(一)出口商延迟装运引起的纠纷案

1. 案例介绍

某公司向日本出口一批玉米, 来证规定装运期不得超过 4 月 30 日, 交单期不得超过 5 月 10 日。该公司接到信用证后即备货准备装运。按原计划, 运输船只应于 4 月 26 日到港, 预计 29 日装完。但因天气原因, 该船舶延至 5 月 1 日到港, 但因下雨无法装船。5 月 5 日天气转晴后开始装船, 预计到 8 日可装运完毕。考虑到在申请修改信用证的装运期后再行装运, 一是手续麻烦, 二是船舶等待时间太长, 不利船舶周转。因此, 为避免提单日期晚于信用证所规定的最迟装运期(4月30日)，该出口公司出具了担保书，愿承担后果与责任，向船公司申请"倒签提单"。于是，货物在5月8日装运完毕，船舶开航，而提单日期则显示为4月30日。5月9日，该出口公司向银行交单。单到开证行后，开证行会同申请人一起审单，进口方发现提单装运日为4月30日，而货物实际到港日期为5月13日，按常规运输时间有失实可能。遂请律师查验航海日志与装货日期，发现提单日期是伪造的。于是，申请人与开证行实施拒付，并附来航海日志等影印件。

该出口公司持以下理由对开证行、进口方反驳：根据UCP600规定，银行所处理的是单据，而不是单据可能涉及的货物、服务(及)或履约行为，并仅基于单据本身确定其是否在表面上构成相符交单等等，坚持要求开证行付款。开证行提出反驳意见，按照UCP规定，银行确实没有义务去鉴定单据的真伪，但如事前已发现单据是伪造的，而且持有可靠的证据，则有权拒绝接受伪造的单据。该出口公司进一步了解到日本进口商实际已于单到开证行前凭保函提取了货物。由于装船延误，错过了最佳销售时间，市场价格下跌，日方损失了51 000美元，要求出口方赔偿。最终该出口公司以"倒签提单"理亏在先，同意赔偿对方损失并结案。

2. 案例分析

在实践中，受益人制作单据因时间引起的不符主要表现为：延迟装运(LATE SHIPMENT)、信用证过期(CREDIT EXPIRED)、未在最迟交单期内提交单据(DOCUMENTS NOT PRESENTED IN TIME)、提早装运(EARLY SHIPMENT)等。本案例的关键点在于出口方在延迟装运的情况下，再伪造单据，反被对方抓住把柄，最终酿成重大损失。

(二)金额方面的不符引起的纠纷案

1. 案例介绍

金额方面的不符主要表现为：超支(OVER DRAWING)、超过信用证金额(CREDIT AMOUNT EXCEEDED)、少开支款金额(SHORT DRAWING)、发票金额与汇票金额不一致(THE AMOUNTS SHOWN ON THE INVOICE AND DRAFT DIFFER)等。

一份英国来证规定的货物名称为粮食，数量为1800公吨，每公吨510美元CIF利物浦，总金额为918 000美元，数量允许5%增减，要求中国出入境检验检疫局签发品质证明书一式三份，在装运时检验(...INSPECTED AT THE TIME OF SHIPMENT)，按照中国保险条款投保，保险如发生赔偿，请付给多布逊有限公司(LOSS IF ANY, PAY TO DOBSON CO., LTD.)。受益人按期将全部货物装运完毕，因货物超装3%，因而汇票金额列为945 540美元，较来证超额27 540美元。开证行来电表示拒付，理由是"交单不符"：一是信用证金额超支，信用证只规定数量允许5%增减，而金额并未做相应规定；二是保险单上未按信用证规定列明"如发生赔偿，付款给多布逊有限公司"；三是品质检验证书签发日期为10

月 23 日，而提单装运日为 10 月 25 日，这不符合信用证的规定即"于装运时检验"。受益人通过交单行向开证行提出反驳：一是既然数量允许 5%增减，金额当然应有同步的 5%增减；二是提交的保险单已明确以多布逊有限公司为被保险人，也就是保险单权益所有人，这与信用证上要求达到的目的完全一样；三是中国出入境检验检疫局于 10 月 23 日先检验商品，合格后才开始装运，10 月 25 日装运完毕，两者并无矛盾，也完全符合来证所要达到的目的。开证行再次来电宣称：银行不管交易双方的实际业务效果，而只管单据表面上是否相符，信用证金额未明确规定允许有 5%的增减，信用证金额超支不允许；保险单上未写明信用证上所要求的文句就是"交单不符"。关于货物检验日期与装运日期不一致，也属于类似的表面上不符，因此无法接受单据并付款。受益人对上述拒付理由再难予以反驳，因为单据的内容已无法修改，最后只得与进口方协商每公吨降价 20 美元，全部货款损失 37 080 美元才使对方接受了不符单据而付款。

2. 案例分析

受益人造成损失的关键是其接受了数量、金额增减条款含糊不清的信用证。既然对货物数量有增减 5%的溢短装条款，则信用证金额也必须有增减相应幅度的条款，如不修改信用证，就只能少装货而不能使金额超支。所以，在受益人多装货物的情况下，对方开证行就有意要拒付该单据，而提交单据中存在的其他不符点又给对方提供了可乘之机，从而导致损失。其实，按照 UCP600 第 18 条 b 款，银行可以接受金额大于信用证允许金额的商业发票，其决定对有关各方均有约束力，只要该银行对超出信用证允许金额的部分未作承付或议付。有关本案的判决，出口商可以要求开证行接受单据，按照信用证金额付款，超出信用证金额的部分可由进口商在信用证外解决。

(三)发票方面的不符引起的纠纷案

1. 案例介绍

发票方面的不符主要表现为：发票的货物描述与信用证不符(DESCRIPTION OF GOODS IN INVOICE DIFFERS FROM THAT IN THE CREDIT)、发票的贸易条件不正确(INVOICE DOES NOT SHOW CORRECT TRADE TERMS)、发票的参考号码与信用证上的号码不一致(REFERENCE NUMBER ON INVOICE NOT IN ACCORDANCE WITH THE CREDIT)、发票没有做成以信用证申请人名称为抬头人(INVOICE NOT MADE OUT TO APPLICANT'S NAME AS SHOWN IN THE CREDIT)等。

某工艺品公司向巴基斯坦 B 公司出口一批货物。6 月 5 日对方开来信用证，其中有下列条款：...350 SETS OF DINNER SET, PRICE USD35.00 PER SET, C&F KARACHI, SHIPMENT FROM QINGDAO TO KARACHI(350 套西餐具，价格每套 35 美元，C&F 卡拉奇，从青岛装运至卡拉奇)。该公司装运货物后立即向银行交单，单到开证行审单后被指出有下列不符点而被拒付：信用证规定价格条款为"USD35.00 PER SET, C&F KARACHI"，而发票上表示的价格条款为"USD35.00 PER SET，CFR KARACHI"。出口公司回电反驳：关于价格条款的"C&F"与"CFR"的不符问题，按照INCOTERMS 2010，C&F术语已被CFR代替。所以，发票内容正确。开证行接电后再次来电坚持认为交单不符而拒付：关于贸易条件，UCP600规定银行只管单据是否与信用证表面上相符，"C&F"与"CFR"就是表面上不符。受益人与交单行共同研究认为，尽管对方属于挑剔单据，但提交的单据存在缺陷也是事实，后几经洽商，以出口方让价10%而结案。

2. 案例分析

从单证表面上看，本案例可以认定为交单不符。在不太了解开证行或进口商经营作风的情况下，应该严格按照来证规定制单，不给对方以拒付把柄。

(四)保险方面的不符引起的纠纷案

1. 案例介绍

保险方面引起不符的主要表现为：提交的保险单据类型与信用证要求不符(PRESENTATION OF AN INSURANCE DOCUMENT OF A TYPE OTHER THAN THAT REQUIRED BY THE CREDIT)，保险险别与信用证规定不符(INSURANCE RISKS COVERED NOT AS SPECIFIED IN THE CREDIT)，投保货币与信用证规定的货币不符(INSURANCE COVER EXPRESSED IN A CURRENCY OTHER THAN THAT OF THE CREDIT)，保险金额不足(UNDER INSURED)，保险生效日期表示方法不对，未自提单装运日期算起(INSURANCE NOT EFFECTIVE FROM THE DATE OF SHIPMENT ON THE B/L)，保险单理赔地点与信用证规定不符(INSURANCE POLICY INDICATING PLACE OF SETTLING CLAIM DIFFERS FROM THAT IN THE CREDIT)，收到保险声明但通知书未交(ACKNOWLEDGEMENT OF INSURANCE DECLARATION NOT PRESENTED)等。

英国A公司通过伦敦某银行开来在中国到期的信用证，有效期为3月15日，最迟装运期为2月28日，所有单据须于装运日后21天内寄达开证行，要求提交保险单一式两份。受益人于1月26日办理装运并取得提单，考虑到信用证有效期至3月15日，时值春节放假，故未急于交单，直到2月10日才向出口地银行交单。开证行于2月26日来电提出拒付，拒付理由如下：一是装运日为1月26日，但所有单据于2月18日才寄到开证行，违反了装运日后21天内必须到达开证行的规定；二是以保险凭证代替保险单，不符合信用证条款要求。受益人提出反驳：我方于1月26日装运，2月10日向议付行交单，其间只有15天，并未超过21天，且在信用证有效期以内，完全符合信用证条款的要求。关于保险凭证(INSURANCE CERTIFICATE)与保险单(INSURANCE POLICY)，两者名称虽不同，但效果一样，并不违反信用证规定。开证行再次来电宣称：信用证规定所有单据必须在装运日后21天内到达开证行，其涵义并非UCP600所指期限。保险凭证与保险单的效果虽一样，但其表明并不相符,故不能接受。受益人在无法反驳的情况下,最后委托其他代理商处理了货物,损失惨重,教训深刻。

2. 案例分析

本案例中的信用证规定"所有单据必须于装运日后21天内寄达开证行"与信用证规定"有效期至3月15日,在中国到期"是矛盾的,但受益人未仔细审核推敲。关于保险单据的问题,必须严格区分保险单和保险凭证的概念。保险单是正式的保险单据,也是保险人与被保险人之间的正式合同,背面印有详细的条款,说明双方的权利与义务。保险凭证只是一种简化的保险单,两者虽有同等效力,但终究有所区别。因此,凡来证要求提供保险单时,应注意不可以保险凭证代替。如来证要求提供保险凭证,一般可用保险单代替,但最好再加上"CERTIFICATE"字样,即写成"INSURANCE POLICY/CERTIFICATE"以求与信用证一致,防止对方吹毛求疵,借口不符而拒付。

(五)单据与单据之间的不符引起的纠纷案

1. 案例介绍

单单之间不一致主要表现为:单据之间唛头和号码不一致(MARKS AND NUMBERS DIFFER BETWEEN DOCUMENTS),汇票、保险单或提单背书不正确(DRAFT, INSURANCE POLICY OR B/L NOT ENDORSED CORRECTLY),缺少信用证要求的单据(ABSENCE OF DOCUMENTS CALLED FOR IN THE CREDIT),单据之间重量不同(WEIGHTS DIFFER BETWEEN DOCUMENTS),各项单据内容矛盾(DOCUMENTS INCONSISTENT WITH EACH OTHER),需要签字的单据却没有签字(ABSENCE OF SIGNATURES WHERE REQUIRED ON DOCUMENTS PRESENTED)等。

PH公司对新加坡出口一批货物。对方于3月5日由N.H.M.银行开来装船期为3月23日、有效期至4月3日的信用证,要求提交"FULL SET OF CLEAR ON BOARD OCEAN BILL OF LADING AND ONE COPY OF NON-NEGOTIABLE B/L...AND GENERALIZED SYSTEM OF PREFERENCES CERTIFICATE OF ORIGIN FORM A",并要求"ALL DOCUMENTS EXCEPT DRAFT AND INVOICE MUST NOT SHOW THE CREDIT NUMBER AND INVOICE NUMBER"。PH公司制单人员在装船前缮制GSP原产地证书时发现信用证要求除汇票和发票外的所有单据不能表示发票号,而GSP原产地证书格式A却要求填写"发票号和日期",遂立即与当地出证机构联系,但出证机构坚决不同意出具发票号留空的GSP原产地证书,其理由是联合国贸发会对于填写GSP原产地证书格式A的有关规定,此栏目不得留空不填。PH公司立即联系新加坡进口商,提出"你方信用证要求一切单据除发票和汇票外,不得表示发票号和信用证号,但是你方又要求我方提供GSP

原产地证书，该证书按照联合国贸发会规定必须填写发票号，故你方信用证与上述规定有抵触，而且我出证当局也不同意接受此条款。请你修改信用证为"ALL DOCUMENTS EXCEPT DRAFT，INVOICE AND GENERALIZED SYSTEM OF PREFERENCES CERTIFICATE OF ORIGIN FORM A MUST NOT SHOW THE CREDIT NUMBER AND INVOICE NUMBER"。

新加坡进口商回复：请立即装船，信用证正在申请办理修改中。PH公司随即安排3月22日装船，装船后一周仍未见其修改的信用证开到，因有效期将至，再次联系新加坡进口商，对方却称已经办理信用证修改。4月3日，PH公司只好出具保函向中国光大银行办理担保议付。PH公司向中国光大银行提交的提单中船名表明："INTENDED VESSEL 'FREESEA'"，但是在"已装船"批注中填有经承运人加注的实际已装船的船名和装船日期，并有承运人签章。单据寄到国外后，开证行提出交单不符，暂代保管单据。不符点有二：其一，GSP原产地证书格式A第10栏表示了发票号，与我方信用证的规定不符；其二，正本提单上承运人加注了实际装船的船名和日期，但是在副本提单上却无此批注。开证申请人不同意接受单据。

PH公司立即通过中国光大银行向开证行提出，对于XXX号信用证项下单据的不符点一事：一，GSP原产地证书表示了发票号系根据联合国贸发会的规定。开证申请人不但同意此不符点，而且已经修改了信用证；二，对于提单的"预期船名"，在提单上已经由承运人批注了实际装船的船名和装船日期，并有承运人签章。根据上述情况，应属交单相符，你方应该接受单据，按时付款。开证行收到PH公司申辩后再次提出反驳意见：对于GSP原产地证书不显示发票号的条款问题，我行并未修改信用证，经查对我申请人也未有申请修改的情况。银行对单据审核的唯一标准就是看单据表面上是否与信用证条款相符，并不考虑什么联合国贸发会的规定。原产地证书上标明了发票号，就是表面上单证不符。正本提单上有承运人批注内容，副本也应该有批注的内容。虽然承运人可以对提单副本不进行签章，但其各方面内容均应与提单正本内容完全一样。正本有，而副本没有，即构成单单不符。根据上述情况，申请人无法接受该单据。请速告对单据处理的意见。最后，买卖双方经过反复交涉，又由于当时货物价格趋涨，买方才决定付款。付款时间比正常收汇拖延了3个月，PH公司损失利息14 000美元。

2. 案例分析

本案例中，买卖双方之所以会产生纠纷的主要原因是卖方考虑不周，忘记了GSP原产地证书格式A要填写"发票号和日期"的要求，接受了信用证要求除汇票和发票外的所有单据不能表示发票号的条款，以至于在缮制结汇单据时遇到麻烦，不能完全按照信用证的要求取得单据。后来又在未收到买方信用证修改通知书的情况下，仅凭对方的口头承诺就发运了货物，结果遭到开证行拒付。好在经过双方反复交涉，又逢当时货价上涨，买方才决定付款，从而避免了巨额损失。但尽管如此，卖方还是损失了相当金额的利息。

由此案，我们可以得出如下教训：第一，在国际结算中，要熟练掌握不同单据的要求，并做好信用证及单据的审核工作，保证单证一致，单单一致。本案中就是由于业务员的疏忽，接受了一个不能完成的信用证条款，给自己造成了麻烦。如果熟悉普惠制原产地证书的缮制方法及其必须要求记载的事项，在审核信用证的过程中就会发现该条款存在的问题，从而及时修改。另外，也要对不同单据进行认真审核，避免单据之间的不一致。本案中，正本提单中有实际已装船的船名、日期，而副本提单上却漏掉了这项记载，从而被对方抓住了把柄。类似这样的情况在外贸公司中是极易产生的，因此需要外贸公司业务人员特别注意。第二，在信用证条款需要进行修改时，一定要等到收到书面修改通知后再发货，不能轻信对方的一面之词。

本 章 小 结

本章先介绍了 UCP600 项下单据的"审核标准"以及"相符交单"与"不符单据"的规定，并说明了银行的具体责任；然后，介绍了审单方法以及各种单据的审核要点；之后通过一份信用证及其具体单据实例来训练如何审核单据；最后，结合相关案例，说明出口公司在制单、审单方面应注意的事项，其中最重要的是在开证行拒付后，出口企业应如何应对。熟知国际贸易惯例，特别是 UCP600 至关重要。

复习思考题

1. 如交单不符，信用证项下涉及的开证行、保兑行、被指定银行实施拒付的必要手续有哪些？

2. 结合 UCP600 的审单标准及具体的实务操作案例，谈谈您对跟单信用证制单的想法。

3. 出口企业应如何抗辩银行有关交单不符而产生的拒付？

第八章

国际贸易结算融资

学习目标： 掌握开证额度、提货担保、信托收据等进口贸易融资方式和出口押汇、福费廷、保理等出口贸易融资方式的具体适用情况以及申请手续；了解出口信用保险项下的融资业务。

关键概念： 开证额度、提货担保、信托收据、进口押汇、出口押汇、打包贷款、出口商业发票贴现、保理、福费廷、出口信用保险

在结算业务中，银行往往向有资格的客户提供融资服务，这类服务与国际结算过程密切相关，从而称为国际结算融资。国际结算融资业务有两种形式：一是银行向客户直接提供资金融通；二是银行为客户提供信用保证，以使客户能从贸易对方或第三方取得融资。

国际结算融资方式根据银行提供融资对象的不同可以分为进口贸易融资和出口贸易融资。

第一节　进口贸易融资

一、开证额度

为方便业务，开证银行对一些资信状况较好、有一定清偿能力、业务往来频繁的进口人，根据其资信状况和提供担保品的数量与质量情况，核定一个相应的开证额度，供客户使用，客户在额度内申请开立信用证时，可免收或少收保证金。

开证额度(LIMITS FOR ISSUING LETTER OF CREDIT)有两类：普通信用额度(GENERAL L/C LIMITS)和一次性开证额度(ONE TIME L/C LIMITS)。普通信用额度是指银行订立额度后，客户可以无限次地在额度内委托银行开立信用证，额度可循环使用；一次性开证额度是指银行为客户的一个或几个贸易合同核定的开证额度，不得循环使用。一次性开证额度可以弥补普通开证额度不能满足大宗交易需要的不足，或可避免普通开证额度

的大量占用对其正常经营带来的影响。

【案例 8-1】开证额度的使用

1. 案例介绍

假设进口企业 A 在 B 银行开户。B 银行根据进口人 A 的情况，给予了 500 万美元的开证额度。在 500 万美元的额度内，保证金比例为 5%，则企业 A 每次从 B 银行开证，交纳的保证金为 5%，不需要再逐笔与 B 银行就保证金比例进行协商。当然，其前提条件是企业 A 在 B 银行的未付余额小于 500 万美元。

2. 案例分析

(1) 为什么开证额度是银行给予的一种融资？假定 B 银行规定，对于普通客户申请开立信用证，要求企业交纳 100%的保证金，以规避日后的垫款风险。对于一般企业来说，如想通过 B 银行对外开证，就必须筹集足够的资金作为保证金。若超出自身资金周转能力，就不得不向银行贷款来交纳保证金，或将用于周转的资金来交纳保证金，而正常周转时又必须向银行贷款。因此，银行给企业的开证额度，其实是一种变相的贷款，是银行给予的一种融资。

(2) 开证行为什么要提供开证额度？银行因竞争的需要不得不考虑进口人办理业务的方便与资金周转的需要。开证行通常根据实际情况对进口人区别对待，要求进口人交纳的保证金比例、担保和抵押要求、授信额度等均有差异。例如中国银行浙江分行将一些客户的资信等级划为 A 级与 B 级。A 类客户开立信用证一般交纳 30%的开证保证金，其余可以用开证额度和担保品；B 类客户则要交纳 40%的开证保证金，其余可用开证额度和担保品。

(3) 银行提供开证额度有否有风险？有的企业认为，银行开立信用证时，开证行并没有对外付款，也就不会有风险。信用证项下开证行承担第一性的付款责任，只要受益人根据信用证的规定和要求提交了相符单据，开证行就必须付款。所以，银行均视开证业务为银行业务中风险较大的一种"授信业务"。

(4) 银行对风险的控制。这其中的核心就是了解客户，了解客户的业务。银行开证前要审核企业的开证额度、货物的性质及变现能力以及货物保险和对物权单据的控制情况。银行根据客户的资信情况变化和业务需求变动随时对额度做必要的调整。

二、提货担保

1. 提货担保的概念与作用

提货担保(SHIPPING GUARANTEE，S/G)是指在跟单信用证或是跟单托收项下，货物运抵目的港(地)后，包括提单在内的单据尚未寄到，而延期提货会使进口商增加额外开支，或者进口商品行情下跌、市价回落。进口商为了报关的需要，事先可以向开证行或代收行签具"申请提货担保书"连同进口商自己的担保函(又称联合凭证)，以求通过银行的担保，及时通关提货。

通常情况下，收货人应凭正本提单向船公司办理提货。由于近海航行航程过短，货物常常先于单据到达。如果收货人急于提货，可采用提货担保方式，请开证行出具书面担保，请船公司先行放货，保证日后及时补交正本提单，并负责交付船公司的各项费用及赔付由此可能遭受的损失。货物到港后，收货人凭提货担保及时提货，而不必要等运输单据到达后提货，节省了收货人因等货运单据没有及时提货而可能产生的滞港费用和额外费用，避免了可能产生的损失。

2. 办理提货担保的业务流程

办理提货担保的业务流程较为简单。

(1) 在货物先于提单到达港口的情况下，开证申请人向开证行提出办理提货担保的申请。申请人应提供与本次提货担保申请有关的副本发票、副本提单和货物到港通知单(如有)，并填写提货担保申请书(见示样 8-1 和示样 8-2)。提货担保申请书表明开证行进行提货担保的一切后果均由开证申请人负责，决不使开证行蒙受损失，并同意一旦正本提单寄到，即将上述担保书换回，交回开证行注销，或由开证行直接将提单交给船公司换回上述提货担保书，以便解除开证行的担保责任，同时开证申请人授权开证行无条件支付上列货物价款和(或)解除有关领取上列款项所提供的保证书。进口商应按提货担保申请书格式内容填列准确、完整的资料。

(2) 开证行根据实际情况，有条件地办理提货担保书(LETTER OF GUARANTEE FOR THE RELEASE OF GOODS)(见示样 8-3 和示样 8-4)。开证行要将申请书和担保书上填写的各项内容与信用证分户账页核对，以证实是该笔信用证项下的货物。银行应对进口商进行审查，确信其为该批货物的收货人，以防进口商借担保骗取货物，同时可以要求进口商提供担保或交纳保证金或抵押品，以维护银行的权益。

(3) 开证申请人收到运输单据后立即向船公司换回提货担保。

示样 8-1　提货担保申请书 1

提货担保申请书

编号：　　年　字　　号

中国银行 XX 分行：

　　兹因有关提单尚未收到，请贵行向承运公司签署提货担保书，以便我公司先行提取下列货物。

信用证/合同号：

货名：

船名：

提单号：

发货人：

装运地点与日期：

总件数(大写)：

唛头：

　　我公司谨此承诺和同意下列事项：

　　1. 我公司在收到有关单据后，无论其是否与有关信用证/合同完全相符，我公司保证立即承付/承兑。贵行向我公司发出单到通知后，如我公司未在合理时间内承付/承兑，贵行有权从我公司账户中扣款，按期对外支付。

　　2. 我公司在收到有关提单后，立即向承运公司换回上述提货担保书，退回贵行。

　　3. 如因出具此提货担保使贵公司遭受任何损失，我公司负责赔偿。

　　4. 如提货担保出具之日到退还之日期间天数超过三个月，则须加收提货担保手续费。

公司(公章)

法定代表人或授权签字人(签字)：_____

日期　　年　　月　　日

联系电话：_____　　　　　　　　　　银行经办：_____

复核：_____

负责人：_____

示样 8-2　提货担保申请书 2

APPLICATION TO LETTER OF GUARANTEE

FOR THE RELEASE OF GOODS

TO :_____(ISSUING BANK)

DEAR SIRS,

WE ENCLOSE HEREWITH FOR YOU COUNTERSIGNING THE LETTER OF GUARANTEE ADDRESSED TO _____ CALLING FOR THE FOLLOWING CARGOS SHIPPED FROM _____ PER S.S._____

L/C NO._____

B/L NO._____

COMMODITY VALUE:_____

MARKS:

THE BILLS OF LADING OF THESE CARGOS HAVE NOT ARRIVED.

IN CONSIDERATION OF YOUR COUNTERSIGNING THIS LETTER OF GUARANTEE, WE HEREBY AGREE TO HOLD YOU HARMLESS FOR ALL CONSEQUENCES THAT MAY ARISE FROM YOU SO DOING. WE FURTHER AGREE THAT ON RECEIPT OF THE ORIGINAL BILLS OF LADING FOR THE ABOVE SHIPMENT, WE WILL DELIVER THE SAID LETTER OF GUARANTEE TO YOU FOR CANCELLATION, OR YOU MAY DELIVER THE ORIGINAL BILLS OF LADING DIRECT TO THE STEAMSHIP COMPANY ON OUR BEHALF TO RELEASE YOUR LETTER OF GUARANTEE. MEANWHILE YOU ARE AUTHORIZED TO PAY UNCONDITIONALLY THE ABOVE MENTIONED AMOUNT, AND/OR RELEASE ANY OTHER GUARANTEE, IF ANY.

YOURS TRUTHFULLY

NAME OF APPLICANT

示样 8-3　提货担保书 1

提 货 担 保 书

编号：　年　字　号

公司：

　　兹因中国银行＿＿＿＿＿＿行开立的＿＿＿＿＿＿号信用证项下全套正本提单尚未收到，请贵公司准许我公司凭此担保书先行提取下列货物。

信用证号/合同号	
发票号	
唛头	
货名	
集装箱号	
船名	
发货人	
承运人	
提单号	
提单日期	
装运地点	
货物数量(大写)	
发票金额(大写)	

　　上述货物属于我公司进口货物。若因我公司未凭提单先行提货致使贵公司遭受任何损失，我公司负完全赔偿责任。

　　正本提单将由：

　　(一)签发提货担保书的银行

　　(二)我公司

交给贵公司，以换回此提货担保书。

＿＿＿＿＿＿＿＿＿＿公司(公章)

法定代表人或授权签字人(签字)：＿＿＿＿＿＿＿＿＿

日期＿＿＿＿年＿＿＿＿月＿＿＿＿日

地点＿＿＿＿＿＿＿＿＿＿

银行签署：

　　当＿＿＿＿＿＿＿＿＿＿公司不能履行上述赔偿责任时，我行承担保证责任。

示样 8-4 提货担保书 2

BANK'S AGREEMENT FOR THE RELEASE OF GOODS
IN LIEU OF ORIGINAL NEGOTIABLE BILL OF LADING

DATE:_____

TO: _____(SHIPPING COMPANY)

GENTLEMEN:

RE: S/S. _____ VOYAGE NO.:_____

PORT OF LOADING:_____

PORT OF DISCHARGE:_____

BILL OF LADING NO. _____DATED _____

DESCRIPTION OF GOODS: _____

CONTAINER/SEAL NO. :_____

ESTIMATED VALUE:_____(OPTION FOR BANKING PURPOSE ONLY)

AS THE ORIGINAL BILL OF LADING IS UNAVAILABLE, UPON PAYMENT OF ALL FREIGHT AND CHARGES, PLEASE DELIVER THE ABOVE MENTIONED GOODS:

TO:_____

FOR ACCOUNT OF_____

IN CONSIDERATION OF YOUR RELEASING THE AFOREMENTIONED GOODS TO THE ABOVE, WE UNDERTAKE TO INDEMNITY AND HOLD HARMLESS YOU AND /OR THE ABOVE CARRIER, ITS OWNERS, CHARTERS, MASTERS AND AGENTS WITH RESPECT TO ANY CLAIMS, DAMAGES, COSTS AND EXPENSES OF ANY NATURE WHATSOEVER AND TO REIMBURSE YOU FOR CARGO VALUE AND ANY ADDITIONAL CLAIM, DAMAGES, COSTS AND EXPENSES IN CONNECTION THEREWITH.

WE FURTHER UNDERTAKE TO DELIVER TO YOU OR TO ARRANGE FOR OUR CUSTOMER TO DELIVER TO YOU, UPON RECEIPT OF THE ORIGINAL BILL OF LADING PROPERLY ENDORSED, AND UPON DELIVERY TO YOU, THIS UNDERTAKING SHALL HAVE NO EFFECT. MEANWHILE PLEASE RETURN THIS INDEMNITY TO US ACCORDINGLY.

FOR_____(ISSUING BANK)

SIGNATURE

3. 办理提货担保书应注意的问题

提货担保有两个当事人：出具赔偿担保的银行(负第一性责任)和运输公司(被担保人)。

1) 船公司要求提货担保具备的要件

船公司要求的提货担保内容包含三个方面：①形式以船公司/承运人或银行抬头预先印制，并且表明它是提货担保以及承诺"不出示提单的交货"。②申请人和开证行二者都可以签署赔偿担保。如果提货担保直接由银行出具，只包含银行签名，应承诺：A. 担保由此产生的损失或损害一律由银行向船公司/承运人赔偿并保证他们不受损失；B. 对任何针对船公司/承运人的诉讼而进行的抗辩提供资金；C. 对由于货物产生的任何运费和/或共同海损/或费用索要时立即支付。③一经收到正本提单马上提交，担保书不能带有限制责任赔偿条款和不能列有到期日。出具人承担不可撤销的赔偿责任。

2) 申请人应注意的事项

进口商凭提货担保书提取了货物，就丧失了拒付的权利，即使单据审核后发现不符点，但因正本提单已经交给船公司，无法退回提单，只能放弃拒付。进口商非万不得已最好不要办理银行担保先行提货。如果货物先到，进口商可以去码头看看货物情况，确有需要才去办理提货担保。本办法仅限于开证行自身开立的信用证项下的商品进口，并且运输方式为海运，并在规定提交全套海运提单的条件下方可办理。对于采用其他结算方式进口的商品、运输方式为非海运、2/3 提单等物权不完整条款的信用证，通常不能办理提货担保。提货担保属于银行的授信业务。进口商收到有关单据后，应立即用正本提单向船公司换回提货担保书并退回开证行。如不及时归还开证行将影响申请人的授信额度和信誉。因出具提货担保而使开证行遭受的任何损失，开证申请人负赔偿之责。

3) 开证行应注意的事项

(1) 银行为了便利进口商及时提货而有提货担保的做法，这是银行的服务项目，不受UCP600 的保护，因 UCP600 未对提货担保做出规定。

(2) 在办理提货担保书时，对于航程较远的进口货物，单据到达开证行的时间一般早于货物到达目的港的时间，此种情况下不需要银行提供提货担保书。如进口商在这种情况下申请提货担保，属于反常情况。开证行应调查情况，谨慎从事。

(3) 开证行收到指定银行寄来的一套正本提单，最好自己交给船公司换回提货担保书。可以先交一份正本提单给船公司，自己保留其他两份。若船公司拖延退回提货担保书，日后又要求开证行履行保证责任时，可以再拿出另一份正本提单，凭以解除保证责任。

(4) 申请提货担保由进口商提出，开证行应该考虑进口商的信用是否可靠，必要时可以向其收取押金或货款，也可要求其他银行或贸易商在申请书上会签，以防受骗。

(5) 提货担保只限用于正常寄送的正本提单晚到开证行的情况，如信用证交单属于副本提单或非全套正本提单，银行不要做提货担保。

三、信托收据

信托收据(TRUST RECEIPT，T/R)(见示样 8-5)是指进口商以信托的方式向银行商借全套商业单据出具的一种保证书。银行是信托人，代表委托人掌握物权；进口商是被信托人或受托人，代表信托人处理单据。进口商以银行受托人的身份代办提货、报关、存仓、保险等手续，物权仍归银行所有。如果货物出售，则货款存入银行。进口商在汇票到期后向银行偿付票款，收回汇票，赎回信托收据。

示样 8-5　信托收据

信托收据

XXX 银行　　　　　　　　　　　　　　　　　　　　编号：

我公司在贵行办理了业务编号为＿＿＿＿＿＿＿、期限为＿＿＿＿＿＿＿天的进口开证/代收业务，现同意以下列方式处理该进口开证/代收项下单据(单据金额：＿＿＿＿＿，货物名称：＿＿＿＿＿，数量：＿＿＿＿＿)及货物：

一、我公司兹确认收到贵行上述进口开证/代收项下单据/货物，自我公司取得该单据之日起，至我公司付清该进口开证/代收项下货款、利息及一切费用之日止，该单据及货物的所有权以及有关的保险权益均归属于贵行，我公司保证办理确认贵行上述权利所必需的手续。未经贵行授权，我公司不以任何方式处理该单据及货物。我公司不因上述转让行为而减少、免除或抵消我公司对贵行所承担的债务。

二、我公司作为贵行的受托人，代贵行保管有关单据，以贵行名义办理该货物的存仓、保管、运输、加工、销售及保险等有关事项，代为保管该货物出售后的货款或将货款存入贵行指定账户。贵行有权以任何合法方式对我公司进行监督，包括随时派员或代理人在任何时候进入仓库检查货物。

三、贵行有权要求我公司立即返还该单据或货物或销售所得款项，或从我公司在贵行系统内各机构开立的账户中直接扣款。该货物折价或销售所得款项不足我公司所欠贵行债务的，贵行有权就差额部分向我公司及保证人进行追索；货物折价或销售所得款项超过我公司所欠贵行债务的，超额部分我公司有权保留。

四、该货物在我公司保管期间产生的所有费用(包括但不限于保险、仓储、运输、码头费用等)由我公司承担。我公司承诺对该货物的市价投保所有可能出现的风险，在保险单上列明贵行为第一收益人，并将保险单交贵行保管，如投保货物发生损失，贵行有权直接向保险公司索赔。

示样 8-5(续)

> 五、未经允许，我公司不以延期付款或任何非货币方式或低于市场价值处理该货物。
>
> 六、我公司保证不将货物销售给我公司无权向其进行索偿的任何人。
>
> 七、我公司不向其他任何人抵押或质押该货物，或使该货物受到任何留置权的约束。
>
> 八、一经贵行要求，我公司即将该货物的账目、任何销售收入或与该货物有关的销售合同详细情况提交给贵行，贵行有权进入仓库对货物的实际情况进行检查或重新占有该货物。
>
> 九、若本公司发生破产清算，以信托收据提取的货物不在本公司债权人可分配的财产范围内。
>
> 十、我公司保证履行上述有关承诺，否则贵行有权采取任何措施(包括处理公司其他财产)清偿我公司在本信托收据项下承担的义务。
>
> 单位名称(公章)：
>
> 有权签字人：
>
> 年　　月　　日

理论上，信托收据是进口人与开证行或代收行之间关于物权处理的一种契约，是将货物抵押给银行的确认书，银行可以凭此办理融资业务。

【案例 8-2】D/P T/R 的风险

1. 案例介绍

我某外贸企业与某国 A 商达成一项出口合同，付款条件为付款交单，见票后 60 天付款，当汇票及所附单据通过托收行寄抵进口地代收行后，A 商在汇票上履行了承兑手续并出具信托收据向代收行借得单据，先行提货转售。汇票到期时，A 商因经营不善，失去偿付能力。代收行以汇票付款人拒付为理由通知托收行，并建议我外贸公司向 A 商收取货款。对此，你认为我外贸公司应如何处理？为什么？

2. 案例分析

信托收据可用于远期付款交单和远期信用证项下。利用信托收据融资时，存在的一个潜在风险是进口商有可能违反信托收据，不愿或无力退回货物或货款。如果进口商凭信托收据借单事先得到出口商同意或授权，风险由出口商承担。如果未经出口商同意，而是由充当信托人的银行主动提供这项融资，则风险由银行承担，视同进口商已经付款，银行必须支付货款。在办理信托收据时，银行应严格审查进口商的资信等级，避免借出单据而不获付款。实际上，进口地银行擅自凭信托收据借单给进口商，这是进口地银行向进口商提供信用，使进口商得到了资金融通，但进口商的信誉必须足够好。

因此本案中，按照 URC522，代收行有保管单据的责任。若代收行自行同意进口商凭信托收据借单，如事先未得到出口商同意，这其实是代收行自行为进口商提供了到期付款的信用担保。如果进口商提货后到期不能付款，则代收行应承担付款责任。

1) 进口人作为被信托人应注意的问题

(1) 进口商应将信托收据项下的货物和其他货物分开存仓、保险，其物权属于开证行或代收行。一旦货物出险，保险赔偿所得应归开证行或代收行所有。

(2) 货物销售后，所得货款应属于开证行或代收行。若款项尚未到期，该款由开证行或代收行保管或另外开立保证金账户，与进口人自己的资金分开，或提前付款，或提前赎回信托收据，利息按借单的实际天数计算，或由双方协商解决。

(3) 物权在未付款前并不属于进口人，进口人不得将该货物抵押给他人。为防止进口人擅自将该货物抵押给他人，银行在借出单据时，应在提单上加盖"UNDER LIEN TO XX BANK"的字样，表明该银行对货物持有留置权，货物随时接受银行的监督与查看。

2) 银行作为信托人的权利及应注意的问题

银行视进口人的信誉而决定是否给予进口商以信托收据的融资。银行如接受了信托收据，借出了单据，其拥有以下权利：①可以随时取消信托，收回借出的商品；②如商品已经被销售，可以随时收回货款；③如进口人破产、倒闭清算，信托人对货物、货款享有优先权。

本案例中，我外贸公司可以直接向代收行索赔，要求其承担全部付款责任。由此可见，银行办理信托收据有一定的风险。只有在进口商的信誉足够好的前提下，银行才受理信托收据借单。在实务中，开证人或代收行是否接受进口人的信托收据应十分慎重，应注意以下事项。

(1) 认真审查进口人的资信状况，根据进口人的信誉、抵押物、质押物的情况，对进口人核定一定的授信额度，并在核定的授信额度内办理。

(2) 借出单据后，应该加强对货物存仓、保险、销售、收款直到赎回信托收据等一系列活动的监控手段，绝不能放任自流，否则将造成"钱、货两空"的后果。

(3) 必须熟悉当地的法律，尽管通常信托人在被信托人破产清算时对货物或货款享有优先权，但不同国家对此的规定有所不同。

① 国家A：破产对象的清算按收支两条线原则。不论信托收据如何规定，货物拍卖所得均作为破产企业资产的增加；若仍资不抵债，根据比例按优先顺序偿付企业的债权人，这将使银行得不到全额的进口款项。

② 国家B：承认信托收据的优先权，但另外也有超越一切优先权的"最优先"项目，如拖欠的税款、员工的工资和国家规定的福利保障等。破产企业必须在扣除以上拖欠款有余额时，才能归还享有优先权的债务。因此，若"最优先"项目不够支付时，根本没有余款可归还开证行或代收行，信托收据的优先权就不能兑现。

③ 国家C：承认开证行或代收行的质押权，在企业破产清算时，质押货物不在清算

范围内，但如货物已经销售，货款并未入开证行或代收行的保证金账户，而是混入了企业的往来账户，一旦清算时被清算人查封账户并作为破产企业的总资产的一部分时，就难以分清，在实务中也难以操作，开证行或代收行往往难以得到应有的款项。

因此，银行必须熟悉进口人所在国的法律，同时要加强监管，随时注意自己的权益不被侵犯。

(4) 正确计算还款期限。由于信托收据的用途是为了在付款前先提货进行转卖或加工。因此，应正确计算还款期限，给予申请人一定的时间收回货款并归还银行的垫款。根据开证申请人的具体情况，该期限可以从半个月到几个月不等，最长可达半年。

3) 出口商应注意的问题

有些进口商希冀凭信托收据借单，会事先征求出口商的同意，可在开立信用证时要求开证行加列"受益人同意开证行凭信托收据放单给申请人"条款，如"ALL DOCUMENTS MUST BE DELIVERED TO THE APPLICANT AGAINST A TRUST RECEIPT IN ORDER TO OBTAIN CLEARANCE OF MECHANDISE TO SECURE INSPECTION BY CANADIAN AUTHORITIES BEFORE PAYMENT/ACCEPTANCE OF DRAFTS"(在汇票付款或承兑前，为确保加拿大授权检验机构检验后并获得货物的允许通关证明，所有的单据必须凭进口商的信托收据交给申请人)，或要求出口商在办理托收时在托收申请书上注明"同意进口商凭信托收据向代收行借单"(OTHER TERMS: THE BUYER MAY OBTAIN THE SHIPPING DOCUMENTS AGAINST A TRUST RECEIPT ISSUED BY THE BUYER TO THE COLLECTING BANK)。如出口商同意，则"货、款两空"的风险由出口商自己承担。

当然，绝大部分进口商希望用信托收据借单时不会直接告知出口商，因为出口商考虑信托收据的风险后，一般不会同意进口商的要求。

必须知道，信托收据是进口商向进口地银行融资的方式，应与出口商无关。但要注意的是，这只在进口地银行信用良好的前提下才能够得到保证，因为信托收据的接受对进口地银行来说是有很大风险的，出口商要防范进口地银行将风险转嫁到出口商身上，就像本案中的代收行一样。出口商在远期付款交单时，要谨慎选择代收行。在远期信用证下，要仔细审核信用证条款，预防开证行在信用证中加列"受益人同意申请人凭信托收据借单"条款。否则，进口地银行会以习惯做法和进口地法律、条款默认为由将货款收不回的风险直接转嫁到出口商头上。

4) 信托收据的习惯用法

在实务中，银行仅凭信托收据办理融资业务的风险较大，因此通常不单独使用。信托收据仅从法律上保证银行对货物的所有权，因而一般作为防范风险的手段，常与进口押汇、提货担保、进口代收押汇等业务结合起来使用。如银行为某开证申请人核定了100万美元的开证额度，其中包括50万美元的信托收据额度。开证申请人应将其开证余额控制在100万美元之内，其中的50万美元的证下单据可凭信托收据释放给开证申请人。信托收据额度与开证额度的比例主要是根据客户的经营范围、商品类别、资金周转速度等因素决定的。

比照开证额度的种类，信托收据额度也可分为普通额度和一次性额度，其使用方法和掌握原则与开证额度相同。在信托收据项下的货款付清之前，有关部分开证额度也不能恢复使用。

四、进口押汇

1. 进口押汇的概念及作用

进口押汇(INWARD BILL)是指信用证开证行在收到出口商或银行寄来的相符单据后先行垫付货款，待进口商得到单据，凭单提货后再收回该货款的融资活动，它是开证行对申请人(进口商)的一种短期资金融通。其发生的主要原因是申请人因资金周转问题，无法在开证行付款前赎单。

实务中，开证行收到单据后，如交单相符，或虽有不符点但申请人同意接受，开证行应立即偿付。进口商以信用证项下代表货权的单据为抵押，并同时向开证行提供必要的抵押、质押或其他担保，由开证行先行代付，这就产生了进口押汇的要求。

2. 进口押汇利息的计算

进口押汇的融资比例为发票/汇票金额的100%。采用"后收利息法"，在押汇到期后，银行从企业账户扣收押汇本金及利息。进口押汇一般使用信用证及单据使用的货币直接对外付款，不可兑换成本币使用(如本币与信用证使用的货币不一致)。开证行办理进口押汇通常不收取押汇手续费，其利息计算公式如下：

押汇利息=本金×融资年利率×押汇天数/360

进口押汇的天数一般以30天、60天计算，但最长不超过90天。

进口押汇与普通商业贷款相比，具有手续简便、融资速度快捷的特点。

3. 进口押汇的步骤

进口押汇的步骤如下所述。

(1) 单据到达开证行后，申请人向开证行提出进口押汇申请并签订有关协议。开证行审查进口押汇申请书(见示样8-6)的内容，如申请人名称、信用证编号、押汇金额及进口商的付款义务、押汇期限和利率、进口商的保证条款、延期还款条款、货权及其转移条款、违约条款等。

(2) 开证行办理进口押汇并对外付款。

(3) 开证行凭信托收据向进口商交付单据，申请人将自己货物的所有权转让给银行。

(4) 进口商凭单据提货及销售货物。

(5) 进口商归还押汇款本息，换回信托收据。

示样 8-6　进口押汇申请书

进口押汇申请书

编号：　年　字　　号

现我公司因业务需要，依据我司与贵行签署的____年____字____号《授信额度协议》及附件，用于进口押汇，向贵行申请叙做进口押汇。由于进口押汇而产生的权利义务，均按照前述协议、附件和本申请书的约定办理。

第一条　信用证有关内容

信用证号码：　　　　　　　　　来单银行名称：

来单编号：　　　　　　　　　　单据金额：

第二条　押汇币种和金额

押汇币种：　　　　　押汇金额为：(大写)　　　　　　　(小写)

第三条　押汇期限

押汇期限为 _____月/天，自贵行对外支付信用证款项之日起连续计算。

押汇到期日为前述期限的截止日或贵行依据相关协议宣布的立即到期日。

进口项下货物出售款项在进口押汇到期日前全部收妥的，贵行有权以货款收妥之日作为押汇到期日。

押汇的最终期限以贵行确认的为准。

第四条　押汇利率和付息

1. 正常进口押汇的利率及付息

请按以下第_____种利率(均为年率)核算贵行为我司办理进口押汇的利息：

(1)双方协商确定的利率_____%；　　(2)押汇时贵行确定/公布的利率_____%；

(3)押汇是 LIBOR/HIBOR+_____基点。

计收利息的方式为第____种：　(1)到期结息；　(2)按季结息。

2. 逾期进口押汇的利率和付息

如我公司未能按照总协议和相关附件的要求偿还贵行对我公司的押汇款项，则该笔押汇的本金、利息及相关费用构成我公司对贵行的逾期债务，贵行可按本条第 1 款确定的利率加 20%的水平核算利息。

对于我公司的逾期债务，贵行有权：

(1)　　根据本条第 1 款的利率按季结息；且

(2)　　对于我公司应付未付的利息按照本条第 1 款的利率计收复利。

第五条　费用(本条为选择性条款，双方的选择：1. 适用；2. 不适用)

我公司将通过以下第_____种方式向贵行交纳本笔业务下的费用：

1. 在贵行接受此申请书后____个银行工作日内主动通过_____向贵行交纳本笔业务下的费用；

2. 请从我公司在贵行开立的人民币账户(账号_____)/外币账户(账号_____)中直接划收本笔业务下的费用；

3. _____。

申请人：　　　　　　　　　　　　银行意见：

授权签字人：　　　　　　　　　　授权签字人：

　　　年　　月　　日　　　　　　　　年　　月　　日

地点：　　　　　　　　　　　　　　地点：

4. 办理进口押汇应注意的问题

办理进口押汇应注意的问题总结如下。

(1) 申请人应注意的事项：①进口押汇款项专款专用，只能用于履行信用证项下的对外付款。②进口押汇是短期融资，期限一般不超过 90 天。③进口押汇需要逐笔申请，逐笔使用，一般不设额度。④押汇比例及期限等根据实际情况与开证行协商解决。

(2) 融资银行应注意的事项：①了解开证申请人的资信情况和经营能力。②了解进口货物的市场行情。若货物畅销、变现能力强，可适当放宽押汇条件。否则，应从严控制。③适当考虑增加其他安全措施，因为进口押汇还款来源单一，风险较大。在需要时，可以要求申请人增加第三方担保、房产抵押、有价证券抵押等，以增加申请人的谨慎程度，并使银行的损失降到最低。④注意押汇后的管理，必要时监控申请人的进口货物资金回笼情况，并采取适当措施，减少损失。

五、进口代收押汇

进口代收押汇是代收行凭包括物权单据在内的进口代收单据为抵押向进口人提供的一种融资性垫款，由于风险较大，一般仅适用于 D/P。押汇比例、期限、收取利息的方法、还款的来源类似于信用证项下的进口押汇。区别在于对于进口代收押汇来说，因某进口人的代收业务较大，代收行通常根据其资信情况和抵押品的情况核定一个押汇额度，以供进口商资金周转使用。

六、汇出汇款项下融资业务

1. 汇出汇款项下融资的概念

在货到付款结算方式下，汇出行(进口地银行)根据进口人申请，并凭其提供的有效凭证及商业单据先行对外支付，从而向进口人提供的一种短期资金融通。该种融资方式开发晚、风险大，目前开办该业务的银行还在少数。进口人申请融资的资格、条件、手续等信用风险控制方面，与普通商业贷款相同；其融资的比例、收取利息的方法、还款的来源类似于进口信用证押汇。

2. 汇出汇款项下融资的业务流程

汇出汇款项下融资的业务流程如下所述。

(1) 进口人备妥汇出汇款所需要的各种单据并交汇出行。这些单据包括：填写完毕的银行格式化《汇出汇款项下融资申请书》和《购汇/用汇申请书》、加盖企业章的副本商业发票和副本提单各两份、正本货物进口报关单一份、进口批文(如需要)、外管所需要的其他单据或文件及与汇出行签订的《汇出汇款项下融资合同》。

(2) 进口人向汇出行(进口地银行)提出办理汇出汇款项下融资业务的申请并签订有关部门协议。

(3) 进口地银行办理汇出汇款项下融资并直接对外付款。

(4) 融资到期后，进口人归还本金并支付利息。

3. 进口地银行应注意的事项

进口地银行应注意的事项总结如下。

(1) 应了解进口人的资信情况。

(2) 应了解进口人的贸易背景。

(3) 应了解进口货物的市场行情。

(4) 应了解汇出汇款项下融资业务应占有该企业(进口人)的流动资金贷款的额度，对于银行没有核定信用等级和核定流动资金贷款的额度的企业，原则上不办理该项融资。

(5) 实行严格的贷后监控管理，必要时考虑增加其他安全措施。

第二节 出口贸易融资方式

一、打包贷款

1. 打包贷款的概念和作用

打包贷款(PACKING LOAN)是信用证(L/C)下的贸易融资方式，出口商在提供货运单据前，以供货合同和从国外收到的、以自己为受益人的信用证向当地银行抵押，从而取得生产或采购出口货物所需的周转资金的一种装船前融资。

打包贷款的金额通常不是信用证的全部金额，而只是部分金额(一般为 70%)，具体金额由打包放款银行根据出口商资信情况、存款数目、抵押品以及在本行的业务来确定。

贷款期限一般自信用证的抵押之日到从开证行收回货款之日为止，收到开证行支付的货款后即扣除贷款本息，然后将余额付给出口商。在实践中，出口商可在办理装运后，向打包贷款银行交单，并以出口押汇融资来替代打包贷款融资。一般来说，企业办理外汇打包贷款的利息远远低于人民币的打包贷款利息。银行办理打包贷款通常不收取手续费，利息计算公式为：打包贷款利息=信用证金额×打包折扣(如 70%)×融资年利率×打包天数/360。打包天数的计算为办理打包日至信用证最迟装运日的天数加 30 天。

2. 打包贷款的业务流程

打包贷款的业务流程如下。

(1) 出口企业将信用证正本交银行，向银行提出打包贷款申请，并同时提供以下文件。①如企业第一次在该银行办理贷款等授信业务，办理打包贷款时必须提供基础资料：企业的营业执照副本、税务登记证、企业组织机构代码证、进出口业务许可证和贷款卡。②填写并提交银行提供的《打包贷款申请书》。③如需要，交纳保证金，落实担保单位、抵押、质押。④签订贷款合同。⑤签订其他需要的协议。

(2) 银行审核信用证和一切出口商提供的资料后，办理打包贷款。

(3) 出口企业收到国外货款后归还打包贷款本金及利息。

3. 办理打包贷款应注意的问题

办理打包贷款应注意的问题如下。

(1) 提供打包贷款的银行应注意的问题：①以正本信用证作抵押，但银行不能仅凭国外信用证就给受益人放款。信用证对开证行是一种"或有负债"，对受益人是一种"或有资产"。银行需要仔细审核信用证的满足条件和要求，例如，开证行的付款承诺是否会得以实现，客户是否能满足信用证的全部条件和要求，或客户是否能履约。②银行应根据客户的资信情况和清偿能力为其核定相应的打包贷款额度，供其循环使用。先审证，审查开证行的资信和印鉴是否合乎开证要求，L/C 条款是否清楚、合理，有否对出口商不利的陷阱条款和出口商难以履行的规定，能否控制物权单据以减少风险等。审查通过后，还要根据融资额度的余额和商品类别来决定放款期限和金额。对于装运单据为非物权单据或不能控制全套正本物权单据者，银行的审核将更加严格。③为保证安全、及时地收回打包资金，贷款期间，银行应与客户保持密切联系，了解、掌握业务的进展和有关合同的执行情况，督促客户及时发货交单，如信用证过期后仍未能提交单据，银行应根据贷款协议的规定，要求客户立即归还银行贷款和利息。

(2) 申请打包贷款的企业应注意的问题：①向银行提交所要求的有关资料。②自身信誉良好，在该行没有不良记录。③关注信用证条款。若信用证在打包贷款时已经过最迟装运期、有效期，或信用证已没有足够的余额，开证行所在国政治、经济不稳定，信用证有软条款、不利条款，付款期限超过一年，均不能轻易地从银行取得打包贷款。④若企业为可转让信用证的第二受益人，也不能轻易地从银行取得打包贷款。

二、出口押汇

1. 出口押汇的概念与作用

出口押汇(OUTWARD BILL)是指出口商将代表物权的单据及其他单据抵押给银行，从

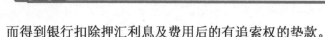

而得到银行扣除押汇利息及费用后的有追索权的垫款。

出口押汇的融资比例通常为100%，但其利息计收采用"预收利息法"，即银行在全额的本金内扣除预收利息及各种手续费后，将余额贷款给受益人。因此，出口商收到的金额不足 100%，还款的来源在正常情况下为信用证或托收项下的收汇款，在企业不能正常从国外收回货款的情况下，企业应偿还押汇本金及利息，或允许银行主动从其账户扣划押汇金额及补收有关费用。

$$押汇利息=本金×融资年利率×押汇天数/360$$

押汇天数的计算通常是：办理出口押汇日到预计收汇日的天数+ 5～7 天。

出口押汇主要是使出口商能向银行申请短期融资。在国外货款到达之前从银行得到垫款，加速资金周转，方便出口商的资金运作。出口押汇与其他融资方式相比，具有手续简便(无须担保、质押、保证金等)、快捷的特点。

出口押汇主要是买单，包括信用证项下的单据押汇和托收单据押汇。

2. 信用证押汇

信用证押汇(NEGOTIATION UNDER DOCUMENTARY CREDIT)是在信用证项下，卖方以出口单据为抵押，要求往来银行提供在途资金融通。

对银行来说，这种融资风险小、收款较有保障，但如交单不符，会失去开证行的信用保障。

出口商要求银行买入其出口单据时，应填写《出口融资申请书》(见示样 8-7)，连同信用证正本和全套单据提交银行。银行核对融资申请书印鉴并验收单据后开始审核单据，除了按信用证条款和规定审核外，银行还要审核以下方面。

(1) 开证行所在国的政治经济情况，有否第三国信用良好的银行加具保兑或确认偿付。

(2) 开证行的资信情况。

(3) 信用证条款是否符合国际惯例。

(4) 对物权的控制。海运提单和货物承运收据是物权凭证，其他运输单据都不是物权凭证。

(5) 出口商的资信情况。

(6) 对于限制议付的信用证、可转让信用证、有不符点的单据、政治经济不稳定的国家来证或 SWIFT 开立的使用无密押格式的信用证，银行要从严控制出口押汇的办理。

(7) 押汇有追索权。若开证行(或保兑行)未能及时付款，不论何种原因，企业作为受益人必须归还出口地银行的押汇融资款项。

(8) 出口押汇期限一般不超过 180 天。

(9) 银行采用预收方式收取押汇利息，押汇利息是根据押汇利率和融资期限计算出来的。如果实际收汇时间超出了预收利息期限，则议付行有权追收迟付利息。

示样 8-7　出口融资申请书

出口融资申请书

(用于出口押汇或远期信用证下承兑汇票贴现)

编号：　　年　　字　　号

现我司因业务需要，依据我司与贵行签署的_____年_____字_____号《授信额度协议》及附件_____：1.附件：用于出口押汇；2.附件：用于远期信用证下承兑汇票贴现，向贵行申请叙做第_____项业务：1.出口押汇；2.远期信用证下承兑汇票贴现。由此而产生的权利义务，均按照前述协议、附件和本申请书的约定办理。

第一条　有关的业务内容

信用证号码：　　　　　　　　　　　开证行名称：

信用证期限：　　　　　　　　　　　寄单编号：

单据/发票金额：　　　　　　　　　　发票号：

托收编号：　　　　　　　　　　　　代收行名称：

对代收行指示：　　　　　　　　　　贵行业务编号：

汇票号：_____、_____、_____、_____。

第二条　融资币种和金额

融资币种为：_____融资金额为：(大写)_____(小写)_____

第三条　融资期限

融资期限为_____月/天，自贵行向我司支付融资款项之日起连续计算。融资到期日为前述期限的截止日或贵行依据相关协议宣布的立即到期日。出口项下应收款项在出口融资到期日前全部收妥的，贵行有权以货款收妥之日作为融资到期日。融资的最终期限以贵行确认的为准。

第四条　融资利息和付息

1. 正常出口融资的利率及付息

请按以下第_____种利率(均为年率)核算贵行为我司办理出口押汇的利息：

(1)双方协商确定的利率____%；(2)押汇时贵行确定/公布的利率____%；

(3)押汇时 LIBOR/HIBOR+_____基点。

计收利息的方式为以下第____种：

(1)预收利息，到期结息；(2)后收利息，到期结息；(3)后收利息，按季结息。

2. 逾期出口融资的利率和付息

如我司未能按照总协议和相关附件的要求偿还贵行对我司的融资款项，则该融资的本金、利息及相关费用构成我司对贵行的逾期债务，贵行可按本条第 1 款确定的利率加 20%的水平核算利息。对于我司的逾期债务，贵行有权：

(1)根据本条第 1 款的利率按季结息；且(2)对于我司应付未付的利息按照本条第 1 款的利率计收复利。

第五条　费用(本条为选择性条款，双方的选择是_____：1. 适用；2. 不适用)

我司将通过以下第_____种方式向贵行交纳本笔业务下的费用：

1. 在贵行接受此申请书后_____个银行工作日内主动通过_____向贵行交纳本笔业务下的费用；

2. 请从我司在贵行开立的人民币账户(账号_____)/外币账户(账号_____)中直接划收本笔业务下的费用；

3._____。

申请人：	银行意见：
授权签字人：	授权签字人：
年　　月　　日	年　　月　　日
地点：	地点：

3. 出口托收押汇

出口商提交单据，委托托收行向进口商收取款项的同时，要求托收行先预支部分或全部货款，待托收款项收妥后归还银行垫款，这种融资方式称为出口托收押汇(ADVANCE AGAINST DOCUMENTARY COLLECTION)。

托收行办理押汇后成为全套单据的正当持有者，有权要求付款人支付货款。如果付款人拒付，托收行有权向出口商追索。如果出口商破产，银行对该款项可以寻求物权的保障，通过处理单据即货物来回笼资金，保留对不足部分索偿并参与破产清理的权利。

一般来说，为控制风险，银行一般要核定额度，在额度内叙做出口托收押汇。银行根据审查出口商的资信情况、清偿能力和履约能力、托收交单方式(D/P 风险比 D/A 小)、是否由出口商办理运输保险等情况来考虑是否接受出口商办理押汇的要求。托收行办理押汇后有权向出口商收取差额押汇利息，有权向出口商索回垫款和由此产生的利息。同时，出口地银行应选择适当的代收行，与出口商签订质押书(LETTER OF HYPOTHECATION)，其押汇利率高于信用证押汇利率。

4. 出口信用证押汇和出口托收押汇的区别

两者的根本区别在于出口信用证押汇有开证行(或保兑行)的付款保证，属于银行信用；而出口托收押汇属于商业信用，收汇风险大。银行为控制风险，通常根据出口方收款人的资信、还款能力等对出口商核定相应的授信额度，仅仅在额度内叙做出口托收押汇。

三、票据贴现

票据贴现(DISCOUNTING)是指票据持有人在票据到期前为获取现款而向银行贴付一定利息的票据转让。贴现票据必须是已承兑的远期汇票，承兑人一般是进口商、开证行或其他付款人，票据持有者一般是出口商。这类票据流动性强，可靠性高。

在办理该业务时，银行要与出口商签订质权书，确定双方的权利和义务。银行根据贴现费率扣减贴现利息和手续费后买下票据，票据到期收回票款，偿还垫款，余下部分为贴现收益。如果到期收不回，银行有权向出口商进行追索。银行一般应对票据的付款人和承兑人的资信进行调查，确认符合条件后才予以贴现。

办理票据贴现应注意的问题如下：

(1) 票据的信誉。银行承兑汇票信誉高于商业承兑汇票。

(2) 票据的风险。L/C 的远期汇票风险低于 D/A 和 D/P 项下的远期汇票。

(3) 要注意各国票据法的不同之处，如持票人享有的权利方面的差异。

(4) 票据本身的质量。加保兑的票据最可靠。如票据为不可流通或限制流通，则不容易被再贴现，影响票据的流通性。

四、银行承兑

银行承兑(BANKER'S ACCEPTANCE)是指银行在远期汇票上签署"承兑"字样，成为票据承兑人，使持票人能在公开市场转让贴现。银行主要承兑有贸易背景的汇票，如 L/C 项下的以银行为付款人的远期汇票、融通汇票等。

银行承兑汇票不必要垫付本行资金，只是将信誉借出，增强汇票的流动性。但是，银行承兑汇票有一定的风险性，银行承担一种"或有付款"的责任。

五、买入票据

买入票据，是指托收银行在光票托收款项收妥前，把票据的金额扣除贴现利息和费用后，将净额付给委托人的一种融资业务。光票托收不一定有贸易背景，难于掌握，融资风险较跟单托收大。因此，在实际业务中很少办理此项业务。银行在买入票据前，一般应注意以下几个方面：

(1) 客户资信可靠，有偿还能力。

(2) 票据没有过期，背书手续清楚，没有发现任何缺陷。

(3) 票据上没有限制流通文句。

(4) 为防止假票，核对出票行印鉴。

(5) 对金额较大者，事先以电讯方式查询证实。

六、出口商业发票贴现

1. 出口商业发票贴现的概念与作用

出口商业发票贴现(DISCOUNT AGAINST EXPORT COMMERCIAL INVOICE)是在"货到付款"结算方式项下，出口地银行以出口商的出口商业发票作为抵押进行融资的业务。中国银行将出口商业发票贴现业务归入国内保理来进行操作。它是从保理业务的融资功能中演变而来的，其融资比例通常为100%，使用与其他押汇相同的"预收利息法"，即银行在全额的本金内扣除预收利息及各种手续费后，将余额贷款给出口方收款人。因此，出口商收到的金额不足 100%，还款的来源在正常情况下为收汇款。在企业不能正常从国外收回货款的情况下，企业应偿还贴现的本金及利息，或允许银行主动从其账户扣划贴现的金额及补收有关费用。银行办理贴现有时不收贴现手续费，其利息计算方法如下：

$$贴现利息=本金×融资年利率×贴现天数/360$$

贴现天数通常是办理贴现日到预计收汇日或发票的到期日的天数+30 天。

2. 出口商业发票贴现的业务流程

出口商业发票贴现的业务流程如下。

(1) 卖方向卖方保理商提交《国内保理业务申请书》(见示样 8-8)。该申请书应由卖方法定代表人或其授权的有权签字人签字并加盖公章。

示样 8-8　　国内保理业务申请书

国内保理业务申请书

编号：

致：中国银行　　　　分行

我司拟在对(买方名称)的信用销售中利用贵行提供的国内保理服务。现请贵行审批信用额度。有关细节详见下表：

卖方名称	
买方名称	
货物名称	
合同/订单号	
合同/订单金额	
预计年赊销额	
付款条件	
申请循环额度金额	
申请单笔额度金额	
申请信用额度效期	

请贵行将审批结果尽快通知我司。
感谢贵行的大力协助。

公司
(签字盖章)

年　　月　　日

---

(2) 卖方保理商审核无误后，填具《国内保理信用评估委托书》(见示样 8-9)，由业务主管行长签字并加盖银行章传真至买方保理商。

示样 8-9　国内保理信用评估委托书

国内保理信用评估委托书

编号：

致：中国银行　　　分行

　　鉴于我行客户_____(卖方名称)拟在对你地客户_____(买方名称)的信用销售中利用我行提供的国内保理服务，根据卖方申请，现委托你行对买方进行信用评估，并于 14 个工作日内将有关评估结果通知我行。有关细节详见下表：

卖方名称	
买方名称	
货物名称	
合同/订单号	
合同/订单金额	
预计年赊销额	
付款条件	
申请循环额度金额	
申请单笔额度金额	
申请信用额度效期	

　　感谢你行的大力协助。

中国银行　　　分行

(签字盖章)

年　　月　　日

　　(3)　买方保理商在收到《国内保理信用评估委托书》后，经过评估和调查后，买方保理商出具《国内保理信用评估意见书》(见示样 8-10)，经主管行长签字并加盖行章后传真至卖方保理商。

　　(4)　卖方保理商在收到买方保理商有关决定全额或部分批准信用额度的《国内保理信用评估意见书》后按总行有关规定向总行报批。

　　(5)　在收到总行的同意批复后，卖方保理商应及时通知买方保理商，并及时向卖方签发《国内保理信用额度核准通知书》(见示样 8-11)并与卖方签订《国内综合保理协议》。

示样 8-10　国内保理信用评估意见书

国内保理信用评估意见书

编号：

致：中国银行　　　　分行

根据你行　年 月 日第　　号《国内保理信用评估委托书》要求，遵循总行有关统一授信管理的规定，我行对_____(买方名称)进行资信调查评估，现复评估结果如下：

卖方名称	
买方名称	
货物名称	
合同/订单号	
合同/订单金额	
付款条件	
批复循环额度金额	
批复单笔额度金额	
批复信用额度效期	
我行费率	

我行将按照《中国银行国内保理业务管理办法》和《中国银行国内保理业务操作规程》的有关规定办理相关业务。

中国银行　　　　分行

(签字盖章)

年　　月　　日

示样 8-11　国内保理信用额度核准通知书

国内保理信用额度核准通知书

编号：

致：　　　　　　　公司

根据你司　年 月 日第　　号《国内保理业务申请书》申请，经审查，我行同意为你司采用信用销售方式向　　(买方名称)销售　　(货物名称)提供国内综合保理服务。现核定信用担保额度详情如下：

信用额度(人民币元)		额度有效期	
保理费率		付款条件	

□此额度为循环信用额度。

□此额度为单笔额度，只适用于第(　　　　)号商务合同/订单下交易，不可循环使用。最迟装运期为 年 月 日。

请你司立即与我行签署《国内综合保理协议》，并按该协议有关规定办理业务。

特此通知。

中国银行　　　　分行

(签字盖章)

年　　月　　日

(6) 买方保理商在接到卖方保理商的通知后与买方签署《国内保理风险承担协议书》(见示样 8-12)。

示样 8-12 国内保理风险承担协议书

国内保理风险承担协议书

编号：

鉴于中国银行_____分行(下称"买方保理商")已同意为_____公司(下称"买方")采用赊购方式从_____公司(下称"卖方")购买_____(货物名称)承担信用风险，买方保理商和买方经友好协商，达成协议条款如下：

1. 买方保理商同意在该项业务中为买方核定信用担保额度(大写金额)_____元人民币。额度有效期至 年 月 日。

□此额度为循环信用额度。

□此额度为单笔额度，只适用于第(_____)号商务合同/订单下交易，不可循环使用。最迟装运期为 年 月 日。

2. 买方保证将按基础交易合同规定付款金额和付款期限将货款付给买方保理商。

若买方无正当理由却未在规定的付款日后 30 天期限内将货款付给买方保理商，买方保理商有权在付款到期日后第 31 天自动从买方在买方保理商开设的账户扣款。

若届时买方账户资金不足，买方保理商有权采取其认为适合的任何方式向买方追偿。

3. 买方对本协议涉及的基础交易存在争议，买方将在基础交易合同规定的付款到期日前做成"委托收款拒付理由书"，说明拒付理由，提供有关证据，连同委托收款凭证交买方保理商。否则，将视为对卖方所交货物无异议。

中国银行 分行 公司
(签字盖章) (签字盖章)
年 月 日 年 月 日

(7) 卖方在规定的时间内发运相关货物。发货后，应立即向卖方保理商提示带有债权转让条款的商业发票一式三份、货运单据正本(如有的话)及其复印件两份。

(8) 卖方保理商在审核卖方提交的单据无误后，将一份商业发票及货运单据正本退还卖方，由其直接寄送买方；自己留存一份商业发票及货运单据复印件，将另一份商业发票及货运单据复印件寄买方保理商。

(9) 买方保理商在收到相关单据后三个工作日内向买方提交《应收账款债权转让通知/确认书》(见示样 8-13)一式两份，请其确认交易的真实性及付款到期日。收到买方交回的两份《应收账款债权转让通知/确认书》后，买方保理商留存一份，将另一份寄送卖方保理商。买方保理商同时应扣减买方相应的授信额度。

(10) 买方保理商根据案卷记录定期向买方催收。对无任何争议产生的应收账款，买方保理商应在付款到期日前 10 天开始采用适当方式敦促买方做好到期付款的准备。

示样 8-13　应收账款债权转让通知/确认书

应收账款债权转让通知/确认书

编号：

致：_____公司(通知书)：

　　根据贵司与_____(卖方名称)签订的第____号购销合同/订单，卖方已于日前完成发货，并将第_____号商业发票项下应收账款债权转让给我行，请确认。

中国银行　　　分行

(签字盖章)

年　月　日

编号：

致：中国银行　　分行(确认书)：

　　我司确认已收到_____(卖方名称)为执行第_____号合同/订单下向我司发货而出具的第____号商业发票。兹向贵行确认该商业发票上所载内容与第_____号合同/订单的要求一致。我司同意贵行为该发票项下应收账款债权的合法受让人，并保证在本发票涉及的基础交易未发生争议的情况下于_____年__月__日将人民币_____元(大写金额)付至贵行指定的账户(账号：_____)。

公司

(签字盖章)

年　月　日

　　(11) 在收到买方付款后，买方保理商在一个工作日内扣除自身费用，将有关款项通过电子联行划往卖方保理商，并恢复买方相应的授信额度，在《买方保理业务登记表》上做好相应的登记。

　　(12) 除非发生争议，如在付款到期日后 30 天买方仍未付款，买方保理商应向卖方保理商做担保付款，并在《买方保理业务登记表》中进行登记。

　　(13) 卖方发货后若申请卖方保理商提供融资应提交《国内保理融资申请书》(见示样 8-14)。

　　(14) 卖方保理商只对卖方受核准的应收账款提供融资。每笔融资金额不超过受核准的发票金额的 80%。

　　(15) 若收到争议通知时，卖方保理商应立即通知卖方，并按《国内保理协议》和《国内保理融资申请书》的有关规定冲回融资本金及利息。

示样 8-14　国内保理融资申请书

国内保理融资申请书

致：中国银行　　　分行

根据贵我双方　年　月　日共同签署的第(　　)号《国内综合保理协议》，我司拟凭下列国内保理项下受核准的应收账款向贵行申请提供资金融通。

我司保证将按贵行要求支付融资利息及费用，并郑重声明若发生上述《国内综合保理协议》提及的情形致使贵行不能按期收回该等款项，贵行有权从我司在贵行开立的账户中主动扣款或采取其他办法强行收款。我司账号为：

公司

(签字盖章)

年　　月　　日

发票日期	付款到期日	发票号码	发票金额	受核准金额	申请融资金额

以下部分由银行填写审批意见：

3. 办理出口商业发票贴现需要注意的问题

出口商业发票贴现中有关当事人的权利与责任参见《出口商业发票贴现协议》。

(1) 出口方应注意的事项：①了解进口方付款人的资信情况和履约能力，但在货款不能正常收回时，出口方收款人作为商业发票贴现项下的债务人仍然不能免除还款责任。若出口方拒不履行还款责任，银行可以如同对待其他逾期贷款一样，采取必要法律手段。②了解进口方付款人所在国的政治、经济及外汇管制情况。

(2) 出口地贴现银行应注意的事项：①了解出口方收款人的资信情况及履约能力；②了解进口方付款人的资信情况；③了解出口货物的行情；④适当考虑其他安全措施；⑤商业发票最好载有债权转让条款；⑥加强贴现后的管理。

4. 业务受理范围

(1) 原则上仅适用于以承兑交单(D/A)或赊销(O/A)为付款方式的业务。

(2) 付款期限原则上不超过 90 天，最长不超过 180 天的国际货物买卖交易。

(3) 在中行办理出口商业发票贴现的出口商应为已纳入中行统一授信管理的客户。为出口商核定的出口商业发票贴现额度应纳入中行为客户核定的授信额度内。

(4) 出口商业发票贴现业务必须有真实的贸易背景，符合国家有关结售汇和国际收支申报的规定。

5. 费用

(1) 手续费：贴现的发票金额的 0.1%～0.4%范围内。手续费应在办理贴现时扣收。

(2) 贴现利率：应执行中国银行总行资产负债管理部和财会部的有关规定。

(3) 中行应逐笔办理贴现，可在扣收贴现利息后，将净额给付出口商，扣息天数按贴现日至发票到期日的实际天数加一定宽限期(不超过 30 天)计算。

(4) 中行亦可采用后收利息的方式。如采用该方式，中行原则上提供不超过发票金额 90%的融资。

6. 报批材料

(1) 有关贸易背景材料，包括近期签约情况、付款条件、有关销售合同、订单等。

(2) 卖方与中行的往来情况，包括在中行的授信情况、存款情况、办理结算业务的情况、业务纠纷情况等。

(3) 买方保理商提供的有关债务人的详细资料，包括对债务人的资信评估材料及同意为债务人划出专项授信额度叙做国内保理业务的书面文件等。

(4) 卖方近三年的财务状况分析(附企业资产负债表、损益表、现金流量表)。

(5) 管辖分行的基本意见。

(6) 总行要求提供的其他材料。

第三节　福　费　廷

一、福费廷的定义及主要内容

1. 定义

福费廷(FORFAITING)，即无追索权出口票据贴现业务，又称为包买票据，是指包买商无追索权地购进已经承兑的并通常由进口所在地银行担保的远期汇票或本票。

2. 主要内容

它是新型的贸易融资工具，融资比例通常为 100%，还款来源为出口项下的收汇款。出口方受益人承担的费用一般由利息、手续费和承诺费三部分构成。有的银行从与同业竞争的需要出发，不收取手续费，而承诺费在客户违约时收取，仅仅收取利息。

福费廷业务的利息计算方法与出口押汇相同。

福费廷利息=本金×利率(根据具体情况而定并高于押汇利率)×天数(办理日至到期日天数+5个工作日)/360

出口方实际入账金额=本金(汇票或发票金额)-利息-手续费-承诺费-出口议付应承担的费用(议付费、邮寄费、电报费)-国外预扣款(通常为300美元,在收汇后多退少补)

二、福费廷的业务特点

(1) 购买的汇票或本票应产生于销售货物或提供技术服务的经常贸易项下,在绝大多数情况下,票据的开立都是以国际贸易为背景的。

(2) 叙做福费廷业务后,出口人必须放弃对所出售债权凭证的一切权益,而包买商也必须放弃对出口人的追索权(出口人欺诈、进口地所在法院收到法院禁付令的情况下例外)。

(3) 出口人在背书转让作为债权凭证的票据时均需加注"无追索权"(WITHOUT RECOURSE)字样,将收取债款的权利、风险和责任转嫁给包买商。

三、福费廷业务的主要作用

对于出口人,福费廷与出口信用证项下的贴现融资条件相仿,而其承担的风险大大降低。福费廷业务越来越为广大出口人所接受,并正在成为新的主要票据融资工具。对出口人来说,该业务的主要作用如下。

(1) 可获得无追索权的中短期贸易融资,能将远期应收账款变成现金销售收入,有效地解决了应收账款的资金占有问题,改善了出口人的财务报告。

(2) 有效地避免了因远期收款而可能产生的利率风险、汇率风险、进口国家的政治和经济风险、外汇管制风险和付款人的信用风险。

(3) 出口人不必再负担应收账款管理和催收的工作及费用。

(4) 手续简单、方便快捷。银行是否同意办理该业务,很大程度取决于担保人(如信用证项下的开证行)的资信状况,只要担保人的资信状况较好,在银行有授信额度,银行在几个小时甚至几分钟内就可办妥该业务。

(5) 在得到票据贴现款的同时,即可获得可供出口收汇核销使用的进账单或结汇水单,加快了企业的收汇和核销,能帮助企业提前办理出口退税。

当然,叙做福费廷业务对银行(包买商)也是有益处的。由于其承担的风险相对比信用证项下的押汇风险大,因此按"高风险、高收益"的原则,在同等条件下,其收款的利率通常较出口押汇高,从而能获得相对较高的收益。

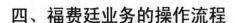
四、福费廷业务的操作流程

出口人办理福费廷业务的流程如下：

(1) 将出口信用证项下的单据交出口地银行议付或处理。

(2) 提供基础资料：企业的营业执照副本、税务登记证、企业组织机构代码证、会计师事务所审计的报表、进出口权批文或外商投资企业的批文。

(3) 逐笔填写并提交银行格式化的《福费廷业务申请书》。

(4) 与出口地银行签订《福费廷业务合同》。

(5) 提交国外银行承兑电报或开证银行承兑的汇票。

在我国，办理福费廷业务目前暂时还局限于信用证项下的票据包买，对于其他的单据暂不予办理。信用证项下的福费廷业务操作流程如下：

(1) 出口人(受益人)将远期信用证项下的单据交出口地银行议付(或处理)。

(2) 出口地银行收到开证行的承兑后通知出口人。

(3) 出口人提交福费廷业务申请，填写《福费廷业务申请书》(见示样8-15)。

示样8-15　福费廷业务申请书

福费廷业务申请书

致：中国银行_____分(支)行　　　　　我公司参考号_____

根据我公司与贵行签订的_____年第_____号《福费廷业务合同》，我公司特向贵行申请叙做福费廷业务。有关交易情况如下：

□远期承兑信用证　　　□延期付款信用证　　　□远期议付信用证

1.信用证号：　　　　　　　　　　　　　　　2.开证行：

3.指定承兑/承付银行(如有)：　　　　　　　4.进口商名称及地址：

5.信用证金额：　　　　　　　　　　　　　　6.远期/延期期限：

7.汇票/发票金额：　　　　　　　　　　　　 8.货物名称：

9.出运及交单日期：

□出口承兑交单托收(D/A)

1.汇票/发票金额：　　　　　　　　　　　　 2.承兑交单期限：

3.进口商名称及地址：　　　　　　　　　　　4.货物名称：

5.保付银行：如果贵行确认可以对上述信用证或托收业务叙做福费廷业务，请向我公司报价。本申请书构成我公司与贵行签订的_____年第_____号《福费廷业务合同》不可分割的一部分。在此，我公司重申遵守上述《福费廷业务合同》的有关承诺、陈述与保证。我公司联系人_____电话_____传真_____

公司名称：　　　　　　　　　　(加盖公章)

有权人签字：

日期：

---

(4) 出口地银行确定价格并通知出口人。

(5) 出口地银行将本金扣除费用及利息后入出口人账户并出具可供国家外汇管理局核销的进账单或"水单"。

(6) 出口地银行收到国外货款后自动还款转账。

五、福费廷业务需要注意的问题

1. 出口人(信用证项下的受益人)应注意的事项

(1) 必须将远期信用证项下的单据交办理福费廷业务的出口地银行议付(或处理),这是一般银行办理福费廷业务的前提条件,否则银行将拒绝受理福费廷业务的申请,即出口人准备在 A 银行办理福费廷业务,就不能将信用证项下的单据交由 B 银行议付(或处理)。

(2) 开证行所在国政局、经济不稳定或开证行信誉欠佳等情况下,银行一般不愿做福费廷业务。

(3) "无追索权"是相对而言的,出口商欺诈或开证行因法院禁付令而未能履行信用证项下付款的情况下,福费廷业务申请人必须归还原融资款。

(4) 承受比出口押汇较高的利息支出。

2. 办理福费廷业务的银行应注意的事项

(1) 对出口受益人提供的资料进行合规性审核。

(2) 信用证项下的单据必须交本行议付或处理,在他行议付(或处理)的单据不予办理福费廷业务。

(3) 充分考虑信用证的开证行及所在国家、地区的风险,原则上不办理高风险国家、地区的福费廷业务。

(4) 认真审核国外开证行或保兑行的承兑电报,对属于开证申请人的承兑、未经加押或有权签字人签字的承兑或含义不明的承兑,不得办理福费廷业务。

(5) 在出口地银行的"代理行管理系统"中,对开证行在出口地银行(或其总行)没有授信额度的,原则上不予以办理福费廷业务。

(6) 对于风险较高的国家或地区,为了避免风险,可考虑转卖,或邀请一家或数家银行对自己拟做的福费廷业务提供风险担保,即"风险参与"(RISK PARTICIPATION)。由于风险参与银行是独立于进口开证行担保以外的,对任何信用风险和国家风险造成的票款迟付或拒付负有不可撤销的责任和无条件的赔付责任。对初级包买商来说,可通过风险参与银行获得开证行之外的第二重保障。

【案例8-3】中国银行福费廷业务的具体办理

1. 案例介绍

浙江省进出口公司6月1日向浙江省中国银行下属某分行申请办理福费廷业务：承兑金额100 000.00欧元，到期日8月27日；福费廷利率为年利5%。假设6月1日欧元买入价为953.09，当日交易如下：

$$100000-100000 \times 5 \times (88+5)/(100 \times 360)= 987083.33(欧元)$$
$$987083.33 \times 9.5309 = 9407792.51(元)$$

2. 案例分析

(1) 出口公司叙做福费廷业务可能出现的结果。

① 假定开证行拖欠付款或付款未达，直到9月7日才收到款项，有利息损失，如果做其他有追索权的融资如押汇，此利息由出口商承担。

② 9月1日欧元贬值到798.00，但由此引起的汇率损失转嫁到中国银行，当然欧元也有升值的可能，关键是锁定了成本。

③ 开证行所在国(如印尼)因政治原因，造成所有的外汇付款推迟。

(2) 福费廷业务的费用。

① 贴现率=LIBOR+MARGIN。

② 承诺费(COMMITMENT FEE)。利率定为贴现率的一半，承诺期间不超过30天，则免收承诺费，如中途取消福费廷业务，承诺费按实际占用额度的天数算收。目前的模式基本无此项费用。

③ 手续费：50.00美元/笔，20万美元以上免收。

(3) 操作流程。如初次办理，需和中行签订《福费廷协议》，每笔按中行的格式提交福费廷申请书。待收到承兑电后报浙江省分行。审批通过后，买入票据并出具水单和出口收汇核销专用联。

(4) 例外条款。①如开证行因当地法院止付令而未能付款，中行根据福费廷协议向出口商行使追索权，并从出口公司收回原融资款、融资利息及相关费用，并要求退回中行出具的出口收汇核销联。②出口商涉嫌欺诈。

(5) 业务掌握要点。业务风险取决于进口国及开证行的风险；进口商的资信状况也比较关键，防遭止付；代理行要选择大银行，如中银集团等。

(6) 在贸易中的深入应用。可以大胆使用远期业务，扩大贸易机会，增强竞争力。要求国外客户通过信誉好的银行开证，可向中国银行咨询进口国信用等级较高的银行。

第四节 保 理 业 务

一、保理的概念及适用范围

保理商(金融企业)买进出口商通常以发票表示的对进口商(债务人)的应收账款债权,并负责信用销售控制、销售分户账管理、债务回收、坏账担保和贸易融资。这种承担较大风险而开展的综合性售后服务,称为保付代理业务,简称保理业务。

出口商可以根据本公司的实际情况,要求保理商提供该项服务的全部服务项目或部分服务项目。保理业务主要是为承兑交单(D/A)、赊销(O/A)方式而设计的一种综合性的金融服务。

二、保理业务的主要内容

(1) 销售分户账管理(MAINTENANCE OF THE SALES LEDGER),是指银行(保理商)利用已销售的账务管理制度、先进的管理技术和丰富的管理经验,为供应商提供优良的售后服务。利用银行的此项服务,供应商可以集中人力、物力进行企业经营与销售,并可相应减少财务管理人员和办公设备。

(2) 债款回收(COLLECTION FROM DEBTORS),是指银行(保理商)利用自己的收债技术和丰富的收债经验,为供应商提供催收应收账款的服务。如需要通过法律途径解决债款,为收回该应收账款而产生的一切诉讼费和律师费由保理商承担。因此,利用银行的这项服务,供应商即节省了营运资金,又免除了其对收债而存在的担忧。

(3) 信用销售控制(CREDIT CONTROL),是指银行(保理商)利用自己的网络和信息,为供应商了解其贸易客户的资信变化情况,制定切合实际的信用销售限额,并采取必要的防范措施,帮助供应商避免或减少潜在的收汇风险的服务。

(4) 坏账担保(FULL PROTECTION AGAINST BAD DEBTS),是指银行(保理商)对在核定的信用销售额度内已核准的应收账款提供担保,当出现坏账时负赔偿之责。保理商通常在保理协议生效前对供应商的客户,一一核定临时的信用销售额度,并可根据客户的资信等情况,随时进行调整。供应商在信用销售额度之内的销售称为已核准的应收账款(APPROVED RECEIVABLES);超出额度部分的销售,称为未核准的应收账款(UNAPPROVED RECEIVABLES)。保理商对已核准的应收账款提供100%的坏账担保,但条件是该应收账款必须基于已被客户所接受的商品销售或技术服务。由于供应商出售给保理商的应收账款必须是正当的、无争议的债务求偿权,所以对由于产品的质量、服务水平、交货期等引起的贸易纠纷所造成的呆账和坏账，保理商不负担赔偿责任。

(5) 贸易融资(TRADE FINANCING)，是指在保理业务项下，保理商为供应商提供的一种融资。保理业务项下的融资手续方便、快捷，供应商在发货或提供技术服务后，将发票通知保理商通常就可以立即获得不超过发票金额90%的融资，以解决货物销售的资金占用问题。

三、保理业务的种类

按照不同的标准，保理业务可以有多种分类法。

(1) 根据是否保留追索权，可分为有追索权的保理(RECOURSE FACTORING)和无追索权的保理(NON-RECOURSE FACTORING)。有追索权的保理，保理商不负责为客户核定信用额度和提供坏账担保，仅提供包括融资在内的其他服务。若债务人因清偿能力不足而形成坏账时，保理商有权向供应商追索。无追索权的保理业务中，保理商负责为客户核定信用额度和提供坏账担保。在该额度内，由债务人资信等问题造成的坏账损失由保理商承担。

(2) 根据是否提供融资，可分为到期保付代理(MATURITY FACTORING)和融资保付代理(FINANCED FACTORING)。在到期保付代理业务中，保理商根据供应商给予的付款期限计算出平均到期日，于该日将应收账款付给供应商。在融资保付代理中，保理商一收到供应商的代表应收账款的销售发票，就立即以预付款方式提供不超过发票额90%的融资，剩下的10%于货款收妥后清算。

(3) 根据是否将销售货款直接付给保理商，可分为公开型保理(DISCLOSED FACTORING)和隐蔽型保理(UNDISCLOSED FACTORING)。在公开型保理业务中，供应商必须以书面形式将保理商的参与通知其所有的客户，并指示他们将货款直接付给保理商。在隐蔽型保理业务中，保理商的参与对外保密，货款直接支付给供应商，融资和清算的费用由供应商承担。

(4) 根据供应商与其客户是否在同一国家或地区，可分为国际保理(INTERNATIONAL FACTORING)和国内保理(DOMESTIC FACTORING)。供应商与其客户在同一国家或地区，称为国内保理；供应商与其客户不在同一国家或地区，称为国际保理。国际保理有单保和双保两种模式，仅涉及一方保理商的称为单保，涉及双方保理商的称为双保。

国际保理业务中一般采用双保理方式。出口人委托本国出口保理商，出口保理商再从进口国的保理商中选择进口保理商，出口人将需要核定信用额度的进口人清单交给出口保理商，由其转交进口保理商。进口保理商负责对进口人的资信状况进行调查，逐一核定相应的信用额度，并通过出口保理商通知出口人执行。然后，出口保理商负责贸易融资和催收账款等。

四、保理业务的操作流程

下面以双保理方式为例来介绍保理业务的操作流程。

(1)　出口人寻找有合作前途的进口人签订出口销售合同，商定以保理作为结算方式，并将进口保理商以寄送介绍信(见示样 8-16)的形式介绍给进口人。

示样 8-16　保理业务介绍信

INTRODUCTORY LETTER

GENGTLEMEN,

BEGINGING_____(DATE), _____(NAME OF IMPORT FACTOR, 进口保理商名称)WILL SERVE AS OUR FACTOR FOR SALES IN _____(IMPORT COUNTRY).

_____(NAME OF IMPORT FACTOR) IS A MEMBER OF FACTORS CHAIN INTERNATIONAL, A WORLDWIDE ASSOCIATUION OF LEADING FACTORS WHO PROVIDED CREDIT AND COLLECTION SERVICES FOR EACH OTHER'S CLIENTS. THIS ENABLES US TO SELL OUR PRODUCTS ON _____(SETTLEMENT METHODS, SUCH AS O/A) TERMS IN_____(IMPORT COUNTRY) AS WELL AS MANY OTHER COUNTRIES.

AS PER THIS ARRANGEMENT, OUR INVOICES TO YOU WILL CONTAIN INSTRUCTIONS TO PAY_____(NAME OF IMPORT FACTOR)AND YOUR CHEQUES SHOULD BE MADE PAYABLE TO THAT COMPANY, PLEASE SEND ALL FUTURE REMITTANCES TO:
_____(NAME AND ADDRESS OF THE IMPORT FACTORS)
ACCOUNT NO._____
SWIFT NO._____
REF. NO._____(VENDOR NAME, INVOICE NO., ETC.)
ANY BILLING DISCREPANCIES MUST BE REPORTED TO THEM AT ONCE.

IF YOU HAVE ANY QUESTIONS REGARDING YOUR ACCOUNT OR THIS ARRANGEMENT, PLEASE CONTACT_____(IMPORT FACTORS) AT THE ADDRESS LISTED ABOVE OR CALL THEM AT _____(TEL. NO.).

WE FEEL SURE THAT THIS NEW ARRANGEMENT WILL HELP US SERVE YOU BETTER AND THAT _____(IMPORT FACTORS) WILL GIVE YOU THE UTMOST ATTENTION AND CONSIDERATION.

YOURS FAITHFULLY
_____(NAME OF THE EXPORTER)
_____(SIGNATURE)

(2) 出口人向出口地保理商申请保理信用额度,须填写《出口保理信用额度申请书》(见示样 8-17)。

示样 8-17　出口保理信用额度申请书

出口保理信用额度申请书

编号：

致：中国银行　　　　分行

我司拟向_____(国际或地区)出口_____(商品的中英文名称),请贵行代为向进口保理商提出初步信用额度评估申请,有关资料如下：

(一)我司(卖方资料)	
卖方名称：	
开户银行(英文)： 银行账户：	
预计年国际和国内贸易总额(万美元)：	
预计对进口国以赊销方式出口的年出口额(万美元)及年出单笔数(单)：	
与进口商以往的业务往来情况(包括近期签约情况、付款条件及贸易关系)：	
(二)贸易背景资料	
进口商名称及详细地址(英文)： 联系电话：	
联系人：	
是否允许进口保理商与进口商直接联系?　　YES (　　)　　　NO(　　)	
有否折扣宽限期/优惠期：YES (　　)　　　NO(　　)如有,请列明方式：	
是否季节性销售商品：YES (　　)　　　NO(　　)如是,请说明情况：	
价格条款：　　FOB(　　)　　CFR(　　)　　CIF(　　)　其他：	
付款方式：　　O/A(　　)　　D/A(　　) DAYS	
进口商的开户银行(英文)： 银行账户：	
出口商代理人/授权人的名称、详细地址、开户银行及其权限(如有)：	
(三)申请额度资料	
□循环额度　　　　发票使用货币：　　　　金额：	
□单笔非循环额度　发票使用货币：　　　　金额：	
备注：	

请贵行将审批结果尽快通知我司。

感谢贵行的大力协助。

公司
(签字盖章)
年　　月　　日

(3) 出口地保理商寻找进口保理商并向进口地保理商转交出口人保理信用额度申请。

(4) 进口地保理商对进口商进行信用评估，并在 14 天内做出答复。如基本符合条件，则须发送《出口保理信用额度评估回复书》。

(5) 出口保理商收到后三个工作日内通知出口人。

(6) 出口保理商与出口人签订《出口保理协议》。

(7) 进口保理商正式批准申请。

(8) 出口保理商向出口人发出正式《出口保理信用额度核准通知书》。

(9) 出口人在额度内出货，全部单据交给保理商。

(10) 出口保理商在发票上加贴有关转让条款并自发票上列明的到期日(如有)后寄送进口保理商。

(11) 如需要融资，可按规定办理。

(12) 出口保理商在收到进口保理商付款后扣除利息、费用，净额入出口人账户。

五、保理业务的作用

国际保理业务能为进出口双方在增加营业额、获得风险保障、节约成本、简化手续、扩大利润等方面带来好处，具体如表 8-1 所示。

表 8-1　国际保理业务的作用

优　点	对出口方而言	对进口方而言
增加营业额	对现有客户或潜在客户提供更具竞争力的 O/A、D/A 付款条件，便于拓展海外市场、增加营业额	利用 O/A、D/A 优惠付款条件，以有限的资本购进更多的货物，加快资金流动，扩大营业额
获得风险保障	进口商的信用风险转由保理商承担，出口方可以得到 100%的收汇保障	以公司的信誉和良好的财务表现而获得卖方的信贷，无须抵押
节约成本	资信调查、账务管理和欠款催收由保理商负责，减轻业务负担，节约管理成本	省略了开立信用证和处理繁杂文件的费用
简化手续	免除了一般信用证交易的繁琐手续	在批准信用额度后，购买手续简化，进货快捷
扩大利润	由于出口额扩大，降低了管理成本，排除了信用风险和坏账损失，利润随之增加	由于加快了资金和货物的流动，生意更加发达，从而增加了利润

六、办理保理业务应注意的问题

保理业务当事人的权利与责任见《出口保理业务协议》的有关内容。

1. 出口方应注意的问题

(1) 进口人的信誉和进口国的政治、经济局势及保理商在该国的网络。

(2) 选择合适的贸易方式。一般来说，信用证项下业务不需要再做保理业务。

(3) 必须在额度内发货。

(4) 是否有追索权。

(5) 须承担较高的费用。

(6) 纠纷自理。不管出口人是否同意进口人的观点，一旦发生贸易纠纷，保理商对核定的应收账款项下发生的贸易纠纷涉及金额，视为未核准的应收账款，不负责担保赔偿。

(7) 付款有时较迟。

2. 出口保理商应注意的问题

(1) 了解出口人情况(信誉、贸易背景、产品销售情况等)，以防风险。

(2) 了解进口人的信誉情况，提高保理业务的成功率。

(3) 加强保理项下的货款催收工作。

(4) 正确对待贸易纠纷。

【案例8-4】中国银行保理业务的具体办理

某出口商预计对进口商年销售额为 120 万美元，支付条件(PAYMENT TERMS):赊销(O/A)30 DAYS，向中国银行申请叙做保理业务。

操作流程分析

(1) 额度申请与核准。

① 出口商寻找有合作前途的进口商。

② 出口商向出口保理商提出叙做保理的需求并要求为进口商核准信用额度。

③ 出口保理商要求进口保理商对进口商进行信用评估。

④ 如进口商信用良好，进口保理商将为其核准信用额度。

(2) 申请循环额度的计算。

申请的额度(CREDIT LINE)：120 万 ÷ (360 ÷ 30)×1.5 =15 万(美元)

(3) 出单与融资。

① 如果进口商同意购买出口商的商品或服务，出口商开始供货，并将附有转让条款的发票寄送进口商。

② 出口商将发票副本交出口保理商。

③ 出口保理商通知进口保理商有关发票详情。

④ 如出口商有融资需求，出口保理商付给出口商不超过发票金额80%的融资款。

(4) 催款与结算。

① 进口保理商于发票到期日前若干天开始向进口商催收。

② 进口商于发票到期日向进口保理商付款。

③ 进口保理商将款项付出口保理商。

④ 如果进口商在发票到期日90天后仍未付款，进口保理商做担保付款。

⑤ 出口保理商扣除融资本息(如有)及费用，将余额付出口商。

3. 保理业务的费用

(1) 费用性质。保理收取的主要是风险承担费，买方(进口)保理商承担风险不需要进口商交保证金或提供抵押担保等。

(2) 收费结构。①出口保理商佣金：发票金额的0.1%～0.4%。②进口保理商佣金：发票金额的0.4%～1%。③银行费用：约30美元。④单据处理费：10美元/单(或有)。

4. 出口商如何降低和消化保理费用

出口商降低和消化保理费用的方法如下：①选择资信较好的进口商；②扩大交易量；③相应提高合同单价；④与进口商分摊保理费用。

5. 保理业务与相关业务的比较

1) 与出口信用险的比较

保理业务与出口信用险的比较如表8-2所示。

表8-2 保理业务与出口信用险的比较

比较项目	出口保理	出口信用保险
最高信用保障(在批准信用额度内)	100%	70%～90%
赔偿期限(从货款到期日起)	90天	120～150天
索赔程序	简单	繁琐
坏账担保	有	有
进口商资信调查与评估	有	有
财务账目管理	有	无
账款催收	有	无
以预支方式提供融资	有	无

2) 与福费廷业务的比较

保理业务与福费廷业务的比较如表 8-3 所示。

表 8-3　保理业务与福费廷业务的比较

项　目	福费廷	保　理
相同点	①都是与贸易融资相关的金融产品 ②都是对应收账的购买 ③固定利率融资 ④出口商将风险转嫁给保理商或包买商	
不同点	①购买的为可流通凭证 ②100%货款融资 ③180 天以上中期融资 ④可有选择性地叙做 ⑤信用证结算方式 ⑥无追索权	①不可流通应收账款 ②约 80%货款融资 ③180 天以内短期融资 ④出售所有合格应收账 ⑤O/A 或 D/A 结算方式 ⑥有/无追索权

6. 贸易纠纷问题的处理

(1) 保理商承担的是进口商的信用风险，而非基础交易风险。

(2) 出口商应在销售合同中加入货物质量认证条款，以避免进口商借货物质量问题拒付。

(3) 进口保理商对纠纷的处理是积极和谨慎的，不必过于担心纠纷问题。

7. 中行开办的保理业务种类和业务流程

业务种类：①国际双保理项下出口保理；②国际双保理项下进口保理；③国内商业发票贴现；④国内综合保理。

以中国银行开办的国际双保理项下进口保理为例，其业务流程如下：①向中国银行提出办理进口保理业务的需求，并提供供货商及相关交易的详细情况；②中国银行对进口企业的资信状况进行评估后将通知评估结果；③若进口企业符合要求，中国银行将通知出口商所在地的保理商，请其联络出口商提出保理信用额度申请；④收到单据并提货后，公司在付款到期日将货款付给中国银行，或授权中国银行从该企业账户中主动借记。

第五节　出口信用保险项下的融资业务

一、出口信用保险的概念及主要内容

出口信用保险是国家为了推动本国的出口贸易，保障出口企业的收汇安全而制定的一项由国家财政提供保险准备金的政策性保险业务。它适用于所有以付款交单(D/P)、承兑交单(D/A)或赊账(O/A)等为商业信用付款条件，信用期不超过 180 天，产品全部或部分在中国制造的出口合同项下的保险。

1. 短期出口信用保险的保险责任分类

(1) 商业风险。短期出口信用保险承保如下商业风险：①买方破产或无力偿还债务；②买方拖欠货款逾期 4 个月以上；③买方拒收货物并拒付货款，但原因并非保险人违约，且被保险人已经采取了措施，包括在必要时向买方起诉，迫使买方收货付款。

(2) 政治风险。短期出口信用保险承保如下政治风险：①买方国家实行外汇管制，禁止或限制汇兑，但在不违反买方所在国法律、法令、命令或条例的前提下，须先由买方按保险公司要求，在指定的银行或机构存入相等于他所欠货款的本国货币；②买方国家实行进口管制；③买方国家撤销已经颁发的进口许可证或不批准进口许可证的展期；④买方所在国或货款须经过的第三国颁布延期付款令；⑤买方所在国或任何有关的第三国发生战争、暴乱或革命；⑥其他被保险人和买方均无法控制的非常事件。

2. 短期出口信用保险的除外责任

短期出口信用保险的除外责任如下：

(1) 货物在运输和储存期间发生磨损、破损、耗损、丢失或毁灭引起的损失，或在货物出口时已经或按常规能够由货物运输保险或其他保险承保的损失。

(2) 由汇率变动引起的损失。

(3) 由被保险人或代表他的任何人违反合同或不遵守法律引起的损失，买方的代理人破产、违约、欺诈、违反法律或其他行为引起的损失。

(4) 在货物交付前，买方已有严重违约行为，被保险人有权停止发货，但仍向其发货而造成的损失。

(5) 在交付货物时由于买方没有遵守所在国的法律、法令、命令或条例，因而未得到各种所需的许可证、批准书、授权或进口许可证无法展期致使销售合同无法继续履行引起的损失。

(6) 由于被保险人或买方的代理人或承运人破产、欺诈、违约或其他行为引起的损失。

(7) 被保险人没有如实、及时申报出口项下发生的损失。

(8) 被保险人在发货前信用限额批复为"零"或信用限额被撤销、失效，或不适用被保险人自行掌握信用限额的买方出口造成的损失。

(9) 货物交付承运人之日起两年内未向保险公司索赔的损失。

(10) 在货物出口前，被保险人已经或应该知道本保单条款所述风险已经发生，或由于买方根本违反销售合同或预期违反销售合同，被保险人放弃其解除或中止履行销售合同的权利，仍继续发货而造成的损失。

另外以下情况也不在出口信用保险的承保责任范围内：银行、运输代理人或承运人擅自放单造成的损失；在货物出口前发生的一切损失；直接或间接由于核辐射或核废料、核燃料引起的放射性污染，或爆炸性核装置或核成分引发的辐射、有毒物、爆炸或其他有害物质所引起的损失；由联合国安理会常任理事国任何两国或两国以上之间的战争所引起的损失；本保单保险责任以外的其他损失。

注意：根本违反销售合同又称根本违约，是指销售合同一方当事人违反销售合同的实质性义务，致使销售合同目的无法实现。在这种情况下，守约方有权解除销售合同。预期违反销售合同，又称预期违约，是指销售合同一方当事人明确表示将不履行销售合同义务，或被证明有经营状况严重恶化、转移财产以逃避债务、丧失商业信誉等丧失或者可能丧失履行债务能力的情形时，另一方当事人有权中止履行销售合同。

3. "买方信用额度"审批制度

保险公司向已投保的出口公司实行"买方信用额度"审批制度，该信用额度将作为保险公司对向该买家出口而承担的保险责任的最高限额。在以下几种情况下不批准限额：

(1) 买方无注册记录或查无此买家。

(2) 资信极为不详，且地区风险系数高。

(3) 买方财务上已出现困难，发生拖欠。

(4) 买方已上"危险买家名单"。

4. 短期出口信用保险的赔偿比例

(1) 一般情况下，买方拒收所致损失的赔偿比例为80%，保险单责任范围内的其他原因所致损失的赔偿比例为 90%。

(2) 对于规模较小且管理素质较差的投保单位，拒收拒付的赔偿比例可视情况低于 80%，破产和拖欠所致损失的赔偿比例可低于 90%。

(3) 政治风险项下所致损失的最高赔偿比例为 95%。

二、短期出口信用保险项下融资业务的概念及作用

短期出口信用保险项下融资是出口地银行基于保险公司短期出口信用保险的一种融资方式，是出口地银行与保险公司合作为出口企业推出的一种新型的贸易融资工具。其融资的比例一般不超过保险公司赔偿的比例，还贷的方法、利息收取的方法和计算公式与流动资金贷款类似，还款的来源为出口人收回的货款，或在非正常的情况下，还款来源为出口信用保险项下的赔款或出口企业的利润。在实际业务中，短期出口信用保险有时被作为其他融资方式的额外担保手段，如在承兑交单(D/A)结算方式下，出口地银行可以凭"出口托收押汇"为出口人提供融资，出口人办理的出口信用保险，仅仅是作为额外的融资担保而已。又如在赊销(O/A)结算方式下，出口地银行可以凭"出口托收押汇"为出口人提供融资，出口人办理的出口信用保险，也作为额外的融资担保。至于信用证项下，更可以使用"打包贷款"、"出口押汇"等方式为出口人提供融资，一般情况下，不需要出口人再办理出口信用保险。

出口信用保险的主要作用是集保险与融资于一体，使出口企业相应降低了出口收汇风险，既可得到付款的保证，又可得到融资的便利。

三、短期出口信用保险项下融资业务的操作流程

短期出口信用保险项下融资业务的操作流程如下。

(1) 进出口双方达成交易意向。

(2) 向保险公司申请办理出口信用保险。

(3) 进出口双方签订合约(也可在办理保险之前签约)。

(4) 出口方发货装运，向保险公司申报，并缴纳保费。

(5) 与出口地签订融资协议(此程序可提前进行)。

(6) 出口方与保险公司、出口地银行签订赔款转让协议(赔款转让授权书)(见示样 8-18)。

(7) 向出口地银行提交相关单据，以获得融资，这些单据包括：①出口贸易合同或订

单；②商业发票；③质量合格证明；④出口保险保险单；⑤买方额度申请表(由办理出口信用证保险的保险公司提供)；⑥出口保险申报单；⑦证明已缴纳保费的凭证；⑧保险赔款授权转让书；⑨海关手册；⑩出口货物报关单、提单或其他运输单据。

(8) 出口地银行根据出口人的信誉、采用的贸易结算方式、货物的销售情况、提供的担保和抵押品情况，决定是否办理融资。

示样 8-18　赔款转让协议

编号：＿＿＿＿＿＿＿＿＿＿

日期：＿＿＿＿＿＿＿＿＿＿

赔 款 转 让 协 议

甲　方：＿＿＿＿＿＿＿＿＿＿＿＿＿＿＿＿＿＿＿(被保险人)

注册地址：＿＿＿＿＿＿＿＿＿＿＿＿＿＿＿＿

企业营业执照号码：＿＿＿＿＿＿＿＿＿＿＿＿

机构代码：＿＿＿＿＿＿＿＿＿＿＿＿＿＿＿＿

电话：＿＿＿＿＿＿＿＿＿　邮编：＿＿＿＿＿＿＿＿＿

传真：＿＿＿＿＿＿＿＿＿＿＿＿＿＿＿＿＿＿

基本存款账户银行：＿＿＿＿＿＿＿＿＿＿＿＿＿＿

账号：＿＿＿＿＿＿＿＿＿＿＿＿＿＿＿＿＿＿

乙　方：中国进出口信用保险公司＿＿＿＿＿＿＿＿分公司

注册地址：＿＿＿＿＿＿＿＿＿＿＿＿＿＿＿＿＿

电话：＿＿＿＿＿＿　邮编：＿＿＿＿＿＿＿＿＿＿

传真：＿＿＿＿＿＿＿＿＿＿＿＿＿＿＿＿＿＿＿

丙　方：＿＿＿＿＿＿＿＿＿＿＿＿＿＿＿＿＿＿银行

注册地址：＿＿＿＿＿＿＿＿＿＿＿＿＿＿＿＿＿＿

电话：＿＿＿＿＿＿　邮编：＿＿＿＿＿＿＿＿＿＿

传真：＿＿＿＿＿＿＿＿＿＿＿＿＿＿＿＿＿＿＿

示样 8-18(续)

鉴于：

甲方向乙方投保短期出口信用保险，保单号为_____(以下简称"保险单")，各方经充分协商，就保险单下赔款转让授权事宜达成如下协议：

一、自本协议生效之日起，且在保险单有限期内，对于甲方(请在下列适用"□"内打对号，不适用"□"内打"X")

□　在保险单适保范围内的全部出口_____

□　向_____地区的全部买方的出口_____

□　向买方代码为_____的买方的出口

项下发生保险责任范围内的损失，甲方授权乙方将按照保险单规定理赔后应付给甲方的赔款直接全额支付给丙方，且同时乙方在上述出口项下的赔偿责任终止。

无论本协议其他条款如何规定，甲方和乙方之间的保险法律关系，以及甲方和丙方之间的出口贸易融资法律关系是两个相互独立的法律关系。乙丙双方在各自与甲方签订的合同中独立享有合同约定的权利并承担合同约定的义务。甲方是否向乙方投保短期出口信用保险并不构成其获得丙方的贷款或其他形式融资的必要条件或充分条件；甲方能否获得丙方的贷款或其他形式的融资并不构成乙方接受其投保短期出口信用保险的必要条件或充分条件。乙、丙双方应根据各自的规定，对甲方的投保申请和贷款或其他形式的融资申请做出独立的判断和决定。

二、甲方义务

1. 未经丙方书面同意，在保险单有限期内不单方面解除和变更保险单。

2. 无论索赔权是否转让，均履行保险单项下被保险人的各项义务。

3. 在得知发生保险单项下的损失或可能导致损失的事件时，立刻通知乙方和丙方，及时采取一切必要的措施避免或减少损失，并且不延误地向乙方和丙方报告有关进展，否则赔偿由此造成的损失。

4. 若出现如下情况，应由甲方向丙方偿还融资协议项下的款项(包括本金、利息、费用以及其他应付款项)，直至丙方完全受偿。

(1) 乙方按照国家有关法律法规、本协议、保险单的规定或基于其他任何原因，作出不支付或不完全支付赔偿的决定；

(2) 乙方向丙方赔偿款项不足以偿还甲方应向丙方偿还的款项；

(3) 甲方任何原因不向乙方索赔或甲方没有按照保险单的规定向乙方索赔及未能按照《索赔单证明细表》的要求提供齐全的索赔单证。

5. 在乙方误将赔款支付给甲方的情况下，甲方应在收到赔款的两个工作日内主动将赔款全额划转至丙方指定的账户(开户行：_____、账户名称：_____、账户号码：_____)

6. 甲方应保证出口贸易的真实性、合法性。乙方不负责审查出口贸易的真实性、合法性。

三、乙方义务

1. 乙方应向丙方介绍其与甲方签订的保险单条款。

2. 按照本协议第一条的规定，将应支付给甲方的赔款直接全额支付到丙方指定的账户(开户行：_____、账户名称：_____、账户号码：_____)

3. 乙方由于其过错未按照本协议第三条第2项的规定向丙方支付基于保险单项下的赔偿款项，对由此给丙方造成的损失承担赔偿责任。

4. 在保险单有限期内，甲方单方面提出变更或解除保险单的请求需事先征得丙方的书面同意，对于甲方向乙方提交的变更或解除保险单的书面申请，如未附有丙方的书面同意材料，乙方将其视为申请材料不完备而不予接受。

5. 乙方依据法律、保险单的规定或被保险人的其他约定作出变更或解除保险单的决定后，应及时书面通知丙方。并且乙方承诺该变更或解除不影响在变更或解除前乙方按照法律和保险单规定应承担的保险责任。

示样 8-18(续)

四、丙方义务

1. 开展此项业务前，已明晰了解乙方的保险单条款。

2. 及时通知乙方有关甲方的贸易融资金额，在每月 15 日之前将上月甲方收汇结算情况(《出口商短期出口信用保险项下贸易融资、收汇结算情况表》)书面通知甲、乙双方。

3. 乙方将赔款支付给丙方后，丙方扣除融资本金、利息等相关费用后仍余额，应将余款及时支付给甲方。

五、关于索赔

1. 在本协议第一条授权范围内，如发生保险责任范围内的损失，应由甲方直接向乙方索赔。因甲方怠于行使索赔权致使丙方利益受到损害的，甲方应承担赔偿责任。乙方也接受甲方委托丙方进行索赔。

在甲方委托丙方索赔的方式下，甲方需与丙方另行签订书面委托代理协议，授权丙方向乙方行使索赔权，同时甲方须向丙方提供甲方签字盖章后的《委托代理协议书》、《Collection Trust Deed》、《出口信用保险赔款收据及利益转让书》和《Export Credit Insurance Payment Receipt and Subrogation Form》交丙方留存。

2. 甲方或丙方行使索赔权时，应按照保险单及其相关单证的规定向乙方提供索赔单证(《索赔单证明细表》)。提供的索赔单证不齐全的，乙方有权不予受理，但索赔单证的完整提供并不是乙方受损赔付的唯一前提条件。

六、任何一方违反本协议的规定给其他各方造成损失的，应对受损方的该损失承担赔偿责任。

七、本协议自三方签字盖章之日起生效，有效期一年。在本协议有效期内，除非法律另有规定，对本协议的变更或解除应经三方协商一致并签署书面协议或采取三方共同认可的其他方式。如本协议的一方希望在本协议有效期届满后终止本协议，应与有效期届满前 30 日内书面通知其他方，否则本协议自动顺延一年。

八、本协议的终止，不影响任何一方在本协议的有效期内依据本协议所获得的权利，也不豁免任何一方在本协议终止前依据本协议应该承担的义务。

九、因履行本协议而引起争议时，各方应通过友好协商解决争议。如果争议经协商仍未能解决，任何一方可将本协议提交中国国际经济贸易仲裁委员会仲裁。

十、本协议适用中华人民共和国法律。

十一、本协议一式三份，甲方、乙方和丙方各执一份，具有同等法律效力。

十二、自本协议生效日起原__年__月__日签订的__号《赔款转让协议》、__年__月__日签订的__号《赔款转让协议》、__年__月__日签订的__号《赔款转让协议》同时全部终止。该终止不影响各方在上述《赔款转让协议》有效期内享有的权利和应承担的义务。

甲方：_____(公章)

法定代表人或授权签字人：_____

日期　年　月　日

乙方：_____(公章)

法定代表人或授权签字人：_____

日期　年　月　日

丙方：_____(公章)

法定代表人或授权签字人：_____

日期　年　月　日

注：赔付通知书见示样 8-19，中英文的《出口信用保险赔款收据及利益转让书》见示样 8-20。

示样 8-19　赔付通知书

贸易融资业务适用	中国出口信用保险公司
	China Export & Credit Insurance Corporation
	立案号：_____

赔 付 通 知 书

致：_____(保单号：　　　　　　　　　)

　　经调查审理，立案号_____的索赔案，因买家_____(代码：_____)拖欠致使贵公司遭

受损失，按保单规定，我公司决定向贵公司赔付(大写)_____

_____(小写：_____)，计算公式：

_____(保险金额) × _____%(赔付百分比)=

　　根据我公司和贵公司、_____ 银行签署的《赔款转让协议》，我公司决定将上述赔款划入

银行指定账户。请将下联回执及中英文《短期出口信用保险赔款收据及利益转让书》<u>正本各两份签字盖章</u>

后退还我公司，以便我公司支付赔款。

　　特此通知。

中 国 出 口 信 用 保 险 公 司_____分 公 司

授权签字人：

年　月　日

回 执　　　　　　　　立案号：

保单号：

中国出口信用保险公司：

　　我公司接受上述赔付决定，根据三方签署的《赔款转让协议》，同意将保险赔款全额划入

银行指定账户。

被保险人授权签字人：　　　　(公章)　　　　　年 月 日

根据《赔款转让协议》，请贵公司将保险赔款划入我银行指定账户：

户　　　　　名：_____

账　　　　　号：_____

我行在中行之往来账号：_____

融资银行授权签字人：　　　　　(公章)　　　　　年 月 日

示样 8-20　出口信用保险赔款收据及利益转让书

贸易融资业务适用

中国出口信用保险公司
China Export & Credit Insurance Corporation

短 期 出 口 信 用 保 险

赔 款 收 据 及 利 益 转 让 书

立案号：

致：中国出口信用保险公司

　　兹证实收到贵公司短期出口信用保险第_____号保险单项下赔款(大写)_____整(小写：　　　　)，此赔款系_____号合同项下之买方_____发生拖欠风险所引起的全部最终的赔款。

　　根据《赔款转让协议》，该赔款直接划入银行指定账户。

　　鉴于已收到上述赔款，该保险人同意将该赔款项下的一切利益转让给贵公司，并全权授予贵公司得以被保险人或贵公司的名义向责任方追偿。为使贵公司实现该项权益，被保险人保证根据贵公司的合理要求，提供充分协助，特立书为凭。

被保险人签字：

(公　章)

年　月　日

中国出口信用保险公司
China Export & Credit Insurance Corporation

Export Credit Insurance
Payment Receipt and Subrogation Form

Loss No. _____　　　Policy No. _____

To: China Export & Credit Insurance Corporation

We, _____(Insured) received from China Export & Credit Insurance Corporation the Sum of _____(in word) in full and final settlement of the claim under our Contract No._____ for the buyer, _____, who was in default.

In consideration of having received this payment, we hereby agree to assign, transfer and subrogate to you, to the extent of your interest, all our rights and remedies in and in respect of the subject matter insured, and to grant you full power and give you any assistance you may reasonably require of us in the exercise of such rights and remedies in our or your name.

Signed at_____, Dated on_____

(place)　　　(date，month，year)

(Signed) _____

(Stamp)

四、办理短期出口信用保险项下融资业务应注意的问题

1. 出口人应注意的事项

(1) 尽可能了解进口人的资信情况，对进口客户有所选择，如进口人的资信情况不明，又处于高风险国家或地区，应采用谨慎的、较为安全的结算方式，不能依托出口信用险的"后盾"而不顾一切。因为高风险，保险公司不一定同意办理保险或者会收取高额的保险费，而出口地银行并不会因为办理了出口信用保险就一定同意向出口人融资。

(2) 应对出口信用险的除外责任有足够的了解。

(3) 赔付时间较长，手续较为繁琐。赔付时间一般在应付款日期后 3 个月，被保险人填报《可能损失通知书》后，尚有 4 个月的"赔偿等待期"。如保险公司得到买方破产或失去偿付能力的证明，则无"赔偿等待期"。因此，实际业务中，从出口人产生损失到保险公司赔款到账，至少需要半年以上，而且还必须提交十多种相关证明文件，有的文件还需要从国外得到，手续繁琐。

(4) 出口信用保险项下的融资有追索权。如果出口地银行将保险单作为一种抵押品办理了融资，当出口人不能按时还款时，可以根据法律、法令等采取"依法收贷"的措施。

(5) 成本、费用负担较高。出口信用保险项下办理融资，除了承担利息，还需要承担高额的保险费。

2. 出口地银行作为融资银行应注意的事项

(1) 了解出口人的资信情况。一般情况下，出口地银行对业务往来不是很频繁的、年出口量较小的出口人(年出口量在 500 万美元以下)，不轻易仅凭出口信用保险办理融资。

(2) 尽可能了解进口人的信用。若进口人是世界知名的大型企业，可适当放宽融资条件。反之，则应从严。

(3) 了解货物的质量、市场情况等。

(4) 了解保险公司的信誉、保险协议内容等。

(5) 加强融资的后期管理，注意掌握出口人的动态，及时采取风险防范措施。

第六节　国际贸易融资相关案例：浙江企业办理出口信用保险的成功与失败案例

近年来，很多外贸公司经常被外国买家欺骗，发货后货款却迟迟不见动静，因此选择了出口信用险这个工具，为自己的出口贸易"装"上保险。出口信用保险是以国家财力为

后盾的政策性保险，是各国鼓励出口，降低出口收汇风险，增强出口企业竞争力的常用手段。外贸企业利用这种保险的风险控制、风险预警、收汇风险保障、追偿等功能，拓展出口渠道，规避收汇风险，减少海外投资风险，已经成为一种国际贸易惯例。在浙江省的出口贸易中，一般贸易占了近80%，单票结算的业务交易方式灵活，但是风险性也较高，因此对出口信用保险的需求就更加迫切。2006年，浙江信保接到杭州地区类似报案近200个，有约15亿美元的出口获得出口信用保险的保障。而杭州市政府已经连续5年出台了相关政策，鼓励出口企业充分利用出口信用保险工具。浙江信保专业人士提醒各出口企业，对海外买家进行风险管理，不仅要关注买家自身的资产状况、赢利能力等，还要关注买家经营策略对其还款能力的影响，尤其是进行多元化经营的海外买家，所进口产品是否是其主营业务，可能会对还款风险造成影响。

1. 案例系列

1) 出口信用保险案例——单笔赔付68.7万美元

中国出口信用保险公司温州办事处已决定向温州市冠盛汽车零部件制造有限公司支付出口信用保险赔款68.7万美元。这是温州地区迄今为止出口信用保险赔付金额最大的一起赔案。日前，冠盛公司向美国一家汽车配件销售有限公司出口了一批价值70多万美元的货物，结果该美国公司被另一家公司兼并，买方趁机赖账，冠盛公司无法得到货款。由于该公司办理了出口信用保险，得到了巨额赔付，避免了贸易风险。

2) 杭企获最大笔出口信用保险赔款——94.3万美元

因为美国买家迟迟不交巨额货款，使得浙江省临安市的浙江天杰实业有限公司面临着资金不能回收的风险。幸运的是，在出口的时候他们专门到中国出口信用保险公司浙江分公司进行投保，因此在催款未果之后，他们申请正式索赔，终于在日前收到了一笔金额为94.3万美元的赔款。据悉，该笔赔款是临安市首笔信用保险赔款，也是浙江信保成立近5年来在杭州地区范围内金额最大的赔款。

短短23天索赔获得成功。实际上，从2007年6月初开始，浙江天杰的相关负责人开始为其美国买家的巨额逾期货款而发愁，美国买家以销售旺季未到、财务困难等为由，迟迟不付款。因为此前曾经为这笔出口贸易合同投保了中国出口信用保险，所以浙江天杰向中国信保浙江分公司报损，同时专程到美国买家处了解情况并催讨货款，但此次美国之行并未达成有效的还款计划。在万般无奈之际，浙江天杰于2007年9月7日向中国信保浙江分公司申请正式索赔。浙江信保接到索赔申请后迅速介入，根据调查，美国买家的主营业务原为电器类产品，从浙江天杰处采购的同轴电缆类产品只占到全部销售额的10%左右，由于美国买家对线缆行业的盲目乐观驱使该买家从浙江天杰大量采购，但是由于刚涉足该行业，此买家的下游线缆销售网络建立尚不完备，造成大批线缆积压在仓库中无法销售。虽然该买家现经营正常，电器业务销售势头良好，但其不愿意挪用其电器销售的款项支付浙江天杰货款。浙江信保在查清了损失原因后23天，进行了快速赔付，有效地解决了企业的燃眉之急。

3)　浙江土畜遭遇大买家拖欠案

此案例的介绍参见图 8-1。

买家情况	风险发生	风险处理
买家 A 为美国大型玩具商，中国信保公司给出的授信额度为 200 万美元。 　2002 年底买家 A 开始与浙江土畜交易，月成交金额约 20 万美元，支付条件是 O/A 。	因市场变化，买家 A 采购的货物无法正常销售，积压严重，短期流动资金趋紧，拖欠浙江土畜货款 18 万美元。浙江土畜于 2003 年 8 月向中国信保报损。	浙江土畜为不影响其与买家关系，希望中国信保公司先不予介入，中国信保给予浙江土畜 1 个月时间自行追讨。浙江土畜自行追讨无果，于 2003 年 9 月委托中国信保追讨，并提起索赔。2003 年 10 月，中国信保追回 2 万美元，同时向浙江土畜赔付 14.4 万美元。

图 8-1　中信保解决浙江土畜遭遇大买家拖欠案

4)　浙江纺织遭遇政治风险案

此案例的介绍参见图 8-2。

买家情况	风险发生	风险处理
买家 B 为美国大型纺织品批发商，与浙江纺织成交多年，商品为罗缎布，每年的交易额在 300 万美元左右，支付条件为 D/P AT SIGHT。	2003 年 3 月，美国海关突然告知浙江纺织原用 CAT#617 配额不能再继续使用，应使用 CAT#625 配额。到港的 40 万美元货物无法进关。	浙江纺织在买家 B 的协助下，把其中 20 万美元的货物在美国保税区进行销售。另有 20 万美元的货物，在中国信保公司的确认下，购买 CAT#625 配额后进关，配额费及滞港费达 13 万美元，中国信保赔付 11.7 万美元。

图 8-2　中信保解决浙江纺织遭遇政治风险案

5)　正泰集团借助出口信用险开拓独联体市场

此案例的介绍参见图 8-3。

案例		结果
2002 年，在正泰集团 80 多亿的销售额中，外销不到 500 万美元，其中没有一分是放账交易。正泰集团虽想尽各种办法，国际市场开拓的步伐仍达不到预期效果。考察南美、前苏联等国后，发现市场很大，但普遍采用放账交易。	出口信用风险	正泰集团对每个接触的新客户都做资信调查，对资信好的买家主动放账并适当提高价格，对资信不佳的买家坚持前 T/T、L/C 或放弃交易，从而成功开拓南美和独联体市场，年出口突破 1500 万美元。

图 8-3　正泰集团借助出口信用保险成功开拓国际市场

6) 借助出口信用险，浙江医保做大市场

此案例的介绍参见图 8-4。

案例		结果
意大利买家，年定单 500 万美元，但提出 O/A 120 天的交易方式。 浙江医保陷入两难困境：不接，丧失成交机会；接，面临巨大收汇风险。	出口信用风险	中国信保对买家做了资信调查和评估，并给出 100 万美元授信额度，浙江医保顺利接单。 两年来，双方合作越来越好，中国信保的授信额度达到 1000 万美元，浙江医保对买家年出口达到 2000 万美元以上。

图 8-4　浙江医保借助出口信用保险成功开拓国际市场

7) 信息共享，避免损失发生

此案例的介绍参见图 8-5。

买家情况	风险发生	风险处理
买家 C 为美国大型营养品批发商，每年在中国大陆的采购金额为 3000 万美元以上，山东、安徽、浙江等地多家企业与其交易，中国信保给出的授信额度达 170 万美元。 浙江中大、医保、土畜等同买家都有交易。	2002 年 11 月，买家接连对山东和安徽卖家拒收和拖欠。 山东和安徽等地停止了对买家的供货，买家转而到江浙一带寻找新的供货商，并找到浙江纺织。 浙江纺织于 2002 年 12 月向中国信保申请信用限额。	在买家对山东和安徽企业拒收和拖欠后，中国信保把其列为"特别关注名单"，同时撤销了浙江中大、医保和土畜的限额，中大、医保、土畜对买家停止了供货。中国信保未批复给浙江纺织限额，并告知其买家已发生拒收和拖欠，浙江纺织未与买家达成交易协议。2002 年 12 月，买家未能有效得到货物供应，主动与中国信保联系。 中国信保答应其在解决山东和安徽企业的货款基础上，恢复限额。2003 年 1 月，买家付款，中国信保恢复其信用限额。

图 8-5　信息共享，避免损失

8) 轻信客户，遭受损失

S 公司为大型省级专业外贸公司。2002 年 12 月，与一日本买家接洽，日本买家表示了大量采购的意愿，并希望 S 公司尽快出运。S 公司第一时间向中国信保申请信用限额，中国信保在未做资信调查的情况下，先行批复 2.5 万美元。S 公司追加信用限额，中国信保即委托日本第一帝国资信公司，对日本买家做资信调查。2003 年 1 月，资信报告显示，买家已经严重资不抵债，中国信保即告知 S 公司该信息，并撤销该限额。S 公司当即与买家联系，表示不再愿意继续交易。买家告知 S 公司：为避税需要，故意把账做小，因此资信调查公司拿到的是不准确的数字。S 公司业务员对买家的解释表示接受，并对买家继续出货达 13 万美元。2003 年 3 月，买家全额拖欠，并表示无力偿付。中国信保在保险责任范围内部分进行赔付，S 公司损失 11 万美元。

9) 借助信用险，金龙电机突破资金瓶颈

此案例的介绍参见图 8-6。

案例		结果
金龙电机是小型电动机的专业生产企业，2001 年还是集体企业，历史包袱重。2001 年底，一澳大利亚买家与金龙电机联系，提出年定单金额 200 万美元，但支付条件为 D/A 180 的要求。金龙电机无法自行解决资金问题，希望开户行工行给予支持，被工行拒绝，转而到中国银行，同样被拒绝。	出口信用风险	金龙电机与台州农行接洽，农行与当时省人保国际部联系，商讨信用保险合作事宜。金龙电机参加投保，通过三方权益转让，农行给予融资。资金问题解决后，金融电机高速发展，2003 年出口近 2000 万美元，并入选台州市重点支持企业。

图 8-6　借助出口信用保险成功融资案

2. 案例分析

1) 国际结算与收汇风险

浙江省出口企业对待收汇风险采用的措施如下。

(1) 选择有利于出口商的结算方式，基本采用前 T/T 或信用证，只对部分大客户、老客户放账，即使放账也在能掌握货权的前提之下。

(2) 竞争激烈，生意难做，客户提出的结算方式一般都接受。

(3) 公司内部设立风险管理部门，对不同的客户采用不同的信用政策。

对 L/C 的重新认识：①收汇安全性；②交易成本；③成交机会。

L/C 交易的风险分析(优点)：①世界一流银行开出的信用证，收汇保障程度比一般商业放账方式高；②买家能开出信用证，意味买家具备一定实力；③有利于获得银行融资。

L/C 交易的风险分析(缺点)：①开证行良莠不齐；②软条款和不符点防不胜防；③信用证中的特殊条款存在风险；④新型的运输方式的潜在风险；⑤近洋贸易中单据直寄客户的快递方式存在风险；⑥不注重政治风险；⑦没有可追索性。

L/C 交易的交易成本分析如图 8-7 所示。

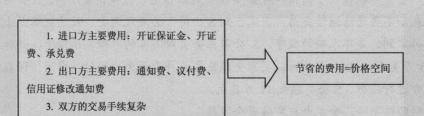

1. 进口方主要费用：开证保证金、开证费、承兑费
2. 出口方主要费用：通知费、议付费、信用证修改通知费
3. 双方的交易手续复杂

节省的费用=价格空间

图8-7　L/C的交易成本

L/C 结算的交易机会分析：①部分大买家不愿意开信用证；②部分小买家无力开信用证；③部分国家没有信用证；④买方市场下，缺乏竞争力；⑤买方的发展受到限制，进而影响卖方发展。

对信用证的看法：①只有一流银行直开的、海运的、条款简单的信用证，具有很好的收汇保证；②信用证在一定程度上促进了国际贸易的发展，特别在国际贸易发展初期以及同新客户初期交易时；③信用证不是收汇保障的代名词，由于交易成本高，使得信用证在一定程度上阻碍了国际贸易的发展。

对大买家和老买家的重新认识：①与我国出口企业真正交易的对象是谁？②通过什么途径了解买家的资信情况？③怎样的买家是大买家、老买家？④大买家和老买家就没有风险吗？

从案例1)中可知：只有具备足够短期偿付能力的买家才是大买家；客户规模不是决定收汇风险的根本要素，收汇风险来自于买家实力、买家信誉和国家风险；买家的信用建立在商业利益之上，而非历史交易之上；交易历史是增加买方信用的参数，但不是防范风险的手段；信保公司的承保经验要注意。因此，避免收汇风险主要依靠出口信用管理，而不是靠哪种支付方式或怎样的买家。

2)　出口信用保险介绍

定义：出口信用保险是各国政府为了扩大本国出口，对海外买家的商业风险和买家所在国政治风险带来的收汇风险进行风险保障的一项政策性的、国际通行的、WTO 补贴与反补贴协议原则上允许的贸易促进工具。

出口信用管理的基本构成如下。①成交前：进行客户资信情况的调查和评估。②成交中：债权保障机制。③成交后：账款管理和追收机制。

出口信用保险对出口信用的管理如下。①成交前：进行专业的买家资信情况的调查和评估。②成交中：风险规避和控制。③成交后：风险转嫁和商账追收。

出口信用保险要点：①对收汇风险的风险保障；②保障商业风险和政治风险；③国际通行做法；④WTO 补贴与反补贴协议允许；⑤政策性；⑥贸易促进工具。

出口信用保险的延伸作用如下：

①　出口助推器。帮助企业转变单一的L/C收汇方式，可使出口企业获得更多的贸易机会；采用商业信用支付方式，可使出口企业提高商品价格，获得更大利益，使企业获得更多的成交机会和更多利润。

②　信息集散地。出口信用保险公司能够提供广泛而有效的买家资信情况调查网络，科学专业的资信分析与评估，动态的买家风险跟踪；提供国家风险报告；利用机构网络优势，实现信息共享；实行灰黑名单制度。

③　搭建融资平台。出口企业可通过保单赔款权益转让获得银行融资支持；银行可通过出口押汇保险，更加放心地给企业提供贷款。

④　海外追账。中信保公司拥有追账优势：政府背景、雄厚的实力和广泛而有效的网络。

3)　出口信用保险实务

(1)　承保的主要风险如表8-4所示。

表8-4　出口信用保险承保的主要风险

商业信用风险	政治风险	责任免除
①买方破产 ②开证行破产 ③买方拖欠货款 ④开证行拖欠 ⑤买方拒绝接受货物 ⑥开证行拒绝承兑	①禁止或限制汇兑 ②禁止买方所购的货物进口 ③发生战争等不可抗力事件，导致买方已无法履行合同 ④其他属于政治风险的非常事件而导致买方已无法履行合同	保险责任以外的其他损失，需要特别指出的是： ①能够由货物运输保险或其他商业保险承保的损失 ②银行或承运人擅自放单造成的损失 ③在货物出口前发生的损失 ④由于被保险人的原因引起的损失

(2)　出口信用保险操作要点如下。

①　信用限额申请：应及时、正确和详细，并填写信用限额申请书。

②　出运申报：应及时、足额、合理。申报要素包括买方代码、支付方式及期限、出运日期。

③　报损后货物处理方案：破产项下，做好债权债务登记，妥善处理好货物；拖欠项下，继续催讨，最好使用书面函电，并保持沟通，切勿擅自做出降价或放弃债权的行为；拒收项下，及时妥善处理货物，或转卖或拉回。处理方案须经中信保公司认可。

④　索赔单证：必需的单证有索赔单证明细表、可能损失通知书、索赔申请书、有关保险证明(保单明细表、限额审批单)、案情说明、销售合同、商业发票、提单、报关单、书面的往来函电。可能需要的相关单证有承兑汇票复印件、银行出具的未收汇证明、外管

局出口收汇未核销证明、其他有关买方的违约证明、质检报告、其他证明文件、中英文委托协议书、保证函。

4) 中信保产品介绍

中国信用保险的业务种类参见图8-8。

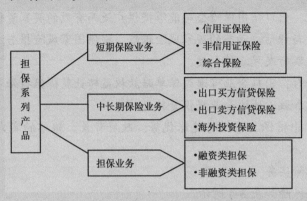

图8-8 中国信用保险的业务种类

充分利用信用保险政策，将会给出口企业带来丰厚的回报，利用政策的潜在收益可使企业：增加贸易成交机会，做大出口规模；提供决策依据，提高风险管理水平；保障收汇安全，解除出口后顾之忧；获得银行融资支持，加快资金周转；加强债权管理，减少企业坏账损失。

本 章 小 结

本章介绍了进出口贸易的融资方式及其具体办理方法。其中，进口贸易融资方式有开证额度、提货担保、信托收据、进口押汇、进口代收押汇和汇出汇款项下融资；出口贸易融资方式有打包贷款、出口押汇、票据贴现、买入票据、银行承兑、出口商业发票贴现、福费廷、保理和出口信用保险项下融资。

出口企业可以根据货物的装运情况、票据及或单据的质量(如汇票是否已被某一银行承兑，单据是否相符等情况)，向出口地银行申请装船前或装船后的融资。融资可以是可被追索的，也可以是不被追索的。当然，各种融资方式的成本是不一样的。

进口企业可以根据货物的运输、单据、资金周转等方面因素综合考虑后选择合适的融资方式。货物装运前的融资是开证额度，但前提是采用信用证结算。货物装运后，如货到目的港而单未到，进口商可以选择提货担保；货到目的港，而单据付款期限未到，可以申请凭信托收据借单；单据或合同付款期限已到，但无资金买单，可以申请进口押汇、进口代收押汇和汇出汇款项下融资。

无论是出口贸易融资，还是进口贸易融资，银行会根据客户的信用、开证行的资信、单据的质量等因素综合考虑后决定是否予以融资。

复习思考题

1. 简述进口押汇、进口代收押汇、出口押汇的异同点。押汇利息如何计算？
2. 简述企业叙做福费廷的条件及其融资的特点。简述保理的业务范围及其分类。
3. 如何理解出口信用保险集保险与融资为一体？
4. 是否所有种类的出口贸易融资，出口商都会被追索？
5. 简述 D/P T/R 应注意的事项。

Chapter 1

Summary of International Settlement

1.1 Definition of International Settlement

International settlements are financial activities conducted among different countries in which either payments are effected or funds are transferred from one country to another for the purpose of settling accounts, debts, claims, etc. It may be involved by tangible trades or by intangible trades, foreign investments, funds borrowed from or lent to other countries and so forth.

In this course, we mainly discuss the international trade settlement caused by tangible trades. The methods of international trade settlement can be usually suitable for non-trade settlement. In practice, non-trade settlement is usually much simpler than international trade settlement.

1.2 Main Contents of International Trade Settlement

Contents of international trade settlement can be divided into four parts: a. negotiable instrument; b. methods of international settlement; c. documentation; d. financing under international trade settlement. All of them make international settlement a complete mechanism.

1. Negotiable Instrument

The negotiable instrument is a kind of credit instrument just as the treasury bill, the bond certificate and the bank debenture. They are known as credit instruments and are widely used in the world capital market. The negotiable intrument is widely used in international businesses for the main purposes of: a. making business standing credit related with notes; b. payment unconditional and formation; c. payment due to maturity or transferred freely in the bills house or market.

2. Methods of International Settlement

Methods of international settlement mean tunnels/ways to pay/receive money. There are five methods of international settlement: remittance, collection, credit, letter of guarantee and standby credit. Please notice that different methods have different ways of financing under international settlement.

Methods of International Settlement can be used independently or in combination. In the current trade practice, the main stream is the combination of two or more methods of international settlement in a sales contract.

Specimen 1-1   Combination of Payment Terms in a Sales Contract

(1) The supplier agrees that the buyer will effect payments under the term of T/T (Telegraphic Transfer) against receipt of B/L by fax.

(2) Hong Kong suppliers agree that the buyer will effect payments under the term of CAD (Cash against Documents).

(3) Only in case of new suppliers and first order to them, the buyer might agree to effect payments under L/C terms. The L/C charges on the buyer's side will be born by the buyer and the L/C charges on supplier's side will be born by the supplier. The Bill of Lading is made out to order and notify the buyer.

(4) In case that the supplier still insists on L/C terms even after the first order, the supplier agrees to take over all L/C charges on him as well as on the buyer's side. In those cases we request a Bill of Lading.

3. Documentation

Documents are tools of paying/receiving money under international settlement. Documents include commercial invoices, packing lists, bills of lading, insurance policies/certificates, certificates of origin, export licenses, etc.

Documentation concerned to international settlement is including issuance & examination of documents. In this course, we will mainly study how to issue main kinds of documents and how to review the quality of documents as per examination principals of documentation.

4. Financing Under International Settlement

International settlement offers great convenience for capital finance and both benefit for the importer and exporter.

According to the form of banker's finance, finance can be divided into three kinds: finance in fund, finance in documents and finance in guarantee. According to parties financed, finance can be divided into two kinds: import finance and export finance. It means that finance under international settlement is very flexible and optional.

Finance under international settlement can help both parties: a. Reduce the capital occupied; b. Grasp the market opportunity; c. Optimize the capital management; d. Improve the cash flow; e. Accelerate the capital circulation; f. Simplify the financing procedure; g. Save the financial expenses; h. Minimize risks or shift risks.

1.3 Laws, Conventions and Rules Concerning International Settlement

1. Laws & Conventions Related to Negotiable Instrument

(1) Bill of Exchange Act, 1882. It is a typical representative of the Anglo-American law.

(2) Geneva Uniform Bill Act. It is a typical representative of the law in the continental law system.

(3) Negotiable Instrument Law of the People's Republic of China.

2. International Practices Related to Methods of International Settlement

(1) ICC Uniform Customs and Practice for Documentary Credits, 2007 Revision, ICC Publication No. 600 (UCP600).

(2) ICC Uniform Rules for Collection, ICC Publication No. 522 (URC522).

(3) ICC Uniform Rules on Demand Guarantees, ICC Publication No. 758 (URDG758).

3. International Practices & Conventions Related to Documents

(1) International Standard Banking Practices for the Examination of Documents under Documentary Credits (ISBP).

(2) Hague Rules.

(3) Hamburg Rules.

(4) International Convention Concerning the Transport of Goods by Rail.

(5) Agreement on International Rail-Road through Transport of Goods.

(6) Uniform Rules for a Combined Transport Documents.

(7) UNCTAD/ICC Rules for Multimodel Transport Documents.

(8) Institute Cargo Clauses (ICC).

(9) Incoterms 2010.

(10) UNCITRAL Arbitration Rules, etc.

1.4　History and Development of International Settlement

The history of international settlement goes back to originate from transactions in the world trade. With the development of international settlement, negotiable instrument as a credit instrument, emerged and became popular to meet the needs of the constantly increasing business activities in geographical regions and volume of the international trade. Negotiable instrument plays a very important role in making international settlement transform from cash settlement to non-cash settlement, from payment against goods to payment against documents.

Nowadays, both the buyers and the sellers are usually to clear their settlement through commercial banks. In order to satisfy both parties' requirements for proceeds transferring and financing, more and more business banks have focused their business on international settlement and trade finance.

1.5　Bank's Network and Clearing Systems

Banks offer credit guarantee, financing and effective funds transferring network for the sellers or the buyers. In order to improve the efficiency of transferring funds and increase market share in the area of international settlement, business bankers have flocked to join the worldwide clearing systems and opened overseas affiliates.

1. Clearing Systems

There are three popular kinds of clearing system in the world:

(1)　Clearing House Interbank Payment System—CHIPS. It is an electronic payment system for US dollar payments worldwide.

(2)　Clearing House Automated Payment System—CHAPS. It is an electronic settlement system between London interbanks with high computer automation instead of clearing.

(3)　The Society for Worldwide Interbank Financial Telecommunication— SWIFT. It is the most popular worldwide clearing system. It can automatically store information, test and check test key. With advantages of cheapness, safty, reliability, fastness, standardization and automation etc., SWIFT has become the most important tool for transferring funds, opening credit and communication between the bankers.

2. Banker's Network

Business bankers always open their overseas affiliates as follows: a. Branches & Sub-branches. We usually call the relations between branches and sub-branches as "Sister-bank"; b. Representative offices; c. Agencies; d. Subsidiaries; e. Affiliated banks; f. Consortium banks.

Besides the above, a business banker always cooperates with other business bankers abroad through an agency agreement. We call both contracted parties under an agency agreement as correspondent banks or correspondents. If the correspondents wish to develop closest partner relationship, one bank can open an account in the other bank.

At one party's end, Nostro Account or Due from Account refers to the account that he opened in the other bank. Meanwhile, Vostro Account or Due to Account refers to the account that the other bank opened in his bank.

Specimen 1-2   Bank of China Ltd. and Its Network (from http://www.boc.cn/)

Global network —With 12529 domestic branches, 560 institutions scattered in Hong Kong, Macao and oversea areas and nearly 4000 agency banks, BOC, exclusively in domestic market, has established a multi-nation and multi-layer high-speed global payment network through 90 years accumulation.

Safe and timely clearing business — With four major clearing centers, that are US dollar clearing center—New York Branch; Hong Kong dollar clearing center—Bank of China (Hong Kong); Euro clearing center—Frankfurt Branch and Japanese yen clearing center—Tokyo Branch. BOC stands as the leader in domestic market for foreign currency clearing businesses.

Advanced technology level — BOC has become one of the first banks to participate SWIFT in 1993. Sophisticated SWIFT system provides our clients with robust guaranty of convenient and high-speed collection service.

BOC, one of the leading banks to bring forth "One day Global Remittance."

Chapter 2

Negotiable Instruments

2.1 General Introduction

Negotiable instrument is a credit instrument to settle international debts from cash settlement to non-cash settlement. In order to improve the circulation of negotiable instruments, countries usually have negotiable instrument laws specially. Bills of exchange, promissory notes and cheques are three kinds of negotiable instruments. Negotiable instrument can act as a tool for settlement, credit instrument, payment and negotiability.

2.2 Bills of Exchange

2.2.1 Definition

According to Bill of Exchange Act, 1882: A bill of exchange (see Figure 2-1) is an unconditional order of writing, addressed by one person to another, signed by the person giving it, requiring the person to whom it is addressed to pay on demand or at a fixed or determinable future time a sum certain in money to or to the order of a specified person or to bearer.

According to article 19 of Negotiable Instrument Law of the People's Republic of China: A draft is a bill signed by the drawer, requiring the entrusted payer to make unconditional payment in a fixed amount at the sight of the bill or on a fixed date to the payee or the holder.

EXCHANGE FOR USD10,000.00   JULY 13, 2010   PARIS

AT THIRTY DAYS AFTER SHIPMENT DATE (SHIPMENT DATE: JULY 10, 2010) PAY TO

THE ORDER OF C COMPANY THE SUM OF USD TEN THOUSAND ONLY

DRAWN UNDER P/O NO. 95E03LC001 DATED ON MAY 13, 2010.

TO: A COMPANY, NEW YORK   FOR B COMPANY, PARIS

                                                  (MANUALLY SIGNED)

Figure 2-1   A Bill of Exchange

2.2.2   Essentials & Non-essentials of a Bill of Exchange

Essentials refer to the important contents on the face of a bill of exchange. They can be divided into two kinds: absolute essentials and relative essentials. Absolute essentials mean the basic conditions of a valid bill of exchange and can not do otherwise. A draft lacking one of the absolute essentials listed is invalid. Relative essentials mean important but not constitute the basic condition of effectiveness to a bill of exchange. Non-essentials belong to non-important contents of a bill of exchange with effectiveness.

1. Absolute Essentials

(1)   The word " Exchange" or "Bill of Exchange" must be clearly indicated. The purpose is to differentiate a bill of exchange from the other negotiable instruments, such as promissory notes or cheques.

(2)   An unconditional order in writing. Payment of a bill of exchange must be unconditional, such as stipulating "Pay to the order of C Company the sum of USD ten thousand only".

(3)   A sum certain in money. The face value shall be definite or calculating definite on the date of payment. For example, a bill of exchange can be indicated to be paid to the order of C Company the sum of USD ten thousand: a. plus interest calculated at the rate of 3% per annum from the date of issue to the date of payment if it bears interest; b. by ten equal consecutive monthly installments if it bears payment by installments; c. converted into HK dollar at current rate of exchange if it bears payment by other kinds of currency.

(4)   Name and address of the drawee. The drawee of a bill of exchange is the potential payer.

(5)   Name or entity of the payee. Payee of a bill of exchange can be designed as follows: a.

restrictive order. A bill of exchange with restrictive order cannot be negotiable as per negotiable instrument law; b. demonstrative order. With demonstrative order, the bill can be negotiable by endorsement and delivery; c. bearer order. A bill of exchange with bearer order can be negotiable by delivery only.

(6)　Drawer's name & signature(s). If the drawer makes a bill of exchange but does not sign on it, he shall bear no liability on it. If the drawer's signature on a bill of exchange is forged, the bill of exchange isn't effective.

(7)　Date of issue. Date of issue is applied to judge due date of a bill of exchange, to define time of presentation, to check validity of a bill of exchange and to vindicate if the drawer is insolvent or not.

2. Relative Essentials

(1)　Tenor. Tenor refers to the payment period of a bill of exchange. A bill of exchange can be paid at sight or at a specified future date. If a draft does not bear the date of payment, it is a draft payable at sight.

A sight bill can be described as "at sight or on demand or on presentation pay to the order of C Company…".

A time bill with payment at a specified future date can be described as follows: a. Dated payment. Payable on a fixed future date, such as "On 9th Aug 2010 pay to the order of C Company…"; b. Payable on a fixed date after draft, such as "At 30 days after date hereof pay to the order of C Company…"; c. Payable on a fixed date after sight, such as "At 30 days after sight pay to the order of C Company…"; d. Payable at a fixed time after the happening of a specified event, such as "At 30 days after bill of lading date pay to the order of C Company…".

(2)　Place of issue. To judge if a bill of exchange is effective or not according to the relative negotiable instrument law of the issuing place. If a draft does not bear the place of draft, the place of draft shall be taken as the business site or the residence of the drawer or the place where the drawer often lives. Such a place will be applied to judge if the bill of exchange is effective.

(3)　Place of payment. Place of payment refers to the place where a bill of exchange will be cashed. If a bill of exchange is dishonored, notice of dishonor or protest should be issued as per the relative negotiable instrument law of the payment place. If a draft does not bear the place of payment, the place of payment shall be the business site or the residence of the payer or the place where the payer often lives.

3. Non-essentials

Usually, there are four main kinds of non-essentials on a bill of exchange. In detail: a. A banker designated as payer; b. Referee in case of need; c. Notice of dishonor excused or protest waived; d. Without recourse.

2.2.3 Acts of a Bill of Exchange

In the life-circle of a bill of exchange, acts of a bill of exchange may concern issuance, endorsement, presentation, acceptance, payment, dishonor, recourse, acceptance for honor supra protest, guarantee and discounting, etc.

1. Issuance

Issuance refers to create rights arising out of a bill of exchange. To issue a draft comprises two acts to be performed by the drawer: the first is to draw and sign a draft, and the second is to deliver it to the payee. By drawing the bill, the drawer commits himself to the following:

The draft will be duly accepted or paid on presentment, and if the draft is dishonored, the drawer will compensate the holder or any endorser for any loss suffered.

2. Endorsement

A bill of exchange with demonstrative order can be transferred by endorsement. Endorsement is an act of negotiation. The payee on the face of a bill of exchange with demonstrative order must be the first endorser if he is willing to transfer rights of a bill to the endorsee. The first endorsee can also endorse over the bill to another one and so on.

Prerequisites for a valid endorsement should be normally effected on the back of a draft and signed by the endorser and must be made for the whole amount of the draft. The endorser must bear liability to the endorsee that the draft will be duly paid upon presentment, and if the draft is dishonored, he will compensate endorsee or the consecutive holder who is compelled to pay the draft.

There are many kinds of endorsement, such as blank endorsement, special endorsement, restrictive endorsement, conditional endorsement, endorsement for collection, endorsement in pledge, reverse endorsement and forged endorsement, etc. Blank endorsement (see Figure 2-2) and special endorsement (see Figure 2-3)are the two most important endorsements. An endorsement in blank is one that shows an endorser's signature only and specifies no endorsee. It is also called a general endorsement. A draft so endorsed becomes payable to bearer. A special endorsement is one that specifies an endorsee to whom or to whose order the draft is to be paid, in addition to the signature of an endorser. As per article 30 of Negotiable Instrument Law of People's Republic of China, the draft shall bear the name of the endorser.

For C Company, Paris

(Signed)

Figure 2-2   Blank Endorsement

Pay to the order of D Company

For C Company, Paris

(Signed)

Figure 2-3   Special Endorsement

3. Presentation

A draft must be duly presented for payment if it is a sight bill or duly presented for acceptance first and then presented for payment at maturity if it is a time bill.

A bill with payment at sight should be presented for payment within one month from the date of issue as per Negotiable Instrument Law of the People's Republic of China and within one year from the date of issue as per the continental negotiable instrument laws.

A time bill with payment after sight should be presented for acceptance within the same period as a sight bill be presented for payment. Meanwhile, it should be presented for payment, within 10 days from maturity as per Negotiable Instrument Law of the People's Republic of China and two days around maturity as per the continental negotiable instrument laws.

4. Acceptance

Acceptance of a draft is a signification by the drawee of his assent to the order given by the drawer. He engages, by signing his name across the face of the bill that he will pay when it falls due. So presentment for acceptance is legally necessary to fix the maturity date of a draft payable after sight. General acceptance (see Figure 2-4) is the most important kind of acceptance. It means that the drawee engages that he will pay a draft unconditionally. Acceptance may be made before endorsement.

ACCEPTED

Date: 19TH JULY 2010

FOR A COMPANY, NEW YORK

（SIGNED）

Figure 2-4   General Acceptance

5. Payment

Act of payment is performed when a bill of exchange is paid. A bill is discharged by payment in due course only when such payment is made by or on behalf of the drawee or the acceptor.

6. Dishonor

Act of dishonor is a failure or refusal to make acceptance on or payment of a draft when presented. When dishonor happens, the holder shall usually make a notice of dishonor or protest in order to recourse as per the relative negotiable instrument law of the drawee's country.

A notice of dishonor refers to a notice on which default of acceptance or of payment by the drawee or the acceptor is advised. It should be given by the holder of a draft to the drawer and all the endorsers whom he seeks to hold liable for payment. It must be given by or on behalf of the holder or an endorsee on the next business day after dishonor of the draft.

A protest refers to a written statement under seal drawn up and signed by a notary public or other authorized person for the purpose of giving evidence that a bill of exchange has been presented by him for acceptance or for payment but dishonored.

7. Recourse

In the event of a draft being dishonored, the holder has a right of recourse against the other parties thereto, that is a right to claim compensation from the drawer or any endorser.

(1) The person subject to recourse. The drawer, endorser, acceptor and guarantor shall bear a joint and several liability with regard to the holder. A holder may exercise the right of recourse against one person or several persons or all the draft debtors in disregard of the sequential order of the debtors. After a holder has exercised the right of recourse against one person or several persons involving in the draft, the holder may also exercise the right of recourse over others involved in the draft. The person against whom the right of recourse has been exercised will enjoy the same right as the holder after the debt has been cleared.

In the case in which the holder is the drawer, the holder has no right of recourse to the prior holder. In the case in which the holder is the endorser, the holder has no right of recourse against the subsequent holders.

(2) Recourse amount. Article 70 & 71 of Negotiable Instruments Law of the People's Republic of China stipulate the following: In exercising the right of recourse, the holder may request the person subject to recourse to pay the following money and expenses: a. The amount of the draft dishonored; b. The interests calculated according to the rate fixed by the People's

Bank of China on the draft amount from the due date or the date of presentation for payment to the date of liquidation; c. The expenses incurred in obtaining the related certificates of dishonor and the issuing of notification.

When the person subject to recourse is clearing his debt, the holder shall deliver the draft and related certificates of dishonor and produce the receipts for the interests and expenses received. After debt clearance according to the provisions of the preceding article, the person against whom the right of recourse has been exercised may exercise the right of re-recourse against other draft debtors and request other debtors to pay the following amount and expenses: a.The complete amount cleared; b.The interests on the amount cleared, calculated according to the rate fixed by the People's Bank of China from the date of liquidation to the date of liquidation for re-recourse; c. Expenses on issuing notifications.

When the person who exercises the right of re-recourse is getting paid, that person shall deliver the draft and related certificates of dishonor and produce the receipts for the interests and expenses received.

8. Acceptance for Honor Supra Protest

It is an act performed by the acceptor for honor, who accepts the bill supra protest, for the honor of any party liable thereon or for the honor of the person for whose account the bill is drawn. A bill may be accepted for honor for only a part of the sum drawn payable.

9. Guarantee

It is performed by a third party called guarantor, who engages that the bill will be paid on presentation if it is a sight bill or accepted on presentation and paid at maturity if it is a time bill. A guarantor shall undertake the liabilities of guaranty for the debt involved in the draft. A guarantor shall be some person other than the debtor of the draft.

A guarantor shall record the following items on the draft or allonge: a. The word "Guarantee", b. Name and residence of the guarantor, c. Name of the guaranteed party, d. Date of guaranty, e. Signature or seal of the guarantor. If a guarantor has failed to record "Name of the guaranteed party" on the draft or allonge, the acceptor shall be the guaranteed party of the accepted draft; and the drawer shall be the guaranteed party for the draft not accepted. If the guarantor has failed to record "Date of guaranty" of the preceding article, the date of draft shall be the date of guaranty.

A guarantor shall guarantee that there are no conditions attached. If conditions have been attached, they shall not affect the liability of guaranty for the draft. A guarantor shall undertake the liability of guaranty for the right to the draft enjoyed by the holder who has acquired the draft according to law, except cases when the debt guaranteed has become invalid due to inadequate recording in the draft. A guarantor shall undertake some liability together with the guaranteed for the draft under guarantee. If the draft is not paid when due, the holder has the right to demand the guarantor for payment and the guarantor shall pay the full amount. If there are two or more guarantors, the guarantors shall undertake a joint and some liability.

After the draft debt is cleared, the guarantor may exercise the right of recourse of the holder against the guaranteed and the prior holder.

10. Discounting

Discounting a bill of draft is to sell a time bill already accepted by the drawee but not yet fallen due to a financial situation at a price less than its face value. It is also an act of negotiable draft. Perfect procedures for a time draft are as follows:

(1) Drawer: To issue a bill, present it for acceptance.

(2) Drawee: To accept it and become an acceptor, then deliver it to the drawer or the payee.

(3) Payee: To sell it to the discounting house as the first endorser through endorsement.

(4) Endorsee: To pay the amount (i.e. less than the face value) and to be the holder.

(5) Holder: To present it for payment at maturity.

(6) Acceptor: To pay the face value.

2.2.4　Classification of a Bill of Exchange

According to tenor, there are sight (demand) bills or time (usance) bills. According to the drawer, a bill of exchange can be a banker's draft or a trader's draft. According to the acceptor, a time trader's draft can be divided into a trader's acceptance draft or a banker's acceptance draft.

According to whether commercial documents are attached thereto, there are clean bills & documentary bills. According to the currency denominated, there are local currency bills & foreign currency bills. According to the place of acceptance and place of shipment, there are inland bills & foreign bills.

2.3　Promissory Notes

2.3.1　Definition

A promissory note is a an unconditional promise in writing made by one person to another signed by the maker engaging to pay on demand or a fixed or determinable future time a sum certain in money to or to the order of a specified person or to bearer.

2.3.2　Characteristics of a Promissory Note

A promissory note (see Figure 2-5) is an unconditional promise in writing. The basic parties to a promissory note are the maker and the payee. The maker corresponds to the drawer as well as the drawee of a bill of exchange. There is no need to accept the instrument if it is payable at a fixed or determinable future time. In all cases the maker is the primarily liable party.

Promissory notes other than those issued by banks are not very widely used in modern commercial transactions. Bearer promissory notes payable on demand and issued by banks are equivalent to bank notes of large denomination, which may cause inflation and are prohibited by the government in many countries. Article 73 of Negotiable Instrument Law of the People's Republic of China stipulates "The term Promissory Note used in this law refers to the bank note".

Promissory note for USD10,000.00　　　13th Jul. 2010 New York

At thirty days after shipment date (shipment date：10 July, 2010) we

promise to pay B Company or order the sum of USD ten thousand only for

value received.

　　　　　　　　　　　　　　　　For A Company，New York

　　　　　　　　　　　　　　　　　　(Signed)

Figure 2-5　A Promissory Note

2.3.3　Essentials of a Promissory Note

A promissory note must be clearly indicated the words "Promissory Note". It must be an unconditional promise to pay, show name of the payee or his order, put the maker's signature on it and have a date of issue. Meanwhile, place of issue, place of payment, tenor and a certain amount of money are relative essentials to a promissory note.

2.3.4　Difference Between a Promissory Note and a Bill of Exchange

Difference between a promissory note and a bill of exchange are as follows:

(1)　A promissory note is a promise to pay, whereas a bill of exchange is an order to pay.

(2)　There are only two parties to a promissory note, namely the maker and the payee (or

the holder in the case of a bearer note), whereas there are three parties to a bill of exchange, namely the drawee, the drawer and the payee.

(3) The maker is primarily liable on a promissory note, whereas the drawer is primarily liable, if it is a sight bill, and the acceptor becomes primarily liable, if it is a time bill.

(4) When issued, a promissory note has an original note only, whereas a bill of exchange may be either a sole bill or a bill in set, i.e. a bill drawn with second of exchange and third of exchange in addition to the original one.

2.4　Cheques

2.4.1　Definition

Briefly speaking, a cheque (see Figure 2-6) is a bill of exchange drawn on a bank payable on demand. Detailedly speaking, a cheque is an unconditional order in writing addressed by the customer to a bank signed by that customer authorizing the bank to pay on demand a sum certain in money or to the order of a specified person or to bearer.

Article 81 of Negotiable Instrument Law of the People's Republic of China stipulates that a cheque is an instrument issued by a drawer, at the sight of which the cheque deposit bank or other financial institutions unconditionally pay the fixed amount to the payee or holder.

```
CHEQUE NO. 123678                        NEW YORK AUG. 9, 2010

PAY TO THE ORDER OF B COMPANY THE SUM OF USD TEN THOUSAND
ONLY                                     USD10,000.00

TO: ABC BANK, NEW YORK         FOR A COMPANY, NEW YORK
                                         (MANUALLY SIGNED)
```

Figure 2-6　A Cheque

A cheque must be unconditional and drawn on a bank at sight. There are three basic parties to a cheque. The drawer is the customer who writes the cheque, the drawee is the banker on whom the cheque is drawn and to whom the order to pay is given, the payee is the person to whom a cheque is stated to be payable.

2.4.2　Essentials of a Cheque

A cheque must be clearly indicated the word " Cheque", an unconditional order in writing, show name of the paying bank and have the drawer's signature. A sum certain in money must be written on a cheque, which should be signed by or by procurement for the drawer. The date of a cheque is not essential in that it can be antedated, post-dated or dated on a non-business day. The payee may be bearer, a specified person or his order.

Processing an international cheque is normally as follows:

(1)　The payee presents the cheque to his own bank and requests the bank to collect it.

(2)　The collecting bank examines the cheque to insure that it is in order.

(3)　The collecting bank presents the cheque to the paying bank.

(4)　The paying bank pays the collecting bank when it is satisfied that the cheque is properly drawn and there are sufficient funds or overdraft balance in the drawer's account.

(5)　The collecting bank credits the payee's account when he receives the funds from the paying bank.

2.4.3　A Banker's Duty to Honor a Cheque

The banker is obliged to honor a customer's cheque up to the amount of his credit balance or available overdraft limit. The banker's duty to honor the check ends: a. On countermanding of payment by the customer, commonly known as "stop"; b. On receiving a notice that the customer has died or dissolved; c. On receiving a notice of bankruptcy or liquidation of the customer; d. On receiving an order that is made against the customer; e. On receiving a notice of mental disorder of the customer; f. On receiving a garnishee order against the customer's account; g. On receiving a court order freezing the customer's account.

Paying bank to honor a cheque will pay more attention to the following points: a. **The cheque is drawn on the paying bank and its branch**; b. The cheque has the correct date; c. The words and figures agree; d. The signature complies with the authority; e. The cheque must be complete and regular; f. There is no material alteration; g. The cheque is payable to a specified person or bearer; h. There is no countermand of payment; i. There are sufficient funds; j. If there is no legal bar.

2.4.4　Differences Between a Cheque and a Bill of Exchange

Differences between a cheque and a bill of exchange are as follows:

(1)　A cheque is a bill of exchange drawn on a bank with payment at sight, whereas the drawee and the tenor of a bill of exchange are more flexible. The drawee of a bill of exchange may be a bank or a trader. The tenor of a bill of exchange may be at sight or at a specified future date.

(2) The drawer is primarily liable on a cheque, whereas the drawer is primarily liable, if it is a sight bill, and the acceptor becomes primarily liable, if it is a time bill.

(3) A cheque only needs presentation for payment and does not need presentation for acceptance as it's at sight, whereas a bill of exchange needs both presentation for acceptance and payment, if it is a time bill.

(4) A bill of exchange may be guaranteed by other third party, whereas a cheque may be certified by the paying bank. Crossing is the act of a cheque that differs from a bill of exchange.

Chapter 3

Remittance and Collection

3.1 Remittance

3.1.1 Definition

On a banker's side, remittance means the remitting bank, entrusted by the remitter, remits funds to his sister-banks or his correspondent banks by the certain instrument and instructs them to pay the certain amount to the nominated payee. With instructions from bank to bank, remittance is faster, more convenient and safer than cash settlement.

In international trade, remittance also means transferring of funds from the buyer to the seller abroad through banks on the buyer's initiative. Remittance has four parties concerned: the remitter, the remitting bank, the payee and the paying bank. The remitter and the payee are contracted parties to a sales contract. The remitting bank and the paying bank usually belong to sister-banks or correspondent banks.

3.1.2 Methods of Remittance

Remittance consists of telegraphic transfer(T/T), mail transfer (M/T) and demand draft (D/D). T/T means remittance by cable/telex/SWIFT. M/T means remittance by airmail. D/D means remittance by banker's demand draft.

Nowadays, T/T becomes the most important and popular remittance. T/T is the quickest remittance and the payee can receive the proceeds earlier than by M/T and D/D. The remitter may establish excellent reputation and win the trust of the remittee. While, demand draft may lost, stolen or destroyed. Fluctuation in the exchange rate and withdrawl may happen during the longer waiting time of M/T than T/T.

3.1.3 Procedure of T/T

If a S/C stipulates terms of payment as T/T, payment procedure (see Figure 3-1) is usually as follows:

(1) According to the time and the amount of the sales contract, the remitter fills the application form of remittance by T/T and delivers a sum certain of money to the remitting bank.

(2) The remitting bank examines and verifies the relative instructions of remittance, then returns a copy of the application form to the remitter with stamp and signature. It means that he accepts the request of the remitter.

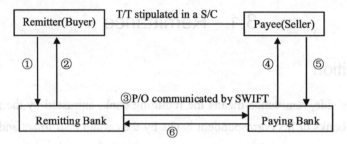

Figure 3-1 Procedure of T/T

(3) The remitting bank makes a payment order to the paying bank by SWIFT/cable/telex as per the instructions received from the remitter. Bank to bank reimbursement methods must be indicated clearly on the payment order. Here are some examples.

a. In cover, we have credited the sum to your account with us. (Crediting vostro account of the paying bank.)

b. In cover, please debit the sum to our account with you, or, in cover, you are authorized to debit the sum to our account with you. (Debiting the remitting bank 's nostro account.)

c. In cover, we have authorized The Bank of Tokyo, New York to debit our account and credit your account with the above sum. (Instructing a reimbursement bank to effect payment by debiting the remitting bank's nostro account.)

d. In cover, we have instructed the Bank of Tokyo, New York to pay the proceeds to your account with the Standard Chartered Bank, New York. (Instructing the paying bank to claim reimbursement from another branch of the same bank or another bank with which the remitting bank opens an account.)

e. In cover, you are authorized to debit our central bank's clearing account with your central bank. Or in cover, we have requested our central bank to credit the sum to the clearing account of your central bank with them (according to the payment agreement between two countries).

(4) The paying bank gives the payee notice to receive the proceeds.

(5)   The payee verifies the identity and obtains the proceeds from the paying bank.

(6)   The paying bank informs the remitting bank of payment. The remittance is terminated.

3.1.4   Application of T/T in International Trade

Remittance belongs to business standing. Compared with credit and collection, remittance has the characteristics of flexibility, simple formality and low charge. Remittance can be made both in advance or after the arrival of the goods.

1. Remittance Made in Advance

In international trade, remittance made in advance means that the buyer must pay earlier than taking delivery. The following examples all belong to remittance made in advance.

(1)   Cash with order. It means payment shall be made once the two parties signed a Sales Contract. It represents the buyer has to bear all risks involved by performance of the sales contract. The terms can be stipulated in a S/C as follows: Cash with order, the buyer shall make payment by T/T within 7 days from the date of contract being signed.

(2)   100% payment at least a certain days before shipment. It means that the seller will ship the goods on the basis of 100% payment made by the buyer before shipment. The terms can be stipulated in a S/C as follows: 100% payment shall be made at least 10 days earlier than shipment; shipment will be arranged against 100% payment.

(3)   100% payment made between the date of shipment and the date of arrival. The buyer insists on payment made after shipment but agrees to make payment on/before the goods arriving at the port or place of destination.

The terms can be stipulated in a S/C as follows: a. 100% payment made within 30 days from the date of B/L, the full set of shipping documents will be released to the buyer by the seller on the basis of 100% payment, if shipment is made by seafreight and the transport period from the port of shipment to the port of destination will take more than 30 days; b. Cash on delivery (COD), if shipment is made by non-waterway transport; c. Cash against documents (CAD), if the buyer deposits the proceeds at a bank in advance and asks the seller to get the proceeds against the shipping documents from the deposit bank.

2. Remittance Made After Arrival of the Goods

In international trade, remittance made after arrival of the goods means that the buyer can take delivery earlier than payment. The following methods belong to remittance after arrival of the goods.

(1) Open account business (O/A). It means that the seller shall ship the goods and deliver the shipping documents to the buyer first and the buyer will make payment at the agreed date. The terms can be stipulated in a S/C as follows: Payment made by T/T within 30 days after shipment. The buyer always sell/use the goods first and pay the proceeds to the seller later.

(2) Consignment. It means that the buyer not only can get the goods before payment but also can return the unsold goods to the seller. On the agreed date of payment, the buyer can make payment wholly if he sold out or in part if he didn't sell out. Consignment represents the greatest risks to the seller.

3.2　Collection

3.2.1　Definition

Collection is an arrangement whereby the goods are shipped and a relevant bill of exchange is drawn by the seller on the buyer, and/or shipping documents are forwarded to the seller's bank with clear instructions for collection through one of its correspondent banks located in the domicile of the buyer. On a banker's side, collection refers to the following: "Entrusted by the exporter, the bank, with the financial and/or commercial documents submitted by the exporter, collects payment from the importer via its foreign correspondent banks or sister-branches."

There are four basic parties and two possible parties concerning collection. Basic parties are the principal (seller/exporter/drawer), the remitting (principal's /seller's /exporter's) bank, the collecting bank and the drawee (buyer/importer). Possible parties are the presenting bank and the representative in case of need.

3.2.2　Methods of Collection

According to collection with commercial documents or not, there are clean collection and documentary collection.

1. Clean Collection

Clean collection means collection with financial documents only and isn't accompanied by commercial documents. It benefits for the payee with safety, convenience, swiftness and low charges. Cheques, promissory notes, clean drafts, acceptances, dividend warrants drawn on foreign banks, certificates of deposit or saving passbook issued by foreign banks, governments or post offices, drafts drawn under a traveler's letter of credit from a foreign bank are usually the items of clean collection.

2. Documentary Collection

Documentary collection is a payment mechanism that allows the exporters to retain ownership of the goods until they receive payment or are reasonably certain that they will receive it. In most cases, documentary collection is made with both financial documents and commercial documents. In some specific cases, it also can be made with commercial documents only. For example, some specific countries like Japan and Germany impose stamp tax on the financial documents. In order to lessen tax burden, documentary collection without financial documents can be applied to business between highly trusted firms with high reputation.

According to the definition given in the Uniform Rules for Collections (ICC Publication No. 522), the purposes for collection are as follows: a. obtain acceptance and/or, as the case may be, payment; b. deliver commercial documents against acceptance or, as the case may be, payment; c. deliver documents on other terms and conditions. So documentary collection can be made: a. Documents against payment (D/P). With D/P, the payment can be made at sight (D/P at sight) or at a specific future date (Usance D/P); b. Documents against acceptance(D/A). With D/A, the payment only can be made at a specific future date.

3.2.3   Application of Documentary Collection

In business practice, utilization of collection is much less than credit and remittance. On the seller's side, collection always only means D/P at sight. D/A is seldom used in actual practice as it has high risks. Usance D/P is not better than D/A. Usance D/P is regarded as an abnormal payment mechanism by ICC. Different bankers have different operational approaches on it (see Table 3-1).

Table 3-1   Operational Approaches of Different Bankers on Usance D/P

Countries	Operational Approaches
USA	There is different understanding among different bankers.
France	There is no legal basis to settle disputes on Usance D/P.
Germany	Refuse to accept.
Canada	Only accept D/P at sight.
Australia	Usance D/P = D/A

Continued

Countries	Operational Approaches
Norway	Refuse to accept.
UAE	Usually refuse to accept Usance D/P.
Chile	Refuse to accept, or equals to D/A.
Thailand	Accept Usance D/P.

3.2.4 Procedure of Documentary Collection

Let's give an example to describe the processing of D/P at sight with financial documents (see Figure 3-2). Financial documents are usually used with bill of exchanges issued by the seller under collection.

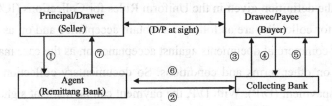

Figure 3-2 Procedure of D/P at sight

(1) The seller ships the goods as schedule stipulated in the S/C, preparing for commercial documents for collection and draws a bill of exchange at sight, fills a collection application form and delivers them to the remitting bank.

(2) The remitting bank checks all the writing materials delivered by the seller, makes a collection order as per the instructions on the application form strictly, then sends all of them to the collecting bank abroad by courier.

(3) The collecting bank shall also check commercial documents, the bill of exchange and the collection order carefully. Then he presents commercial documents and the bill of exchange at sight to the drawee (the buyer) as per instructions on the collection order.

(4) The buyer examines the presenting documents according to the sales contract. Then he makes payment of the sight draft to the nominated account of the collecting bank.

(5) The collecting bank delivers all of commercial documents to the buyer against payment.

(6) The collecting bank reimburses the proceeds to the account instructed by the remitting bank.

(7)　The remitting bank pays the proceeds to the seller. Business with D/P at sight is terminated.

3.2.5　Comments on Collection

Collection gives the buyer time to pay for the shipment but gives the seller assurance that the title to the shipment will not be handed over until payment or acceptance has been made. If the buyer refuses to accept the bill or does not honor payment at maturity, the exporter will have time to take appropriate measures or possibly to look for another customer for the goods.

1. Banks

Acting as the seller's agent, the bank regulates the timing and sequence of the exchange of goods for value by holding the title documents until the importer either pays the draft or accepts the obligations to do so. Banks will act in good faith and exercise with reasonable care and must verify that the documents received appear to be as listed in the collection order and must immediately advice the party from whom the collection was received of any documents missing.

However, the banker in documentary collection is the most important role for successful collection, specially the collecting bank.

2. The Seller

On the seller's side, he may accept D/P at sight only for documentary collection with a lot of constraints: a. Cooperate parties including the buyer, the bank and its network and the trade country shall be trusted, safe and with high reputation; b. The cargo shall be general. Specific cargo such as fresh cutting flowers, foods, the seasonable goods and the goods with market fluctuation shall be avoided to transact under collection; c. Trade term shall be CIF and shipped by seafreight. Bill of lading (transport documents) is title to the goods and the seller covers transport insurance by himself.

3. The Buyer

On the buyer's side, he may worry about the goods being shipped not as ordered, while payment may have to be made prior to the arrival of the goods. The buyer under documentary collection depends on the exporter's credit standing only. However, he shall bear two separate legal liabilities both on the bill of exchange and on the sales contract. Non-acceptance or non-payment on the part of the buyer will be worse than anything else. He may face ruining the reputation of a trade and it may be considered an act of bankruptcy if a bill of exchange is protested.

Finally, the buyer may protect himself against faulty merchandise by requiring an inspection certificate as part of the documentation.

Chapter 4

Documentary Credits

4.1 Definition

Credit means any arrangement, however named or described, that is irrevocable and thereby constitutes a definite undertaking of the issuing bank to honor a complying presentation, as per The Uniform Customs and Practice for Documentary Credits, 2007 Revision, ICC Publication No. 600(UCP600).

In brief, a credit is a conditional undertaking of payment by a bank. Complying presentation is the definite undertaking condition of the issuing bank. Complying presentation means a presentation that is in accordance with the terms and conditions of the credit, the applicable provision of these rules and international standard banking practice.

4.2 Features of a Credit

A credit places a bank's credit standing on the basis of commercial credit standing. It is guaranteed by the issuing bank's creditworthiness. Its main characteristics are as follows:

(1) The issuing bank undertakes to effect payment, quite independent of whether the applicant is bankrupt or in fault or not, provided the documents presented are in compliance with the terms and conditions of the credit. Meanwhile, banks dealing with credit business assume no responsibilities for the acts of third parties taking part in one way or another in the credit transaction.

(2) A credit stands independent of the sales contract. A credit by its nature is a separate transaction from the sales or other contract on which it may be based. Banks are in no way concerned with or bound by such contract, even if any reference whatever to it is included in the credit. Consequently, the undertaking of a bank to honor, to negotiate or to fulfill any other obligation under the credit is not subject to claims or defenses by the applicant resulting from its relationship with the issuing bank or the beneficiary. A beneficiary can in no case avail itself of the contractual relationships existing between banks or between the applicant and the issuing bank. (As per article 4 of UCP600, Credits v. Contracts)

(3)   In credit business, banks deal with documents and not with goods, services or other performances to which the documents may relate.(article 5 of UCP600). Banks engaged in credit business also assume no responsibilities for the form, sufficiency, accuracy, genuineness, falsification or legal effect of any documents presented. Their main responsibility in this respect is to examine each document presented to see whether it appears on the face to be in compliance with the credit terms.

4.3   Parties to a Credit

According to article 2 of UCP 600, there are two kinds of parties to a credit as follows:

1. Basic Parties to a Credit

Issuing bank and beneficiary are the basic parties of a credit. Issuing bank means the bank that issues a credit at the request of an applicant or on its own behalf. Beneficiary means the party in whose favour a credit is issued. A credit constitutes a payment arrangement between issuing bank and beneficiary. If the beneficiary makes a complying presentation under a credit, the issuing bank must honor.

Provided that the stipulated documents are presented to the nominated bank or to the issuing bank and that they constitute a complying presentation, the issuing bank must honor if the credit is available by: a. Sight payment, deferred payment or acceptance with the issuing bank; b. Sight payment with a nominated bank and that nominated bank does not pay; c. Deferred payment with a nominated bank and that nominated bank does not incur its deferred payment undertaking or, having incurred its deferred payment undertaking, does not pay at maturity; d. Acceptance with a nominated bank that does not accept a draft drawn on it or, having accepted a draft drawn on it, does not pay at maturity; e. Negotiation with a nominated bank and that nominated bank does not negotiate.

2. General Parties to a Credit

General parties to a credit are applicant, advising bank, nominated bank, presenter, confirming bank and so on. Applicant means the party on whose request the credit is issued. Advising bank means the bank that advises the credit at the request of the issuing bank. Confirming bank means the bank that adds its confirmation to a credit upon the issuing bank's authorization or request. Nominated bank means the bank with which the credit is available or any bank in the case of a credit available with any bank. Presenter means a beneficiary, bank or other party that makes a presentation.

4.4 Honor & Negotiation of a Credit

The issuing bank may issue a credit that can be available with himself or with a nominated bank by sight payment, deferred payment, acceptance or negotiation. A credit can be available with a nominated bank and also can be available with the issuing bank. The issuing bank must honor a complying presentation, whereas the nominated bank may honor or negotiate a complying presentation as per the issuing bank's nomination.

A nominated bank other than a confirming bank may negotiate with recourse, whereas a bank honors a complying presentation must not recourse.

1. Honor

Honor means a. to pay at sight if the credit is available by sight payment; b. to incur a deferred payment undertaking and pay at maturity if the credit is available by deferred payment; c. to accept a bill of exchange ("draft") drawn by the beneficiary and pay at maturity if the credit is available by acceptance.

2. Negotiation

Negotiation means the purchase by the nominated bank of drafts (drawn on a bank other than the nominated bank) and/or documents under a complying presentation by advancing or agreeing to advance funds to the beneficiary on or before the banking date on which reimbursement is due to the nominated bank.

4.5 Procedure of a Credit

Procedure of a credit can be partitioned into three parts: issuance, amendment and availability.

1. Issuance of a Credit

An issuing bank is irrevocably bound to honor as of the time it issues the credit. The procedure of opening a credit is as follows (see Figure 4-1):

(1) The applicant, the buyer of a sales contract with payment by credit, must fill an application form (see Specimen 4-1) for opening a credit during the reasonable time as per the S/C stipulated, sign a security agreement with the issuing bank, deposit a certain percentage of credit value into the issuing bank's margin account as per the issuing bank's requirement.

(2) The issuing bank will examine contents of the application in earnest to assure its accuracy, completeness and consistency before issuing the credit, and issue a credit (see Specimen 4-2) according to the application strictly, then send the credit to the advising bank by specific communication, such as by SWIFT/telex/cable/airmail/express.

(3) On receipt of a credit, the advising bank must examine the apparent authenticity of the credit before advising the credit, then advise accurately to reflect the terms and conditions of the credit. If a bank is requested to advise a credit but cannot satisfy itself as to the apparent authenticity of the credit, it must so inform, without delay, the bank from which the instructions appear to have been received.

An advising bank may utilize the services of another bank("second advising bank") to advise the credit to the beneficiary. By advising the credit, the second advising bank signifies that it has satisfied itself as to the apparent authenticity of the credit it has received and that the advice accurately reflects the terms and conditions of the credit or amendment.

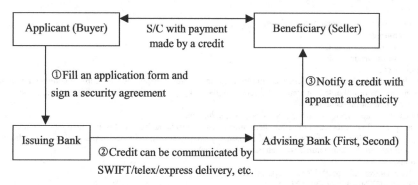

Figure 4-1   The Procedure of Opening a Credit

Specimen 4-1   Application for Issuing a Credit

APPLICATION FOR ISSUING LETTER OF CREDIT

DATE: 20080129

To: BANK OF CHINA LTD. ZHEJIANG BRANCH

Please issue on our behalf and for our account the following ☒IRREVOCABLE ☐TRANSFERABLE ☐UNTRANSFERABLE LETTER OF CREDIT SUBJECT TO UCP600.

L/C No.: 63211020049

Applicant: (full name & detailed address) BNP PARIBAS (CANADA) MONTREAL	Advising Bank: (left for bank to fill)	
Beneficiary: (full name & detailed address) NANJING TANG TEXTILE GARMENT CO., LTD. HUARONG MANSION RM2901 NO. 85 GUANJIAQIAO, NANJING 210005, CHINA	Expiry date:20080410 Place: IN CHINA Partial shipments: NOT ALLOWED Transhipment: ALLOWED Loading in Charge: ANY PORT IN CHINA	For transport to: MONTREAL Latest date of shipment:20080325
Amount: USD32640.00		

Credit available with: any bank by negotiation Against the documents detailed herein and Beneficiary's Draft(s) drawn ☒at sight ☐ at   days after ☐B/L Date ☐

Documents required: (marked with X)
☒ Manually signed Commercial Invoice in 3 COPIES ☐ indicating L/C No. and Contract No.
☒ Full set 3/3 plus 2 non-negotiable copies of clean on board ocean Bills of Lading made out to order of BNP PARIBAS (CANADA) marked "freight prepaid" notifying applicant's full name and address.
☐ Air Waybills consigned to applicant marked "freight ☐prepaid/☐collect" indicating actual flight no., actual flight date and notifying
☒ 2 of original Insurance Policy/Certificate for 110% of the invoice value, showing claims payable in Canada, in currency of the draft, issued or endorsed to the order of BNP PARIBAS (CANADA) covering INSTITUTE CARGO CLAUSES A, INSTITUTE WAR CLAUSES AND INSTITUTE STRIKES, CIVIL COMMOTIONS CLAUSES as per ICC clause/ ☐   .
☒ Certificate of Origin Form A in   issued by
☒ Packing List in 3 issued by Beneficiary indicating ☒quantity ☒gross and net weight of each package.
☐ Weight Memo in   issued by   indicating gross and net weight of each package.
☐ Certificate of Quality in   issued by   .
☐ Beneficiary's certified copy of fax sent to applicant within ☐   days / ☐ 5 beneficiary's working days after shipment indicating contract No., L/C No., goods name, quantity, invoice value, vessel's name. ☐flight No., ☐container No., ☐package, ☐ loading port ☐dispatch place, shipping date ☐ B/L No. and etc.
☐ Beneficiary's statement attesting that one set of non-negotiable documents have been sent to applicant by   within ☒ 3 days/ ☐   beneficiary's working days after   .
☐ Fumigation Certificate in duplicate.
☐ Certificate of non-wood packing material in duplicate.
Other Documents required:
  +Canada customs invoices in 4 copies.
  +Copy of Certificate of Origin Form A.
  +Copy of export licence.
  +Beneficiary's letter stating that original Certificate of Origin Form A, original export licence, copy of commercial invoice, detailed packing lists and a copy of bill of lading were sent direct to applicant by courier within 5 days after shipment. The relative courier receipt is also required for presentation.
  +Copy of applicant's fax approving production samples before shipment.
  +Letter from shipper on their letterhead indicating their name of company and address, bill of lading number, container number and that this shipment, including its container, does not contain any non-manufactured wooden material, dunnage, bracing material, pallets, crating or other non-manufactured wooden packing material.
Description of goods:
  SALES CONDITIONS: CIF MONTREAL/CANADA
  SALES CONTRACT NO. F01LCB05127
  LADIES COTTON BLAZER (100% COTTON, 40SX20/140X60)
  STYLE NO.   PO NO.   QTY/PCS   USD/PC
  46-301A   10337   2550   12.80

  ☐FOB   ☐C&F   ☒CIF   ☐OTHER TERMS CFR

  Packing: Shipping mark:
Additional instructions:
☐All documents must indicate contract No.   .
☒All banking charges ☐except L/C opening and /or acceptance charges ☒outside the issuing bank are for beneficiary's account.
☒Both quantity and amount ☐for each item 3% more or 3% less allowed.
☒Documents must be presented within 15 days after the date of shipment but within the validity of this credit.
☒ + Third party as shipper is acceptable.
☒ + Shipment date earlier than L/C issuing date is acceptable.
☒ +Correction to B/L made by a separate document signed by the issuer of the B/L, indicating the corrections are acceptable.
☒ +Bill of Lading and commercial invoice must certify the following: This shipment, including its container does not contain Any non-manufactured wooden material, dunnage, bracing material, pallets, crating or other non-manufactured wooden packing material.

                        Signature of authorized person:

                              Tel: Fax:

Specimen 4-2   A Credit Available with any Bank by Negotiation at Sight

2008 JAN31 15:23:46		LOGICAL TERMINALE102
MT S700	ISSUE OF A DOCUMENTARY CREDIT	PAGE 00001
FUNC MSG700		
		UMR
		06607642

MSGACK   DWS765I AUTH OK, KEY B110106173BAOC53B, BKCHCNBJ BNPA**** RECORO

BASIC HEADER		F 01 BKCHCNBJA940 0542 725524
APPLICATION HEADER		0 700 1122 010129 BNPACAMMAXXX 4968 839712 010130 0028 N *BNP PARIBAS (CANADA) *MONTREAL
USER HEADER		SERVICE CODE 103: BANK PRIORITY 113: MSG USER REF. 108: (银行盖信用证通知专用章) INFO. FROM CI 115:
SEQUENCE OF TOTAL	*27 :	1 / 1
FORM OF DOC. CREDIT	*40 A:	IRREVOCABLE
DOC. CREDIT NUMBER	*20 :	63211020049
DATE OF ISSUE	31C:	080129
EXPIRY	*31D:	DATE 080410 PLACE IN BENEFICIARY'S COUNTRY
APPLICANT	*50:	FASHION FORCE CO., LTD. P.O.BOX 8935 NEW TERMINAL, ALTA, VISTA OTTAWA, CANADA
BENEFICIARY	*59:	NANJING TANG TEXTILE GARMENT CO., LTD. HUARONG MANSION RM2901 NO. 85 GUANJIAQIAO, NANJING 210005, CHINA
AMOUNT	*32B:	CURRENCY USD AMOUNT 32640,
AVAILABLE WITH/BY	*41D:	ANY BANK BY NEGOTIATION
DRAFTS AT ...	42 C:	SIGHT
DRAWEE	42 A:	BNPACAMMXXX
		*BNP PARIBAS (CANADA) *MONTREAL
PARTIAL SHIPMENTS	43P:	NOT ALLOWED
TRANSSHIPMENT	43T:	ALLOWED
LOADING ON BOARD/ TAKING IN CHARGE	44A:	CHINESE MAIN PORT
FOR TRANSPORT TO...	44 B:	MONTREAL
LATEST DATE OF SHIP.	44 C:	080325
DESCRIPT. OF GOODS	45 A:	SALES CONDITIONS: CIF MONTREAL/CANADA SALES CONTRACT NO. F01LCB05127 LADIES COTTON BLAZER (100% COTTON, 40SX20/140X60) STYLE NO. PO NO. QTY/PCS USD/PC 46-301A 10337 2550 12.80
DOCUMENTS REQUIRED	46 A:	
	+COMMERCIAL INVOICES IN 3 COPIES SIGNED BY BENEFICIARY'S REPRESENTATIVE.	
	+CANADA CUSTOMS INVOICES IN 4 COPIES.	
	+FULL SET OF ORIGINAL MARINE BILLS OF LADING CLEAN ON BOARD PLUS 2 NON-NEGOTIABLE COPIES MADE OUT TO ORDER OF BNP PARIBAS (CANADA) MARKED FREIGHT PREPAID AND NOTIFY APPLICANT'S FULL NAME AND ADDRESS.	
	+DETAILED PACKING LISTS IN 3 COPIES.	

	+COPY OF CERTIFICATE OF ORIGIN FORM A.	
	+COPY OF EXPORT LICENCE.	
	+BENEFICIARY'S LETTER STATING THAT ORIGINAL CERTIFICATE OF ORIGIN FORM A, ORIGINAL EXPORT LICENCE, COPY OF COMMERCIAL INVOICE, DETAILED PACKING LISTS AND A COPY OF BILL OF LADING WERE SENT DIRECT TO APPLICANT BY COURIER WITHIN 5 DAYS AFTER SHIPMENT.THE RELEATIVE COURIER RECEIPT IS ALSO REQUIRED FOR PRESENTATION.	
	+COPY OF APPLICANT'S FAX APPROVING PRODUCTION SAMPLES BEFORE SHIPMENT.	
	+LETTER FROM SHIPPER ON THEIR LETTERHEAD INDICATING THEIR NAME OF COMPANY AND ADDRESS, BILL OF LADING NUMBER, CONTAINER NUMBER AND THAT THIS SHIPMENT, INCLUDING ITS CONTAINER, DOES NOT CONTAIN ANY NON-MANUFACTURED WOODEN MATERIAL, DUNNAGE, BRACING MATERIAL, PALLETS, CRATING OR OTHER NON-MANUFACTURED WOODEN PACKING MATERIAL.	
	+INSPECTION CERTIFICATE 1 ORIGINAL SINGED AND ISSUED BY FASHION FORCE CO., LTD. STATING THE SAMPLES OF FOUR STYLE GARMENTS HAVE BEEN APPROVED, WHICH IS SEND THROUGH DHL BEFORE 15 DAYS OF SHIPMENT.	
	+INSURANCE POLICY OR CERTIFICATE IN 2 ORIGINAL ISSUED OR ENDORSED TO THE ORDER OF BNP PARIBAS (CANADA) FOR THE CIF INVOICE VALUE PLUS 10 PERCENT, COVERING INSTITUTE CARGO CLAUSES A, INSTITUTE WAR CLAUSES AND INSTITUTE STRIKES, CIVIL COMMOTIONS CLAUSES.	
ADDITIONAL COND.	47 A:	
	+IF DOCUMENTS PRESENTED ARE FOUND BY US NOT TO BE FULL COMPLIANCE WITH CREDIT TERMS, WE WILL ASSESS A CHARGE OF USD 55.00 PER SET OF DOCUMENTS.	
	+ALL CHARGES IF ANY RELATED TO SETTLEMENTS ARE FOR ACCOUNT OF BENEFICIARY.	
	+3 PCT MORE OR LESS IN AMOUNT AND QUANTITY IS ALLOWED.	
	+ALL CERTIFICATES/LETTERS/STATEMENTS MUST BE SIGNED AND DATED.	
	+FOR INFORMATION ONLY, PLEASE NOTE AS OF JANUARY 4, 1999 THAT ALL SHIPMENTS FROM CHINA THAT ARE PACKED WITH UNTREATED WOOD WILL BE BANNED FROM CANADA DUE TO THE THREAT POSED BY THE ASIAN LONGNORNED BEETLE.	
	+THE CANADIAN GOVERNMENT NOW INSIST THAT EVERY SHIPMENT ENTERING CANADA MUST HAVE THE ABOVE DOCUMENTATION WITH THE SHIPMENT.	
	+BILL OF LADING AND COMMERCIAL INVOICE MUST CERTIFY THE FOLLOWING: THIS SHIPMENT, INCLUDING ITS CONTAINER DOES NOT CONTAIN ANY NON-MANUFACTURED WOODEN MATERIAL, DUNNAGE, BRACING MATERIAL PALLETS, CRATING OR OTHER NON-MANUFACTURED WOODEN PACKING MATERIAL.	
	+BENEFICIARY'S BANK ACCOUNT NO. 07773108201140121	
CHARGES	71 B:	OUTSIDE COUNTRY BANK CHARGES TO BE BORNE BY THE BENEFICIARY, OPENING BANK CHARGES TO BE BORNE BY THE APPLICANT
PRESENTATION PERIOD	:48:	15 DAYS AFTER SHIPMENT DATE BUT WITHIN VALIDITY OF THIS CREDIT
CONFIRMATION	*49:	WITHOUT
INSTRUCTIONS	78 :	
	+WE SHALL COVER THE NEGOTIATING BANK AS PER THEIR INSTRUCTIONS	
	+FORWARD DOCUMENTS IN ONE LOT BY SPECIAL COURIER PREPAID TO BNP PARIBAS (CANADA) 1981 MCGILL COLLECE AVE. MONTREAL QC H3A 2W8 CANADA.	
TRAILER		ORDER IS <MAC:> <PAC:> <ENC:> <CHK:> <TNG:> <PDE:> MAC:F344CA36 CHK:AA6204FFDFC2

2. Amendment of a Credit

On receipt of a credit, the beneficiary must examine the terms and conditions of the credit as per the relative contract stipulated. The beneficiary may ask the applicant to amend the credit if the credit needs to be amended. Otherwise, the beneficiary holds the credit and waits to be available after shipment.

A credit can neither be amended nor cancelled without the agreement of the issuing bank, the confirming bank, if any, and the beneficiary, except as otherwise provided by article 38 for transferable credit.

If the beneficiary wants to amend a credit, the procedure is as follows (see Figure 4-2):

(1)   The beneficiary informs the applicant for amendment.

(2)   The applicant sends an application for amendment to the issuing bank.

(3)   The issuing bank amends the credit as the application for amendment, then sends it to the advising bank. The issuing bank is irrevocably bound by an amendment as of the time it issues the amendment.

(4)   If the advising bank or second advising bank elects nonetheless to advise the amendment, it must inform the beneficiary or second advising bank that it has not been able to satisfy itself as to the apparent authenticity.

(5)   The beneficiary examines the amendment. Partial acceptance of an amendment is not allowed and will be deemed to be notification of rejection of the amendment. The terms and conditions of the original credit (or a credit incorporating previously accepted amendments) will remain in force for the beneficiary until the beneficiary communicates its acceptance of the amendment to the bank that advises such amendment. The beneficiary should give notification of acceptance or rejection of an amendment. If the beneficiary fails to give such notification, a presentation that complies with the credit and to any not yet accepted amendment will be deemed to be notification of acceptance by the beneficiary of such amendment. As of that moment the credit will be amended. So, a provision in an amendment to the effect that the amendment shall enter into force unless rejected by the beneficiary within a certain time shall be disregarded.

(6)   The advising bank informs the issuing bank the amendment of any notification of acceptance or rejection.

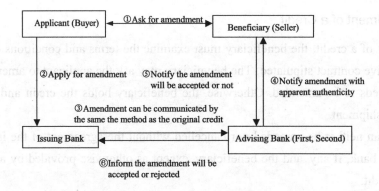

Figure 4-2   The Procedure of Amending a Credit

Please be kindly noticed that a confirming bank may extend its confirmation to an amendment and will be irrevocably bound as of the time it advises the amendment. It may, however, choose to advise an amendment without extending its confirmation and, if so, it must inform the issuing bank without delay and inform the beneficiary in its advice.

3. Availability of a Credit

Here is an example for explaining the procedure of a credit available with the nominated bank (see Figure 4-3):

(1)   The beneficiary ships the goods as scheduled.

(2)   The beneficiary prepares all relative documents stipulated, and delivers the presentation to the nominated bank for negotiation within presenting period but before maturity of the credit.

(3)   The nominated bank examines the presentation. When a nominated bank other than a confirming bank determines that the presentation is complying, it may honor or negotiate. When a confirming bank determines that a presentation is complying, it must honor or negotiate.

(4)   After the nominated bank honors or negotiates, it must forward the documents to the confirming bank (if any) or the issuing bank. After the confirming bank honors or negotiates, it also must forward the documents to the issuing bank.

(5)   The issuing bank examines the presentation.When the issuing bank determines that a presentation is complying, it must honor.

(6)   The issuing bank presents the presentation to the applicant for reimbursement.

(7)   The applicant examines the presentation. When the applicant determines that a presentation is complying, it must honor.

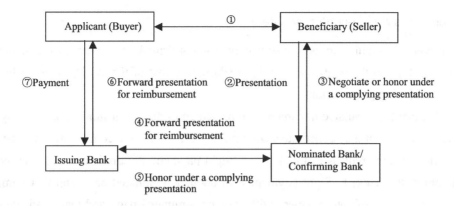

Figure 4-3   The Procedure of Making a Credit Available

Please notice that

(1)   A nominated bank acting on its nomination, a confirming bank, if any, and the issuing bank shall each have a maximum of five banking days following the day of presentation to determine if a presentation is complying. This period is not curtailed or otherwise affected by the occurrence on or after the date of presentation of any expiry date or last day for presentation.

(2)   Whatever a nominated bank, a confirming bank(if any) or the issuing bank determines that a presentation does not comply, it may refuse to honor or negotiate.

(3)   When the issuing bank determines that a presentation does not comply, it may in its sole judgment approach the applicant for a waiver of the discrepancies.

(4)   The issuing bank undertakes to reimburse a nominated bank that has honored or negotiated a complying presentation and forwarded the documents to the issuing bank. Reimbursement for the amount of a complying presentation under a credit available by acceptance or deferred payment is due at maturity, whether or not the nominated bank prepays or purchases before maturity. An issuing bank's undertaking to reimburse a nominated bank is independent of the issuing bank's undertaking to the beneficiary.

4.6   Classification of a Credit

A credit is irrevocable even if there is no indication to that effect (article 3 of UCP600). An issuing bank is irrevocably bound to honor as of the time it issues the credit (article 7 of UCP600).

1. Confirmed & Non-confirmed Credit

An irrevocable credit can be confirmed or non-confirmed. A confirmed credit means a definite undertaking of the confirming bank, in addition to that of the issuing bank, to honor or negotiate a complying presentation.

Provided that the stipulated documents are presented to the confirming bank or to any other nominated bank and that they constitute a complying presentation, the confirming bank must

(1) honor, if the credit is available by: a. Sight payment, deferred payment or acceptance with the confirming bank; b. Sight payment with another nominated bank and that nominated bank does not pay; c. deferred payment with another nominated bank and that nominated bank does not incur its deferred payment undertaking or, having incurred its deferred payment undertaking, does not pay at maturity; d. Acceptance with another nominated bank and that nominated bank does not accept a draft drawn on it or , having accepted a draft drawn on it, does not pay at maturity; e. negotiation with another nominated bank and that nominated bank does not negotiate.

(2) Negotiate, without recourse, if the credit is available by negotiation with the confirming bank.

A confirming bank is irrevocably bound to honor or negotiate as of the time it adds its confirming to the credit.

A confirming bank undertakes to reimburse another nominated bank that has honored or negotiated a complying presentation and forwarded the documents to the confirming bank. Reimbursement for the amount of a complying presentation under a credit available by acceptance or deferred payments is due at maturity, whether or not the another nominated bank prepays or purchases before maturity. A confirming bank's undertaking to reimburse another nominated bank is independent of the confirming bank's undertaking to the beneficiary.

If a bank is authorized or requested by the issuing bank to confirm a credit but is not prepared to do so, it must inform the issuing bank without delay and may advise the credit without confirmation.

2. Credit Available by Sight Payment, Deferred Payment, Acceptance or Negotiation

A credit must state whether it is available by sight payment, deferred payment, acceptance or negotiation (see Specimen 4-3). For issuing a credit, the applicant shall fill the drawing clause in application form. Drawing clause is containing: Credit available with_____by: ☐sight payment ☐acceptance ☐negotiation ☐deferred payment against the documents detailed herein □and beneficiary's draft (s) for ____ % of invoice value at_____days after sight □date of shipment □_____drawn on_____.

The applicant can select a bank with which it is available or whether it is available with any bank. A credit available with a nominated bank is also available with the issuing bank. A credit with a nominated bank in the exporting country is better for the exporter. The credit shall not be issued available by a draft drawn on the applicant.

Unless a nominated bank is the confirming bank, an authorization to honor or negotiate does not impose any obligation on that nominated bank to honor or negotiate, except when expressly agreed to by that nominated bank and so communicated to the beneficiary. By nominating a bank to accept a draft or incur a deferred payment undertaking, an issuing bank authorizes that nominated bank to prepay or purchase a draft accepted or a deferred payment undertaking incurred by that nominated bank. Receipt or examination and forwarding of documents by a nominated bank that is not a confirming bank does not make that nominated bank liable to honor or negotiate, nor does it constitute honor or negotiation.

> ### Specimen 4-3　Credit Available by Sight Payment, Deferred Payment, Acceptance or Negotiation
>
> (1)　This credit is available with advising bank by sight payment against the documents detailed herein.
>
> (2)　This credit is available with advising bank by deferred payment at 30 days after date of bill of lading against the documents detailed herein.
>
> (3)　This credit is available with issuing bank by acceptance against beneficiary's draft at 30 days after sight drawn on us.
>
> (4)　This credit is available with advising bank by negotiation at sight, or, negotiation under this credit is restricted to advising bank.
>
> (5)　This credit is available with any bank by negotiation at sight.

3. Transferable Credit

A bank is under no obligation to transfer a credit except to the extent and in the manner expressly consented to by that bank. Transferable credit means a credit that specifically states it is "transferable". A transferable credit may be made available in whole or in part to another beneficiary ("second beneficiary") at the request of the beneficiary ("first beneficiary").

Transferring bank means a nominated bank that transfers the credit, in a credit available with any bank, a bank that is specially authorized by the issuing bank to transfer the credit. An issuing bank may be a transferring bank. Transferred credit means a credit that has been made available by the transferring bank to a second beneficiary. Unless otherwise agreed at the time of transfer, all charges (such as commissions, fees, costs or expenses) incurred in respect of a transfer must be paid by the first beneficiary.

A credit may be transferred in part to more than one second beneficiary provided partial drawing or shipments are allowed. Any request for transfer must indicate if and under what conditions amendments may be advised to the second beneficiary. The transferred credit must clearly indicate those conditions. If a credit is transferred to more than one second beneficiary, rejection of an amendment by one or more second beneficiary does not invalidate the acceptance by any other second beneficiary, with respect to which the transferred credit will be amended accordingly. For any second beneficiary that rejected the amendment, the transferred credit will remain un-amended.

The transferred credit must accurately reflect the terms and conditions of the credit, including confirmation, if any, with the exception of the amount of the credit, any unit price stated therein, the expiry date, the period for presentation, or the latest shipment date or given period for shipment. Any or all which may be reduced or curtailed. The percentage for which insurance cover must be effected may be increased to provide the amount of cover stipulated in the credit of these articles. The name of the first beneficiary may be substituted for that of the applicant in the credit. If the name of the applicant is specifically required by the credit to appear in any document other than the invoice, such requirement must be reflected in the transferred credit.

4.7   Attentions for a Credit

1. Attentions for an Export Credit

The seller is enjoyed with lower risks, high initiative, free transfer and easy finance under a credit. When discussing business terms with the seller, soft clauses (see Specimen 4-4) should be avoided. At the same time, a safe and convenient way of reimbursement should be confirmed to guarantee a safe collection of payment. Under a credit, the seller needs to present full set of commercial documents and original credit to the nominated bank. If the presentation has discrepancies, it is difficult to handle trade financing.

The bank will also deal with operations such as collection of payment, settlement of payment, credit account according to the state regulations concerning foreign exchange control.

If the seller wants to withdraw a credit, he needs to present trust instrument in written form and full set of original credit to the advising bank. If a credit is available by a nominated bank located at the export country, the credit is benefit for the beneficiary instead of the applicant. The seller may choose the best kind of credit, just as sight payment credit is better than negotiable credit.

Specimen 4-4 Soft Clauses in a Credit

(1) Inspection certificate of quality and quantities issued by the applicant.

(2) This credit is not operative, it will become operative as soon as the applicant obtains the Italian import license.We shall advise you of the receipt of import license after which date the credit will become valid.

(3) This credit will not be operative until we receive L/G for 10% of the credit value issued by first class bank in China and accepted by buyers and valid for 3 months from shipment date to guarantee supplying a specification of goods.

(4) This credit is only a preliminary advice and will become effective upon receipt of our authenticated cable to the advising bank confirming that applicants have received and approved the advanced sample.

(5) This credit will become operative provided that the necessary authorization will be obtained from exchange authority, we shall inform you as soon as the authorization is obtained.

2. Attentions for an Import Credit

The Chinese buyer shall surrender the application form, the contract, import permit (e.g., import registration form of mechanical and electrical products and various files as per the foreign exchange control regulation to the issuing bank for a credit.

When issuing a credit, the buyer provides the seller with extra guarantee on payment in cost of more bank charge born by it, so the buyer had better ask the seller for preferential prices during the commercial negotiation concerning this point.

The buyer may bear risks of fraudulence caused by the seller, such as shipping the un-ordered goods or juggling the original B/Ls.

Chapter 5

Letters of Guarantee & Standby Credits

5.1 Overview

Although a credit is a perfect payment mechanism, it cannot solve all of problems for the seller, the buyer and the banker. On the seller's side, such as a presentation with discrepancy(ies) , or a credit with payment exceeding 180 days, or a credit with soft clauses will make him difficult to receive the proceeds and finance. A credit also always brings to the seller high costs. The seller may give up a credit from the trusted buyer initiatively. On the buyer's side, to issue a credit will tie his money into a margin account of the issuing bank until the credit is being paid. In theory, the buyer must pay without recourse earlier than taking the delivery, whereas the goods may be found faulty. So, the buyer isn't willing to conclude a contract with payment by a credit. On the issuing bank's side, an issuing bank is irrevocably bound to honor as of the time it issues the credit or an amendment. The issuing bank undertakes to effect payment under a credit, quite independent of whether the applicant is bankrupt or in fault or not, provided the documents presented are in compliance with the terms and conditions of the credit. If a credit is available with the nominated bank, the issuing bank's undertaking to reimburse a nominated bank is independent of the issuing bank's undertaking to the beneficiary, and the issuing bank himself may be refused to reimburse by the applicant.

In consideration of the above, a substitute method of a credit that the bank can still involve trade settlement as a credit but his undertaking is a little weaker than a credit appears. Letters of guarantee and standby credits are the substitute methods with more flexibility than a credit.

5.2 Letters of Guarantee

5.2.1 Definition

Letters of guarantee can be issued by a bank or a trader. Normally, a letter of guarantee refers to a bank guarantee considered to the guarantor's standing.

A bank guarantee is used as an instrument for securing performance or payment especially in international business. A bank guarantee is a written promise issued by a bank at the request of its customer, undertaking to make payment to the beneficiary within the limits of a stated sum of money in the event of default by the principal.

A bank guarantee may also be defined as an independent obligation where the guarantor (a bank/financial institution/security) has to make a special agreement with its customer, ensuring that it will be refunded by him for any payment to be effected under the contract of guarantee.

5.2.2   Functions of a Bank Guarantee

Bank guarantees are used widely and flexibly in international business, complicated transactions, non-credit available transactions, etc. A guarantee does not consist in assuming the debtor's liability (by the guarantor) in the latter's interest, but in recouping the beneficiary for any damage caused by faulty performance. A guarantee is used as a secure mechanism for payment of the contract amount. A contractor uses a bank guarantee as default instrument that covers the risk of non-performance or defective performance by the contractor.

5.2.3   Parties to a Bank Guarantee

There are three basic parties and one possible party to a bank guarantee. The basic parties are principal, beneficiary and guarantor. The possible party is instructing party. The parties and their obligations are as follows:

1. Beneficiary

The beneficiary refers to the party in whose favor the guarantee is issued. He is secured against the risks of the principal's not fulfilling his obligations towards the beneficiary in respect of the underlying transaction for which the demand guarantee is given. He will not obtain a sum of money if the obligations are not fulfilled.

2. Principal

The principal refers to the party at whose request the guarantee is issued. The principal will be claimed if he is in breach of his obligations.

3. Guarantor

The guarantor refers to the party who issues a guarantee undertaking to make payment to the beneficiary in the event of default of the principal against the presentation of a written

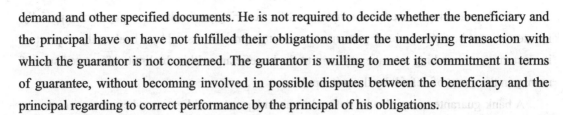

demand and other specified documents. He is not required to decide whether the beneficiary and the principal have or have not fulfilled their obligations under the underlying transaction with which the guarantor is not concerned. The guarantor is willing to meet its commitment in terms of guarantee, without becoming involved in possible disputes between the beneficiary and the principal regarding to correct performance by the principal of his obligations.

4. Instructing Party

The instructing party refers to a bank or a financial institution or any other body acting as an instructing party that issues a counter guarantee acting on the instruction of a principal in favor of a bank or a financial institution located in the beneficiary's country.

5.2.4 Classfication of Bank Guarantee

In terms of the relationship with the underlying transaction, the guarantor's liability to a bank guarantee may be primary or second. Primary obligation can be called independent undertaking of payment, and second obligation can be called accessory obligation. Uniform Rules on Demand Guarantees, ICC Publication No. 758 (URDG 758) was formally brought into effect from July 01, 2010, and it highlights its independent undertaking of payment and documentary features and emphasizes "Claims first, debate later". It becomes the common international practice just as UCP600, and is recognized by International Federation of Consulting Engineers (FIDIC), World Bank and United Nations Commission on International Trade Law, etc. In consideration of the above, a bank guarantee with independent undertaking of payment and unconditional payment is the basic kind.

In addition, bank guarantees can be divided into the following types:

1) Direct Guarantees & Indirect Guarantees

A bank guarantee may be issued by the guarantor (the issuing bank) directly or indirectly. An direct guarantee means that the issuing bank opens a guarantee by himself and sends it to the beneficiary by specific communication. He may send the guarantee to the beneficiary directly or through an advising bank just as a credit.

An indirect guarantee means that the bank entrusted by the principal instructs another bank (issuing bank, ususlly located at the place of the beneficiary) to issue a guarantee to the beneficiary. The bank entrusted by the principal, as the instructing party, shall issue a counter guarantee acting on the instruction of a principal in favor of the issuing bank of the guarantee.

2)   Guarantees for Payment & Guarantees for Credit

In terms of the payment prerequisite under a guarantee, a guarantee may become a guarantee for payment or for credit. Payment bonds, deferred payment bonds, guarantees for compensation trade, loan guarantees, overdraft guarantees, leasing guarantees, payment guarantees for commission or any other charges belong to guarantees for payment. A guarantee for credit is a default instrument that covers the risk of non-performance or defective performance by the contractor. Bid bonds, performance bonds, advance payment guarantees, quality guarantees and maintenance guarantees belong to guarantees for credit. In terms of the purpose of guarantee, it can be used in international trade and international construction/engineering contracting. For example, tender/performance/advance/down payment/quality/maintenance/payment/deferred payment guarantee is usually used in international trade. Tender/duty free/retention money/overdraft/payment/performance/maintenance/customs guarantee is usually used in international construction/engineering contracting.

Introduction to Some Specific Guarantees

(1)   Tender guarantee. It is a written undertaking issued by the bank at the request of tenderee in projects of construction works or material procurement subject to bidding, guaranteeing that the tenderer will not withdraw or modify his tender within the validity period, and, if awarded the tenderer, will sign the contract or submit the performance guarantee within a specified period. It is applicable to public bidding or tender evaluation, when the employer requires the tenderer to submit tender security.

(2)   Performance guarantee. It is a written undertaking issued by the guarantor to the employer or buyer at the request of the contractor or supplier, guaranteeing that the latter will strictly perform his contractual obligations. It is applicable to provide guarantee for the performance of contractual obligations by the principal. Common cases include projects involving construction or material procurement.

(3)   Advance payment guarantee. It is a written undertaking issued by the guarantor to the employer or buyer at the request of the contractor or supplier, guaranteeing that the latter will perform his contractual obligations after the employer or buyer has effected the advance payment. It is applicable to provide guarantee for the performance of contractual obligations by the principal. Common cases include projects involving construction or material procurement.

(4)   Retention money guarantee. It is a written undertaking issued by the guarantor to the employer or buyer at the request of the contractor or supplier, guaranteeing that the latter will

perform his contractual obligations after the latter has drawn the final payment in advance. Retention money guarantee is also called "final payment guarantee". It is applicable to the later stage of contract execution when the employer or buyer retains the final payment and the contractor or supplier has to draw the final payment in advance with the bank's letter of guarantee.

(5) Warranty guarantee. It is a written undertaking issued by the guarantor to the employer or buyer at the request of the contractor or supplier, guaranteeing that the latter will perform his contractual obligations during the warranty or maintenance period. Warranty guarantee is also called "maintenance guarantee". It is applicable to the warranty or maintenance period of the contract on construction or goods supply, when the employer or buyer requires the contractor or supplier to perform the warranty obligation. After contracting or supply projects enter the warranty or maintenance period, the employer or buyer, in order to prevent the inconformity of the quality of works or goods with the contractual stipulations, or the reluctance or failure on the contractor or supplier's part to carry out repair, replacement or maintenance, often asks the contractor or supplier to provide warranty guarantee before the performance guarantee expires, thereby binding the contractor or supplier to the obligations in the warranty period.

(6) Customs guarantee. It is a written undertaking issued by the guarantor to the customs at the request of the importer (including processing trade enterprises), guaranteeing that the latter will perform his obligation of duty payment. The customs guarantee offered mainly includes two types: guarantees for payment of customs duty, guarantees for payment of taxes on processing trade.

(7) Payment guarantee. It is a written undertaking issued by the guarantor to the seller at the request of the buyer, guaranteeing that the buyer will perform his payment obligations under contracts for purchase of commodity, technology, patent or labor. It is applicable to commodity trade, technical service trade, or construction projects involving payment. In commodity trade, the guarantee is for the buyer's timely payment after the seller has delivered goods as agreed in the contract. Its functions are similar to the credit, but it has simpler procedures, flexible formats to fit different needs. A credit has to follow fixed format and conventions while the format of payment guarantee can be tailored for specific projects or customers. In construction project, the guarantee is for the employer's timely and full payment for construction progress to the contractor under terms of construction contracting. The payment guarantee has a wider application scope than the credit because it can be used for both commodity trade and construction project.

(8) Financing guarantee. It is a written undertaking issued by the guarantor to the lender at the request of the borrower, guaranteeing that the borrower will perform his obligation of repaying the loan fund. It includes loan guarantee, overdraft guarantee, guarantee for securities issuance and credit line guarantee. It is applicable when the borrower intends to gain all forms of financing from banks or other financial institutions or to issue securities in the financial market.

(9) Leasing guarantee. It is a written undertaking issued by the guarantor to the lessor at the request of the lessee, guaranteeing that the lessee will timely pay the rent. It can be divided into guarantee for financing leasing and guarantee for operating leasing by leasing mode. In leasing projects, the leaser often asks the bank to make guarantee for the timely payment of rent by the lessee to safeguard against the failure of the lessee to make timely rent payment (especially under financial leasing, when the lease term is long, and object of leasing is of specific nature, the leaser has to take big risk).

(10) Guarantee for compensation. Under terms of contract on compensation trade, guarantee for compensation is a written undertaking issued by the guarantor to the licensor of equipment and technology at the request of the licensee, guaranteeing that the licensee will pay for the equipment or technology with products or spot exchange. In compensation trade, the licensor of equipment and trade asks the bank to make guarantee for the licensee's payment with products or spot exchange to protect against the licensee's failure to produce as per the contract or to make payment with proceeds from product sales.

5.2.5   Contents of a Bank Guarantee

Contents are the most important parts of the guarantee. All instructions for the issuance, amendments thereto should be clear, precise and avoid excessive details. Main contents of a bank guarantee include guarantee purpose, parties involved, the underlying transaction requiring the issue of guarantee, amount of the guarantee (the maximum amount and its currency), the expiry date or expiry event of the guarantee, payment mechanism or terms for demanding payment, assignment and other provisions, such as reduction of the amount, the governing law and jurisdiction, etc. Please notice that

(1) Functional terms and conditions shall be indicated in some kinds of guarantee. For example, a performance bond is issued when the contract has been awarded. It gives the employer an indication of the contractor's creditworthiness and affords a remedy in case of default. A performance bond payable on demand is issued for a specified sum, usually between 5% and 10% of the project value.

(2) Since the bank guarantee is independent of the underlying transaction, a precise definition of how the principal defaults on the contract in question is not necessary, and the beneficiary's claim is all that is needed to elicit payment.

(3) The amount payable under a guarantee shall be reduced by the amount of any payment made by the guarantor in satisfaction of a demand in respect thereof.

(4) The expiry date or expiry event of the guarantee can be indicated as follows: a. Be worded to expire on a definite date for the guarantor's benefit; b. State that the claim must be received not later than the specified date and where it must be presented; c. May be on a specified calendar date or on presentation to the guarantor of the documents specified for the purpose of expiry; d. Show expiry date or expiry event occurs first.

(5) For payment mechanism or terms for demanding payment, the guarantee may insert the required conditions to trigger payment. Any demand for payment under the guarantee shall be in writing and shall be supported by a written statement stating that the principal is in breach and other documents specified in the guarantee.

(6) For assignment, depending on the applicable law the benefit of a guarantee may be assignable by the beneficiary. The guarantors generally do not like such assignments, preferring to restrict their guarantee undertaking to beneficiaries who are known at the time of issue.

5.3   Standby Credits

5.3.1   Definition

A Standby Letter of Credit is any letter of credit, or similar arrangement however named or described, which represents an obligation to the beneficiary on the part of the issuer: a. to repay money borrowed by or advanced to or for the account of the account party or b. to make payment on account of any indebtedness undertaken by the account party or c. to make payment on account of any default by the account party in the performance of an obligation. Standby credits are originated in USA for banker's restrictions to issue L/G outward.

5.3.2   Functions & Features of a Standby Credit

A standby credit can act as an independent guarantee, a financial tool as well as a payment tool. It can be called "an independent guarantee with features like a credit" or "a credit with features like an independent guarantee".

As per the above stated, a standby credit is a kind of independent documentary business, and the issuing bank of a standby credit engages payment on the first position and its payment made against representing documents in compliance with the terms and conditions of credit.

5.3.3　Classification of a Standby Credit

A standby credit may be issued for performance or for payment. Standby credits for payment can be divided into three kinds, that is, financial standby credits, direct pay standby credits and commercial standby credits.

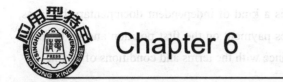

Chapter 6

Documents Related to International Settlement

6.1 Overview

As per Incoterms 2010, the seller must provide the goods and the commercial invoice in conformity with the contract of sale and other evidence of conformity that may be required by the contract. Any document may be an equivalent electronic record or procedure if agreed between the parties or customary. It is general obligation for the seller to deliver the goods and relative documents to the buyer in international trade.

Documents are the tools of collecting payment, especially under collection and documentary credit, the seller shall present documents to the bank. A complying presentation under a credit is the payment condition for the seller to receive the proceeds successfully. So how to issue a complying presentation is top important for the seller under a credit.

6.2 Classification of Documents

According to the functions of documents, documents may be basic documents or additional documents. With the development of international trade practices and application of electronic record, the importance of bill of lading and insurance policy is becoming weaker. Nowadays, only commercial invoice is worthy of basic documents.

According to the issuer, documents can be divided into commercial documents, transport documents, insurance documents and government documents.

6.3 Issuance of Documents

6.3.1 Issuer

Article 3 of UCP600 stipulates "Terms such as first class, well known, qualified, independent, official, complete or local used to describe the issuer of a document allow any issuer except the beneficiary to issue that document."

6.3.2 Originals & Copies

Article 17 of UCP600 stipulates "At least one original of each document stipulated in the credit must be presented." An original document must be bearing an apparently original signature, mark,stamp, or label of the issuer of the document. Unless a document indicates otherwise, an original document is written, typed, perforated or stamped by the document issuer's hand, or with the issuer's original stationery, or is stated that it is original, unless the statement appears not to apply to the document presented.

Regarding to copies of documents, either originals or copies are permitted. If a credit requires presentation of mutiple documents by using terms such as "in duplicate", "in two fold" or "in two copies", this will be satisfied by the presentation of at least one original and the remaining number in copies, except when the document itself indicates otherwise.

6.3.3 Signed Documents

If a document required by a credit need to be signed, article 3 of UCP600 stipulates "A document may be signed by handwriting, fascimile signature, perforated signature, stamp, symbol or any other mechanical or electronic method of authentication." Article 18 of UCP600 stipulates " A commercial invoice need not be signed." Transport documents (articles 19, 20, 21, 22, 23, 24, 25, 26, 27 of UCP600) and insurance documents(article 28 of UCP600) all need be signed.

6.3.4 Date of Issuance

Article 14 of UCP600 stipulates "A document may be dated prior to the issuance date of the credit, but must not be dated later than its date of presentation." In actual international practice, the seller usually prepares the goods for shipment after he receives the credit. The date of documents generally will be later than the date of issuance of the credit.

Logically, the date of commercial invoice must be the earliest, the date of draft must be the latest, whereas the date of transport document is between the date of commercial invoice and the date of draft in a presentation under a credit. Meanwhile, the date of transport document must be no later than the latest date of shipment stipulated in the credit, the date of draft shall be no later than the latest date for presentation but within maturity of the credit. The date of an insurance document must be no later than the date of shipment, unless it appears from the insurance document that the cover is effective from a date not later than the date of shipment (article 28 of UCP600). The date of beneficiary's certificate may be earlier or later than the date of transport document based on what need to be certificated.

Besides the above, the date of other documents, such as certificate of origin, export license, inspection certificate, etc., may be between the date of commercial invoice and the date of transport documents generally.

6.3.5 Expiry Date and Place for Presentation

A presentation by or on behalf of the beneficiary must be usually made on or before the expiry date and delivered to the place for presentation.

1. Expiry Date

A credit usually have four dates: date of issue, expiry date for presentation, latest date of shipment and presenting period. Expiry date for presentation is the most important.

A credit must state an expiry date for presentation. An expiry date stated for honor or negotiation will be deemed to be an expiry date for presentation. If the credit is stated with an expiry date only but without neither latest date of shipment nor presenting period, it means that the beneficiary shall both make shipment and presentation before the maturity date of the credit. The expiry date is normally stipulated to be 15 days or 21 days later than the latest date of shipment, while the period of presentation is usually stipulated "within 15 days after shipment date." Shipment date means the date of actual shipment made.

A presentation including one or more original transport documents subject to articles 19, 20, 21, 22, 23, 24, or 25 of UCP600 must be made by or on behalf of the beneficiary not later than 21 calendar days after the date of shipment as described in this rule, but in any event not later than the expiry date of the credit.

2. Place for Presentation

The place of the bank with which the credit is available is the place for presentation. The place for presentation under a credit available with any bank is that of any bank. A place for presentation other than that of the issuing bank is in addition to the place of the issuing bank.

6.3.6 Drawing Amount

Article 30 of UCP600 is titled as "Tolerance in Credit Amount, Quantity and Unit prices". It

stipulates that

(1) The words "about" or "approximately" used in connection with the amount of the credit or the quantity or the unit price stated in the credit are to be construed as allowing a tolerance not to exceed 10% more or 10% less than the amount, the quantity or the unit price to which they refer.

(2) A tolerance not to exceed 5% more or less than the quantity of the goods is allowed, provided the credit does not state the quantity in terms of a stipulated number of packing units or individual items and the total amount of the drawings does not exceed the amount of the credit.

(3) Even when partial shipments are not allowed, a tolerance not to exceed 5% less than the amount of the credit is allowed, provided that the quantity of the goods, if stated in the credit, is shipped in full and a unit price, if stated in the credit, is not reduced or that sub-article 30 (b) is not applicable. This tolerance does not apply when the credit stipulates a specific tolerance or uses the expressions referred to in sub-article 30 (a).

Specimen 6-1   Combined Training

In this part, we will study how to review a credit, judge what kinds of documents should be presented and how to draft documents required by the credit.

1)   A credit

BASIC HEADER		F O1 BKCHANBJA5XX 9828 707783
:MT: 700-----------------------------------	-------	NOSCCATTAXXX 3775 931472 0008010718 N +BANK OF CHINA, TORONTO, CANADA +TORONTO, ONTARIO, CANADA ISSUE OF A DOCUMENTARY CREDIT ------------
SEQUENCE OF TOTAL	:27:	1/1
FORM OF DOCUMENTARY CREDIT	:40A:	IRREVOCABLE TRANSFERABLE
DOCUMENTARY CREDIT NUMBER	:20:	I01800/146791
DATE OF ISSUE	:31C:	080731
DATE AND PLACE OF EXPIRY	:31D:	080915 IN CHINA
APPLICANT	:50:	WENSCO FOODS LTD., 1191 GREEN LAND STREET, WELL D.,.COQUITLAM, B.C., CANADA, V3K 5Z1
BENEFICIARY	:59:	HUANGHAI CEREALS, OILS AND FOODSTUFFS IMP. AND EXP. CORP., NO. 7 HEPING ROAD, HANGZHOU, CHINA
CURRENCY CODE, AMOUNT	:32B:	USD10830.00
MAXIMUM CREDIT AMOUNT	:39B:	NOT EXCEEDING
AVAILABLE WITH...BY	:41D:	ANY BANK BY NEGOTIATION
DRAFTS AT...	:42C:	DRAFTS AT 75 DAYS AFTER BILL OF LADING DATE FOR 100 PERCENT OF INVOICE VALUE

DRAWEE	:42D:	THE BANK OF NOVA SCOTIA, 650 WEST GEORGIA ST., PO BOX 11502, VANCOUVER, B.C., CANADA V6B 4P6
PARTIAL SHIPMENT	:43P:	ALLOWED
TRANSSHIPMENT	:43T:	ALLOWED
LOADING/DISPATCH/TAKING FROM	:44A:	SHIPMENT FROM NINGBO,CHINA
FOR TRANSPORTATION TO	:44B:	VANCOUVER, B.C., CANADA
LATEST DATE OF SHIPMENT	:44C:	080831
DESCRPT. OF GOODS/SERVICES	:45A:	EVIDENCING SHIPMENT OF P.O. NO. 2027 950 CARTONS TROPIC ISLE CANNED MANDARIN ORANGES LS-WHOLE SEGMENTS 6/2.84KG AT USD11.40 PER CARTON CIF VANCOUVER, B.C., CANADA
DOCUMENTS REQUIRED	:46A:	
		+SIGNED COMMERCIAL INVOICE IN TRIPLICATE. +SIGNED PACKING LIST IN TRIPLICATE. +CANADA CUSTOMS INVOICE IN QUADRUPLICATE FULLY COMPLETED. +CERTIFICATE OF ORIGIN FORM A IN TRIPLICATE. +BENEFICIARY'S LETTER OF GUARANTEE STATING THEY WILL REIMBURSE ALL EXPENSES IN CASE OF REJECTION BY CANADIAN FOOD INSPECTION AGENCY IN TRIPLICATE. +BENEFICIARY'S CERTIFICATE IN TRIPLICATE STATING 1. THE SHIPMENT DOES NOT INCLUDE NON-MANUFACTURED WOOD DUNNAGE, PALLETS, CRATING OR OTHER PACKING MATERIALS. 2. THE SHIPMENT IS COMPLETELY FREE OF WOOD BARK, VISIBLE PESTS AND SIGNS OF LIVING PESTS. +FULL SET OF CLEAN "ON BOARD" OCEAN BILL OF LADING TO THE ORDER OF THE BANK OF NOVA SCOTIA MARKED FREIGHT COLLECT AND NOTIFY WENSCO FOODS LTD., 1191 GREEN LAND STREET, WELL D. COQUITLAM, B.C., CANADA, V3K 5Z1. + INSURANCE POLICY IN DUPLICATE COVERING ALL RISKS AND WAR RISKS AS PER CIC(1/1/1980).
ADDITIONAL CONDITIONS	:47A:	
		+THIS LETTER OF CREDIT IS TRANSFERABLE. IF TRANSFERRED, THE DRAFT MUST BE ACCOMPANIED BY A LETTER BY THE BANK EFFECTING THE TRANFFER STAING THE NAME OF THE TRANSFEREE AND THAT THIS CREDIT HAS BEEN TRANSFERRED.

+THE ADVISING BANK IS THE DESIGNATED TRANSFERRING BANK.

+THIRD PARTY DOCUMENTS ARE ACCEPTABLE ONLY IF L/C IS TRANSFERRED.

+AMENDMENT CHARGES (IF ANY) WILL BE FOR THE BENEFICIARY'S ACCOUNT IF THE CAUSE OF AMENDMENT OCCURRED FROM THE BENEFICIARY'S SIDE.

+ IT IS A CONDITION OF THE LETTER OF CREDIT THAT PAYMENT WILL BE EFFECTED AT MATURITY BUT ONLY UPON RECEIPT OF WRITTEN NOTIFICATION FROM THE BUYER STATING THE GOODS HAVE PASSED CANADIAN AUTHORITIES INSPECTION. THE REMITTING BANK/NEGOTIATING BANK MUST INDICATE ON THEIR COVERING LETTER TO SCOTIABANK THAT ALL DOCUMENTS MUST BE DELIVERED TO THE APPLICANT AGAINST A TRUST RECEIPT IN ORDER TO OBTAIN CLEARANCE OF MERCHANDISE TO SECURE INSPECTION BY CANADIAN AUTHORITIES.

+ PAYMENT /ACCEPTANCE OF DRAFTS WILL ONLY BE MADE AFTER RECEIPT OF WRITTEN ADVICE FROM THE APPLICANT STATING THAT THE MERCHANDISE HAS PASSED INSPECTION AND HAS BEEN RELEASED FOR SALE IN CANADA BY THE CANADIAN AUTHORITIES.

+ IF THE GOODS DO NOT PASS INSPECTION, THEN NOTICE TO THIS EFFECT MUST BE GIVEN IN WRITING BY THE CANADIAN AUTHORITIES WHO MUST PRESENT SAME TO SCOTIABANK. UPON RECEIPT OF THE REJECTION NOTICE, THE NEGOTIATING BANK/REMITTING BANK WILL BE ADVISED ACCORDINGLY AND SCOTIABANK'S LIABILITY WILL BECOME NULL AND VOID.

+ PLEASE DIRECT ALL ENQUIRIES AND FORWARD DOCUMENTS IN ONE LOT(VIA COURIER) TO THE BANK OF NOVA SCOTIA, VANCOUVER INTERNATIONAL

		TRADE SERVICES, MAL LEVEL, 650 WEST GEORGIA STREET, VANCOUVER, B.C., CANADA V6B 4P6. + A DISCREPANCY HANDLING FEE OF USD45.00 WILL BE ADDRESSED BY THE BANK OF NOVA SCOTIA ON EACH PRESENTATION OF DOCUMENTS NOT IN STRICT COMPLIANCE WITH THE TERMS AND CONDITIONS OF THE CREDIT. THIS FEE IS FOR THE ACCOUNT OF BENEFICIARY AND WILL BE DEDUCTED FROM THE PROCEEDS WHEN PAYMENT IS EFFECTED, IN ADDITION TO ANY OUT OF POCKET EXPENSES INCURRED BY THE BANK OF NOVA SCOTIA IN THIS CONNECTION. + THIS IS THE OPERATIVE INSTRUCTION. + DRAFT(S)MUST INDICATE THE NUMBER AND DATE OF THIS CREDIT.
CHARGES:	:71B:	ISSUING BANK CHARGES ARE FOR THE ACCOUNT OF THE APPLICANT. ALL OTHER BANK CHARGES INCLUDING REIMBURSING BANK CHARGES ARE FOR THE BENEFICIARY'S ACCOUNT.
PERIOD FOR PRESENTATIONS	: 48:	DOCUMENTS MUST BE PRESENTED AT PLACE OF EXPIRATION WITHIN 15 DAYS AFTER ON BOARD DATE OF OCEAN BILL OF LADING BUT WITHIN THE L/C VALIDITY.
CONFIRMATION INSTRUCTION	:49:	WITHOUT
TRAILER:		MAC: BA00E6EA CHK: 9E5503EE1810

2) Review of the credit

(1) This is an irrevocable, transferable, non-confirmation, available with any bank by negotiation, issued by SWIFT and usance credit. On the beneficiary's side, this credit has high risks, such as terms and conditions stipulated in the credit as "If the goods do not pass inspection, then notice to this effect must be given in writing by the Canadian authorities who must present same to Scotiabank. Upon receipt of the rejection notice, the negotiating bank/remitting bank will be advised accordingly and Scotiabank's liability will become null and void."

(2) The date of issue is July 31, 2008, the expiry date and place is Sept. 15, 2008 in China.

The latest date of shipment is Aug. 31, 2008, period for presentation is within 15 days after the date of B/L but within validity of the credit. If the beneficiary shipped the goods on Aug. 20, 2008, the presentation must be made on/before Sept. 04, 2008.

(3)   The credit should be amended, as description of goods/services (area: 45A) indicated trade term as "CIF Vancouver, B.C., Canada". So the freight clause in"Documents required (area: 46A) " should be changed from "freight collect" to "freight prepaid".

(4)   Documents required & their issuing date

Table 6-1 shows the documents required by the specimen credit, copies and restrictions about the date of issuance.

Table 6-1   Documents Required and Their Dates

Documents	Total Copies	Date of Issue	Remarks
Commercial invoice	In triplicate	From the credit's date of issue to date of bill	Signed, at least one original
Packing list	In triplicate	May without date or apply date of commercial invoice	Signed, at least one original
Canada customs invoice	In quadruplicate	From date of commercial invoice to date of B/L	Fully completed, at least one original
GSP Form A	In triplicate	From date of commercial invoice to date of B/L	Usually one original plus 2 copies
Letter of guarantee issued by the beneficiary	In triplicate	From date of commercial invoice to date of draft	At least one original, contents reflect requirements of the credit
Beneficiary's certificate	In triplicate	From date of commercial invoice to date of draft	At least one original, contents reflect requirements of the credit
Bill of lading	3 originals (full set)	Actual date of shipment made but no later than latest date of shipment in the credit	Clean on board, contents reflect requirements of the credit
Insurance policy	In duplicate	From date of commercial invoice to date of B/L	Normally in 2 originals, covering all risks and war risks
Bill of draft	In duplicate	From date of B/L to the latest date of presentation but within validity of the credit	Contents reflect requirements of the credit

3) Issuance of documents

(1) Commercial invoice

ISSUER HUANGHAI CEREALS, OILS AND FOODSTUFFS IMP. AND EXP. CORP., NO. 7 HEPING ROAD, HANGZHOU, CHINA	商业发票 **COMMERCIAL INVOICE** **ORIGINAL**		
TO WENSCO FOODS LTD., 1191 GREEN LAND STREET, WELL D., COQUITLAM, B.C., CANADA, V3K 5Z1	NO.: CMO234		DATE: AUG. 10, 2008
TRANSPORT DETAILS FROM NINGBO, CHINA TO VANCOUVER, B.C., CANADA BY SEAFREIGHT	S/C NO.: P.O. NO. 2027		L/C NO.: I01800/146791
	TERMS OF PAYMENT CREDIT IS AVAILABLE BY NEGOTIATION AT 75 DAYS AFTER BILL OF LADING DATE		
Marks and Numbers	Number and kind of package; Description of goods	Quantity	Unit Price	Amount

Marks and Numbers	Number and kind of package; Description of goods	Quantity	Unit Price	Amount
N/M	NINE HUNDRED AND FIFTY (950) CARTONS OF TROPIC ISLE CANNED MANDARIN ORANGES LS-WHOLE SEGMENTS 6/2.84KG, EVIDENCING SHIPMENT OF P.O. NO. 2027, CIF VANCOUVER, B.C., CANADA	950 CARTONS	AT USD11.40 PER CARTON	USD10830.00
	TOTAL:	950 CARTONS		USD10830.00

TOTAL AMOUNT SAY USD TEN THOUSAND EIGHT HUNDRED AND THIRTY ONLY.

CREDIT NO. I01800/146791   DATE OF ISSUE: 080731
THE NAME OF ISSUING BANK: BANK OF NOVA SCOTIA, TORONTO, CANADA

WE HEREBY EVIDENCE THAT THE SHIPMENT OF THE ABOVE GOODS IS UNDER P.O. NO. 2027.

TOTAL PACKAGES: 950 CARTONS
TOTAL GR.WT.   :   18050.0 KGS
TOTAL NT. WT.   :   16188.0 KGS
TOTAL MEAS.   :   25.0 CBM

HUANGHAI CEREALS, OILS AND FOODSTUFFS IMP. AND EXP. CORP.
SIGNED

(2)　Packing list

ISSUER HUANGHAI CEREALS, OILS AND FOODSTUFFS IMP. AND EXP. CORP., NO. 7 HEPING ROAD, HANGZHOU, CHINA			装箱单 PACKING LIST ORIGINAL			
TO WENSCO FOODS LTD., 1191 GREEN LAND STREET, WELL D., COQUITLAM, B.C., CANADA,V3K 5Z1			INVOICE NO.: CMO234		DATE: AUG. 10, 2008	
Marks and Numbers	Number and kind of package; Description of goods	Quantity	Packages	G.W.	N.W.	Meas.
N/M	NINE HUNDRED AND FIFTY (950) CARTONS OF TROPIC ISLE CANNED MANDARIN ORANGES LS-WHOLE SEGMENTS 6/2.84 KG, EVIDENCING SHIPMENT OF P.O. NO. 2027 CIF VANCOUVER, B.C., CANADA	950 CARTONS	950 CARTONS	18050.0 KGS	16188.0 KGS	25.0 CBM
	TOTAL:	950 CARTONS	950 CARTONS	18050.0 KGS	16188.0 KGS	25.0 CBM

TOTAL PACKAGES SAY NINE HUNDRED AND FIFTY (950) CARTONS ONLY.

CREDIT NO.: I01800/146791

DATE OF ISSUE: 080731

THE NAME OF ISSUING BANK: BANK OF NOVA SCOTIA, TORONTO, CANADA

WE HEREBY EVIDENCE THAT THE SHIPMENT OF THE ABOVE GOODS IS UNDER P.O. NO. 2027.

TOTAL PACKAGES:　　950 CARTONS

TOTAL GR.WT.:　　18050.0 KGS

TOTAL NT. WT.:　　16188.0 KGS

TOTAL MEAS.:　　25.0 CBM

HUANGHAI CEREALS, OILS AND FOODSTUFFS IMP. AND EXP. CORP.

SIGNED

(3) Canada customs invoice

Revenue Canada Customs and Excise	Revenue Canada Douanes et Accise	CANADA CUSTOMS INVOICE FACTURE DES DOUANES CANADIENNES	Page	of de

1. Vendor (Name and Address) Vendeur (Nom et adresse)		2. Date of Direct Shipment to Canada/Date d' expedition directe vers ie Canade		
HUANGHAI CEREALS, OILS AND FOODSTUFFS IMP. AND EXP. CORP., NO.7 HEPING ROAD, HANGZHOU, CHINA		AUG 22, 2008		
		3. Other References (include Purchaser's Order No.) Autres reterences(inclure ie n de commande de Í acheteur) P.O. NO. 2027		

4. Consignee (Name and Address) Destinataire (Nom et adresse)	5. Purchaser's Name and Address(if other than Consignee) Nom et adresse de Í acheteur(S'll differe du destinataire)
WENSCO FOODS LTD., 1191 GREEN LAND STREET, WELL D., COQUITLAM, B.C., CANADA, V3K 5Z1	SAME AS CONSIGNEE
	6. Country of Transhipment/Pays de transbordement N/A

7. Country of Origin of Goods pays d' origine des marchandises CHINA	IF SHIPMENT INCLUDES GOODS OF DIFFERENT ORIGINS ENTER ORIGINS AGAINST ITEM A IN 12 SIL' EXPEDON COMPREND DES MARCHANDISES D' ORIGINESDIFFERENTES PRECISER LEUR PROVENANCE EN 12

8.Transportation Give Mode and Place of Direct Shipment to Canada Transport Preciser mode et point d' expedition directe vercte vers ie canada FROM NINGBO CHINA TO VANCOUVER, B.C., CANADA BY SEAFREIGHT	9. Conditions of Sale and Terms of Payment (i.e. Saie, Consignment Shipment, Leased Goods, etc.) Conditions de vente et modaitites de paiement (P.ex vente, expedition en consignation, location, de marchandises, etc) CIF VANCOUVER, B.C., CANADA
	10. Currency of Settlement/Devises du paiement USD

11. No. of Pkgs Colis	12. Specification of Commodities (Kind of Packages, Marks, and Numbers, General Description and Characteristics, i.e. Grade, Quality) Designation des articles (Nature des colis, marques et numeros, description ger erale et caracteristiques, P. ex classe, qualite)	13. Quantity (State Unit) Quantite (Preciser Í unite)	Selling Price/Prix de vente	
			14. Unit Price	15. Total
950 CARTONS	NINE HUNDRED AND FIFTY(950) CARTONS TROPIC ISLE CANNED MANDARIN ORANGES LS-WHOLE SEGMENTS 6/2.84KG N/M	950 CARTONS	USD11.40/CTN	USD10830.00

18. If any of fields 1 to 17 are included on an attached commercial invoice, ☐ check this box Si tout renseignement relatIvement aux zones 1 e 17 ligure sur une ou des tactures commerciaies ci-attachees cocher cette case commercial invoice No. 1 N de la factre commerciaie		16. Total Weight/Poids Total		17. Invoice Total
		Net	Gross/Brut	Total de la facture
	CMO234	16188.0 KGS	18050.0 KGS	USD10830.00

19. Exporter's Name and Address(if other than Vendor) Nom et adresse de Í exportateur(s'll differe du vendeur) SAME AS VENDOR	20. Originator (Name and Address)/Expediteur d' origine(Nom et adresse) SAME AS VENDOR	
21. Departmental Ruling (if applicable)/Decision du Ministere(S' lly a lieu N/A	22. If fields 23 to 25 are not applicable, check this box Si ies zones 23 e 25 sont sans objet, cocher cette case N/A	
23. If included in field 17 indicate amount Si compris dans ie total a ia zone 17, preciser (I)Transportation charges, expenses and insurance from the place of direct shipment to Canada Les frais de transport, depenses et assurances a partir du point of expedition directe vers is Canada.	24. If not included in field 17 indicate amount Si non compris dans le total a ie zone 17, Dreciser (I)Transportation charges, expense and insurance to the place of direct shipment to Canada Les frais de transport, depenses et assurances Iusqu' au point d' of expedition directd vers ie Canada	25.Check (if applicable) Cochet (s'lly a liso) (I)Royalty payments or subsequent proceeds are paid or payable by the purchaser Des redevances ou produits ont ete ou seront Verses par Í acheteur
CNY 18900.00	CNY18900.00	N/A
(II)Costs for construction, erection and assembly incurred after importation into Canada Les couts de construction, d' erection et d' assemblage,, pres imporaation au.Canada	(II)Amounts for commissions other than buying commissions Les commissions autres que celles versees Pour Í achat	(II)The purchaser has supplied goods or services for use in the production of these goods. L'acheteur a fouml des merchandises ou des Services pour ia production des merchandises
N/A	N/A	N/A
(III)Export packing Le cout de Í emballage d' exportation	(III)Export packing Le cout de Í emballage d' exportation	
CNY5800.00	N/A	

(4) GSP Form A

1. Goods consigned from (Exporter's business name, address, country)	Reference No.	
HUANGHAI CEREALS, OILS AND FOODSTUFFS IMP. AND EXP. CORP., NO.7 HEPING ROAD, HANZGHOU, CHINA	GENERALIZED SYSTEM OF PREFERENCES CERTIFICATE OF ORIGIN (Combined declaration and certificate)	
2. Goods consigned to (Consignee's name, address, country)	FORM A	
WENSCO FOODS LTD., 1191 GREEN LAND STREET, WELL D., COQUITLAM, B.C., CANADA,V3K 5Z1	Issued in CHINA (country)	THE PEOPLE'S REPUBLIC OF CHINA
	See notes overleaf	
3. Means of transport and route (as far as known)	4. For official use	
FROM NINGBO, CHINA TO VANCOUVER, B.C.,CANADA BY SEAFREIGHT		

5. Item number	6. Marks and numbers of packages	7. Number and kind of packages; description of goods	8. Origin criterion (See notes overleaf)	9. Gross weight or other quantity	10. Number and date of invoices
1	N/M	NINE HUNDRED AND FIFTY(950) CARTONS OF TROPIC ISLE CANNED MANDARIN ORANGES LS-WHOLE SEGMENTS 6/2.84KG **********************************	"P"	QUANTITY 950 CARTONS	CMO234 AUG. 10, 2008

11. Certification	12. Declaration by the exporter
It is hereby certified, on the basis of control carried out, that the declaration by the exporter is correct.	The undersigned hereby declares that the above details and statements are correct, that all the goods were
	produced in CHINA (country)
	and that they comply with the origin requirements specified for those goods in the Generalized System of Preferences for goods exported to
	CANADA
HANGZHOU CHINA AUG. 14, 2008	HANGZHOU CHINA AUG. 12, 2008
Place and date, signature and stamp of certifying authority	Place and date, signature and stamp of authorized signatory

(5)　Beneficiary's letter of guarantee

黄海粮油食品进出口公司

HUANGHAI CEREALS , OILS AND FOODSTUFFS IMP. AND EXP. CORP.

中国杭州和平路 7 号

NO.7 HEPING ROAD, HANGZHOU, CHINA

TO WHOM IT MAY CONCERN

RE: INVOICE NO. CMO234

CREDIT NO.: I01800/146791

DATE: AUG. 20, 2008

BENEFICIARY'S LETTER OF GUARANTEE

WE HEREBY STATE THAT WE WILL REIMBURSE ALL EXPENSES IN CASE OF REJECTION BY CANADIAN FOOD INSPECTION AGENCY.

BEST REGARDS

HUANGHAI CEREALS, OILS AND FOODSTUFFS IMP. AND EXP. CORP.
SIGNED

(6)　Beneficiary's certificate

黄海粮油食品进出口公司

HUANGHAI CEREALS, OILS AND FOODSTUFFS IMP. AND EXP. CORP.

中国杭州和平路 7 号

NO.7 HEPING ROAD, HANGZHOU, CHINA

TO WHOM IT MAY CONCERN

RE: INVOICE NO. CMO234

CREDIT NO.: I01800/146791

DATE: AUG. 20, 2008

BENEFICIARY'S CERTIFICATE

WE HHEREBY STATE THAT 1. THE SHIPMENT DOES NOT INCLUDE NON-MANUFACTURED WOOD DUNNAGE, PALLETS, CRATING OR OTHER PACKING MATERIALS; 2. THE SHIPMENT IS COMPLETELY FREE OF WOOD BARK, VISIBLE PESTS AND SIGNS OF LIVING PESTS.

BEST REGARDS

HUANGHAI CEREALS, OILS AND FOODSTUFFS IMP. AND EXP. CORP.
SIGNED

(7) Bill of lading

1. Shipper Insert Name, Address and Phone	B/L No. 200818
HUANGHAI CEREALS, OILS AND FOODSTUFFS IMP. AND EXP. CORP., NO.7 HEPING ROAD, HANGZHOU, CHINA	中国海运(集团)公司 CHINA OCEAN SHIPPING (GROUP) CO. Port-to-Port or Combined Transport **BILL OF LADING** **ORIGINAL**

2. Consignee Insert Name, Address and Phone
TO THE ORDER OF THE BANK OF NOVA SCOTIA

3. Notify Party Insert Name, Address and Phone (It is agreed that no responsibility shall attach to the Carrier or his agents for failure to notify.)
WENSCO FOODS LTD., 1191 GREEN LAND STREET, WELL D., COQUITLAM, B.C., CANADA,V3K 5Z1

RECEIVED in external apparent good order and condition except as otherwise noted. The total number of packages or units stuffed in the container, the description of the goods and the weights shown in this Bill of Lading are furnished by the Merchants, and which the carrier has no reasonable means of checking and is not a part of this Bill of Lading contract. The carrier has issued the number of Bills of Lading stated below, all of this tenor and date, one of the original Bills of Lading must be surrendered and endorsed or signed against the delivery of the shipment and whereupon any other original Bills of Lading shall be void. The Merchants agree to be bound by the terms and conditions of this Bill of Lading as if each had personally signed this Bill of Lading.See clause 4 on the back of this Bill of Lading (Terms continued on the back hereof, please read carefully).*Applicable Only When Document Used as a Combined Transport Bill of Lading.

4. Combined Transport * Pre-carriage by	5. Combined Transport* Place of Receipt
6. Ocean Vessel Voy. No. BEAUTY V23	7. Port of Loading NINGBO, CHINA
8. Port of Discharge	9. Combined Transport *

VANCOUVER, B.C., CANADA		10. Place of Delivery	VANCOUVER, B.C., CANADA

Marks & Nos. Container / Seal No.	No. of Containers or Packages	Description of goods	Gross Weight Kgs	Measurement
N/M 00631/127X CY TO CY 1X20' GP	950 CARTONS	TROPIC ISLE CANNED MANDARIN ORANGES LS-WHOLE SEGMENTS 6/2.84KG FREIGHT PREPAID **SHIPPED ON BOARD** **AUG. 20, 2008**	18050.0 KGS	25.000 CBM

Description of Contents for Shipper's Use Only (Not part of This B/L Contract)

11. Total number of containers and/or packages (in words)   TOTAL NINE HUNDRED AND FIFTY CARTONS ONLY.
Subject to Clause 7 Limitation

12. Freight & Charges		Revenue Tons	Rate	Per	Prepaid	Collect
Declared Value Charge THE SHIPPING COMPANY AGENT IN CANADA NAME: ADDRESSS: TELEPHONE NUMBER:						

Ex. Rate:	Prepaid at NINGBO	Payable at	Place and date of issue NINGBO, CHINA AUG. 20, 2008
	Total Prepaid	No. of Original B(s)/L 3	Signed for the Carrier, CHINA OCEAN SHIPPING (GROUP) CO.
			CHINA OCEAN SHIPPING (GROUP) CO. **(SIGNED)**

LADEN ON BOARD THE VESSEL			
DATE	AUG. 20, 2008	BY	BEAUTY V23

(8) Insurance Policy

PICC	中国人民保险公司杭州市分公司 The People's Insurance Company of China, Hangzhou Branch 总公司设于北京　一九四九年创立 Head Office Beijing　Established in 1949

货物运输保险单 CARGO TRANSPORTATION INSURANCE POLICY

发票号(INVOICE NO.)	CMO234	保单号次 POLICY NO.	
合同号(CONTRACT NO.)	P.O. NO. 2027		
信用证号(L/C NO.)	I01800/146791		
被保险人：Insured:	HUANGHAI CEREALS, OILS AND FOODSTUFFS IMP. AND EXP. CORP.		

中国人民保险公司(以下简称本公司)根据被保险人的要求，由被保险人向本公司缴付约定的保险费，按照本保险单承保险别和背面所载条款与下列特款承保下述货物运输保险，特立本保险单。

THIS POLICY OF INSURANCE WITNESSES THAT THE PEOPLE'S INSURANCE COMPANY OF CHINA (HEREINAFTER CALLED "THE COMPANY") AT THE REQUEST OF THE INSURED AND IN CONSIDERATION OF THE AGREED PREMIUM PAID TO THE COMPANY BY THE INSURED, UNDERTAKES TO INSURE THE UNDERMENTIONED GOODS IN TRANSPORTATION SUBJECT TO THE CONDITIONS OF THIS POLICY AS PER THE CLAUSES PRINTED OVERLEAF AND OTHER SPECIAL CLAUSES ATTACHED HEREON.

标 记 (MARKS & NOS)	包装及数量 (QUANTITY)	保险货物项目 (DESCRIPTION OF GOODS)	保险金额 (INSURED AMOUNT)
N/M	950 CARTONS	TROPIC ISLE CANNED MANDARIN ORANGES LS-WHOLE SEGMENTS 6/2.84KG	USD11913.00

总保险金额 TOTAL AMOUNT INSURED:	SAY USD ELEVEN THOUSAND NINE HUNDRED AND THIRTEEN ONLY.

保费： PREMIUM:	AS ARRANGED	启运日期 DATE OF COMMENCEMENT:	AUG. 20, 2008	装载运输工具： PER CONVEYANCE:	BEAUTY V23
自 FROM:	HANGZHOU, CHINA	经 VIA		至 TO	VANCOUVER

承保险别(CONDITIONS):
COVERING ALL RISKS AND WAR RISKS AS PER CIC (1/1/1980)

所保货物，如发生保险单项下可能引起索赔的损失或损坏，应立即通知本公司下述代理人查勘。如有索赔，应向本公司提交保单正本(本保险单共有__份正本)及有关文件。如一份正本已用于索赔，其余正本自动失效。

IN THE EVENT OF LOSS OR DAMAGE WHICH MAY RESULT IN A CLAIM UNDER THIS POLICY, IMMEDIATE NOTICE MUST BE GIVEN TO THE COMPANY'S AGENT AS MENTIONED HEREUNDER. CLAIMS, IF ANY, ONE OF THE ORIGINAL POLICY WHICH HAS BEEN ISSUED IN	2	ORIGINAL(S)

TOGETHER WITH THE RELEVENT DOCUMENTS SHALL BE SURRENDERED TO THE COMPANY. IF ONE OF THE ORIGINAL POLICY HAS BEEN ACCOMPLISHED, THE OTHERS TO BE VOID.

赔款偿付地点 CLAIM PAYABLE AT	VANCOUVER	IN USD	中国人民保险公司杭州分公司 The People's Insurance Company of China Hangzhou Branch		
出单日期 ISSUING DATE	AUG. 16, 2008		授权签字人(SIGNATURE)		

INSURANCE AGENT IN CANADA:
NAME:
ADDRESS:
CONTACT PERSON:
TEL: FAX: CABLE:

(9) Bill of exchange

BILL OF EXCHANGE

凭 Drawn Under	BANK OF NOVA SCOTIA, TORONTO, CANADA		不可撤销信用证 Irrevocable L/C No.					I01800/146791		
日期 Date	080731		支 取 Payable With interest	@		%	按		息	付款
号码 No.	CMO234	汇票金额 Exchange for	USD10830.00		杭州 HANGZHOU		AUG. 24, 2008			

见票 at	75 DAYS AFTER BILL OF LADING DATE BILL OF LADING DATE : AUG . 20, 2008	日后 (本 汇 票 之 副 本 未 付) 付 交 sight of this FIRST of Exchange (Second of Exchange

being unpaid) Pay to the order of	BANK OF CHINA, ZHEJIANG

金额 the sum of	TOTAL AMOUNT SAY USD TEN THOUSAND EIGHT HUNDRED AND THIRTY ONLY.

此致 To	THE BANK OF NOVA SCOTIA, 650 WEST GEORGIA ST., PO BOX 11502, VANCOUVER, B.C., CANADA V6B 4P6	HUANGHAI CEREALS, OILS AND FOODSTUFFS IMP. AND EXP. CORP. MANUALLY SIGNED

Chapter 7

Examination of Documents

7.1　Complying Presentation

Complying presentation means a presentation that is in accordance with the terms and conditions of the credit, the applicable provision of these rules and international standard banking practice. When a nominated bank determines that a presentation is complying and honors or negotiates, it must forward the documents to the confirming bank or the issuing bank. When a confirming bank determines that a presentation is complying, it must honor or negotiate and forward the documents to the issuing bank. When an issuing bank determines that a presentation is complying, it must honor (article 15 of UCP600).

7.2　Standard for Examination

Whatever a credit stipulated must be carried out!

There are no specific terms and conditions regarding "Standard for examination of documents" in UCP500, you can find many articles connecting with standard for examination and the contents cannot be understood well. In practice, principle "Mirror Image" is adopted by the beneficiary, nominated bank, confirming bank (if any) and issuing bank for the purpose of drafting documents and its examination. However, article 14 of UCP600 is regarding to "Standard for Examination of Documents" especially. It makes documents making and examination much more clarified, flexible and practical. Standard for examination of documents is as follows:

7.2.1　Highlighting Documents

A nominated bank acting on its nomination, a confirming bank, if any, and the issuing bank must examine a presentation to determine, *on the basis of the documents alone*, whether or not *the documents appear on their face* to constitute a complying presentation (article 14(a) of UCP600).

Banks deal with documents exclusively. However, banks assume no responsibility both for authenticity, form or validity of the document and for the act of the third parties taking part in the credit operations.

7.2.2 Period for Examination

A nominated bank acting on its nomination, a confirming bank, if any, and the issuing bank shall *each have a maximum of five banking days following the day of presentation* to determine if a presentation is complying. This period is not curtailed or otherwise affected by the occurrence on or after the date of presentation of any expiry date or the last day for presentation (article 14(b) of UCP600).

7.2.3 Period for Presenting Original Transport Documents

A presentation including one or more original transport documents subject to articles 19, 20, 21, 22, 23, 24 or 25 must be made by or on behalf of the beneficiary *not later than 21 calendar days after the date of shipment* as described in these rules, but in any event not later than the expiry date of the credit (article 14(c) of UCP600).

This sub-article only refers to original transport documents that are included in a presentation. If a presentation isn't including any original transport document, this sub-article won't be applicable.

7.2.4 Conformity of Documents

(1) *Data* in a document, when read in context with the credit, the document itself and international standard banking practice, need not be identical to, but must not conflict with, data in that document, any other stipulated document or the credit (article 14(d) of UCP600).

(2) In documents other than commercial invoice, the *description of the goods, services or performance*, if stated, may be in general terms not conflicting with their description in the credit (article 14(e) of UCP600).

(3) When *the address of the beneficiary and the applicant* appear in any stipulated document, they need not be the same as those stated in the credit or in any other stipulated document, but must be within the same country as the respective addresses mentioned in the

credit. Contact details (telefax, telephone, email and the like) stated as part of the beneficiary's and the applicant's address will be disregarded. However, when the address and contact details of the applicant appear as part of the consignee or notify party details on a transport document subject to articles 19, 20, 21, 22, 23, 24 or 25, they must be as stated in the credit (article 14(j) of UCP600).

(4) *The shipper or consignor* of the goods indicated on any document need not be the beneficiary of the credit (article 14(k) of UCP600).

7.2.5　Issuer

(1) If a credit requires presentation of *a document other than a transport document, insurance document or commercial invoice*, without stipulating by whom the documents is to be issued or its data content, banks will accept the document as presented if its content appears to fulfill the function of the required document and otherwise complies with sub-article 14(d) (article 14(f) of UCP600).

(2) A *transport document* may be issued by any party other than a carrier, owner, master or charter provided that the transport document meets the requirements of articles 19, 20, 21, 22, 23 or 24 of these rules (article 14(l) of UCP600).

(3) Terms such as "first class", "well known", "qualified", "independent", "official", "competent" or "local" used to describe the issuer of a *document* allow *any issuer except the beneficiary* to issue that document (article 3 of UCP600).

7.2.6　Documents & Conditions Not Required

(1) A document presented but not required by the credit will be disregarded and may be returned to the presenter (article 14(g) of UCP600).

(2) If a credit contains a condition without stipulating the document to indicate compliance with the condition, banks will deem such conditions as not stated and will disregard it (article 14(h) of UCP600).

7.2.7　Date of Documents

A document may be dated prior to the issuance date of the credit, but must not be dated later than its date of presentation (article 14(i) of UCP600).

7.3 Discrepant Documents, Waiver and Notice

7.3.1 Refusal of Discrepant Documents

Whatever a nominated bank, a confirming bank (if any) and the issuing bank shall each have a maximum of five banking days following the day of presentation to determine if a presentation is complying. When a bank determines that a presentation does not comply, it may refuse to honor or negotiate.

When a bank decides to refuse to honor or negotiate a presentation with discrepancy(ies), it must give a single notice to that effect to the presenter no later than the close of the fifth banking day following the day of presentation.

If an issuing bank or a confirming bank fails to act in accordance with the above mentioned, it shall be precluded from claiming that the documents do not constitute a complying presentation.

When an issuing bank refuses to honor or negotiate and has given notice to that effect in accordance with the above, it shall then be entitled to claim a refund, with interest, of any reimbursement made.

7.3.2 Waiver

When an issuing bank determines that a presentation does not comply, it may in its sole judgment approach the applicant for a waiver of the discrepancies. This does not, however, extend the period mentioned in sub-article 14(b) of UCP600. It means that the issuing bank still need to determine without exceeding five banking days following the day of presentation.

7.3.3 Notice

When a bank decides to refuse to honor or negotiate a presentation with discrepancy(ies), it must give a single notice to that effect to the presenter.

1. Contents of the Notice

The notice must state

(1) Determination of the bank: the bank is refusing to honor or negotiate;

(2) Reasons for refusing: each discrepancy in respect of which the bank refuses to honor or

negotiate;

(3) Disposal way of discrepant documents. There are four ways for disposal of the discrepant documents: a. the bank is holding the documents pending further instructions from the presenter; b. the issuing bank is holding the documents until it receives a waiver from the applicant and agrees to accept it, or receiving further instructions from the presenter prior to agreeing to accept a waiver; c. the bank is returning the documents; d. the bank is acting in accordance with instructions previously received from the presenter.

The first one mentioned above is the most popular. A bank may return the documents to the presenter at any time after providing notice required.

2. Notice Communication

The notice required must be given by tele-communication or, if that is not possible, by other expeditious means no later than the close of the fifth banking day following the day of presentation.

Specimen 7-1 Combined Practices

As per the following given specimen credit and it's relative presentation, to examine the presentation. The presentation was made on Jun. 15, 2011(Wednesday), including 2 copies of commercial invoice, 2 copies of insurance policy without endorsement and 3 copies of original bill of lading.

1. The Credit

ADVISING BANK: THE BANK OF NEW YORK, INTERNATIONAL BANKING DEPARTMENT, NEW YORK, N. Y.

SEQUENCE OF TOTAL	:27: 1/1
FORM OF DOC. CREDIT	:40B: IRREVOCABLE WITHOUT OUR CONFIRMATION
SENDER'S REFERENCE	:20 : XXXXXXXXX
DOC. CREDIT NUMBER	:21: 110032
DATE OF ISSUE	:31C: 110501
EXPIRY	:31D: 110620 IN NEW YORK
ISSUING BANK	:52D: BANK IN PERU, LIMA, PERU
APPLICANT	:50: BUILDERS, S.A., LIMA, PERU
BENEFICIARY	:59: HENRY CLYDE PRECISION PARTS, ROCHESTER, NEW YORK
AMOUNT	: CURRENCY USD AMOUNT 6000.00
AVAILABLE WITH/BY	:41D: WITH THE BANK OF NEW YORK, NEW YORK, N.Y. BY PAYMENT
DRAFTS AT...	:42C: 60 DAYS SIGHT
PARTIAL SHIPMENT	:43P: NOT ALLOWED

```
TRANSHIPMENT          :43T: ALLOWED
LOADING IN CHARGE     :44A: NEW YORK
FOR TRANSPORT TO      :44B: CALLAO
LATEST DATE OF SHIP.  :44C: 110605
DESCRIPT. OF GOODS    :45A: TOOLS
DOCUMENTS REQUIRED :46A:
    +SIGNED COMMERCIAL INVOICE IN TRIPLICATE
    +CONSULAR INVOICE
    +MARIN INSURANCE POLICY OR CERTIFICATE TO ORDER OF BUILDERS, S.A.,COVERING
      MARINE AND WAR RISKS AND SRCC RISKS, IF ANY ,
      PAYABLE IN LIMA, PERU, IN U.S. DOLLARS.
    +FULL SET OF CLEAN ON BOARD OCEAN BILL OF LADING MADE OUT TO ORDER OF
      ISSUING BANK , MARKED NOTIFY BUYERS AND "FREIGHT PREPAID".
ADDITIONAL CON.       :47A:
    + DRAFTS DRAWN MUST BE DESCRIBED WITH THE NUMBER AND DATE OF THIS L/C.
CONFIRMATION          :49: WITHOUT
INSTRUCTIONS          :78:
+ DRAFTS AND DOCUMENTS TAKEN UP UNDER THIS CREDIT ARE TO BE FORWARDED IN
  ONE LOT TO BANK IN PERU, LIMA, PERU.
+UPON RECEIPT OF L/C CONFIRMATION DOCUMENTS COVER WILL BE SENT AT YOUR
  CONVENIENCE.
```

2. Presentation

(1) Bill of exchange

a. On the face of the bill of exchange

Exchange for USD6000.00   NEW YORK 15 JUNE 2011

    At 30 DAYS   sight of this FIRST of Exchange (SECOND of Exchange) being unpaid

    to the order of OURSELVES the sum of USD SIX THOUSAND ONLY

Drawn under   L/C NO. 110032   dated on 110501

To: HENRY CLYDE PRECISION PARTS

                                            Eleanor Pye
                                            Manager

---

b. On the back of bill of exchange

> HENRY CLYDE PRECISION PARTS
>
>
> Eleanor Pye
> Manager

(2)　Commercial Invoice

ISSUER HENRY CLYDE PRECISION PARTS 42 SAFEWAY BLVD., ROCHESTER, NEW YORK	商业发票 COMMERCIAL INVOICE ORIGINAL		
TO BUILDERS, S.A., LIMA, PERU			
	NO.: 9609		DATE: JUNE 11, 2011
TRANSPORT DETAILS FROM NEW YORK TO CALLAO BY SEA	S/C NO.:		L/C NO.: 110032
	TERMS OF PAYMENT: L/C AT 60 DAYS BY PAYMENT		
Marks & Numbers	Number and kind of package; Description of goods	Quantity	Unit Price	Amount
AIB 471	400 GRADE "B" #7 ROUTER BITS PACKED IN 25 CTNS		USD6,000.00 CIF CALLAO	
	TOTAL: AMOUNT SAY USD SIX THOUSAND ONLY.			

HENRY CLYDE PRECISION PARTS

Eleanor Pye

Manager

(3)　Insurance Policy

XXX　INSURANCE COMPANY
CARGO TRANSPORTATION INSURANCE POLICY

Invoice No.	9609	Policy No.	
Contract No.			
L/C No.	110032		

Insured:	HENRY CLYDE PRECISION PARTS

This Policy Of Insurance Witnesses That xxx Insurance Company (Hereinafter Called "The Company")

at the request of the insured and in consideration of the agreed premium paid to the company by the insured,

undertakes to insure the undermentioned goods in transportation subject to the conditions of this policy as per the

clauses printed overleaf and other special clauses attached hereon.

It is hereby understood and agreed that in the case of the loss, such a loss is payable to the order of bank in Peru,

Lima, Peru, in US Dollars.

MARKS&NOS	QUANTITY	DESCRIPTION OF GOODS	INSURED AMOUNT
AIB 471	25 CARTONS	TOOLS	USD5500.00

总保险金额	US DOLLARS FIVE THOUSAND FIVE HUNDRED ONLY.			
PREMIUM:	AS ARRANGED	DATE OF COMMENCEMENT: 12 JUNE 2011	PER CONVEYANCE:	S.S. TOM
FROM:	NEW YORK	VIA	TO	CALLAO，PERU

CONDITIONS:
ALL RISKS INCLUDING SRCC RISKS AND WAR RISKS.
IN THE EVENTS OF LOSS OR DAMAGE WHICH MAY RESULT IN A CLAIM UNDER THIS POLICY, IMMEDIATE NOTICE MUST BE GIVEN TO THE COMPANY'S AGENT AS MENTIONED HEREUNDER. CLAIMS , IF ANY, ONE OF THE ORIGINAL POLICY WHICH HAS BEEN ISSUED IN TOGETHER WITH THE RELEVENT DOCUMENTS SHALL BE SURRENDERED TO THE COMPANY. IF ONE OF THE ORIGINAL POLICY HAS BEEN ACCOMPLISHED, THE OTHERS TO BE VOID. THE INSURANCE POLICY IS ISSUED IN TWO ORIGINALS.

	2	ORIGINAL(S)

CLAIMS PAYABLE IN LIMA, PERU IN USD	XXX INSURANCE COMPANY BROWN ELLEN
DATE :13 JUNE 2011	

(ADD.):……………NEW YORK

(4)　Bill of lading

1. Shipper Insert Name, Address and Phone				A&P SHIPPING COMPANY LTD.		
HENRY CLYDE PRECISION PARTS ROCHESTER, NEW YORK.				RECEIVED BY THE CARRIER FROM THE SHIPPER IN APPARENT GOOD ORDER AND CONDITION (UNLESS OTHERWISE NOTED HEREIN). THE TOTAL NUMBER OR QUANTITY OF CONTAINER OR OTHER ____ .		
2. Consignee Insert Name, Address and Phone						
TO ORDER OF BANK IN PERU, LIMA, PERU						
3. Notify Party Insert Name, Address and Phone				IN WITNESS OF THE CONTRACT HEREIN CONTAINED THE NUMBER OF ORIGINALS STATED OPPOSITE HAS BEEN ISSUED, ONE OF WHICH BEING ACCOMPLISHED, THE OTHER(S) TO BE VOID.		
BANK IN PERU, LIMA, PERU						
4. Combined Transport *		5. Combined Transport*		ORIGINAL	B/L NO.	0001
Pre - carriage by		Place of Receipt		6. Ocean Vessel Voy. No.	SS ROSALIND	
				7. Port of Loading	NEW YORK	
9. Combined Transport *		10. Place of Delivery		8. Port of Discharge	CALLAO	
		CALLAO				
Marks & Nos. Container / Seal No.	No. of Containers or Packages	Description of Goods, If Dangerous Goods, See Clause 20)		Gross Weight(Kgs)	Measurement	
AIB 471	25 CTNS	TOOLS SHIPPED ON BOARD DATE: 12 JUNE 2011 GEORGE GATES AS MASTER		413 KGS	8.0 CBM	
11. Total Number of containers and/or packages (in words) TOTAL TWENTY FIVE CARTONS ONLY.						
Subject to Clause 7 Limitation						
12. Freight & Charges	Revenue Tons	Rate	Per	Prepaid	Collect	
COLLECT Declared Value Charge						
Ex. Rate:	Prepaid at	Payable at	PLACE AND DATE OF ISSUE	NEW YORK, 12 JUNE 2011		
	Total Prepaid	No. of Original B(s)/L 3	A & P SHIPPING COMPANY LTD. GEORGE GATES AS MASTER			
DATE		BY				

3. Result of Examining Documents

The presentation is discrepant. There are following discrepancies:

(1) Discrepancies in commercial invoice: a. DESCRIPT. OF GOODS in the credit was "TOOLS", whereas the commercial invoice showed as "400 GRADE "B" #7 ROUTER BITS"; b. Date of commercial invoice was later than the latest date of shipment stipulated in the credit; c. The credit stipulated "Commercial invoice in triplicate", while the beneficiary only presented 2 copies.

(2) The presentation was lacking of "CONSULAR INVOICE".

(3) Discrepancies in bill of lading: a. The credit stipulated notify party to be shown as "BUYERS"(BUILDERS, S.A., LIMA, PERU), whereas notify party shown on the B/L was actually "BANK IN PERU, LIMA, PERU"; b.The credit stipulated B/L to be shown as "FREIGHT PREPAID", whereas that actually shown on the B/L was "FREIGHT COLLECT"; c. Late shipment. The credit stipulated the latest date of shipment is June 05, 2011, whereas the date of B/L is June 12, 2011. It means late shipment occurred.

(4) Discrepancies in insurance policy: a. Date of insurance policy was later than that of B/L; b. The insured amount shall be USD6600.00 instead of USD5500.00; c. Name of vessel and voyage shown on the insurance policy was different with that shown on the B/L; d. The insured should be shown "TO ORDER OF BUILDERS, S.A.," instead of the beneficiary, or could be shown as the beneficiary but must be with endorsement.

(5) Discrepancies in draft: a.The credit was available with THE BANK OF NEW YORK, NEW YORK, N.Y. BY PAYMENT at 60 days after sight, whereas tenor of the draft is at 30 days after sight; b. The draft didn't indicate drawee "THE BANK OF NEW YORK, NEW YORK, N.Y.".

Chapter 8

International Trade Financing

8.1　Overview

International trade continues to grow every year as nations expand their global sales and new nations join in. Today, over 225 nations are active in international trade resulting in over $9 trillion dollars in global business every year. Trade-related financial services have developed and expanded in depth, complexity and effectiveness to support the expansion of world trade.

Many trade finance options are now available. However, the small to mid-sized enterprises (SME) trading community is relatively unaware of many of the more sophisticated and/or the sources of the more effective trade finance services. Traders commonly believe that the major international banks are the primary providers of these services.

Compared with general loan, international trade financing is usually with less risks to the financing bank and can provide the customer with diversified financing products and less costs. In order to compete for "soft gold business" (international settlement business called by the banks), the banks often provide the customers with preferential financing. Meanwhile, international trade financing is usually tied to new business by the banks.

According to financing forms, international trade financing can be divided into three kinds: financing in fund, financing in documents and financing in guarantee. Both the sellers and the buyers can be financed by export trade financing and import trade financing at pre and post shipment stages. Financing under international settlement is very flexible and optional.

Lacking money is only one relatively important reason for both parties' application for financing. To a great extent, international trade financing results in difference of three points of time, such as "date of documents of title to the goods arriving at the issuing bank/collecting bank" , "date of the shipped goods arriving at destination" and "date of payment". Negotiable instruments can be made at sight or on a specific future day; the goods shall be usually shipped by short range transportation or mid and long range transportation; full set of commercial documents including documents of title to the goods will be delivered by the seller to the buyer through the banks by courier under collection or credit.

This part is intended to be an introduction to the key types of import trade financing and export trade financing. Understanding these options will help businesses select the most appropriate and effective import trade financing and export trade financing to fit a company's unique financial circumstances.

8.2 Import Trade Financing

The buyer may apply for import trade financing from a bank by selecting from limits for issuing credit, trust receipts (T/R), shipping guarantees (S/G) and inward bills.

8.2.1 Limits for Issuing Credit

1. Application

There is a special credit line for issuing credit. The credit line is authorized by a bank according to the customer's creditworthiness, deposit, assets and mortgage or pledge, trade background, etc. With no exceeding limits for issuing credit, the buyer may apply for issuing a credit with a lower percentage of margin.

2. Risks to a Financing Bank

It means that the issuing bank must honor a complying presentation against a certain percentage of credit amount, such as 30%, deposited in margin account. The balance of credit amount is paid by the issuing bank only against a payment promise provided by the buyer.

3. Consideration for a Financing Bank

Before issuing a credit, the bank will check a. to examine if limits for issuing a credit and credit line of the customer are sufficient or not; b. to control the information about the seller's creditworthiness; c. to analyze situations of the goods' liquidity, market, price, transport & insurance, etc.; d. to judge if the presentation is including full set of transport documents of title to the goods.

4. Mitigating Risks of a Financing Bank

In order to mitigate risks, an issuing bank will a. ask a certain percentage of cash deposited in the bank. It means that limits for issuing credit cannot substitute margin completely; b. take the assets as a mortgage or pledge of the customer or accept a qualified guarantor; c. adjust limits for issuing credit according to the customer's creditworthiness at any time; d. during the life of the letter of credit, the bank should keep it informative and follow each step of the operation, and put the whole process of operation under its supervision.

8.2.2 Trust Receipts

1. Definition

Trust receipt (T/R) means a guarantee issued by the buyer drawn upon a bank by the means of trust for the purpose of borrowing full set of commercial documents, including documents of title to the goods before its payment. The buyer requires the bank to lend bill of lading to him and takes the goods under the goods title held by the bank and promises to the bank that he will fulfill his obligation for payment after he sells the goods.

The legal title to the goods remains with the entruster under an operation of "trust".

2. Application

Trust receipt may be applicable under a specific circumstance, such as the shipped goods and relative documents have arrived at destination/issuing bank/collecting bank, but the bill of exchange drawn by the seller does not fall due under D/P or a credit with payment on a specific future date. The bank regulates the timing and sequence of the exchange of goods for value by holding the title documents until the buyer pays the draft.

3. Parties to a Trust Receipt

There are two parties involved with a trust receipt.

(1) The bank, as the entruster or principal, possessor of title to the goods. He entrusts the buyer to handle the goods under its name and the buyer gets the right to sell the goods with trust receipt.

(2) The buyer, as the trustee, bears obligations to a. arrange for the goods to be warehoused and insured in the bank's name; b. pay all the proceeds of sale to the bank or to hold them on behalf of the bank; c. not to put the goods in pledge to other persons; d. return the goods or the proceeds to the bank at any time when requested; e. settle claims of the bank before liquidation in case of the trustee's bankruptcy.

4. Risks to a Financing Bank and How to Mitigate Them

The bank bears the risk of losing the goods while it grants authority to the importer to handle the goods on its behalf. A financing bank may mitigate risks under T/R through

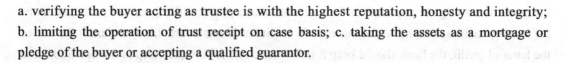

a. verifying the buyer acting as trustee is with the highest reputation, honesty and integrity; b. limiting the operation of trust receipt on case basis; c. taking the assets as a mortgage or pledge of the buyer or accepting a qualified guarantor.

8.2.3　Shipping Guarantees

1. Definition

Shipping guarantee is a written guarantee signed by the bank and issued to the shipping company for the importer's picking up the goods in the case of arrival of cargo prior to the shipping documents.

2. Application

Such a kind of trade financing is especially applicable in the case of short range shipping voyage, arrival of cargo prior to the documents. As the goods arrives ahead of the bill of lading and the market of imported goods is booming, the buyer is anxious to take delivery.

3.　Attentions for Issuing a Shipping Guarantee

(1)　At the issuing bank's end, basic prerequisites for issuing a shipping guarantee are as follows: a. The method of international settlement is restricted to credits only; b.The goods must be shipped by seafreight; c. All documents of title to the goods must be included in the presentation under a credit.

(2)　The buyer is required to submit the following to the issuing bank for a shipping guarantee: a. the application for shipping guarantee; b. letter of shipping guarantee; c. duplication of invoice; d. duplication of bill of lading.

(3)　The buyer is required to maintain credit line or have single credit extension approved by the issuing bank.

(4)　The buyer is required to pledge to the issuing bank that the presentation would not be rejected even if it has discrepancy(ies).

(5)　When the original bill of lading arrives, the buyer is required to substitute the shipping guarantee with bill of lading at the shipping company and return the shipping guarantee to the issuing bank for cancellation.

8.2.4　Inward Bills

1. Definition

Inward bill is a kind of short-term financing offered by the bank to the buyer according to his demand upon receiving a presentation under a credit or collection. It is the best choice of the short-term financing for the buyer and is also called an import bill advance.

2. Application

An inward bill is applicable when the buyer cannot make payment owing to short of work capital, or having other investment opportunities and the prospective earning rate of the investment is higher than the interest rate of the inward bill, while the imported goods market is booming.

3. Classification of Inward Bills

Based on the fundamental settlement methods, the inward bill can be classified into the inward bill under collection and the inward bill under credit.

Based on the currency variety, the inward bills can be classified into those in foreign currency and those in local currency, such as Chinese currency (CNY) for the Chinese buyer.

4. Attentions for Inward Bills

(1)　The buyer is required to maintain the credit line or have a single credit extension approved by the financing bank, put forward a written application for inward bills to the issuing bank or the authorized collecting bank.

(2)　The buyer is required to sign the formal finance agreement with the bank and determine the amount, term, rate, maturity and etc.

(3)　Pay attention to the market interest rate of local currency and the paying currency at all time and choose the currency with the lowest cost for inward bills.

(4)　Inward bill is a kind of special financing which can only be used to carry out the responsibility of payment under trade items.

(5)　The financing period is always matched with the durance of resale of imported goods, and the received payment is the main source to pay off the bill advance.

8.3　Export Trade Financing

Export trade financing is a specific topic within the financial services industry. A product is sold and shipped overseas, therefore, it takes longer to get paid. Extra time and energy is required to make sure that buyers are reliable and creditworthy. In addition, the foreign buyers, just like domestic buyers, prefer to delay payment until they receive and resell the goods.

There are seven kinds of financing products for exportation: packing loan, outward bills, discounting, banker's acceptance, forfaiting, factoring and financing under export credit insurance.

8.3.1 Packing Loan

1. Definition

It is a special loan offered by the local bank to the seller who has received a qualified credit, to be used under items of procurement, production and shipment, so as to support the seller to implement the contract and effect delivery as scheduled.

Packing loan is a pre-loading short-term financing, which enables the exporter to purchase, prepare the material, produce and trade without difficulty even the self-owned capital is not sufficient.

2. Application

Packing loan is applicable when the seller is short of work capital of procurement and production for performance of a sales contract, while the buyer agrees to issue a credit instead or a prepayment terms.

3. Attentions to Packing Loan

(1) Packing loan may be applied under a qualified credit only.

(2) The presentation must be submitted to the financing bank.

(3) The seller must sign formal "Loan Contract (Packing Loan)" with the financing bank.

(4) The original credit must be retained in the financing bank for the purpose of pledge after application of packing loan.

(5) In normal cases, the received remittance should be deemed as the first resource to repay the packing loan.

(6) The seller should present the documents to the financing bank for honor or negotiation as soon as possible.

(7) Financial amount must be less than the credit amount.

4. Risks for the Financing Bank

The bank gives a packing loan to the seller under a credit on its initiative and without an issuing bank's undertaking. The risks to a packing loan are about equal to a general loan. It only depends on the seller's creditworthiness that the financing bank agrees to a packing loan.

As a packing loan is a kind of pre-loading financing, the seller may conspire against the buyer to open a credit without trade background, and won't ship the goods as per the credit stipulated.

5. Mitigating Risks for the Financing Bank

The financing bank puts himself at a disadvantage for a packing loan. The bank bears risks for a financing with a sum certain percentage of credit amount only against an original credit for pledge, waiting for the seller to deliver the presentation and the receivables as the first resource to repay the packing loan.

For mitigating risks, the financing bank may put the whole process of operation under its supervision, require the seller to remain a minimum deposit amount in the financing bank or take the assets as a mortgage or pledge of the seller or accept a qualified guarantor.

8.3.2   Outward Bills

1. Definition

The bank, required by the seller after he makes a presentation under a credit or collection, supplies a financing of money in transit to the seller, with the export bill as a mortgage. It is one kind of export trade financing with the broadest usage, and is also called export bill purchase.

2. Application

It is applicable when the seller has limited current capital, and relies on rapid capital circulation to develop the business, or encounters temporary difficulty in capital circulation after delivering goods and before getting the proceeds, or faces a new investment opportunity after delivering goods and before getting the proceeds and the prospective income rate is surely higher than the interest rate of outward bills.

3. Classification of Outward Bills

Outward bills may be applied under a credit or collection. It can be financed in foreign currency or local currency.

4. Attentions to Handle Outward Bills

(1)   The seller must sign a general financing agreement with the bank.

(2)   The seller must submit the formal financing application to the bank, commonly the

nominated bank.

(3)　The party to be financed under a credit must be the beneficiary of the credit.

(4)　Financing under a credit with restriction to be available with a specific bank will not be handled by a non-specific bank.

(5)　The presentation under a credit should be in compliance with the terms and condition of the credit.

(6)　If a seller wishes to be financed by outward bills, it's better to avoid such conditions as follows: a. To deliver non-negotiated transport documents; b. Failure to submit full set of negotiated bills of lading; c. The credit is transferred; d. A credit with soft clauses; e. Documents with essential discrepancy(ies). Essential discrepancy(ies) can be amended.

8.3.3　Discounting of a Bill of Exchange

Discounting of a bill of exchange refers to the holder sells a time bill already accepted by the drawee but not yet fallen due to a financial situation at a price less than its face value.

In international trade, discounting is a financial mechanism in which a buyer obtains the right to delay payments to a seller, in exchange for a bill of exchange with payment made on a defined future date, drawn by the seller, drawn upon the buyer or the buyer's bank and accepted by him, the sum definite certain amount may with or without calculating interest for a charge or fee of delay payment. Essentially, the buyer that owes money in the present purchases the right to delay the payment until some future date.

As the holder of the accepted bill of exchange that has not fallen due, the seller may discount the daft to his financing bank at a favorable interest rate. The seller gets paid ahead of the draft being paid, and the financing bank becomes the bona-fide holder. Usually, the draft will be finally paid by the acceptor on the definite future date to settle the debt. In case of the draft being dishonored, the financing bank has right to recourse on the seller.

8.3.4　Banker's Acceptance

A banker's acceptance makes a transaction between two parties who do not know each other safer because it allows the parties to substitute the bank's credit worthiness for that who owes the payment. It is used widely in international trade for payments that are due for a future shipment of goods and services. For example, an importer may draft a banker's acceptance when he does not have a close relationship with and cannot obtain credit from an exporter. Once the importer and the bank have completed an acceptance agreement, whereby the bank accepts liabilities of the importer and the importer deposits funds at the bank (enough for the future payment plus fees), the importer can issue a time draft to the exporter for a future payment with the bank's guarantee.

A banker's acceptance is a promised future payment, or time draft, which is accepted and guaranteed by a bank and drawn on a deposit at the bank. The banker's acceptance specifies the amount of money, the date, tenor (typically within six months), and the party to which the payment is due. After acceptance, the draft becomes an unconditional liability of the bank.

A banker's acceptance starts as a time draft drawn on a bank to pay money at a future date, the bank accepts (guarantees) payment to the holder of the draft. The party that holds the banker's acceptance allows the bank to make the promised payment and may wait for the acceptance until it matures, or may sell the acceptance at a discount rate to any party willing to wait for the face value payment of the deposit on the maturity date. The rates at which they trade, calculated from the discount prices relative to their face values, are called banker's acceptance rates. Finally, the holder may be a buyer who is willing to wait until the maturity date for the funds in the deposit.

8.3.5 Forfaiting

1. Definition

Forfaiting is a method of trade financing that allows the exporter to sell its medium/long-term receivables (180 days to 10 years) under a bill of exchange or a promissory note to the forfaiter at a discount, in exchange for cash.

Forfaiters usually work with capital goods, commodities and large projects. On the parties' side, forfaiting also called a bill buy-up or a bill buy-out, is a kind of trade financing that forfaitor, as the buyer-up, purchases without recourse from the exporter the accepted usance draft so as to provide finance to the exporter. It's an indispensable condition that the bill of exchange or the promissory note with medium/long-term payment, must carry the guarantee of the foreign government or the forfaiting houses or the bank with high reputation. Normally, forfaiting is done without recourse.

2. Advantages of Forfaiting

(1) Forfaiting is a kind of non-recourse medium/long-term financing to thoroughly improve the cash flow of the exporter. For example, Bank of China is enjoying an

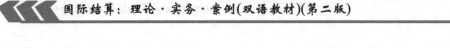

ever-increasing demand from Chinese exporters for forfaiting. The financial crisis saw a considerable number of defaults in the western world, which whetted the Chinese clients' appetite for trade financing on a non-recourse basis.

(2) The forfaiter assumes all the risks, such as interest rate risk, currency risk, credit risk and political risk. The consistent trend of the Chinese currency's appreciation against the US dollar, and lower borrowing costs in US dollars in the past few years, also pushed that demand.

(3) It enables the exporter to extend open account terms and incorporate the discount into the selling price. It saves the administration costs, increases trade opportunity for both parties and the seller also can realize price transfer.

3. Attentions for Forfaiting

(1) The seller shall sign a forfaiting contract with the forfaiter before the sales contract being signed. Further more, forfaiting business must be agreed by the buyer.

(2) Select a bank with good credit standing as the guarantor of a bill of exchange or promissory note with payment at a medium/long-term so as to benefit from forfaiting service and gain a preferable financing interest rate.

(3) Forfaiting can be used widely under open account or D/A. Under collection, the draft needs to be signed and accepted by a proper bank.

(4) Forfaiting business is not only applicable to large capital transactions but also small transactions, but the less the amount is, the higher the financing cost will be, and the seller should weigh the financing cost and facility brought about by forfaiting business.

(5) In accordance with international conventions, in the following cases, the financing bank may reserve its recourse: a. Due to stop payment orders received, the forfaiting bank fails to repay the matured bill; b. The export merchant is suspected of being involved in cheating.

4. Processes of Forfaiting

In international trade, forfaiting is a common form of financing export-related receivables with features of non-recourse and advance payment. The negotiable instrument may be a bill of exchange or a promissory note. Let's take a promissory note for an example to state the process of forfaiting.

(1) The exporter sells the goods to the importer on a deferred payment basis spread over 180 days up under a Sales Contract and a Forfaiting Contract.

(2) The importer draws a series of promissory notes in favor of the exporter for the payments to be made inclusive of interest charges.

(3)　The promissory notes are an aval or guaranteed by a reputed international bank which can also be the importer's bank. An aval is an endorsement on the promissory notes by the guarantor bank that it covers any default of payment by the buyer.

(4)　The exporter sells the notes with an aval to a forfaiter (which can be exporter's bank) at a discount and without recourse. The discount rate applied by the forfaiter will depend upon the terms of the promissory notes, the currencies in which they are denominated, the credit rating of the avalling bank, the country risk of the importer, and the prevailing market rate of interest on medium-term loans.

(5)　The forfaiter may hold these notes till maturity or sell these notes to groups of investors who are interested in taking up such a high-yielding unsecured paper.

8.3.6　Factoring

1. Definition

Once a product has been shipped, that inventory is converted to an account receivable (A/R). A list of all accounts receivable is maintained on an aging report while the exporter waits for final payment. If there is a need for immediate cash, it's possible to sell the A/R at a discount. This solution is called Factoring.

The seller assigns his receivables to the factoring bank and the seller will enjoy one or more of the following services: a. trade finance; b. buyer credit risk control and bad debt protection; c. sales ledger management; d. collection.

Factoring in international trade is the discounting of a short-term receivable (up to 180 days). The exporter transfers title to its short-term foreign accounts receivable to a factoring house for cash at a discount from the face value. It allows an exporter to ship on open account as the factor assumes the financial ability of the importer to pay and handles collections on the receivables. The factoring house usually works with consumer goods.

2. Advantages of Factoring

Factoring is a kind of easy financing with low cost. The seller may also enjoy credit protection, improve market shares and increase total profits.

Factoring is the discounting of foreign accounts receivable that do not involve drafts as the method of payment. A factor (an organization that specializes in the financing of accounts receivable) takes title for immediate cash at a discount from the face value.

The factors typically provide 70% of the face value within 3-5 working days, and assume responsibility for collection from the buyer. After final payment, the factor will pay the remaining 30% less a service fee of 4% - 5%.

3. Ranges of Factoring

(1) Factoring may be done without recourse or with recourse to the exporter, verifying these specific arrangements. For example, if the seller selects trade finance and the buyer's credit risk control and bad debt protection under a factor business, the seller enjoys financing without recourse with not exceeding the buyer's sales credit limit verified by the factor. If the seller selects trade financing only, factoring is usually with recourse.

(2) Factoring may be done by one-factor or two-factor. Two-factor refers to the factor entrusted by the seller nominates another factor at the buyer's place in close cooperation with an appropriate division of factoring services, if the seller selects one or more kinds of services that the factor provides, such as the buyer's credit risk control and bad debt protection, sales ledger management and collection. One-factor is suitable for the seller who only selects trade financing under factor.

(3) Factoring may be bulk factoring or confidential factoring, if the buyer is not informed of the arrangement whose debts have been purchased by the factor. The factor provides the seller for a prepayment against the purchase of book debts and charges interest for the period spanning the date of pre-payment to the date of collection. The sales ledger administration and collection are carried out by the seller. The seller provides the factor with periodical reports on the value of unpaid invoices and the aging schedule of debts. This facility is usually kept confidential. Therefore, this arrangement is referred to as confidential factoring. Factoring may not be confidential in nature. The buyer is advised to make payment directly to the factor and this facility is referred to as bulk factoring. The need for this facility arises when the factor finds that the seller does not fulfill the criteria laid down for invoice discounting and requires the security associated with direct payments from the buyers. Bulk factoring offered with a non-recourse feature is referred to as agency factoring in some countries, because the seller acts as an agent of the factor in collecting the debts.

(4) Factoring may be used both in domestic trade and international trade, such as domestic invoice discounting and export invoice discounting. A variant of invoice discounting is the protected invoice discounting arrangement where the factor bears the credit risk of the receivables purchased. Put differently, the factor purchases the debts without recourse but does not offer the services of sales ledger administration and debt collection. Invoice discounting in

general and protected invoice discounting in particular are offered to the sellers with a sound financial position and with no serious problem of debt collection and debt write-offs.

4. Main Differences Between Factoring and Forfaiting

Factoring and forfaiting are not identical. The basic differences are as follows(see Table 8-1):

(1)　In a factoring transaction, the factor does not provide hundred percent finance; he maintains a factor reserve. On the other hand, in a forfaiting transaction the forfaiter discounts the entire value of the promissory notes.

(2)　In a non-recourse factoring transaction, the factor participates in the credit granting decision of the exporter, whereas in a forfaiting transaction, the forfaiter relies on the unconditional and irrevocable guarantee provided by the avalling bank. So he is more concerned about the financial standing of the avalling bank than with the credit standards applied by the exporter.

(3)　While the factor takes on the responsibilities of receivables accounting, monitoring and collection, the forfaiter does not assume any of these responsibilities.

(4)　The factor purchases receivables which are of a short maturity period, whereas the forfaiter buys bills/promissory notes arising out of deferred credit transactions.

Table 8-1   Main Differences Between Factoring and Forfaiting

Basis of Differences	Factoring	Forfaiting
Extent of finance	Typically 70% of the value of the invoice is considered for advance.	100% financing.
Credit worthiness	Factor does the credit rating of the counterparty in case of a non-recourse factoring transaction.	The forfaiting bank relies on the credibility of the guarantor bank of a bill of exchange or a promissory note.
Financing facility	May with recourse or non-recourse.	Usually without recourse.
	May be bulk or confidential.	Usually be agreed by the buyer.
	Works with consumer goods.	Works with capital goods, commodities and large projects.
	Be suitable in all trade.	Be suitable in international trade or projects.
	Usually without a bill.	Must be with a bill.
Services provided	Day-to-day administration of sales and other allied services are provided.	No services are provided.
Maturity	Advances are short-term in nature.	Advances are generally medium/long-term.

8.3.7　Financing Under Export Credit Insurance

Export credit insurance provides protection against commercial losses caused by default, insolvency or bankruptcy and political losses caused by war, nationalization, currency inconvertibility, etc. It allows exporters to increase sales by offering liberal open account terms to new and existing customers. Insurance also provides security for banks providing working capital and financing exports.

It is a kind of short-term export trade financing, with recourse, sometimes as an additional security under cooperation of an export credit insurance company and the local bank.

The seller (insured) shall sign a tripartite agreement with the insurance company (insurer) and the local bank (the financing bank).

参 考 文 献

[1] 国际商会中国国家委员会(ICC CHINA). International Standard Banking Practice for the Examination of Documents under Documentary Credits (ISBP)(中英文对照本)[M]. 北京：中国民主法制出版社，2003.

[2] 国际商会中国国家委员会(ICC CHINA). UNCTAD/ICC Rules for Multimodel Transport Documents [M]. 北京：中国民主法制出版社，2004.

[3] ICC. Uniform Customs and Practices for Documentary Credits(UCP600).中国银行内部印刷.

[4] 中国银行国际结算部编写. 国际结算文件汇编(2007 年上下册).

[5] 姚新超. 国际贸易惯例与规则实务[M]. 北京：对外经济贸易大学出版社，2005.

[6] 对外经济贸易合作部对外贸易司编. 最新对外贸易法规汇编. 2002.

[7] 佟志广，张志刚，徐秉金. WTO 基础知识读本[M]. 北京：中国对外经济贸易出版社，2002.

[8] 沈瑞年，尹继红，庞红. 国际结算[M]. 北京：中国人民大学出版社，2001.

[9] 吴百福，舒红. 国际贸易结算实务[M]. 北京：中国对外经济贸易出版社，2002.

[10] 庄乐梅. 国际结算实务精要[M]. 北京：中国纺织出版社，2004.

[11] 李晓洁，徐曙娜. 国际贸易结算[M]. 上海：上海财经大学出版社，2003.

[12] 姜学军. 国际结算[M]. 大连：东北财经大学出版社，2002.

[13] 徐进亮. 国际备用信用证与保函[M]. 北京：对外经济贸易大学出版社，2004.

[14] 王益平. 国际支付与结算(英语)[M]. 北京：清华大学出版社，2004.

[15] 曲韬. 外贸单证处理技巧[M]. 广州：广东经济出版社，2003.

[16] 赵玲华. 外汇业务常用英语译答[M]. 北京：经济科学出版社，2008.

[17] Hill C W L. International Business [M]. 北京：中国人民大学出版社，2005.

[18] Pugel T A. International Trade [M]. 北京：中国人民大学出版社，2005.

[19] 金赛波. 中国信用证和贸易融资司法案例选编[M]. 北京：中国纺织出版社，2005.

[20] 顾宏远. 国际贸易结算——实务操作与案例分析[M]. 杭州：浙江大学出版社，2006.

[21] 邹根宝. 外贸信用风险管理及案例分析[M]. 上海：上海人民出版社，2002.

[22] 苏宗祥. 国际结算辅导与练习[M]. 北京：中国金融出版社，2005.

[23] 苏宗祥，张林森. 国际结算练习解答[M]. 北京：中国金融出版社，2001.

[24] 孟祥年. 国际贸易实务习题集[M]. 北京：对外经济贸易大学出版社，2003.

[25] 卓骏. 国际贸易理论与实务[M]. 北京：机械工业出版社，2006.

[26] 胡丹婷. 国际贸易实务[M]. 北京：机械工业出版社，2007.

[27] 黎孝先. 进出口合同条款与案例分析[M]. 北京：对外经济贸易大学出版社，2003.

[28] 陈冠任. 犹太人的智慧[M]. 呼和浩特：内蒙古人民出版社，2002.

[29] 赛妮亚. 世界十大民族生意经[M]. 北京：中国友谊出版社，2004.